QUASI RATIONAL ECONOMICS

Richard H. Thaler

RUSSELL SAGE FOUNDATION / NEW YORK

THE RUSSELL SAGE FOUNDATION

Library of Congress Cataloging-in-Publication Data

Thaler, Richard H., 1945–
    Quasi rational economics / Richard H. Thaler.
        p.   cm.
    Includes bibliographical references and index.
    ISBN 0-87154-846-1
    1. Economics.   I. Title.
    HB171.T47   1991   91-9797
    330—dc20

RUSSELL SAGE FOUNDATION
112 East 64th Street, New York, New York 10021

10   9   8   7   6   5   4   3   2   1

To Daniel Kahneman, who has inspired me, advised me, consoled me, encouraged me, discouraged me, humored me, prodded me, and who spends every seventh year doing all of these things full time. Thanks.

ACKNOWLEDGMENTS

One of the nicest aspects of academic life is the opportunity of writing papers with your friends and becoming friends with your coauthors. I have had more than my share of this pleasure, and the coauthored papers included here are merely the formal output of our extended conversations. Thanks to all of them. Of course, many others have helped improve these papers, too many to name here, but I would especially like to thank the people in behavioral decision theory who were so friendly and encouraging when I was getting started: Maya Bar-Hillel, the late Hillel Einhorn, Baruch Fischhoff, Sarah Lichtenstein, Paul Slovic, and, of course, Daniel Kahneman and Amos Tversky. Vernon Smith and Charlie Plott played a similar role in introducing me to experimental economics. Both invited me to their labs and tried to convert me to experimental methods. Finally, I would like to thank Eric Wanner who, while at the Sloan Foundation, funded my sabbatic in Vancouver to work with Kahneman, and has been the best friend behavioral economics could ever ask for.

CONTENTS

Part Three
EXPERIMENTAL ECONOMICS

Part Four
FAIRNESS

Part Five
FINANCIAL MARKETS

INTRODUCTION

BEGINNINGS

I am an economist interested in how people make decisions. This book is a collection of papers that try to incorporate the psychology of decision making into economic models of behavior. I am sometimes asked, usually by an economist with a worried look, how I became interested in such matters. After all, I got my Ph.D. in economics at the University of Rochester under Sherwin Rosen's guidance, and no one would call Sherwin a heretic. Afterwards I taught for a while at Rochester's Graduate School of Management, then called a University of Chicago farm club, and hardly a place to get interested in psychology. In fact, while I was there, all the behavioral scientists were fired. Luckily, I was still considered a real economist in those days. So, how and why did I go astray?

I think it all started while I was doing the research for my dissertation on the value of a human life. The idea of my thesis was that the correct measure of the value of a life-saving program is the amount people would be willing to pay to have it. I ended up measuring this by investigating how much more people got paid to work in risky occupations like mining and logging. However, as a diversion from running regressions, I decided to see what would happen if you just asked people some questions. (I don't think I told anyone—especially Sherwin—that I was going to do this.) Anyway, I asked people two questions. First, how much would you be willing to pay to eliminate a one in a thousand risk of immediate death. Second, how much would you have to be paid to willingly accept an extra one chance in a thousand of immediate death. To mitigate the effects of possible wealth and liquidity constraints on the willingness-to-pay question, I told the subjects that they could pay off their bid over thirty years interest-free. In spite of this, the differences between the answers to the two questions were astonishing. A typical answer was: "I wouldn't pay more than $200, but I wouldn't accept an extra risk for $50,000!" I came to two conclusions about these answers: (1) I better get back to running regressions if I want to graduate; and (2) The disparity between buying and selling prices was *very* interesting.

After I finished my thesis I continued to do traditional economics, but I also became preoccupied with watching how people made decisions. What I kept noticing was that people did not seem to behave the way they were supposed to. I think being at the Rochester business school helped a lot because I was surrounded by people who really took economic analyses seriously. I was constantly confronted with the contrast between the models my colleagues were constructing and the behavior I was so frequently observing. My observations soon took the form of a list of "anomalous behaviors" that I posted on a wall in my office. After a while, the list began to have categories: buying prices much less than selling prices; paying attention to sunk costs; eliminating options to deal with self control problems, etc. In 1976 I finally had the courage to write some of these ideas up in a paper to which I gave the low key title: "Consumer Theory: A Theory of Economists' Behavior." (This would eventually turn into Chapter 1.) I showed this paper only to close friends and to colleagues I wanted to annoy.

Though I found the ideas intriguing, I did not think that it was possible to earn a living thinking about such things. Then I had some luck. In the summer of 1976 I attended a conference in California on risk (more value of life stuff) where I met Baruch Fischhoff and Paul Slovic who were then both at an outfit called Decision Research. I ended up giving Fischhoff a ride from Monterey to San Francisco and got to learn a bit about what he did for a living. He promised to send me a few papers, and I promised to send him my consumer theory paper. Among the papers in the package I got from Fischhoff was a recent survey article in *Science* by two Israeli psychologists, Daniel Kahneman and Amos Tversky. The paper was called "Judgment Under Uncertainty: Heuristics and Biases." When I read this paper I could hardly contain myself. I still vividly remember rushing to the library to track down the original papers. (First I had to find the psychology section of the university library—I had never been there before.) As I excitedly read all of these (now classic) papers I kept thinking that somehow there was some way I could use these ideas to help my joke paper into something serious. Indeed, there was one very important idea in these papers that was tremendously useful, the idea that the use of judgmental heuristics (shortcuts) would lead to systematic errors or biases. This concept, I thought, is what was necessary to make the psychology of decision making relevant for economics.

Fischhoff also wrote back with some nice comments on my joke paper, and mentioned that K&T had a new paper they were working on called "Value

Theory" (the name would soon change to prospect theory). Unfortunately, he couldn't send me a copy, since his was quite preliminary. Somehow, I did manage to get a copy from Howard Kunreuther (who was then a friend of a friend). While I had high hopes about this paper, I could never have anticipated what was in it. The theory of decision making under uncertainty that was proposed there had an S-shaped "value function" that could make sense out of many of the examples I was carrying around in my head. For example, what I was calling the "endowment effect" (buying prices less than selling prices) dropped right out of their value function which was steeper for losses than for gains. At this point I decided to try and take these ideas seriously.

I soon learned that Kahneman and Tversky were going to be visiting Stanford the following academic year. I had been planning to go to the National Bureau of Economic Research at Stanford for the summer of 1977 to work with Rosen, so I tried to arrange a way to stay longer and meet them. Thanks to the generosity of Victor Fuchs, I actually ended up staying there for fifteen months, and tried to learn as much as I could from Kahneman and Tversky. The papers in this book are all, in some ways, derived from that year in Stanford.

QUASI RATIONAL ECONOMICS

There are five basic themes that have emerged from the research activity I have been engaged in since that year in Stanford. The papers in this book are grouped according to these themes. What I will try to do here is give some indication as to why these might be considered interesting topics to investigate.

Mental Accounting and Consumer Choice

The first two sections of the book are about spending and saving, two of the three most important economic decisions individuals must make (the other being career selection). The economic theory of consumer behavior is frustratingly stark and very difficult to test. Although all economic models of consumer choice are based on rational behavior, most empirical work boils down to testing whether demand curves slope down, or more precisely, whether the sign of the substitution effect is negative. As Becker has shown, in the aggregate demand curves will slope down even if people choose at random, so long as they have binding budget constraints. What then is the economic theory of the consumer? Testing whether people equate price ratios to marginal rates of substitution is, of course, impossible, since we have no direct way of measuring preferences. Even testing for consistency, via revealed preference theory, is not really possible since if someone did buy something they had previously turned down they might be expressing a taste for variety. The trick, then, for testing the theory is to find some prediction about behavior that is independent of preferences. Chapter 1 focuses on these types of predictions.

One example of such a prediction is derived from the economics dictum: Thou shalt ignore sunk costs. Suppose someone sits through an entire 42–3 football game in a 40 degree rainstorm simply because he paid $37 for a ticket and didn't want to waste the money. At least in this case there is an appropriate thought experiment to do. (Would he have sat through the game if he had gotten the ticket for free?) That is some progress. It is also possible, though not easy, to design an experiment to test this proposition. Take a random sample of people who agreed to pay full price for the ticket and give them back their money. Then see if they are less likely to watch the game to the end.[1] But in some ways we don't really have to run such experiments. We know, just from watching people and from trying to teach our students, that the principle of ignoring sunk costs is not immediately obvious. Indeed, some have argued that the failure to ignore sunk costs substantially prolonged the Vietnam War.[2]

But why do people have so much trouble ignoring sunk costs? To understand why it is necessary to introduce the concept of mental accounting. Consider this example: You have paid $120 for a fancy dinner for two at a local restaurant. You had to pay in advance, and there are no refunds. At the last minute you are invited to a friend's house for dinner where there will be an out-of-town visitor whom you would dearly love to see. If you had to choose between these two events for free you would choose the dinner with friends. Do you go to the restaurant? Most people (even economists?) would have trouble ignoring the sunk cost here. They feel that $120 is a lot to pay to eat dinner, and it is even more to pay *not* to eat dinner. Skipping the restaurant meal feels like wasting money, and if you go to your friends' house you will feel that you paid $120 for nothing. It is almost as if you have a debt to yourself that will linger around for a considerable time if you don't pay it off by eating the dinner. This is mental accounting at work. Chapter 2 discusses this concept in some detail.[3]

Mental accounting is applied to the problem of decision making under

---

[1] An experiment of this type is described in footnote 8 of Chapter 1. A series of such experiments were subsequently conducted by Arkes and Blumer (1985). (Hal R. Arkes, and C. Blumer. "The Psychology of Sunk Costs." *Organizational Behavior and Human Performance* 35:124–140.)

[2] See Staw (1976). (Barry Staw. "Knee Deep in the Big Muddy: A Study of Escalating Commitment to a Chosen Course of Action." *Organizational Behavior and Human Performance*, 16:27–44.)

[3] The concept was introduced first in Chapter 1, but I referred to it as "psychological accounting." Kahneman and Tversky suggested the better term "mental accounting" in their 1981 paper. (Amos Tversky and Daniel Kahneman. "The Framing of Decisions and the Psychology of Choice." *Science* 211:453–463.)

uncertainty in Chapter 3. This chapter was prompted by many years of playing low stakes poker with a group of economists and business school faculty members. What I noticed over the years was that though my colleagues knew better, their betting behavior was definitely influenced by how they were doing in the poker game that evening. Players who were ahead would tend to become more reckless, feeling perhaps that they could only lose the money that they had just won. In casinos gamblers call these winnings "house money" (as opposed to "real money"). The behavior of players behind was more difficult to describe. They would become cautious about losing substantially more money (especially those who were married), but would find a bet that gave them some chance of getting back to break even very attractive. Chapter 3 documents these house money and break-even effects in more carefully controlled (but less realistic) settings.

Intertemporal Choice and Self-Control

Chapters 4 and 5 continue a theme started in Chapter 1, the economics of self-control. My interest in this issue was prompted by an incident described in Chapter 1. A group of economists had gathered at my house for dinner. While we were waiting for the food in the oven to finish cooking, I brought a large bowl of cashew nuts into the living room where people were having cocktails. In a few minutes, half the bowl of nuts was gone, and I could see that our appetites were in danger. Quickly, I seized the bowl of nuts and put it back in the kitchen (eating a few more nuts along the way, of course). When I returned, my fellow economists generally applauded my quick action, but then we followed our natural inclinations which was to try to analyze the situation to death. The burning question was: how could removing an option possibly have made us better off? After all, if we wanted to stop eating cashews, we could have done that at any time.

When I began to consider this issue more seriously, I realized that almost all the instances I could think of where people intentionally restrict their options involve intertemporal choice: choosing over time. Specifically, people restrict their *current* choices when they think that they will later regret them. The domains where this behavior is common include dieting (don't keep desserts in the house), smoking (buying cigarettes by the pack), and, most important for economics, saving. Indeed, almost all the individual saving in the United States is accomplished through the use of so-called forced saving vehicles: pensions, whole life insurance, home equity, and especially social security. In Chapter 1, I suggested that to model self-control behavior it was necessary to think of the individual as having two components, a far-sighted planner, and a myopic doer. Self-control is observed when the planner somehow restricts the actions of the doer. Naturally, it seemed incongruous to work on this kind of idea alone, so I conned Hersh Shefrin, a mathematical economist who had heretofore shown no deviant tendencies (at least as an economist), to join me. (Hersh was a quick convert. He has since written an interesting series of papers on behavioral finance with Meir Statman.) Chapter 4 represents our first attempt to model the self-control problem. Chapter 5, written several years later, makes much more use of mental accounting, and offers considerable empirical evidence to support what we call the behavioral life-cycle hypothesis.

Chapter 6 is a short piece on intertemporal choice from a different perspective. The question addressed here is whether people choose over time as if they were using a constant exponential discount function, as is normally assumed in economic analysis. I found three important deviations from a constant discount rate: (1) The discount rate is inversely related to the size of the amount being discounted (the bigger the prize, the lower the discount rate); (2) The discount rate is inversely related to the length of time being waited (the longer the wait, the lower the rate); and (3) Discount rates were much lower for negative amounts than for positive amounts. In fact, some subjects would not be willing to pay anything extra to postpone the payment of a fine.[4]

Experimental Economics

Demonstrating that the predictions of economic theory are false is a daunting task, especially if the usual economic data sets are used. No matter how strange a particular economic action might seem to be, some economist can usually construct a rational explanation for it. For this reason, experiments are often the most attractive domain for theory testing. Chapter 7 is a survey article written for a conference organized by Al Roth, one of the most thoughtful and creative practitioners of the experimental art. The article surveys the experimental work done to test the basic tenets of rational choice. Much of the work I survey was conducted by Kahneman and Tversky. This chapter could serve as an introduction to the more psychological literature for the uninitiated.

Chapter 8 was written directly as a result of attending Roth's conference with Kahneman. At the conference, I presented experimental evidence on the disparity between buying and selling prices. Some of the other participants, particularly Vernon Smith and Charlie Plott, raised some objections. They argued that the existence of this effect had not yet been established. They, in effect, challenged us to demonstrate this disparity in an experimental market setting where subjects had both opportunities and incentives to learn. Kahneman and I teamed up with Jack Knetsch (who had been working on this problem for years) to see whether the endowment effect would exist under

---

[4]For an update on the research along these lines, see George Loewenstein and Richard H. Thaler. "Anomalies: Intertemporal Choice." *Journal of Economic Perspectives* 3 (Fall 1989): 181–193; and George Loewenstein and Jon Elster. *Choice Over Time*. New York: Russell Sage Foundation, forthcoming.

such conditions. In fact, we found that the strength of the effect surprised even us, the true believers. Simply putting a Cornell coffee mug on the desk of a student creates an endowment effect. Students endowed with a mug demanded twice as much to sell it as other students who were not given mugs were willing to pay to get one.

Chapter 9 is a set of comments I delivered at another conference organized at the University of Chicago by Robin Hogarth and Mel Reder. My nominal task was to discuss papers by Hillel Einhorn and Robin Hogarth; Kahneman and Tversky; and Herbert Simon. The other discussant was Gary Becker, so there was one pro-rationality discussant, and one con. I chose to base my remarks on a clever article by George Stigler called "The Conference Handbook." Stigler's piece, in turn, is based on the old joke about the prisoners who have heard the same jokes told so often that they just call them out by number.[5] Stigler points out that many seminar remarks are also a bit worn out, so it would save some time to just call them out by number. In my piece, I offer a few of the most common knee-jerk comments made by economists about the work of psychologists, as well as my own recommended responses. I also recommended the use of Wilem Hofstee's reputational betting paradigm for settling academic disputes. Indeed, the mugs paper (Chapter 8) is essentially our response to a reputational bet. Unfortunately, I am not sure anyone is keeping score.

Fairness

One of the basic principles of economic theory is that, in the absence of government interference or other impediments to efficient markets, prices will adjust to eliminate shortages or surpluses. Yet, as was pointed out in Chapter 2, many markets do fail to clear. Tickets to the Super Bowl and major concerts, and dinner reservations for Saturday night at 8 at Lutece, are all priced too low. The explanation in Chapter 2 was based on the notion of transaction utility. If a customer pays more for a good than is considered normal or fair, she feels "ripped off"; the utility of the transaction per se is negative. Chapters 10 and 11, written in collaboration with Daniel Kahneman and Jack Knetsch, investigate the question of what makes a transaction seem fair or unfair. Chapter 10 concentrates on the results of a large-scale telephone survey conducted in Toronto and Vancouver. (Most of the research was conducted during the glorious year I spent visiting Kahneman at the University of British Columbia in Vancouver.) For several months we had access to a telephone polling bureau, so we ended up asking hundreds of fairness questions to groups of 100–150 respondents. There were two reasons why we

---

[5]The punchline of the joke is this: A newcomer has the system explained to him and decides to try it himself. He calls out "22!," but no one laughs. When he asks his roommate why, his roommate tells him, "Well, I guess you just don't know how to tell a joke."

asked so many different questions: (1) Some theories we had about what determines the fairness of a transaction were wrong; and (2) Some questions (most actually) had alternative interpretations which could be eliminated only by asking many variations. The questions we ultimately reported were those that were most robust, which illustrated the key determinants of fairness.

Chapter 11 reports some additional results for the telephone poll plus some experimental results using a paradigm called the "ultimatum game." One subject (the allocator) makes an offer to divide a sum of money (say, $10) between herself and another subject, the recipient. The recipient can then either accept the offer (and take what he was offered) or reject the offer, in which case both players get nothing. Our interest in this game (which had been first investigated by Werner Guth) was in the behavior of the recipients. How much money would they be willing to turn down in order to punish an allocator who was too greedy. We felt that this game captures the essence of the enforcement mechanism that induces firms to behave fairly. That is, firms that behave unfairly will be punished by their customers, who will be willing to pay a little more to take their business elsewhere.

Financial Markets

The title of this book is taken from Chapter 12, written with my long-time friend Tom Russell. In this article we investigate the conditions in which less than fully rational behavior, or quasi rational behavior as we call it, matters in competitive markets. Is it true that in competitive markets, quasi rational behavior is eliminated or rendered irrelevant? We begin the article with a Shel Silverstein poem, surely the best feature of this book, which illustrates the concept of quasi rationality. In it, a boy makes a series of trades, a dollar for two quarters, then a two quarters for three dimes, etc., all based on the premise that more is better than less. Notice that such behavior is systematic, and therefore predictable. We find that the conditions for markets to eliminate quasi rational behavior of this sort are rarely observed. Indeed, even financial markets, thought by most economists to be the most efficient, leave room for quasi rational behavior to persist.

The rest of this section of the book is a series of chapters about financial markets and quasi rational behavior. I was drawn to the study of financial markets for two reasons. First, because these markets are thought by many to be so efficient,[6] finding evidence of quasi rational behavior in this domain would be particularly telling. The other reason why financial markets are attractive to study is that the data are so good. Stock price data are available on computer tape going back to the 1920s. Actually, there is an important third

---

[6]A Rochester colleague of mine, Mike Jensen, now at the Harvard Business School, once wrote that the efficient market hypothesis was the best documented fact in social science.

reason: Werner De Bondt. Werner was a doctoral student of mine at Cornell (he is now at the University of Wisconsin), who shared my interest in behavioral decision research and who also knew the financial economics literature. Werner soon learned how to spin tapes, so we were off and running.

Chapter 13 is derived from Werner's thesis. It has the following history. There is a well-known anomaly in finance called the P/E effect (price/earnings). The anomaly is that for many years, going back at least to the 1930s, stocks with low price/earnings ratios have had higher rates of return than stocks with high price/earnings ratios. David Dreman, in a popular book called the *New Contrarian Investment Strategy*, offered an interesting theory of the P/E effect based on behavioral decision theory. Essentially, he argued that the market overreacted to the bad events that produce a low P/E and to the good events that lead to a high P/E. He cited the work of Kahneman and Tversky to support his theory. De Bondt and I found his theory plausible, and we felt that if he were right then we should be able to predict a new anomaly, namely that stocks with extreme past price performance should display mean reverting prices in the future. That is, big losers should outperform the market, and big winners should underperform the market. With considerable anticipation, Werner set about to test his idea, and to our great relief it actually worked. A portfolio of 35 big losers outperforms a portfolio of big winners by almost 40 percent over five years.

These results supporting overreaction were greated with considerable skepticism by the financial economic community. Initially, the leading alternative hypothesis was that we had made a programming error. Fortunately, however, Werner did all the programming, and there were no mistakes discovered. At this point, our critics turned their attention to our interpretation of the results. Chapter 14 is our response to this criticism. In this paper we investigate whether the excess returns to the losers is actually a manifestation of another anomaly (equally mysterious) called the size effect. Over long periods of time, (though not in the late 80s) small firms have outperformed large firms. Since big losers have lost much of their market value in the process of becoming big losers, they have, by the standard measure of firm size, market value of equity, become smaller. Therefore, some argued, our losing firm effect was simply the size effect. We did find that the two effects are related. The small firm effect is helped by the fact that many small firms are prior losers, and losing firms are indeed smaller than average, but we concluded that both effects are present. We also investigated whether the losing firm effect can be explained by risk. Do the excess returns to the losers occur because the losing firms are especially risky? Here we found a very striking result. In the test period, after the portfolios are formed, the losing firms have high betas (the risk measure used in the standard capital asset pricing model) only in periods when the market is going up! When the market falls, the losers have betas less than one. This means that the losers go up faster than the market when the market rises, and fall more slowly than the market when it falls. At least to us, this does not seem too risky.

Chapter 15, also written with Werner De Bondt, asks a simple question: Is there any evidence that security analysts overreact in making their predictions of earnings? We test for this by regressing the actual change in earnings for a given firm on the average change forecasted by security analysts. We find strong evidence of overreaction. For one-year forecasts, actual changes are only 65 percent of the predicted change. For two-year forecasts, there is even more overreaction.

The final paper on financial markets concerns the curious institution of closed-end mutual funds. In the case of the more common open-end fund, an investor can withdraw money from the fund at any time just by asking the fund to sell his or her shares at market value. In contrast, investors in a closed-end fund are issued shares in the fund that are traded on the exchanges. An investor who wants to sell her shares must sell them on the market at the going price. This means that the price of the shares of the fund can diverge from the value of the assets that the fund owns. Not only can the prices diverge, they do. The prices of closed-end fund shares typically sell at a discount, compared to the value of the underlying securities, though sometimes premia are also observed. I have found the closed-end fund anomaly interesting for a long time. A student at Rochester, Rex Thompson, wrote an interesting thesis on this topic while I was there. Closed end funds are interesting because they represent the only case in which it is possible to test the efficient market hypothesis prediction that prices should be equal to the intrinsic value of the security. (It is testable in this case because intrinsic value is observable, namely, the value of the assets held by the fund.)

Two events led to the paper that appears as Chapter 16. First, Charles Lee, then an accounting graduate student at Cornell, now a professor at the University of Michigan, wrote a term paper on closed-end funds for a seminar I was teaching. Then, during the seminar we read a working paper by De Long, Shleifer, Summers, and Waldmann that introduced a new model of financial markets with "noise traders" (quasi rational investors). In their paper, they discussed closed-end funds as an interesting application of the model in which the discounts and premia are determined by changes in the sentiment of noise traders. Charles and I decided to collect a data set on closed-end fund discounts and try to test this model. Soon we had the good sense to ask Andrei Shleifer to join us. (This way, if we rejected the noise trader model, he wouldn't blame us!) One of the most interesting implications of the noise trader model is that closed-end fund discounts should be related to the prices of other securities in which noise traders are important investors. Indeed, we report in Chapter 16 that changes in the average discount on closed-end funds helps explain the magnitude of the small firm effect mentioned above. Specifically, in months when the average discount on closed-end funds narrow, small firms have higher excess returns. In the paper we also examine several standard explanations for closed-end fund discounts and premia and find them lacking.

CONCLUSIONS

I would summarize what I have learned so far this way: Quasi rational behavior exists, and it matters. In some well-defined situations, people make decisions that are systematically and substantively different from those predicted by the standard economic model. Quasi rational behavior can be observed under careful laboratory controls and in natural economic settings such as the stock market. Market economies and their institutions are different from the way they would be if everyone were completely rational.

How should economists react to this? First let me suggest what I think is the wrong answer. Once, after a talk I gave at a meeting of economists, I was asked a question by a member of the audience, a respected macroeconomic theorist. He said: "If I take what you say seriously, what am I supposed to do? I only know how to solve optimization problems!" Am I suggesting that economic theorists fold up their tents and go home to make room for psychoeconomists? Just the opposite. I think that there is much to do, and only economists have the tools to do it.

Some of the work that needs to be done is theoretical. What happens in a standard economic model if we relax the assumption that everyone is rational all of the time? Suppose some of the people are rational and some are not, as in Chapter 12. The recent series of papers by De Long, Shleifer, Summers, and Waldmann on "noise traders" is in this spirit. They show that the economists' intuition that irrational investors will automatically go broke is incorrect. In some situations, the irrational investors actually end up with more wealth. Dumb and rich can happen. A similar thrust is coming in game theory. Experiments have shown that real people do not play games according to the predictions of game theory. In complex games, people use simplifying strategies, and they care about acting fairly and being treated fairly. These factors need to be incorporated into new game theoretic models. Only economists can construct such models. And then there is macroeconomics. Over the postwar period a new criterion emerged as a basis of evaluating macroeconomic models: The more rational the agents in a model are assumed to be, the better. It is time to recognize that there can be too much of a good thing, even rationality. Perhaps we can construct better macroeconomic models by recognizing that the agents in the economy are human. They overwithhold on their income tax in order to get a refund. Then they treat the refund as a windfall. They have positive balances in their savings accounts earning 5 percent *and* outstanding balances on their credit card for which they pay 18 percent. Where are these people in macroeconomic models?

In many cases, new theory must be done in conjunction with empirical work, especially experimental research. One of the most important questions to be addressed is learning. I am talking about real learning here, not optimal learning. How do people really learn about the world around them? It is true that most of us do tolerably well at learning how to read and drive a car. Some people can even learn to play the piano or cook a soufflé. But this is all easy compared to choosing a mortgage, much less a career. How do people really search for a job when they are unemployed? Do those who experience frequent spells of unemployment search more optimally? How do firms learn about the elasticity of demand for one of their products? I simply want to make the following claim: It is impossible to build descriptive models of learning without watching people learn.

So, progress has been made, there is lots to do. If you read and enjoy this book, I hope you will pitch in and help. There is more than enough work to go around.

Part One

MENTAL ACCOUNTING AND CONSUMER CHOICE

1

TOWARD
A POSITIVE THEORY
OF CONSUMER CHOICE

Richard H. Thaler

The economic theory of the consumer is a combination of positive and normative theories. Since it is based on a rational maximizing model it describes how consumers *should* choose, but it is alleged to also describe how they *do* choose. This paper argues that in certain well-defined situations many consumers act in a manner that is inconsistent with economic theory. In these situations economic theory will make systematic errors in predicting behavior. Kahneman and Tversky's prospect theory is proposed as the basis for an alternative descriptive theory. Topics discussed are underweighting of opportunity costs, failure to ignore sunk costs, search behavior, choosing not to choose and regret, and precommitment and self-control.

1. INTRODUCTION

Economists rarely draw the distinction between normative models of consumer choice and descriptive or positive models. Although the theory is normatively based (it describes what rational consumers *should* do), economists argue that it also serves well as a descriptive theory (it predicts what consumers in fact do). This paper argues that exclusive reliance on the normative theory leads economists to make systematic, predictable errors in describing or forecasting consumer choices.

In some situations the normative and positive theories coincide. If a consumer must add two (small) numbers together as part of a decision process then one would hope that the normative answer would be a good predictor. So if a problem is sufficiently simple the normative theory will be acceptable.

Reprinted with permission from *Journal of Economic Behavior and Organization* 1 (1980): 39–60.
© North-Holland Publishing Company.

Furthermore, the sign of the substitution effect, the most important prediction in economics, has been shown to be negative even if consumers choose at random (Becker, 1962). Recent research has demonstrated that even rats obey the law of demand (Kagel and Battalio, 1975).

How does the normative theory hold up in more complicated situations? Consider the famous birthday problem in statistics: if 25 people are in a room what is the probability that at least one pair will share a birthday? This problem is famous because everyone guesses wrong when he first hears it. Furthermore, the errors are systematic—nearly everyone guesses too low. (The correct answer is greater than 0.5.) For most people the problem is a form of mental illusion. Research on judgment and decision making under uncertainty, especially by Daniel Kahneman and Amos Tversky (1974, 1979), has shown that such mental illusions should be considered the rule rather than the exception.[1] Systematic, predictable differences between normative models of behavior and actual behavior occur because of what Herbert Simson (1957, p. 198) called "bounded rationality":

> The capacity of the human mind for formulating and solving complex problems is very small compared with the size of the problems whose solution is required for objectively rational behavior in the real world—or even for a reasonable approximation to such objective rationality.

This paper presents a group of economic mental illusions. These are classes of problems where consumers are particularly likely to deviate from the predictions of the normative model. By highlighting the specific instances in which the normative model fails to predict behavior, I hope to show the kinds of changes in the theory that will be necessary to make it more descriptive. Many of these changes are incorporated in a new descriptive model of choice under uncertainty called prospect theory (Kahneman and Tversky, 1979). Therefore I begin this paper with a brief summary of prospect theory. Then several types of predicted errors in the normative theory are discussed. Each is first illustrated by an anecdotal example. These examples are intended to illustrate the behavior under discussion in a manner that appeals to the reader's intuition and experiences. I have discussed these examples with hundreds of friends, colleagues, and students. Many of the examples have also been used as questionnaires—I can informally report that a large majority of non-economists say they would act in the hypothesized manner. Yet I am keenly aware that more formal tests are necessary. I try to provide as many kinds of evidence as possible for each type of behavior. These kinds of evidence range from questionnaires, to regressions using market data, to laboratory experiments, to market institutions that exist apparently to exploit these actions. I hope to gather more evidence in future experimental research. For readers who remain

---

[1] Some of these studies have recently been replicated by economists. See Grether and Plott, 1979, and Grether, 1979.

unconvinced, I suggest they try out the examples on some non-economist friends.

2. PROSPECT THEORY

Not very long after expected utility theory was formulated by von Neumann and Morgenstern (1944) questions were raised about its value as a descriptive model (Allais, 1953). Recently Kahneman and Tversky (1979) have proposed an alternative descriptive model of economic behavior that they call prospect theory. I believe that many of the elements of prospect theory can be used in developing descriptive choice models in deterministic settings. Therefore, I will present a very brief summary of prospect theory here.

Kahneman and Tversky begin by presenting the results of a series of survey questions designed to highlight discrepancies between behavior and expected utility theory. Some of these results are presented in Table 1. A prospect is a gamble (x, p, y, q) that pays x with probability p and y with probability q. If $q = 0$ that outcome is omitted. A certain outcome is denoted (z). N refers to number of subjects who responded, the percentage who chose each option is given in parentheses, and majority preference is denoted by *. Subjects were also given problems such as these:

Problem 11. In addition to whatever you own you have been given 1,000. You are now asked to choose between

A: (1,000, 0.5) and   B: (500) $N = 70$.
(16)   (84)

Problem 12. In addition to whatever you own, you have been given 2,000. You are now asked to choose between

C: (−1,000, 0.5) and   D: (−500) $N = 68$.
(69)   (31)

TABLE 1 Preferences Between Positive and Negative Prospects

	Positive Prospects			Negative Prospects	
Problem 3	(4,000, 0.80)	<(3,000)	Problem 3′	(−4,000, 0.80)	>(−3,000)
N = 95	(20)	(80)*	N = 95	(92)*	(8)
Problem 4	(4,000, 0.20)	>(3,000, 0.25)	Problem 4′	(−4,000, 0.20)	<(−3,000, 0.25)
N = 95	(65)*	(35)	N = 95	(42)	(58)
Problem 7	(3,000, 0.90)	>(6,000, 0.45)	Problem 7′	(−3,000, 0.90)	<(−6,000, 0.45)
N = 66	(86)*	(14)	N = 66	(8)	(92)*
Problem 8	(3,000, 0.002)	<(6,000, 0.001)	Problem 8′	(−3,000, 0.002)	>(−6,000, 0.001)
N = 66	(27)	(73)*	N = 66	(70)*	(30)

SOURCE: Kahneman and Tversky (1979).

The results of these questionnaires led to the following empirical generalizations.

1. Gains are treated differently than losses. (Notice the reversal in signs of preference in the two columns in Table 1.) Except for very small probabilities, risk seeking is observed for losses while risk aversion is observed for gains.
2. Outcomes received with certainty are overweighted relative to uncertain outcomes. (Compare 3 and 3′ with 4 and 4′.)
3. The structure of the problem may affect choices. Problems 11 and 12 are identical if evaluated with respect to final asset positions but are treated differently by subjects.

Kahneman and Tversky then offer a theory that can predict individual choices, even in the cases in which expected utility theory is violated. In expected utility theory, an individual with initial wealth w will value a prospect $(x, p; y, q)$ as $EU = pU(w + x) + qU(w + y)$ if $p + q = 1$. In prospect theory the objective probabilities are replaced by subjective decision weights $\pi(p)$. The utility function is replaced by a value function, v, that is defined over changes in wealth rather than final asset position. For "regular" prospects (i.e., $p + q < 1$ or $x \geq 0 \geq y$ or $x \leq 0 \leq y$) then the value of a prospect is given by

$$V(x, p; y, q) = \pi(p)v(x) + \pi(q)v(y). \tag{1}$$

If $p + q = 1$ and either $x > y > 0$ or $x < y < 0$ then

$$V(x, p; y, q) = v(y) + \pi(p)[v(x) - v(y)]. \tag{2}$$

The value function is of particular interest here since I will discuss only deterministic choice problems. The essential characteristics of the value function are:

1. It is defined over gains and losses with respect to some natural reference point. Changes in the reference point can alter choices as in Problems 11 and 12.
2. It is concave for gains and convex for losses. The shape of the value function is based on the psychophysical principle that the difference between 0 and 100 seems greater than the difference between 1,000 and 1,100 irrespective of the sign of the magnitudes. This shape explains the observed risk-seeking choices for losses and risks averse choices for gains.[2]

---

[2] The loss function will be mitigated by the threat of ruin or other discontinuities. See Kahneman and Tversky (1979, p. 279).

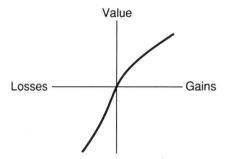

Figure 1. *A hypothetical value function.*

3. It is steeper for losses than for gains. "The aggravation that one experiences in losing a sum of money appears to be greater than the pleasure associated with gaining the same amount."[3]

A hypothetical value function with these properties is pictured in Figure 1. Insurance purchasing and gambling are explained through the π function which is regressive with respect to objective probabilities and has discontinuities around 0 and 1. For details, of course, the reader is encouraged to read the original paper.

3. OPPORTUNITY COSTS AND THE ENDOWMENT EFFECT

Example 1. Mr. R bought a case of good wine in the late 50s for about $5 a bottle. A few years later his wine merchant offered to buy the wine back for $100 a bottle. He refused, although he has never paid more than $35 for a bottle of wine.

Example 2. Mr. H mows his own lawn. His neighbor's son would mow it for $8. He wouldn't mow his neighbor's same-sized lawn for $20.

Example 3. Two survey questions: (a) Assume you have been exposed to a disease which if contracted leads to a quick and painless death within a week. The probability you have the disease is 0.001. What is the maximum you would be willing to pay for a cure? (b) Suppose volunteers were needed for research on the above disease. All that would be required is that you expose yourself to a 0.001 chance of contracting the disease. What is the minimum

[3]Kahneman and Tversky (1979, p. 279).

payment you would require to volunteer for this program? (You would not be allowed to purchase the cure.)

The Results. Many people respond to questions (a) and (b) with answers which differ by an order of magnitude or more! (A typical response is $200 and $10,000.)

These examples have in common sharp differences between buying and selling prices. While such differences *can* be explained using income effects or transactions costs, I will argue that a more parsimonious explanation is available if one distinguishes between the opportunity costs and out-of-pocket costs.

The first lesson of economics is that all costs are (in some sense) opportunity costs. Therefore opportunity costs *should* be treated as equivalent to out-of-pocket costs. How good is this normative advice as a descriptive model? Consider Kahneman and Tversky's Problems 11 and 12. In Problem 11 the gamble is viewed as a chance to gain while in Problem 12 it is viewed as a chance to avert a loss. We know the problems are viewed differently since the majority responses are reversed. Kahneman and Tversky incorporate this in their model by focusing on gains and losses (rather than final asset positions which are identical in these two problems) and by having the loss function steeper than the gains function, $v(x) < - v(x)$. This shape of the value function implies that if out-of-pocket costs are viewed as losses and opportunity costs are viewed as foregone gains, the former will be more heavily weighted. Furthermore, a certain degree of inertia is introduced into the consumer choice process since goods that are included in the individual's endowment will be more highly valued than those not held in the endowment, *ceteris paribus*. This follows because removing a good from the endowment creates a loss while adding the same good (to an endowment without it) generates a gain. Henceforth, I will refer to the underweighting of opportunity costs as the *endowment effect*.

Clearly the endowment effect can explain the behavior in Examples 1–3. In Example 1 it works in two ways. First, as just mentioned, giving up the wine will induce a loss while purchasing the same bottle would create a (less highly weighted) gain. Second, the money paid for a bottle purchased might be viewed as a loss,[4] while the money received for the sale would be viewed as a gain.

The endowment effect is a hypothesis about behavior. What evidence exists (aside from Kahneman and Tversky's survey data) to support this hypothesis? Unfortunately, there is little in the way of formal tests. One recent study by SRI International does provide some supporting evidence. Weiss, Hall, and

---

[4]More about the psychology of spending appears in Section 4.

Dong (1978) studied the schooling decision of participants in the Seattle-Denver Income Maintenance Experiment. They found that variation in the out-of-pocket costs of education had effects which were "stronger and more systematic than that of a controlled change in opportunity costs."[5]

An experimental test was conducted by Becker, Ronen, and Sorter (1974). They asked MBA students to choose between two projects that differed only in that one had an opportunity cost component while the other had only out-of-pocket costs. The students systematically preferred the projects with the opportunity costs. However, some problems with their experimental design make this evidence inconclusive. (See Neumann and Friedman, 1978.)

Other kinds of evidence in support of the endowment effect hypothesis are less direct but perhaps more convincing. I refer to instances in which businesses have used the endowment effect to further their interests.

Credit cards provide a particularly clear example. Until recently, credit card companies banned their affiliated stores from charging higher prices to credit card users. A bill to outlaw such agreements was presented to Congress. When it appeared likely that some kind of bill would pass, the credit card lobby turned its attention to form rather than substance. Specifically, it preferred that any difference between cash and credit card customers take the form of a cash discount rather than a credit card surcharge. This preference makes sense if consumers would view the cash discount as an opportunity cost of using the credit card but the surcharge as an out-of-pocket cost.[6]

The film processing industry seems also to have understood the endowment effect. Some processing companies (notably Fotomat) have a policy whereby they process and print any photographs no matter how badly exposed they are. Customers can ask for refunds (on their next trip if they wish) for any pictures they do not want. The endowment effect helps explain why they are not besieged by refund requests.

Other marketing strategies can be understood with the use of the endowment effect. Consider the case of a two-week trial period with a money-back guarantee. At the first decision point the consumer thinks he can lose at most the transactions costs of taking the good home and back. If the transactions costs are less than the value of the utilization of the good for two weeks, then the maximizing consumer pays for the good and takes it home. The second decision point comes two weeks later. If the consumer has fully adapted to the

---

[5]Weiss, Hall, and Dong (1978).

[6]In his testimony before the Senate Committee on Banking, Housing and Urban Affairs, Jeffrey Bucher of the Federal Reserve Board argued that surcharges and discounts should be treated the same way. However he reported that 'critics argued that a surcharge carries the connotation of a penalty on credit card users while a discount is viewed as a bonus to cash customers. They contended that this difference in psychological impact makes it more likely that surcharge systems will discourage customers from using credit cards . . .' This passage and other details are in United States Senate (1975).

purchase, he views the cost of keeping the good as an opportunity cost. Once this happens the sale is more likely. Of course, it is entirely possible that were the good to be stolen and the price of the good refunded by his insurance company he would fail to repurchase the good.[7]

A final application of the endowment effect comes from the field of sports economics. Harold Demsetz (1972) argues that the reserve clause (which ties a player to a team for life) does not affect the distribution of players among teams. His argument is as follows. Resources go to their highest valued use. Teams are free to sell or trade players to other teams. Thus, if a player is owned by one team but valued more highly by another, a transaction will take place. Since the transaction costs appear to be low, the argument seems correct, but the facts clearly contradict the conclusion!

Consider first the free agent draft in football. Teams take turns selecting players who have finished their collegiate eligibility. The teams pick in a specified order. Demsetz (and economic theory) would suggest that teams should draft at their turn the player with the highest market value and then trade or sell him to the team that values him most. Thus we should expect to see a flurry of trades right after the draft. Instead, while drafting rights (i.e., turns to pick) are frequently traded, players drafted are virtually never traded during the period between the draft and the start of the season. Why? Before offering an answer, consider another empirical observation. In baseball over the last few years the reserve clause has been weakened and many players (starting with "Catfish" Hunter) have become free agents, able to sign with any team. If players are already on the teams where their value is highest these free agents should all re-sign with their former teams (at new higher salaries that give the rents to the player rather than the owner). Yet this has not happened. Instead, virtually all of the players who have become free agents have signed with new teams.

I believe that the endowment effect can explain at least part of these puzzles. When a player is drafted he becomes part of the fans' endowment. If he is sold or traded this will be treated by the fans as a *loss*. However, when a player is declared a free agent he drops out of the endowment, and the fans will recognize that he can only be regained at substantial *out-of-pocket* expense. Similarly, trading the rights to draft a player will be preferred to trading the player since he will never enter the fans' endowment.

---

[7]Suppose your neighbors are going to have a garage sale. They offer to sell any of your household goods for you at one half of the original purchase price. You must only tell them which goods to sell and they will take care of everything else, including returning any unsold items. Try to imagine which goods you would decide to sell and which goods you would decide to keep. Now imagine that some of the goods you decided to keep are stolen, and that your insurance will pay you half the original price. If you could also replace them at half price how many would you replace? (Assume identical quantity.) Many people say that there would be some items which they would not sell in the first case *and* wouldn't buy in the second case, even though transactions costs have been made very low in this example.

4. SUNK COSTS:
MODELING PSYCHIC COSTS

Example 4. A family pays $40 for tickets to a basketball game to be played 60 miles from their home. On the day of the game there is a snowstorm. They decide to go anyway, but note in passing that had the tickets been given to them, they would have stayed home.

Example 5. A man joins a tennis club and pays a $300 yearly membership fee. After two weeks of playing he develops a tennis elbow. He continues to play (in pain) saying, "I don't want to waste the $300!"

Economic theory implies that only incremental costs and benefits *should* affect decisions. Historical costs should be irrelevant. But do (non-economist) consumers ignore sunk costs in their everyday decisions? As Examples 4 and 5 suggest, I do not believe that they do. Rather, I suggest the alternative hypothesis that paying for the right to use a good or service will increase the rate at which the good will be utilized, *ceteris paribus*. This hypothesis will be referred to as the *sunk cost effect*.

Gathering evidence to test this hypothesis is complicated by problems of selectivity bias. People who have paid to join a tennis club are likely to enjoy tennis more than those who have not, and thus they are likely to use it more than another group who didn't have to pay the membership fee. This problem makes market tests difficult. Other evidence does exist, however, and it is generally supportive.

First, some of Kahneman and Tversky's survey questions indicate a sunk cost effect. For example, one set of subjects preferred (0) to (-800, 0.2; 200, 0.8), while a different set preferred ($-1,000$, 0.2) to (-200). This suggests that the 200 subtracted from the first problem to obtain the second is not viewed as sunk by the subjects. Kahneman and Tversky also cite the empirical finding that betting on long shots increases during the course of a racing day, again implying that bettors have not adapted to their losses. Similar behavior is well known to anyone who plays poker.

Second, social psychologists have done experiments on a related concept. Aronson and Mills (1959) tested to see whether people who had to undertake considerable effort to obtain something would like it better. Their procedure was to advertise for students to participate in a discussion group. Subjects were then assigned to one of three groups: severe initiation, mild initiation, and control. Those in the severe initiation group had to read aloud an embarrassing portion of some sexually oriented material. Those in the mild condition read aloud some more timid material. Those in the control group had no initiation. Basically, the results confirmed the hypothesis of the experimenters. Those in the severe initiation group reported enjoying the subsequent group discussion (which, in fact, was deadly dull) more than those in the other group. These results were later replicated by Gerard and Mathewson (1966).[8]

Third, there are many examples of the governmental failing to ignore sunk costs. A dramatic example of this was revealed in a Congressional investigation of the Teton Dam disaster.[9] One part of the hearings was devoted to an analysis of the *theory of momentum*—"that is, the inclination on the part of the Bureau of Reclamation to continue dam construction, once commenced, despite hazards which might emerge during the course of construction."[10] The commissioner of the Bureau of Reclamation denied that such a problem existed. However, when asked to "give an example of any dam whose construction was halted or even paused or interrupted temporarily once the physical construction processes actually began on the dam itself,"[11] the commissioner came up empty-handed.

Finally, perhaps the strongest support for the sunk cost hypothesis can be found in the classroom. Anyone who has ever tried to teach this concept knows that it is not intuitively obvious, even to some experienced businesspeople.

4.1. Modeling Sunk Costs

If the sunk cost effect does exist, it is interesting to speculate on the thought process that produces it. A reasonable explanation can be offered using prospect theory. First, however, we must consider the individual's psychic accounting system. To do this it is necessary to introduce a psychic equivalent to debits and credits which, for lack of better terms, I will call pleasure and pain. In terms of prospect theory, pleasure can be thought of as the value function in the domain of gains while pain corresponds to the value function in the domain of losses. (Henceforth, for expository purposes, I will refer to the value function for losses as $\tilde{v}$.) When will a customer feel pain? Pain will *not* be felt when a purchase is made for immediate consumption (like buying a hamburger for lunch) as long as the price is "reasonable." If the value of the hamburger is g and the cost is c, then the net pleasure will be $v(g) + \tilde{v}(-c)$.[12] Only in the event of a loss will there be actual net pain.

---

[8]I also plan some experiments to test the sunk cost effect. In one pilot study undertaken by one of my students, Lewis Broad, customers at an all-you-can-eat pizza restaurant were randomly given free lunches. They, in fact, ate less than the control group who paid the $2.50 normal bill.

[9]This example was suggested by Paul Slovic.

[10]U.S. Government (1976, p. 14). This issue was raised because the Bureau had in fact received such warnings about the Teton Dam.

[11]*Ibid*, p. 14.

[12]What if the price is "unreasonable?" In this case the customer will feel pain that is a function of the difference between the price paid and some reference (or just) price. Similarly, if the price is especially low there will be extra pleasure that is related to the difference between the reference price and the price paid. A complete analysis of these issues will be presented in a future paper.

Now, however, consider the case described in Example 4. When the basketball tickets are purchased the consumer just exchanges cash for an asset (the tickets). At this point the consumer *could* experience $40 worth of pain with the expectation of feeling pleasure at the game as if the tickets had been free, but this seems unlikely. A much more plausible story is that no pain or pleasure is felt at this point except perhaps in anticipation of the game. Then when the game is attended the consumer feels net pleasure as in the case of the hamburger. The snowstorm, however, creates a problem. If the tickets aren't used then their value has become zero and the consumer should feel a $40 loss ($\tilde{v}(-40)$). But, the economist would say, how does going to the game help? Let's assume that the cost of going to the game through the snow is c and the value of seeing the game is g. (I will ignore uncertainty about getting to the game as it would add nothing to the analysis.) Further, assume that had the tickets been free, the consumer would have been indifferent about going, i.e., $v(g) = -\tilde{v}(-c)$. In this case the $40 paid for the tickets will induce the consumer to go since $v(g) + \tilde{v}(-(c + 40)) > -\tilde{v}(-40)$ due to the convexity of $\tilde{v}$.

4.2. Sunk Costs and Multipart Pricing

Example 5 can be used to illustrate an application of the sunk cost effect in microeconomics. The tennis club uses a two-part pricing scheme. The membership fee is $300 and the court fees are $10 per hour. Suppose the membership fee is raised to $400 keeping the court fees fixed. The standard theory would predict the following effects: (1) some members will drop out, (2) those who remain will use the club slightly less because of the income effect of the increased membership fee (assuming tennis playing is normal), and (3) *average* utilization will rise if the change in the mix of members toward higher demanders outweighs the income effect, otherwise average utilization will fall. Total utilization will certainly fall.

If the sunk cost effect is valid then the analysis of effect (2) must be changed. The sunk cost effect will increase utilization, which is in the opposite direction of the income effect. If the sunk cost effect is large enough in magnitude, then raising the membership fee could increase *total* utilization. Given the wide ranging uses of multipart pricing this analysis could have many important applications.

5. SEARCHING
AND THE PSYCHOPHYSICS OF PRICES

Example 6. (a) You set off to buy a clock radio at what you believe to be the cheapest store in your area. When you arrive, you find that the radio costs $25, a price consistent with your priors (the suggested retail price is $35). As you are about to make the purchase, a reliable friend comes by and tells you that the same radio is selling for $20 at another store ten minutes away. Do you go to the other store? What is the minimum price differential which would induce you to go to the other store? (b) Now suppose that instead of a radio you are buying a color television for $500 and your friend tells you it is available at the other store for $495. Same questions.

On the second page of his price theory text, George Stigler (1970) states a traditional theory of consumer search behavior:

> To maximize his utility the buyer searches for additional prices until the expected saving from the purchase equals the cost of visiting one more dealer. Then he stops searching, and buys from the dealer who quotes the lowest price he has encountered.

Example 6 suggests an alternative to Stigler's theory. The alternative theory states that search for any purchase will continue until the expected amount saved as a proportion of the total price equals some critical value.

This hypothesis is a simple application of the Weber–Fechner law of psychophysics.[13] The law states that the just noticeable difference in any stimulus is proportional to the stimulus. If the stimulus is price then the law implies that

$$\Delta p / p = k,$$

where Δp is the just noticeable difference, p is the mean price, and k is a constant.

Again, this hypothesis is difficult to test empirically. However, a recent paper by Pratt, Wise, and Zeckhauser (1977) studied price dispersions of consumer goods and found nearly a linear relationship between the mean price of a good and its standard deviation. They interpret this result as inconsistent with the standard search theory: "If search costs were constant, we might expect that the expected gains from searching would lead to ratios between standard deviation and price that declined rather rapidly with mean price."[14] While these results are supportive, they are inconclusive because the observed price dispersions represent an equilibrium resulting from both buyer *and* seller behavior. Thus, even if consumers searched optimally, firm behavior could produce this result. A cleaner test may only be possible experimentally.

Because of its psychophysical foundation, prospect theory can be used to

---

[13]For more on the Weber-Fechner Law see Stigler (1965).
[14]Pratt, Wise, and Zeckhauser (1977, p. 22).

model search behavior as observed in Example 6. To see how, reconsider Equation (2) (repeated here for convenience),

$$V(x, p; y, q) = v(y) + \pi(p)[v(x) - v(y)].$$ (2)

Notice that the decision weight given to the chance of winning, $\pi(p)$, is multiplied by the difference in the valuation of the alternative prizes $(v(x) - v(y))$ rather than the value of the monetary differences $(v(x - y))$ because of the concavity of $v, v(x) - v(y) < v(x - y)$. Similarly, the value of obtaining the clock radio at $20 instead of $25 would be $\bar{v}(-25) - \bar{v}(-20)$ which is greater (in absolute value) than $\bar{v}(-500) - \bar{v}(-495)$ because of the convexity of $\bar{v}$. Put simply, $5 seems like a lot to save on a $25 radio but not much on a $500 TV. Needless to say, it would be virtually unnoticed on a $5,000 car.

Market behavior consistent with this hypothesis is easy to find. An old selling trick is to quote a low price for a stripped-down model and then coax the consumer into a more expensive version in a series of increments each of which seems small relative to the entire purchase. (One reason why new cars have whitewall tires and old cars do not is that $20 seems a small extra to equip a *car* with whitewalls but a large extra for a new set of *tires*.) Funeral parlors, as well as automobile dealers, are said to make a living off this idea.[15]

6. CHOOSING NOT TO CHOOSE: REGRET

Example 7.[16] Members of the Israeli Army display a resistance to trading patrol assignments, even when it would be convenient for both individuals to do so.

Example 8.[17] Mr. A is waiting in line at a movie theater. When he gets to the ticket window he is told that as the 100,000th customer of the theater he has just won $100.

Mr. B is waiting in line at a different theater. The man in front of him wins $1,000 for being the 1,000,000th customer of the theater. Mr. B wins $150.

Would you rather be Mr. A or Mr. B?

---

[15]Madison Avenue also seems to understand this principle. An advertisement appeared on television recently for a variable-month car loan (46 months, say, instead of the usual 48). The bank wanted to stress the amount of interest that could be saved by financing the car over two fewer months. In the advertisement an actor had about $5,000 in bills stacked up on a table to represent the total amount of money repaid. He then took $37 representing the interest saved, removed it from the pile, and said, "It may not seem like a lot here . . ." (pointing to the pile) ". . . but it will feel like a lot here" (pointing to his wallet).

[16]This example is due to Daniel Kahneman and Amos Tversky.

[17]This example is due to Ronald Howard.

This and the following section discuss situations where individuals voluntarily restrict their choices. In Section 5 the motive is self-control. Choices in the future are reduced because the current self doesn't trust the future self. In this section we consider a motive for reducing choice which is a special kind of decision-making cost. Here the act of choosing or even just the knowledge that choice exists induces costs, and these costs can be reduced or eliminated by restricting the choice set in advance. These costs fall into the general category of *regret* which will be defined to include the related concepts of *guilt* and *responsibility*.

That responsibility can cause regret is well illustrated by Example 7. If two men trade assignments and one is killed, the other must live with the knowledge that it could (should?) have been he. By avoiding such trades these costs are reduced. Since the opportunity to exchange assignments must surely be a valued convenience, the observed resistance to trading suggests that the potential responsibility costs are non-trivial.

Sometimes just information can induce psychic costs. This is obvious, since it is always possible to make someone feel terrible just by relating a horror story of sufficient horror. Example 8 illustrates the point in a more interesting way. There seems little doubt that were the prizes won by Mr. A and Mr. B the same, Mr. A would be better off. The knowledge that he just missed winning causes regret to Mr. B, enough to cause some people to prefer Mr. A's position in the example as stated!

Whenever choice can induce regret consumers have an incentive to eliminate the choice. They will do so whenever the expected increase in utility (pleasure) derived from making their own choices is less than the expected psychic costs which the choices will induce.

Regret, in prospect theory, can be modeled through induced changes in the reference point. In Example 8, Mr. A simply gains \$100 or $v(100)$. Mr. B however must deal with the near miss. If, for example, the person in front of him cut into the line he may feel he has gained \$150 but lost \$1,000 yielding $v(150)+\bar{v}(-1,000)$.

Two markets seem to have been strongly influenced by this preference for not choosing: the health care industry, and the vacation and recreation industry.

Choosing not to choose is apparent at many levels in the health care industry. It explains, I believe, two major institutional features of the health delivery system. A puzzle for many economists who have studied the industry is the popularity of shallow, first dollar (no deductible or low deductible) coverage which is precisely the opposite pattern which would be predicted by a theoretical analysis of the problem. Many economists have criticized the system because the insurance creates a zero marginal cost situation for most consumers and this, it is argued, helps create the massive inflation we have experienced in this sector in recent years. The analysis may be correct, but an important issue seems ignored. Why do consumers want the first dollar coverage? I believe the reasons involve regret. Most consumers find decisions involving trade-offs between health care and money very distasteful. This is especially true when the decision is made for someone else, like a child. A high deductible policy would force individuals to make many such decisions, at considerable psychic costs. The costs can occur no matter which way the decision is made. Consider a couple who must decide whether to spend $X for a diagnostic test for their child. There is some small probability p that the child has a serious disease which could be treated if detected early enough. There will surely be regret if the decision is made not to get the test and the child later is found to have the disease. If the disease can be fatal, then the regret may loom so large that the test will be administered even for very large values of X or very small values of p. Yet once the test is ordered and the likely negative result is obtained, the couple may regret the expenditure, especially if it is large relative to their income. Obviously, these costs are avoided if all health care is prepaid, via either first dollar coverage or a prepaid health organization.

Though many individuals seem averse to explicit trade-offs between money and health, money does not have to be at stake for regret to enter the picture. The health industry has frequently been criticized for failing to involve the patient in the decision-making process, even when no out-of-pocket expenses are involved. Again, regret seems to provide an attractive explanation for this characteristic of the system. Suppose that a patient must have an operation, but two different procedures are possible. Assume that only one of the procedures can ever be attempted on any individual, that each has the same probability of success and (to make the case as clean as possible) that physicians know that if one procedure doesn't work the other would have. Clearly, in this situation a rational consumer would want the physician to make the choice, and furthermore, he would not want to know that a choice existed! In less dramatic examples there will still be an incentive to let the physician choose, particularly if the physician knows the patient well (and thus can do a good job of reflecting the patient's preferences).

Of course, the physician must then bear all the responsibility costs so there may be advantages to further delegation. One method is to obtain a second opinion, which at least divides the responsibility. Another is to utilize rules-of-thumb and standard-operating-procedures which may eliminate the costs altogether.[18]

The other major example of the market yielding to consumer preferences to not choose is the recreation industry. An excellent case in point is Club Med, which is actually not a club but rather a worldwide chain of resort hotels.[19] One heavily promoted characteristic of the resorts is that they are virtually

---

[18]I should add here that these comments about the health sector are strictly of a *positive* nature. I am simply offering an explanation of why the institutions are structured as they are. Policy implications must be drawn carefully.

[19]This example was suggested by Paul Joskow.

cashless. Almost all activities including food and drink are prepaid, and extra drinks are paid for via poppit beads which are worn necklace style.[20] This example presents an interesting contrast with the health example. Consumers may feel guilty about not buying health and guilty about spending on their vacation. Having everything prepaid avoids decisions about whether to *spend* to do something, and reduces the psychic costs of engaging in the costly activities. The reduction in psychic costs may be enough so that a consumer would prefer to spend $1,000 for a vacation than to spend $400 on plane fare and another $500 in $20 increments, especially given the hypothesis of the preceding section. Club Med has taken the prepaid concept furthest, but the basic idea is prevalent in the recreation industry. Other examples include ocean cruises, "package travel tours," and one-price amusement parks, such as Marriot's Great America.

7. PRECOMMITMENT AND SELF-CONTROL[21]

Example 9. A group of hungry economists is awaiting dinner when a large can of cashews is opened and placed on the coffee table. After half the can is devoured in three minutes, everyone agrees to put the rest of the cashews into the pantry.

Example 10. Professor X agreed to give a paper at the AEA meetings "to ensure that the paper would get written by the end of the year."

A basic axiom of economic theory is that additional choices can only make one better-off (and that an additional constraint can only make one worse-off). An exception is sometimes made due to decision-making costs, a concept that was expanded to include regret in the previous section. This section demonstrates that the axiom is also violated when self-control problems are present.

The question examined now is why individuals impose rules on themselves. This question was brought to economists' attention by Strotz (1955/56)

---

[20]"Cash is useless at Club Med. You prepay your vacation before leaving home. Included in the price are room accommodations, three fabulous meals each day, all the wine you can drink, lunch and dinner, scores of sports activities, plus expert instruction and use of rent-free sporting equipment. The only extras, if there are any, are totally up to you. Drinks at the bar, boutique purchases, optimal excursions, beauty salon visits—simply sign and then pay for them before leaving the village. And there's no tipping. So it couldn't be easier to stick to your vacation budget" (from a Club Med brochure).

[21]The ideas in this section are explored in detail in Thaler and Shefrin (1979). Details on the formal model appear in Shefrin and Thaler (1979). Others who have written in this area are Ainslee (1975), Schelling (1978), Elster (1977), and Scitovsky (1976).

in his now classic paper on dynamic inconsistency. Strotz begins his article with a famous quote from the *Odyssey:*

> . . . but you must bind me hard and fast, so that I cannot stir from the spot where you will stand me . . . and if I beg you to release me, you must tighten and add to my bonds.

Strotz described Ulysses' problem as one of *changing tastes*. He now would prefer not to steer his ship upon the rocks, but he knows that once he hears the Sirens he will want to get closer to their source and thus to the rocks. The solution Ulysses adopts is to have his crew tie him to the mast. Strotz refers to this type of solution as *precommitment*.

Strotz's formal model concerns savings behavior. How should an individual allocate a fixed exhaustible resource over his lifetime? The major finding in Strotz's paper is that unless the individual has an exponential discount function, he will not follow his own plan. That is, if at time t the individual reconsiders a plan formulated at time $t' < t$, he will change the plan. Thus people will be *inconsistent* over time. While changing tastes can explain inconsistency, they cannot explain precommitment. Why should the person with changing tastes bind himself to his *current* preferences, knowing that he will wish to break the binds in each succeeding period? Yet there is no denying the popularity of precommitment devices. One such device which has always been an enigma to economists is Christmas clubs which currently attract over one billion dollars a year in deposits from millions of depositors. Other examples of precommitment are discussed below.

The key to understanding precommitment is to recognize that it is a device used to solve problems of *self-control*. While this seems obvious, it has not been incorporated in the formal models of dynamic choice behavior. Yet it is not difficult to do so. The concept of self-control suggests the existence of a controller and a controllee. To capture this, the individual can be modeled as an organization with a *planner* and a series of *doers*, one for every time period. Conflict arises because the current doer's preferences are always myopic relative to the planner's. This conflict creates a *control problem* of the same variety as those present in any organization. Since the planner's preferences are consistent over time it does make sense for him to adopt rules to govern the doers' behavior. These rules are adopted for the same reasons employees are not given complete discretion: the existence of a conflict of interest.

Since the full details of the model are available elsewhere I will limit my discussion here to the predictions of the model regarding market behavior. One immediate implication of the model is that self-control problems will be most important for those consumption activities which have a time dimension. Since the planner maximizes a function that depends on the doers' utilities, if all the costs and benefits of a particular activity occur in the present there will be no conflict. Of course, as long as there is a finite budget constraint, any current consumption will reduce future consumption, but the conflicts are likely to be greatest for saving per se and for those activities which have an explicit time dimension. For lack of a better term, I will refer to such activities as *investment goods*. Further, goods whose benefits accrue later than their costs (such as education and exercise) are termed *positive investment goods*, while those with the opposite time structure (such as tobacco and alcohol) are termed *negative investment goods*.

Since precommitment usually requires external help (Ulysses needed his crew to tie him to the mast), if it is an important phenomenon we should expect to see evidence of market provision of precommitment services in the investment goods industries. Indeed, such evidence is abundant.

Negative investment goods provide the most dramatic examples: Alcoholics Anonymous, drug abuse centers, diet clubs, "fat farms," and smoking clinics. Note that addiction is not the only factor involved in these services. Calling food addictive is stretching the definition somewhat, so the diet clubs and fat farms can be considered pure self-control administrators. Even the drug examples, such as Alcoholics Anonymous, perform most of their activities for individuals who are "on the wagon." The problem is not that they are addicted to alcohol, rather that they would quickly become readdicted. The problem is to avoid the first drink, and AA helps them do that. One extreme technique of precommitment used by alcoholics is taking the drug Antabuse which makes the individual sick if he ingests any alcohol.

The most obvious positive investment good is saving itself, and here we find an industry dominated by precommitment devices. Christmas clubs, which have already been mentioned, were particularly noteworthy in previous years because they paid no interest and were thus a "pure" self-control device.[22] Another curious savings institution is the passbook loan. A typical example would be of an individual who had $8,000 in a savings account and wanted to buy a $5,000 car. Rather than withdraw the $5,000 and lose the 5½ percent interest it was earning, the individual uses the money in the account as collateral for a loan at 8 percent. These loans are reasonably popular, in spite of the obvious interest costs, because they guarantee that the money in the savings account will be replaced and not spent. A final example is whole life insurance which is often alleged to be a bad investment but again provides a specific savings *plan*.

Other investment goods, such as education and exercise, evidence self-control considerations in their pricing policies. Virtually all such services are sold via prepaid packages. This device lowers the cost to the doer of engaging

---

[22]The vice president of one savings bank has reported to me the results of a survey his bank completed on Christmas club users. They found that the average savings account balance of Christmas club users was over $3,000. This suggests that Christmas clubs should not be considered as a device for people who can't save but as a tool of people who do!

in the investment activity on a day-to-day basis. If the sunk cost effect is also present then the membership fee will also act as an actual inducement to go.

8. CONCLUSION

Friedman and Savage (1948) defined economic theory as a positive science using an analogy to a billiard player:

> Consider the problem of predicting, before each shot, the direction of travel of a billiard ball hit by an expert billiard player. It would be possible to construct one or more mathematical formulas that would give the direction of travel that would score points and, among these, would indicate the one (or more) that would leave the balls in the best positions. The formulas might, of course, be extremely complicated, since they would necessarily take account of the location of the balls in relationship to one another and to the cushions and of the complicated phenomena introduced by "english." Nonetheless, it seems not at all unreasonable that excellent predictions would be yielded by the hypothesis that the billiard player made his shots *as if* he knew the formulas, could estimate accurately by eye the angles etc., from the formulas, and could then make the ball travel in the direction indicated by the formulas. It would in no way disprove or contradict the hypothesis or weaken our confidence in it, if it should turn out that the billiard player had never studied any branch of mathematics and was utterly incapable of making the necessary calculations: unless he was capable in some way of reaching approximately the same result as that obtained from the formulas, he would not in fact be likely to be an expert billiard player.[23]

I would like to make two points about this passage and the relationship between Friedman and Savage's position and mine. First, I do not base my critique of the economic theory of the consumer on an attack of the assumptions. I agree with Friedman and Savage that positive theories should be evaluated on the basis of their ability to predict behavior. In my judgment, for the classes of problems discussed in this paper, economic theory fails this test.

Second, Friedman and Savage only claim that their mathematical model would be a good predictor of the behavior of an *expert* billiard player. It is instructive to consider how one might build models of two non-experts.

A novice who has played only a few times will mainly be concerned with the choice of what ball to try to sink, which will depend primarily on the *perceived* degree of difficulty of the shot. (In contrast, an expert can make nearly any open shot and is likely to sink 50 or more in a row. Thus he will be concerned with planning several shots ahead.) The novice will use little or no "english," will pay little attention to where the cue ball goes after the shot, and

---

[23]Friedman and Savage (1948, p. 298).

may be subject to some optical illusions that cause him to systematically mishit some other shots.

An intermediate player who has played an average of two hours a week for twenty years may only average 4 or 5 balls per turn (compared with the expert's 50). He will have much less control of the cue ball after it strikes another ball and will have some shots that he knows cause him trouble (perhaps long bank shots or sharp angles). He will plan ahead, but rarely more than one or two shots.

Clearly, descriptive models for the novice or intermediate will have to be quite different than the model for the expert. If one wanted to model the behavior of the *average* billiard player, the model selected would be for some kind of intermediate player, and would probably resemble the model of the novice more than the model of the expert. Rules-of-thumb and heuristics would have important roles in this model.

It is important to stress that both the novice and intermediate players described above behave rationally. They choose different shots than the expert does because they have different technologies. Nonetheless, the expert model has a distinct normative flavor. The model chooses from all the shots available the *best* shot. Thus the novice and intermediate players choose rationally and yet violate a normative model. The reason, of course, is that the model is not an acceptable normative (or positive) model for *them*. The novice model (aim at the ball that seems easiest to sink—don't worry about much else) is also a normative model. It is the best the novice can do. Clearly the relationship between rationality and normative models is a delicate one.

How does consumer behavior relate to billiard behavior? Again there will be various classes of consumers. Some will be experts (Ph.Ds in economics?), others will be novices (children?). What I have argued in this paper is that the orthodox economic model of consumer behavior is, in essence, a model of robot-like experts. As such, it does a poor job of predicting the behavior of the average consumer.[24] This is not because the average consumer is dumb, but rather that he does not spend all of his time thinking about how to make decisions. A grocery shopper, like the intermediate billiard player, spends a couple of hours a week shopping and devotes a rational amount of (scarce) mental energy to that task. Sensible rules-of-thumb, such as don't waste, may lead to occasional deviations from the expert model, such as the failure to ignore sunk costs, but these shoppers are doing the best they can.

Prospect theory and the planner-doer model attempt to describe *human* decision-makers coping with a very complex and demanding world. Failure to develop positive theories such as these will leave economists wondering why people are frequently aiming at the balls lined up right in front of the pockets

---

[24]Some related issues have been discussed in the literature on the theory of the firm. See, for example, Winter (1975) and the references cited therein.

rather than at the three-ball carom their computer model has identified as being optimal.

REFERENCES

The author wishes to acknowledge the many people who have made this paper possible. Colleagues, too numerous to name individually, at the Center for Naval Analyses, Cornell University, The National Bureau of Economic Research-West, Decision Research, and the University of Rochester have contributed importantly to the final product. Special thanks go to Daniel Kahneman, Amos Tversky, H.M. Shefrin, Thomas Russell, and particularly Victor Fuchs, who has supported the research in every possible way. Of course, responsibility for remaining deficiencies is the author's. He also wishes to acknowledge financial support from the Kaiser Family Foundation, while he was a visiting scholar at NBER-West.

Ainslie, George. "Specious Reward: A Behavioral Theory of Impulsiveness and Impulse Control." *Psychological Bulletin* 82, 4 (July 1975): 463–496.

Allais, M. "Le compartement de l'homme rationnel devant le risque: Critique des postulats et axiomes de l'ecole Américaine." *Econometrica* 21 (1953): 503–546.

Aronson, Elliot, and Judson Mills. "The Effects of Severity of Initiation on Liking for a Group." *Journal of Abnormal and Social Psychology* 59 (1959): 177–181.

Becker, Gary S. "Irrational Behavior and Economic Theory." *Journal of Political Economy* (February 1962): 1–13.

Becker, S.; J. Ronen; and G. Sorter. "Opportunity Costs—An Experimental Approach." *Journal of Accounting Research* (1974): 317–329.

Demsetz, Harold. "When Does the Rule of Liability Matter." *Journal of Legal Studies* (January 1972): 28.

Elster, Jon. "Ulysses and the Sirens: A Theory of Imperfect Rationality." *Social Science Information* XVI, 5 (1977): 469–526.

Friedman, M., and L.J. Savage. "The Utility Analysis of Choices Involving Risks." *Journal of Political Economy* 56 (1948): 279–304.

Gerard, Harold B., and Groves C. Mathewson. "The Effects of Severity of Initiation on Liking for a Group: A Replication." *Journal of Experimental Social Psychology* 2 (1966): 278–287.

Grether, David M. "Bayes Rule as a Descriptive Model: The Representativeness Heuristic." Social Science Working Paper no. 245 (California Institute of Technology, January 1979).

Grether, D., and C. Plott. "Economic Theory of Choice and the Preference Reversal Phenomenon." *American Economic Review* (September 1979): 623–638.

Kagel, John, and Raymond Battalio. "Experimental Studies of Consumer Behavior Using Laboratory Animals." *Economic Inquiry* (March 1975): 22–38.

Kahneman, Daniel, and Amos Tversky. "Prospect Theory: An Analysis of Decision Under Risk." *Econometrica* 47 (March 1979).

McGlothin, W.H. "Stability of Choices Among Uncertain Alternatives." *American Journal of Psychology* 69 (1956): 604–615.

Neumann, B.R., and L.A. Friedman. "Opportunity Costs: Further Evidence Through an Experimental Replication." *Journal of Accounting Research* (Autumn 1978): 400–410.

Pratt, John; David Wise; and Richard Zeckhauser. "Price Variations in Almost Competitive Markets." (Cambridge, MA: Harvard University, Kennedy School of Government, 1977).

Schelling, T.C. "Egonomics, or the Art of Self-management." *The American Economic Review* 63 (May 1978): 290–294.

Scitovsky, Tibor. *The Joyless Economy*. (New York: Oxford University Press, 1976).

Shefrin, H.M., and Richard Thaler. *Rules and Discretion in Intertemporal Choice* (Ithaca, NY: Cornell University, 1979). See Chapter 5 in this book, pages 91–126.

Simon, Herbert. *Models of Man* (New York: Wiley, 1957).

Stigler, George. *Essays in the History of Economics* (Chicago: University of Chicago Press, 1965).

———. *The Theory of Price* (New York: Macmillan, 1970).

Slovic, Paul; Baruch Fischhoff; and Sarah Lichtenstein. "Behavioral Decision Theory." *Annual Review of Psychology* 28 (1977): 1–39.

Strotz, Robert. "Myopia and Inconsistency in Dynamic Utility Maximization." *Review of Economic Studies* 23 (1955/56): 165–180.

Thaler, Richard, and H.M. Shefrin. *An Economic Theory of Self-Control* (Ithaca, NY: Cornell University, 1979). See Chapter 4 in this book, pages 77–90.

Tversky, Amos, and Daniel Kahneman. "Judgment Under Uncertainty: Heuristics and Biases." *Science* (1974): 1124–1131.

United States Congress Committee on Government Operations, Teton Dam Disaster. Union Calendar no. 837, House Report no. 94-1667, Sept. 23, 1976.

United States Senate Hearings before the Subcommittee on Consumer Affairs of the Committee on Banking, Housing and Urban Affairs, Oct. 9, 1975.

Von Neumann, J., and O. Morgenstern. *Theory of Games and Economic Behavior* (Princeton, NJ: Princeton University Press, 1944).

Weiss, Y.; A. Hall; and F. Dong. *The Effect of Price and Income in the Investment in Schooling: Evidence from the Seattle-Denver NIT Experiment*. Menlo Park, CA: SRI International.

Winter, Sidney. "Optimization and Evaluation in the Theory of the Firm." in Richard Day and Theodore Groves, eds. *Adaptive Economic Models* (New York: Academic Press, 1975).

2

MENTAL ACCOUNTING AND CONSUMER CHOICE

Richard H. Thaler

A new model of consumer behavior is developed using a hybrid of cognitive psychology and microeconomics. The development of the model starts with the mental coding of combinations of gains and losses using the prospect theory value function. Then the evaluation of purchases is modeled using the new concept of "transaction utility." The household budgeting process is also incorporated to complete the characterization of mental accounting. Several implications to marketing, particularly in the area of pricing, are developed.

1. INTRODUCTION

Consider the following anecdotes:

1. Mr. and Mrs. L and Mr. and Mrs. H went on a fishing trip in the Northwest and caught some salmon. They packed the fish and sent them home on an airline, but the fish were lost in transit. They received $300 from the airline. The couples took the money, went out to dinner and spent $225. They had never spent that much at a restaurant before.
2. Mr. X is up $50 in a monthly poker game. He has a queen high flush and calls a $10 bet. Mr. Y owns 100 shares of IBM, which went up ½ today, and is even in the poker game. He has a king high flush but he folds. When X wins, Y thinks to himself, "If I had been up $50 I would have called too."
3. Mr. and Mrs. J have saved $15,000 toward their dream vacation home. They hope to buy the home in five years. The money earns 10 percent in a

Reprinted with permission from *Marketing Science* 4,3 (Summer 1985): 199–214. © Operations Research Society of America and the Institute of Management Sciences, 290 Westminster Street, Providence, RI 02903.

money market account. They just bought a new car for $11,000 which they financed with a three-year car loan at 15 percent.
4. Mr. S admires a $125 cashmere sweater at the department store. He declines to buy it, feeling that it is too extravagant. Later that month he receives the same sweater from his wife for a birthday present. He is very happy. Mr. and Mrs. S have only joint bank accounts.

All organizations, from General Motors down to single person households, have explicit and/or implicit accounting systems. The accounting systems often influence decisions in unexpected ways. This paper characterizes some aspects of the implicit mental accounting system used by individuals and households. The goal of the paper is to develop a richer theory of consumer behavior than standard economic theory. The new theory is capable of explaining (and predicting) the kinds of behavior illustrated by the four anecdotes above. Each of these anecdotes illustrate a type of behavior where a mental accounting system induces an individual to violate a simple economic principle. Example 1 violates the principle of fungibility. Money is not supposed to have labels attached to it. Yet the couples behaved the way they did because the $300 was put into both "windfall gain" and "food" accounts. The extravagant dinner would not have occurred had each couple received a yearly salary increase of $150, even though that would have been worth more in present value terms. Example 2 illustrates that accounts may be both topically and temporally specific. A player's behavior in a poker game is altered by his current position in that evening's game, but not by either his lifetime winnings or losings nor by some event allocated to a different account altogether, such as a paper gain in the stock market. In example 3 the violation of fungibility (at obvious economic costs) is caused by the household's appreciation for their own self-control problems. They are afraid that if the vacation home account is drawn down it will not be repaid, while the bank will see to it that the car loan is paid off on schedule. Example 4 illustrates the curious fact that people tend to give as gifts items that the recipients would not buy for themselves, and that the recipients by and large approve of the strategy. As is shown in §4.3, this also violates a microeconomic principle.

The theory of consumer behavior to which the current theory is offered as a substitute is the standard economic theory of the consumer. That theory, of course, is based on normative principles. In fact, the paradigm of economic theory is to first characterize the solution to some problem, and then to assume the relevant agents (on average) act accordingly.

The decision problem which consumers are supposed to solve can be characterized in a simple fashion. Let $z = \{z_1, \ldots, z_i, \ldots, z_n\}$ be the vector of goods available in the economy at prices given by the corresponding vector $p = \{p_1, \cdots p_i, \cdots p_n\}$. Let the consumer's utility function be defined as $U(z)$ and his income (or wealth) be given as I. Then the consumer should try to solve the following problem:

$$\max_{z} U(z) \quad \text{s.t.} \quad \sum p_i z_i \leq I.$$

Or, using Lagrange multipliers:

$$\max_{z} U(z) - \lambda(\sum p_i z_i - I). \tag{1}$$

The first order conditions to this problem are, in essence, the economic theory of the consumer. Lancaster (1971) has extended the model by having utility depend on the characteristics of the goods. Similarly, Becker (1965) has introduced the role of time and other factors using the concept of household production. These extended theories are richer than the original model, and, as a result, have more to offer marketing. Nevertheless, the economic theory of the consumer, even so extended, has not found widespread application in marketing. Why not? One reason is that all such models omit virtually all marketing variables except price and product characteristics. Many marketing variables fall into the category that Tversky and Kahneman (1981) refer to as *framing*. These authors have shown that often choices depend on the way a problem is posed as much as on the objective features of a problem. Yet within economic theory, framing cannot alter behavior.

To help describe individual choice under uncertainty in a way capable of capturing "mere" framing effects as well as other anomalies, Kahneman and Tversky (1979) have developed "prospect theory" as an alternative to expected utility theory. Prospect theory's sole aim is to describe or predict behavior, not to characterize optimal behavior. Elsewhere (Chapter 1), I have begun to develop a similar descriptive alternative to the deterministic economic theory of consumer choice. There I argued that consumers often fail to behave in accordance with the normative prescriptions of economic theory. For example, consumers often pay attention to sunk costs when they shouldn't, and underweight opportunity costs as compared to out-of-pocket costs.[1]

This paper uses the concept of mental accounting to move further toward a behaviorally based theory of consumer choice. Compared to the model in equation (1) the alternative theory has three key features. First, the utility function $U(x)$ is replaced with the *value function* $v(\cdot)$ from prospect theory. The characteristics of this value function are described and then extended to apply

---

[1] These propositions have recently been tested and confirmed in extensive studies by Arkes and Hackett (1985), Gregory (1982) and Knetsch and Sinden (1984).

to compound outcomes. Second, price is introduced directly into the value function using the concept of a *reference* price. The new concept of *transaction utility* is developed as a result. Third, the normative principle of *fungibility* is relaxed. Numerous marketing implications of the theory are derived. The theory is also used to explain some empirical puzzles.

2. MENTAL ARITHMETIC

2.1. The Value Function

The first step in describing the behavior of the representative consumer is to replace the utility function from economic theory with the psychologically richer *value function* used by Kahneman and Tversky. The assumed shape of the value function incorporates three important behavioral principles that are used repeatedly in what follows. First, the function $v(\cdot)$ is defined over perceived gains and loses relative to some natural reference point, rather than wealth or consumption as in the standard theory. This feature reflects the fact that people appear to respond more to perceived changes than to absolute levels. (The individual in this model can be thought of as a pleasure machine with gains yielding pleasure and losses yielding pain.) By using a reference point the theory also permits framing effects to affect choices. The framing of a problem often involves the suggestion of a particular reference point. Second, the value function is assumed to be concave for gains and convex for losses. ($v''(x) < 0$, $x > 0$; $v''(x) > 0$, $x < 0$.) This feature captures the basic psychophysics of quantity. The difference between \$10 and \$20 seems greater than the difference between \$110 and \$120, irrespective of the signs of the amounts in question. Third, the loss function is steeper than the gain function ($v(x) < -v(-x)$, $x > 0$). This notion that losses loom larger than gains captures what I have elsewhere called the endowment effect: people generally will demand more to sell an item they own than they would be willing to pay to acquire the same item (Thaler, 1980).

2.2. Coding Gains and Losses

The prospect theory value function is defined over single, unidimensional outcomes. For the present analysis it is useful to extend the analysis to incorporate compound outcomes where each outcome is measured along the same dimension (say dollars).[2]

---

[2]Kahneman and Tversky are currently working on the single outcome, multi-attribute case. It is also possible to deal with the compound multi-attribute case but things get very messy. Since this paper is trying to extend economic theory which assumes that all outcomes can be collapsed into a single index (utils or money), sticking to the one-dimensional case seems like a reasonable first step.

The question is how does the joint outcome (x, y) get coded? Two possibilities are considered. The outcomes could be valued jointly as $v(x + y)$ in which case they will be said to be *integrated*. Alternatively they may be valued separately as $v(x) + v(y)$ in which case they are said to be *segregated*. The issue to be investigated is whether segregation or integration produces greater utility. The issue is interesting from three different perspectives. First, if a situation is sufficiently ambiguous how will individuals choose to code outcomes? To some extent people try to frame outcomes in whatever way makes them happiest.[3] Second, individuals may have preferences about how their life is organized. Would most people rather have a salary of $30,000 and a (certain) bonus of $5,000 or a salary of $35,000? Third, and most relevant to marketing, how would a seller want to describe (frame) the characteristics of a transaction? Which attributes should be combined and which should be separated? The analysis which follows can be applied to any of these perspectives.

For the joint outcome (x, y) there are four possible combinations to consider:

1. Multiple Gains. Let $x > 0$ and $y > 0$.[4] Since v is concave $v(x) + v(y) > v(x + y)$, so segregation is preferred. Moral: don't wrap all the Christmas presents in one box.

2. Multiple Losses. Let the outcomes be $-x$ and $-y$ where x and y are still positive. Then since $v(-x) + v(-y) < v(-(x + y))$ integration is preferred. For example, one desirable feature of credit cards is that they pool many small losses into one larger loss and in so doing reduce the total value lost.

3. Mixed Gain. Consider the outcome $(x, -y)$ where $x > y$ so there is a net gain. Here $v(x) + v(-y) < v(x - y)$ so integration is preferred. In fact, since the loss function is steeper than the gain function, it is possible that $v(x) + v(-y) < 0$ while $v(x - y)$ must be positive since $x > y$ by assumption. Thus, for mixed gains integration amounts to *cancellation*. Notice that all voluntarily executed trades fall into this category.

4. Mixed Loss. Consider the outcome $(x, -y)$ where $x < y$, a net loss. In this case we cannot determine without further information whether $v(x) + v(-y) \gtrless v(x - y)$. This is illustrated in Figure 1. Segregation is preferred if $v(x) > v(x - y) - v(-y)$. This is more likely, the smaller is x relative to y. Intuitively, with a large loss and a small gain, e.g., ($40, -$6,000) segregation is preferred since v is relatively flat near $-6,000$. This will be

---

[3]This is illustrated by the following true story. A group of friends who play poker together regularly had an outing in which they played poker in a large recreational vehicle while going to and from a race track. There were significant asymmetries in the way people (honestly) reported their winnings and losings from the two poker games and racetrack bets. Whether the outcomes were reported together or separately could largely be explained by the analysis that follows.

[4]For simplicity I will deal only with two-outcome events, but the principles generalize to cases with several outcomes.

referred to as the "silver lining" principle. On the other hand, for ($40, −$50) integration is probably preferred since the gain of the $40 is likely to be valued less than the reduction of the loss from $50 to $10, nearly a case of cancellation.

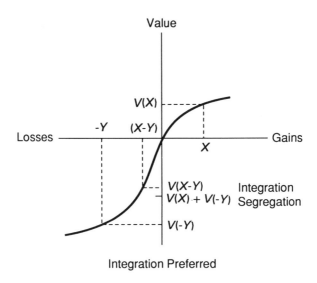

Integration Preferred

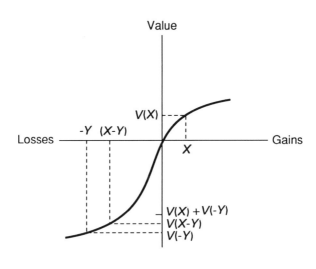

Silver Lining,
Segregation Preferred

Figure 1.

2.3. Evidence on Segregation and Integration

The previous analysis can be summarized by four principles: (a) segegrate gains, (b) integrate losses, (c) cancel losses against larger gains, (d) segregate "silver linings." To see whether these principles coincided with the intuition of others, a small experiment was conducted using 87 students in an undergraduate statistics class at Cornell University. The idea was to present subjects with pairs of outcomes either segregated or integrated and to ask them which frame was preferable. Four scenarios were used, one corresponding to each of the above princples.

The instructions given to the students were:

> Below you will find four pairs of scenarios. In each case two events occur in Mr. A's life and one event occurs in Mr. B's life. You are asked to judge whether Mr. A or Mr. B is happier. Would most people rather be A or B? If you think the two scenarios are emotionally equivalent, check "no difference." In all cases the events are intended to be financially equivalent.

The four items used and the number of responses of each type follow.

1. Mr. A was given tickets to lotteries involving the World Series. He won $50 in one lottery and $25 in the other.

    Mr. B was given a ticket to a single, larger World Series lottery. He won $75.

    Who was happier?   56 A   16 B   15 no difference
2. Mr. A received a letter from the IRS saying that he made a minor arithmetical mistake on his tax return and owed $100. He received a similar letter the same day from his state income tax authority saying he owed $50. There were no other repercussions from either mistake.

    Mr. B received a letter from the IRS saying that he made a minor arithmetical mistake on his tax return and owed $150. There were no other repercussions from his mistake.

    Who was more upset?   66 A   14 B   7 no difference
3. Mr. A bought his first New York State lottery ticket and won $100. Also, in a freak accident, he damaged the rug in his apartment and had to pay the landlord $80.

    Mr. B bought his first New York State lottery ticket and won $20.

    Who was happier?   22 A   61 B   4 no difference
4. Mr. A's car was damaged in a parking lot. He had to spend $200 to repair the damage. The same day the car was damaged, he won $25 in the office football pool.

    Mr. B's car was damaged in a parking lot. He had to spend $175 to repair the damage.

    Who was more upset?   19 A   63 B   5 no difference

For each item, a large majority of the subjects chose in a manner predicted by the theory.[5]

2.4. Reference Outcomes

Suppose an individual is expecting some outcome x and instead obtains $x + \Delta x$. Define this as a reference outcome $(x + \Delta x: x)$. The question then arises how to value such an outcome. Assume that the expected outcome was fully anticipated and assimilated. This implies that $v(x: x) = 0$. A person who opens his monthly pay envelope and finds it to be the usual amount is unaffected. However, when $\Delta x = 0$ there is a choice of ways to frame the outcome corresponding to the segregation/integration analysis of simple compound outcomes. With reference outcomes the choice involves whether to value the unexpected component Δx alone (segregation) or in conjunction with the expected component (integration). An example, similar to those above, illustrates the difference:

- Mr. A expected a Christmas bonus of $300. He received his check and the amount was indeed $300. A week later he received a note saying that there had been an error in this bonus check. The check was $50 too high. He must return the $50.
- Mr. B expected a Christmas bonus of $300. He received his check and found it was for $250.

It is clear who is more upset in this story. Mr. A had his loss segregated and it would inevitably be coded as a loss of $50. Mr. B's outcome can be integrated by viewing the news as a reduction in a gain $-[v(300) - v(250)]$. When the situation is structured in a neutral or ambiguous manner then the same four principles determine whether segregation or integration is preferred:

1. An increase in a gain should be segregated.
2. An increase in (the absolute value of) a loss should be integrated.
3. A decrease in a gain should be integrated (cancellation).
4. A small reduction in (the absolute value of) a loss should be segregated (silver lining).

The concept of a reference outcome is used below to model a buyer's reaction to a market price that differs from the price he expected.

---

[5]Two caveats must be noted here. First, the analysis does not extend directly to the multi-attribute (or multiple account) case. It is often cognitively impossible to integrate across accounts. Thus winning $100 does not cancel a toothache. Second, even within the same account, individuals may be unable to integrate two losses that are framed separately. See Johnson and Thaler (1985).

3. TRANSACTION UTILITY THEORY

In the context of the pleasure machine metaphor suggested earlier, the previous section can be thought of as a description of the hard wiring. The machine responds to perceived gains and losses in the way described. The next step in the analysis is to use this structure to analyze transactions. A two-stage process is proposed. First, individuals evaluate potential transactions. Second, they approve or disapprove of each potential transaction. The first stage is a judgment process while the second is a decision process. They are analyzed in turn.

3.1. Evaluating Transactions

Consider the following excerpt from a movie review:

> My sister just found out that for a $235 per month sublet she shares with another woman, she pays $185 per month. The other woman justifies her $50 per month rent two ways: one, she is doing my sister a favor letting her live there given the housing situation in New York City, and, two, everyone with a room to sublet in NYC will cheat her at least as badly. Her reasons are undeniably true, and that makes them quadruply disgusting. (*Cornell Daily Sun*, Feb. 21, 1983)

Notice that the writer's sister is presumably getting a good value for her money (the room is worth $185 per month) but is still unhappy. To incorporate this aspect of the psychology of buying into the model, two kinds of utility are postulated: *acquisition utility* and *transaction utility*. The former depends on the value of the good received compared to the outlay, the latter depends solely on the perceived merits of the "deal."

For the analysis that follows, three price concepts are used. First, define p as the actual price charged for some good z. Then for some individual, define $\bar{p}$ as the *value equivalent* of z, that is, the amount of money which would leave the individual indifferent between receiving $\bar{p}$ or z as a gift.[6] Finally, let p^* be called the *reference* price for z. The reference price is an expected or "just" price for z. (More on p^* momentarily.)

Now define acquisition utility as the value of the compound outcome $(z, -p) = (\bar{p}, -p)$. This is designated as $v(\bar{p}, -p)$. Acquisition utility is the net utility that accrues from the trade of p to obtain z (which is valued at $\bar{p}$). Since $v(\bar{p}, -p)$ will generally be coded as the integrated outcome $v(\bar{p} - p)$, the cost of the good is not treated as a loss. Given the steepness of the loss function near

---

[6]In the standard theory, p equals the reservation price, the maximum the individual would pay. In this theory, p can differ from the reservation price because of positive or negative transaction utility. Acquisition utility is comparable in principle to consumer surplus.

the reference point, it is hedonically inefficient to code costs as losses, especially for routine transactions.

The measure of transaction utility depends on the price the individual pays compared to some reference price, $p*$. Formally, it is defined as the reference outcome $v(-p: -p*)$, that is, the value of paying p when the expected or reference price is $p*$. Total utility from a purchase is just the sum of acquisition utility and transaction utility.[7] Thus the value of buying good z at price p with reference price $p*$ is defined as $w(z, p, p*)$ where:

$$w(z, p, p*) = v(\hat{p}, -p) + v(-p: -p*). \tag{2}$$

Little has been said as to the determinants of $p*$. The most important factor in determining $p*$ is fairness. Fairness, in turn, depends in large part on cost to the seller. This is illustrated by the following three questionnaires administered to first-year MBA students. (The phrases in brackets differed across the three groups.)

> Imagine that you are going to a sold-out Cornell hockey play-off game, and you have an extra ticket to sell or give away. The price marked on the ticket is $5 (but you were given your tickets for free by a friend) [which is what you paid for each ticket] {but you paid $10 each for your tickets when you bought them from another student}. You get to the game early to make sure you get rid of the ticket. An informal survey of people selling tickets indicates that the going price is $5. You find someone who wants the ticket and takes out his wallet to pay you. He asks how much you want for the ticket. Assume that there is no law against charging a price higher than that marked on the ticket. What price do you ask for if
> 1. he is a friend _____
> 2. he is a stranger _____
> What would you have said if instead you found the going market price was $10?
> 3. friend _____
> 4. stranger _____

The idea behind the questionnaire was that the price people would charge a friend would be a good proxy for their estimate of a fair price. For each question, three prices were available as possible anchors upon which people could base their answers: the price marked on the ticket, the market price, and the price paid by the seller, i.e., cost. As can be seen in Table 1, the modal

---

[7]A more general formulation would be to allow differing weights on the two terms in (2). For example, equation (2) could be written as

$$w(z, p, p*) = v(p, -p) + \beta v(-p: -p*),$$

where β is the weight given to transaction utility. If $\beta = 0$ then the standard theory applies. Pathological bargain hunters would have $\beta > 1$. This generalization was suggested by Jonathan Baron.

answers in the friend condition are equal to the seller's costs except in the unusual case where seller's cost was above market price. In contrast, the modal answers in the stranger condition are equal to market price with the same lone exception. The implication of this is that buyers' perceptions of a seller's costs will strongly influence their judgments about what price is fair, and this in turn influences their value for p^*.

The next questionnaire, given to those participants in an executive development program who said they were regular beer drinkers, shows how transaction utility can influence willingness to pay (and therefore demand). Consider the following scenario:

> You are lying on the beach on a hot day. All you have to drink is ice water. For the last hour you have been thinking about how much you would enjoy a nice cold bottle of your favorite brand of beer. A companion gets up to go make a phone call and offers to bring back a beer from the only nearby place where beer is sold (a fancy resort hotel) [a small, run-down grocery store]. He says that the beer might be expensive and so asks how much you are willing to pay for the beer. He says that he will buy the beer if it costs as much or less than the price you state. But if it costs more than the price you state he will not buy it. You trust your friend, and there is no possibility of bargaining with (the bartender) [store owner]. What price do you tell him?

The results from this survey were dramatic. The median price given in the fancy resort hotel version was $2.65 while the median for the small run-down grocery store version was $1.50. This difference occurs despite the following three features of this example:

1. In both versions the ultimate consumption act is the same—drinking one beer on the beach. The beer is the same in each case.

TABLE 1 Percent of Subjects Giving Common Answers to Hockey Ticket Question

Cost	Market Value		Friend				Stranger		
		0	5	10	Other	0	5	10	Other
0	5 $N = 31$	68	26	3	3	6	77	10	6
0	10	65	26	6	3	6	16	58	19
5	5 $N = 28$	14	79	0	7	0	79	7	14
5	10	7	79	4	9	0	14	57	29
10	5 $N = 26$	0	69	23	8	0	42	46	12
10	10	0	15	69	15	0	0	73	27

NOTE: Modal answer is underlined.

2. There is no possibility of strategic behavior in stating the reservation price.[8]
3. No "atmosphere" is consumed by the respondent.

The explanation offered for these choices is based on the concept of transaction utility. (Acquisition utility is constant between the two cases.) While paying $2.50 for a beer is an expected annoyance at the resort hotel, it would be considered an outrageous "rip-off" in a grocery store. Paying $2.50 a bottle is $15.00 a six-pack, considerably above the reference price.

3.2. Purchase Decisions—Multiple Accounts

The introduction of $w(\cdot)$ as the purchase evaluation device requires additional changes to the standard theory described in the introduction. Since $w(\cdot)$ is defined over individual transactions it is convenient to give each unit of a specific good its own label. Optimization would then require the individual to select the set of purchases that would maximize $\Sigma\ w(\cdot)$ subject to the budget constraint $\Sigma\ p_i z_i \leq I$ where I is income. A solution to this integer programming problem would be to make purchases if and only if

$$w(z_i,\ p_i,\ p_i^*)/p_i \geq k \tag{3}$$

where k is a constant that serves a role similar to that of the Lagrange multiplier in the standard formulation.

Notice that if k is selected optimally then (3) can be applied sequentially without any explicit consideration of opportunity costs. This sort of sequential analysis seems to be a good description of behavior.[9] First, the consumer responds to local temporal budget constraints. That is, the budget constraint that most influences behavior is the current income flow rather than the present value of lifetime wealth. For many families, the most relevant time horizon is the month since many regular bills tend to be monthly. Thus, the budgeting process, either implicit or explicit, tends to occur on a month-to-month basis. Second, expenditures tend to be grouped into categories. Potential expenditures are then considered within their category. (Families that take their monthly pay and put it into various use-specific envelopes to be allocated during the month are explicitly behaving in the manner described

---

[8]The question is what economists would call "incentive compatible." The respondent's best strategy is to state his or her true reservation price. Subjects given extensive explanations of this feature nevertheless still display a large disparity in answers to the two versions of the problem.
[9]The model that follows is based, in part, on some extensive, open-ended interviews of families conducted in 1982. The families were asked detailed questions about how they regulate their day-to-day expenditures, and what they have done in various specific situations such as those involving a large windfall gain or loss.

here. Most families simply use a less explicit procedure.) The tendency to group purchases by category can violate the economic principle of fungibility.

Given the existence of time and category specific budget constraints, the consumer evaluates purchases as situations arise. For example, suppose a couple is called by friends who suggest going out to dinner on Saturday night at a particular restaurant. The couple would have to decide whether such an expenditure would violate either the monthly or the entertainment constraints. Formally, the decision process can be modelled by saying the consumer will buy a good z at price p if

$$\frac{w(z, p, p^*)}{p} > k_{it}$$

where k_{it} is the budget constraint for category i in time period t.

Of course, global optimization would lead all the k_{it}'s to be equal which would render irrelevant the budgeting process described here. However, there is evidence that individuals do not act as if all the ks were equal. As discussed elsewhere (Thaler and Shefrin, 1981), individuals face self-control problems in regulating eating, drinking, smoking, and consumption generally. The whole mental accounting apparatus being presented here can be thought of as part of an individual's solution to these problems. For example, the rule of thumb to restrict monthly expenditures to no more than monthly income is clearly nonoptimal. Yet, when borrowing is permitted as a method of smoothing out monthly ks, some families find themselves heavily in debt. Restrictions on borrowing are then adopted as a second-best strategy. The technology of self-control often implies outright prohibitions because allowing a little bit eventually leads to excesses. (Although smoking cigarettes is undoubtedly subject to diminishing marginal utility, almost no one smokes between 1 and 5 cigarettes a day. That level, while probably preferred by many smokers and former smokers to either zero or 20, is just unattainable.)

Unusually high category specific ks are most likely to be observed for goods that are particularly seductive or addictive. Unusually low ks are observed for goods viewed to be particularly desirable in the long run such as exercise or education. Application of these ideas to gift giving behavior is discussed below.

4. MARKETING IMPLICATIONS

The previous sections have outlined a theory and presented some survey evidence to support its various components. The following sections discuss the implications of this theory to marketing. There are two types of implications presented here. First, the theory is used to explain some empirical puzzles such as why some markets fail to clear. Second, some advice for sellers is derived, based on the presumption that buyers behave according to the theory. This advice is illustrated with actual examples. The implications are derived from each of the three main components of the theory: compounding principles, transaction utility, and budgetary rules.

4.1. Compounding Rule Implications

This section will illustrate how the results from the analysis of mental arithmetic can influence marketing decisions either in the design of products or in the choice of how products are described. The results of section 2-2 can be summarized by two principles: segregate gains and integrate losses. Each principle also has a corollary: segregate "silver linings" (small gains combined with large losses) and integrate (or cancel) losses when combined with larger gains.

Segregate gains   The basic principle of segregating gains is simple and needs little elaboration or illustration. When a seller has a product with more than one dimension it is desirable to have each dimension evaluated separately. The most vivid examples of this are the late-night television advertisements for kitchen utensils. The principle is used at two levels. First, each of the items sold is said to have a multitude of uses, each of which is demonstrated. Second, several "bonus" items are included "if you call right now." These ads all seem to use the same basic format and are almost a caricature of the segregation principle.

   The silver lining principle can be used to understand the widespread use of rebates as a form of price promotion. It is generally believed that rebates were first widely used because of the threat of government price controls. By having an explicitly temporary rebate it was hoped that the old price would be the one for which new regulations might apply. Rebates for small items have the additional feature that not all consumers send in the form to collect the rebate. However, rebates continue to be widely used in the automobile industry in spite of the following considerations:

1. Price controls seem very unlikely during the Reagan administration, especially with inflation receding.
2. All purchasers claim the rebate since it is processed by the dealer and is worth several hundred dollars.
3. Consumers must pay sales tax on the rebate. This can raise the cost of the purchase by 8% of the rebate in New York City. While this is not a large amount of money relative to the price of the car, it nonetheless provides an incentive to adopt the seemingly equivalent procedure of announcing a temporary sale.

Why then are rebates used in the automobile industry? The silver lining principle suggests one reason. A rebate strongly suggests segregating the saving. This can be further strengthened for those consumers who elect to have the rebate mailed to them from the corporate headquarters rather than applied to the down payment.[10]

Integrate losses When possible, consumers would prefer to integrate losses. The concavity of the loss function implies that adding $50 less to an existing $1000 loss will have little impact if it is integrated. This means that sellers have a distinct advantage in selling something if its cost can be added on to another larger purchase. Adding options to an automobile or house purchase are classic, well-known examples. More generally, whenever a seller is dealing with an expensive item the seller should consider whether additional options can be created since the buyers will have temporarily inelastic demands for these options. The principle also applies to insurance purchases. Insurance companies frequently sell riders to home or car insurance policies that are attractive (I believe) only because of this principle. One company has been advertising a "paint spill" rider for its homeowner policy. (This is apparently designed for do-it-yourselfers who have not yet discovered drop cloths.) Another example is credit card insurance which pays for the first $50 of charges against a credit card if it is lost or stolen. (Claims over $50 are absorbed by the credit card company.)

The principle of cancellation states that losses will be integrated with larger gains where plausible. The best example of this is withholding from pay-checks. In the present framework the least aversive type of loss is the reduction of a large gain. This concept seems to have been widely applied by governments. Income taxes would be perceived as much more aversive (in addition to being harder to collect) if the whole tax bill were due in April. The implication for sellers is that every effort should be made to set up a payroll withdrawal payment option. Probably the best way to market dental insurance, for example, would be to sell it as an option to group health insurance through employers. If the employee already pays for some share of the health insurance then the extra premium would be framed as an increase in an existing deduction; this is the ultimate arrangement for a seller.

4.2. Transaction Utility Implications

Sellouts and scalping The tool in the economist's bag in which most economists place the greatest trust is the supply and demand analysis of simple

---

[10]In the first year that rebates were widely used, one manufacturer reported (to me in personal communication) that about one-third of the customers receiving rebates chose the option of having the check sent separately. My impression is that this has become less common as rebates have become widespread.

commodity markets. The theory stipulates that prices adjust over time until supply equals demand. While the confidence put in that analysis is generally well founded, there are some markets which consistently fail to clear. One widely discussed example is labor markets where large numbers of unemployed workers coexist with wages that are not falling. Unemployment occurs because a price (the wage) is too high. Another set of markets features the opposite problem, prices that are too low. I refer to the class of goods and services for which demand exceeds supply: Cabbage Patch dolls in December 1983 and 1984, tickets to any Super Bowl, World Series, World Cup Final, Vladimir Horowitz or Rolling Stones concert, or even dinner reservations for 8:00 p.m. Saturday evening at the most popular restaurant in any major city. Why are these prices too low? Once the Cabbage Patch rage started, the going black market price for a doll was over $100. Why did Coleco continue to sell the dolls it had at list price? Why did some discount stores sell their allotted number at less than list price? Tickets for the 1984 Super Bowl were selling on the black market for $300 and up. Seats on the 50-yard line were worth considerably more. Why did the National Football League sell all of the tickets at the same $60 price?

There are no satisfactory answers to these questions within the confines of standard microeconomic theory. In the case of the Super Bowl, the league surely does not need the extra publicity generated by the ticket scarcity. (The argument that long lines create publicity is sometimes given for why prices aren't higher during first week's showing of the latest *Star Wars* epic.) The ticket scarcity occurs every year so (unlike the Cabbage Patch Doll case) there is no possible surprise factor. Rather, it is quite clear that the league *knowingly* sets the prices "too low." Why?

The concept of transaction utility provides a coherent, parsimonious answer. The key to understanding the puzzle is to note that the under-pricing only occurs when two conditions are present. First, the market clearing price is much higher than some well-established normal (reference) price. Second, there is an ongoing pecuniary relationship between the buyer and the seller. Pure scarcity is not enough. Rare art works, beachfront property, and 25-carat diamonds all sell at (very high) market clearing prices.

Once the notion of transaction (dis)utility is introduced, then the role of the normal or reference price becomes transparent. The goods and services listed earlier all have such norms: prices of other dolls similar to Cabbage Patch dolls, regular season ticket prices, prices of other concerts, dinner prices at other times or on other days, etc. These well-established reference prices create significant transaction disutility if a much higher price is charged.

The ongoing relationship between the buyer and the seller is necessary (unless the seller is altruistic), else the seller would not care if transaction disutility were generated. Again that ongoing relationship is present in all the cases described. Coleco couldn't charge more for the dolls because it had plans

TABLE 2 Recent Prices for Major Sporting Events

1983 World Series	$25–30
1984 Super Bowl	all seats $60
1984 Indianapolis 500	top price $75
1981 Holmes–Cooney fight	top price $600

for future sales to doll customers and even non-doll buyers who would simply be offended by an unusually high price. Musical performers want to sell record albums. Restaurants want to sell dinners at other times and days. When a well-established reference price exists, a seller has to weigh the short-run gain associated with a higher price against the long-run loss of goodwill and thus sales.

The pricing of sporting events provides a simple test of this analysis. For major sporting events, the price of tickets should be closer to the market clearing price; the larger is the share of total revenues the seller captures from the event in question. At one extreme are league championships such as the World Series and the Super Bowl. Ticket sales for these events are a tiny share of total league revenue. An intermediate case is the Indianapolis 500. This is an annual event, and is the sponsor's major revenue source, but racegoers frequently come year after year so some ongoing relationship exists. At the other extreme is a major championship fight. A boxing championship is a one-time affair involving a promoter and two fighters. Those three parties are unlikely to be a partnership again. (Even a rematch is usually held in a different city.) There is no significant long-run relationship between the sellers and boxing fans.

While it is impossible to say what the actual market clearing prices would be, the figures in Table 2 indicate that the predictions are pretty well confirmed. Good seats for the Super Bowl are probably the single item in greatest demand and are obviously underpriced since even the worst seats sell out at $60.

Of course, some Super Bowl tickets and Cabbage Patch dolls do change hands at high prices through scalpers. Since the black market price does rise to the market clearing level, why do the sellers permit the scalpers to appropriate these revenues? There are two reasons. First, the transaction disutility generated by a high black market price is not attributed to the original seller. The NFL sets a "fair" price; it is the scalper who is obtaining the immoral rents.[11] Second, in many cases the seller is really getting more than the face

---

[11]Transferring the transaction disutility is often a good strategy. One way this can be done is to turn over an item for sale to an agent who will sell it at auction. The seller then bears less responsibility for the price.

value of the tickets. Tickets to the Super Bowl are distributed to team owners in large numbers. Many of these tickets are resold to tour operators (see the next section) at prices which are not made public. Similarly, tickets to the NCAA basketball tournament finals are distributed in part to the qualifying teams. These tickets are sold or given to loyal alumni. The implicit price for such tickets is probably in the thousands of dollars.

Methods of raising price   A seller who has a monopoly over some popular product may find that the price being charged is substantially less than the market clearing price. How can price be raised without generating excessive negative transaction utility (and thus loss of good will)? The theory provides three kinds of strategies that can be tried. First, steps can be taken to increase the perceived reference price. This can be done in several ways. One way is to explicitly suggest a high reference price (see next section). Another way is to increase the perceived costs of the product, perhaps by providing excessive luxury. As the hockey question showed, perceptions of fairness are affected by costs. In the beer on the beach example, the owner of the run-down grocery store could install a fancy bar. Notice that the extra luxury need not increase the value of the product to the buyer; as long as p^* is increased then demand will increase holding acquisition utility constant. An illustration of this principle is that short best-selling books tend to have fewer words per page (i.e., larger type and wider margins) than longer books. This helps to raise p^*.

A second general strategy is to increase the minimum purchase required and/or to tie the sale of the product to something else. Because of the shape of the value function in the domain of losses, a given price movement seems smaller the larger is the quantity with which it is being integrated. The Super Bowl provides two illustrations of this phenomenon. Tickets are usually sold by tour operators who sell a package including airfare, hotel and game ticket. Thus the premium price for the ticket is attached to a considerably larger purchase. Also, hotels in the city of the Super Bowl (and in college towns on graduation weekend) usually impose a three-night minimum. Since the peak demand is for only one or two nights this allows the hotel to spread the premium room rate over a larger purchase.

The third strategy is to try to obscure p^* and thus make the transaction disutility less salient. One simple way to do this is to sell the product in an unusual size or format, one for which no well-established p^* exists. Both of the last two strategies are used by candy counters in movie theaters. Candy is typically sold only in large containers rarely seen in other circumstances.

Suggested retail price[12]   Many manufacturers offer a "suggested retail price" (SRP) for their products. In the absence of fair trade laws, SRPs must be only

---

[12]This paragraph was motivated by a discussion with Dan Horsky several years ago.

suggestions, but there are distinct differences across products in the relationship between market prices and SRPs. In some cases the SRP is usually equal to the market price. In other cases the SRP exceeds the market price by as much as 100 percent or more. What is the role of an SRP that is twice the typical retail price? One possibility is that the SRP is being offered by the seller as a "suggested reference price." Then a lower selling price will provide positive transaction utility. In addition, inexperienced buyers may use the SRP as an index of quality. We would expect to observe a large differential between price and the SRP when both factors are present. The SRP will be more successful as a reference price the less often the good is purchased. The SRP is most likely to serve as a proxy for quality when the consumer has trouble determining quality in other ways (such as by inspection). Thus, deep discounting relative to SRP should usually be observed for infrequently purchased goods whose quality is hard to judge. Some examples include phonograph cartridges which usually sell at discounts of at least 50 percent, home furniture which is almost always "on sale," and silver flatware where "deep discounting—selling merchandise to consumers at 40 percent to 85 percent below the manufacturer's 'suggested retail price' has become widespread in the industry."[13]

4.3. Budgeting Implications: A Theory of Gift Giving

The analysis of budgeting rules suggests that category and time specific shadow prices can vary. This implies that individuals fail to undertake some internal arbitrage operations that in principle could increase utility. In contrast, the standard theory implies that all goods that are consumed in positive quantities have the same marginal utility per dollar, and in the absence of capital market constraints, variations over time are limited by real interest rates. Observed patterns of gift giving lend support to the current theory. Suppose an individual G wants to give some recipient R a gift. Assume that G would like to choose that gift which would yield the highest level of utility to R for a given expenditure. (Other nonaltruistic motives are possible, but it seems reasonable to start with this case.) Then the standard theory implies that G should choose something that is already being consumed in positive quantities by R.

How does this compare with common practice? Casual observation and some informal survey evidence suggest that many people try to do just the opposite, namely buy something R would not buy for himself. Flowers and boxed candy are items that are primarily purchased as gifts. "Gift shops" are filled with items that are purchased almost exclusively as gifts. Did anyone buy a pet rock for himself?

[13]See *Business Week*, March 29, 1982. This example was suggested by Leigh McAlister.

Once the restriction that all shadow prices be equal is relaxed, the apparent anomaly is easily understood. Categories that are viewed as luxuries will tend to have high ks. An individual would like to have a small portion of the forbidden fruit, but self-control problems prevent that. The gift of a small portion solves the problem neatly.

A simple test of the model can be conducted by the reader via the following thought experiment. Suppose you have collected $100 for a group gift to a departing employee. It is decided to give the employee some wine since that is something the employee enjoys. Suppose the employee typically spends $5 per bottle on wine. How expensive should the gift wine be? The standard theory says you should buy the same type of wine currently being purchased. The current theory says you should buy fewer bottles of more expensive wine, the kind of wine the employee wouldn't usually treat himself to.

One implication of this analysis is that goods which are priced at the high end of the market should be marketed in part as potential gifts. This suggests aiming the advertising at the giver rather than the receiver. "Promise her anything but give her Arpege."

The gift-giving anomaly refers to those goods in categories with high ks. Individuals may also have categories with low ks. Suppose I like to drink expensive imported beer but feel it is too costly to buy on a regular basis. I might then adopt the rule of drinking the expensive beer only on specific occasions, such as at restaurants or while on vacation.[14] Advertisers may wish to suggest other occasions that should quality as legitimate excuses for indulgence. One example is Michelob's theme: "Weekends are made for Michelob." However, their follow-up campaign may have taken a good idea too far: "Put a little weekend in your week." Lowenbrau's ads stress a different category, namely, what beer to serve to company. "Here's to good friends, tonight is something special." While impressing your friends is also involved here, again the theme is to designate specific occasions when the beer k should be relaxed enough to purchase a high cost beer.

Another result of this analysis is that people may sometimes prefer to receive a gift in kind over a gift in cash, again violating a simple principle of microeconomic theory. This can happen if the gift is on a "forbidden list." One implication is that employers might want to use gifts as part of their incentive packages. Some organizations (e.g., Tupperware) rely on this type of compensation very heavily. Dealers are paid both in cash and with a multitude of gift-type items: trips, furniture, appliances, kitchen utensils, etc. Since many

---

[14]One bit of evidence that people on vacation adopt temporarily low ks is that all resorts seem to have an abundance of gift and candy shops. Some of their business, of course, is for gifts to bring home, but while on vacation, people also seem to buy for themselves at these shops.

Tupperware dealers are women who are second-income earners, the gifts may be a way for a dealer to:

1. mentally segregate her earnings from total family income;
2. direct the extra income toward luxuries; and
3. increase her control over the spending of the extra income.[15]

Another similar example comes from the National Football League. For years the league had trouble getting players to come to the year-end All-Star game. Many players would beg off, reporting injuries. A few years ago the game was switched to Hawaii and a free trip for the player's wife or girlfriend was included. Since then, no-shows have been rare.

CONCLUSION

This paper has developed new concepts in three distinct areas: coding gains and losses, evaluating purchases (transaction utility), and budgetary rules. In this section I will review the evidence presented for each, describe some research in progress, and suggest where additional evidence might be found.

The evidence on the coding of gains and losses comes from two kinds of sources. The "who is happier" questions presented here are a rather direct test, though of a somewhat soft variety. More research along these lines is under way using slightly different questions such as "two events are going to happen to you; would you rather they occurred on the same day or two weeks apart?" The two paradigms do not always lead to the same results, particularly in the domain of losses (Johnson and Thaler, 1985). The reasons for the differences are interesting and subtle, and need further investigation. The other source for data on these issues comes from the investigation of choices under uncertainty. Kahneman and Tversky originally formulated their value function based on such choices. In Johnson and Thaler (1985) we investigate how choices under uncertainty are influenced by very recent previous gains or losses. We find that previous gains and losses do influence subsequent choices in ways that complicate any interpretation of the loss function. Some of our data comes from experiments with real money and so are in some sense "harder" than the "who is happier" data. Kahneman and Tversky are also investigating the multiattribute extension of prospect theory, and their results suggest caution in extending the single attribute results.

The evidence presented on transaction utility was the beer on the beach and

---

[15]Tax evasion may be another incentive if recipients (illegally) fail to declare these gifts as income.

hockey ticket questionnaires, and the data on sports pricing. The role of fairness is obviously quite important in determining reference prices. A large-scale telephone survey undertaken by Daniel Kahneman, Jack Knetch, and myself is underway and we hope it will provide additional evidence on two important issues in this area (see Chapter 10). First, what are the determinants of people's perceptions of fairness? Second, how are market prices influenced by these perceptions? Evidence on the former comes directly from the survey research, while evidence on the latter must come from aggregate economic data. The latter evidence is much more difficult to obtain.

Both the theory and the evidence on the budgetary processes are less well developed than the other topics presented here. The evidence comes from a small sample of households that will not support statistical tests. A more systematic study of household decision making, perhaps utilizing UPC scanner data, should be a high priority.

More generally, the theory presented here represents a hybrid of economics and psychology that has heretofore seen little attention. I feel that marketing is the most logical field for this combination to be developed. Aside from those topics just mentioned there are other extensions that seem promising. On the theory side, adding uncertainty and multiple attributes are obviously worth pursuing. Regarding empirical tests, I would personally like to see some field experiments which attempt to implement the ideas suggested here in an actual marketing environment.

REFERENCES

An earlier version of a portion of this paper was presented at the Association for Consumer Research conference in San Francisco, October 1982, and is published in the proceedings of that meeting. The author wishes to thank Hersh Shefrin, Daniel Kahneman, and Amos Tversky for many useful discussions. Financial support from the Alfred P. Sloan Foundation is gratefully acknowledged.

Arkes, Hal R., and Catherine Blumer. "The Psychology of Sunk Cost." *Organizational Behavior and Human Decision Processes* 35, 1 (1985): 124–140.

Becker, Gary S. "A Theory of the Allocation of Time." *Economic Journal* 75 (September 1965).

Gregory, Robin. "Valuing Non-Market Goods: An Analysis of Alternative Approaches." Unpublished Diss. University of British Columbia, 1982.

Johnson, Eric, and Richard Thaler. "Hedonic Framing and the Break-Even Effect." Working paper. Cornell University, 1985.

Kahneman, Daniel, and Amos Tversky. "Prospect Theory: An Analysis of Decision Under Risk." *Econometrica*, 47 (March 1985): 263–291.

Knetsch, Jack L., and J. A. Sinden. "Willingness to Pay and Compensation Demanded: Experimental Evidence of an Unexpected Disparity in Measures of Value." *Quarterly Journal of Economics* 99 (1984).

Lancaster, Kelvin J. *Consumer Demand, A New Approach.* New York: Columbia University Press, 1971.

Thaler, Richard. "Toward a Positive Theory of Consumer Choice." *Journal of Economic Behavior and Organization* 1 (March 1980): 39–60.

Thaler, Richard, and H. M. Shefrin. "An Economic Theory of Self-Control." *Journal of Political Economy* 39 (April 1981): 392–406.

Tversky, Amos, and Daniel Kahneman. "The Framing of Decisions and the Rationality of Choice." *Science* 211 (1981): 453–458.

3

GAMBLING WITH THE HOUSE MONEY AND TRYING TO BREAK EVEN: THE EFFECTS OF PRIOR OUTCOMES ON RISKY CHOICE

Richard H. Thaler and Eric J. Johnson

1. INTRODUCTION

Imagine that you are attending a convention in Las Vegas, and you walk into a casino. While passing the slot machines, you put a quarter into one machine and, surprisingly, you win $100. Now what? Will your gambling behavior for the rest of the evening be altered? Might you make a few more serious wagers, even if you usually abstain? Suppose instead that you had $100 in cash stolen from your wallet while taking a swim at the pool. How will that alter your behavior? Are either of these events equivalent to discovering, just before entering the casino, that a stock in which you own 100 shares has gone up (down) one point that day?

  Or, consider the case of a manager whose division has lost $10 million under her administration, and who must choose between two projects. Project A will earn a sure $5 million. Project B will earn $20 million with probability .5 and lose $5 million with probability .5. Does this past history influence the decision? Suppose instead that these projects were described using their final asset positions: A produces a sure loss of $5 million and B yields a 50 percent

Reprinted by permission, "Gambling with the House Money and Trying to Break Even: The Effects of Prior Outcomes on Risky Choice," Richard H. Thaler and Eric J. Johnson, *Management Science* 36,6 (June 1990): 643–660. © 1990, The Institute of Management Sciences, 290 Westminster Street, Providence, RI 02903.

chance to lose $15 million and a 50 percent chance to earn $10 million. Does this change in description make a difference?

These examples illustrate the basic question investigated in this paper: How is risk-taking behavior affected by prior gains and losses? The question is quite general since decisions are rarely made in temporal isolation. Current choices are often evaluated with the knowledge of the outcomes which have preceded them. Such knowledge can often be a handicap. While students of economics and decision theory are implored to concentrate only on incremental costs, it is well established that real decision makers are often influenced by historical or sunk costs (Arkes and Blumer, 1985; Staw, 1981; Thaler, 1980). Laughhunn and Payne (1984) have investigated the effect of both sunk costs and what they call sunk gains on decisions under uncertainty. We continue here in the same spirit. We begin by recognizing that most decision makers are influenced by prior outcomes. Our goal then is to investigate how prior gains and losses affect choices. We will offer empirical evidence to support the intuitions evoked in the above scenarios. Specifically, prior gains and losses can dramatically influence subsequent choices in systematic ways. For example, we find that under some circumstances a prior gain can increase subjects' willingness to accept gambles. This finding is labeled the *house money effect*. In contrast, prior losses can decrease the willingness to take risks. We also find that when decision makers have prior losses, outcomes which offer the opportunity to "break even" are especially attractive.

We attempt to explain these phenomena using a framework based on Kahneman and Tversky's (1979) prospect theory. Their analysis of decision making under uncertainty has led them to conclude that "the location of the reference point, and the manner in which choice problems are coded and edited, emerge as critical factors in the analysis of decisions" (1979, p. 288). We agree with this assessment, and our paper extends their earlier work on this topic.

While the ultimate goal of the paper is to investigate the role of prior outcomes on risky choice, we begin with a set of more primitive questions. How are gains and losses encoded by decision makers? When are prior outcomes combined with the potential payoffs of current prospects and when are they ignored or neglected? We formulate several hypotheses about this portion of the decision-making process and call the hypotheses *editing rules*. While we will consider many such rules, special consideration is given to a simple rule which suggests that people edit outcomes in the way that makes them happiest. Tests of this rule give it only partial support. These tests lead us to propose another editing rule, the *quasi-hedonic editing hypothesis*. All the editing rules are then tested experimentally by giving subjects real decisions in which they can win or lose money. The experiments provide some support for our proposed quasi-hedonic editing rule, as well as providing interesting new results on decision making in the presence of prior outcomes.

2. VALUING GAINS AND LOSSES

All theories of decision under uncertainty make, implicitly at least, some assumptions about how problems are represented. Subjective Expected Utility (SEU) theory, for example, assumes that all outcomes are integrated with current wealth. This amounts to the following editing rule: add every possible outcome to existing wealth, then evaluate gambles in terms of their final end states. Given this editing rule, prior outcomes can only influence choice via a wealth effect, and choices must be invariant across problem descriptions. Thus, SEU theory cannot be used to describe the behavior we observe in our experiments.

Prospect theory, in which outcomes are coded as gains and losses relative to a reference point, and in which problem representation can matter, offers a better framework for analyzing the phenomena under study. Therefore, we begin this section by briefly summarizing prospect theory. Two editing rules consistent with prospect theory are presented, plus two additional editing rules that code gains and losses but are not consistent with prospect theory. One of the non-prospect theory rules portrays decision makers as extremely passive, accepting any problem representation that they are given. The other rule characterizes decision makers as hedonic optimizers, coding outcomes to maximize pleasure and minimize pain. Tests of this rule indicate that it is not consistent with behavior, and so at the end of this section we propose a fifth editing rule based on our empirical findings.

2.1. Prospect Theory

Prospect theory uses two functions to characterize choices: the value function, $v(\cdot)$, which replaces the utility function in SEU theory, and the decision weight function, $\pi(p)$, which transforms probabilities into decision weights. The key property of the decision weighting function is that small probabilities are overweighted ($\pi(p) > p$), and that decision weights need not add up to unity (that is, $\pi(p) + \pi(1 - p) \neq 1.0$). For our purposes, however, the value function is of greater interest.

The value function has three important characteristics:

1. It is defined over gains and losses (i.e., changes from the status quo) rather than final asset positions.
2. It is "S" shaped: concave for gains and convex for losses.
3. It displays loss aversion, that is, the loss function is steeper than the gain function, $v(x) < -v(-x)$.

Define a prospect $(x,p; y, 1 - p)$ as a gamble that yields x with probability p and y with probability $1 - p$. Then, according to prospect theory if x and y are of opposite signs (either $x \geq 0 \geq y$ or $y \geq 0 \geq x$), the value of this prospect, V, is given by:

$$V = \pi(p)v(x) + \pi(1 - p)v(y). \tag{1}$$

However, this is not the only representation used in prospect theory. The valuation of prospects is assumed to be preceded by an editing phase in which prospects are simplified. For example, in comparing alternative prospects, decision makers are assumed to look for dominance and select the dominating alternative when the dominance is transparent; outcomes that are extremely unlikely are ignored; and both probabilities and outcomes may be rounded. The editing phase also produces an evaluation rule different from equation (1) for strictly positive or strictly negative options. Kahneman and Tversky state that "In the editing phase such prospects are segregated into two components: (1) the riskless component, i.e., the minimum gain or loss which is certain to be obtained or paid; (2) the risky component, i.e., the additional gain or loss which is actually at stake" (1979, p. 276).

So, if either $x > y > 0$ or $x < y < 0$, then

$$V = v(y) + \pi(p)\,[v(x) - v(y)]. \tag{2}$$

In this formulation the certain gain is valued separately, and the value difference between the two risky outcomes is multiplied by the appropriate decision weight.

2.2. Prior Gains and Losses

How can prior gains or losses be accommodated in this framework? In their original formulation of prospect theory, and also in their subsequent research, Kahneman and Tversky have stressed that the presence of prior gains and losses raises complicated issues. Indeed, they suggest two ways prior outcomes might be coded. First, all events might be coded separately: ". . . people generally evaluate acts in terms of a minimal account which includes only the direct consequences of the act" (Tversky and Kahneman, 1981, p. 456). If this coding is used, prior outcomes have no effect on subsequent choices.

However, Kahneman and Tversky (1979, p. 286) also recognize that "there are other situations in which gains and losses are coded relative to an expectation or aspiration level that differs from the status quo." In these situations, "the outcomes of an act affect the balance in an account that was previously set up by a related act" (Tversky and Kahneman, 1981, p. 457). For example, "a person who has not made peace with his losses is likely to accept gambles that would be unacceptable to him otherwise" (Kahneman and Tversky, 1979, p. 287).

To summarize, prospect theory includes an editing phase in which prospects are simplified and encoded. However, within the prospect theory framework, there is some flexibility in how prospects are edited, particularly when a prior outcome might influence the reference point. In the section that follows, we propose specific alternative representations of prospects that can emerge from the editing phase; we term these *editing rules.*

2.3. Editing Rules

To get a sense of the types of problems to which the editing rules might be applied, consider the following choice:
  You have just won $30. Now choose between:

(a) No further gain or loss.
(b) A gamble in which you have a 50 percent chance to win $9 and a 50 percent chance to lose $9.

This problem is presented in what we term the *two-stage* version since the prior gain of $30 is presented separately from the gamble.[1] Compare it to the following *one-stage* presentation of the same gamble:
  Choose between:

(a) A sure gain of $30.
(b) A 50% chance to win $39 and a 50% chance to win $21.

In contrast to SEU theory, the transformations predicted by the editing rules we consider are contingent on the characteristics of the decision problem. For example, some of the editing rules depend on the signs and magnitudes of the outcomes, and some depend on the problem representation.

2.3(1). Prospect theory with memory When prior outcomes are incorporated into the perceived "balance" of the relevant mental account, choices can be affected. In problems such as those above, where the prior gain exceeds the largest potential loss, equation (2) applies. Therefore, the two-stage gamble presented above is edited as

$$v(21) + \pi(.5)[v(39) - v(21)]. \tag{3}$$

---

[1]Notice that the wording of this problem does suggest segregating the prior outcome as it is presented separately, but it also suggests that the prior gain is in the same (mental) account as the subsequent choices. In contrast, Kahneman and Tversky have reported results using more neutral wording such as "In addition to whatever you own you have been given 1000, now choose . . ." (Kahneman and Tversky, 1979, p. 273). With this wording, subjects may be more likely to consider the prior outcome as being in a different mental account.

The way to read this in words is: "If I accept this gamble I win $21 for sure, plus I have a 50 percent chance of increasing my gain from $21 to $39." The same editing would apply to the one-stage presentation of the gamble.

2.3(2). Prospect theory, no memory An alternative editing rule that is consistent with prospect theory is the "no memory" rule which says that prior outcomes are encoded, valued, and then forgotten. Prior outcomes do not alter the coding of subsequent gambles. Under this editing hypothesis, the presentation of the gambles makes a difference. If the gamble is presented in the two-stage version, it will be edited as

$$\{v(30)\} + \pi(.5)v(9) + \pi(.5)v(-9). \tag{4}$$

This can be read as follows: "I have already won $30. I can now take this gamble which will yield me a 50 percent chance to gain $9 and a 50 percent chance to lose $9." If the one-stage version is presented, however, then the gamble will be coded as in equation (3); that is, applying prospect theory's equation (2). The gamble is edited in this way because in the one-stage presentation there is no prior outcome to be (coded and) forgotten.

2.3(3). Concreteness Another plausible editing rule states that subjects do no active editing per se, but rather accept the problem as presented to them. This hypothesis is suggested by Paul Slovic's (1972) *concreteness* principle, ". . . a judge or decision maker tends to use only the information that is explicitly displayed in the stimulus object, and will use it only in the form in which it is displayed" (p. 14). If the concreteness editing rule is used, then the two-stage version would be encoded the same way as under prospect theory, no memory, i.e., as in (4) above.

The one-stage version would be encoded as

$$\pi(.5)v(39) + \pi(.5)v(21). \tag{5}$$

2.3(4). Hedonic editing The editing rules considered so far characterize decision makers as either mechanical or passive (or both). The rules presume that decision makers take the frames presented to them, as the concreteness hypothesis suggests, or use the same rule irrespective of the signs and magnitudes of the prior and subsequent outcomes. An alternative rule with quite a different flavor is based on the hypothesis that people edit the gambles in a way that would make the prospects appear most pleasant (or least unpleasant). We call this the hedonic editing hypothesis.[2]

---

[2]There are obvious limits to hedonic editing. For example, we assume that decision makers take the actual outcomes at face value. Also, the only operations we permit are combining and separating. That is, when there are two events x and y, we assume that people either *integrate* the two and code the joint event as $v(x + y)$, or they *segregate* the events and code them as $v(x) + v(y)$.

The shape of prospect theory's value function implies that the signs and magnitudes of x and y determine whether hedonic editing calls for segregation or integration. The rules for hedonic editing follow from four principles (see Thaler, 1985):

1. Segregate gains.
2. Integrate losses.
3. Segregate small gains from larger losses (the "silver lining" principle).
4. Integrate (cancel) smaller losses with larger gains.

The hedonic editing hypothesis assumes that these four principles are applied whenever possible. This hypothesis yields the following editing of the two-stage gamble:

$$v(21) + \pi(.5)v(18). \tag{6}$$

This can be read as: "If I win the gamble I will win $21 for sure, and I have a 50 percent chance to also win another $18." The hedonic editing hypothesis suggests the same coding of the one-stage gamble.

3. DIRECT TESTS OF HEDONIC EDITING

Of the editing rules proposed so far, the hedonic editing rule is by far the most radical. There are several reasons why one might expect the hypothesis to be false. First, the hedonic editing hypothesis suggests that decision makers are quite active in their editing of potential outcomes. This may require more cognitive effort than decision makers are willing to expend. Second, hedonic editing predicts that the same coding will be used regardless of the presentation format. There is good reason to believe that presentation matters. Third, hedonic editing is a maximizing process, though perhaps not a rational one. Actual editing may fall short of the hedonic ideal. In spite of these reservations, the hypothesis is worth investigating because it is potentially very powerful. If correct, the hedonic editing hypothesis would provide a canonical representation of any prospect which would make the task of prediction much easier. Also, by discovering the specific ways in which the hypothesis fails, we may be able to formulate alternative (more realistic) hypotheses. Therefore, this section presents tests of the hedonic editing hypothesis, and, based on the results we obtain, offers an alternative editing rule.

3.1. A Previous Test of the Hedonic Framing Hypothesis

In a previous paper, Thaler (1985) investigated an issue related to hedonic editing. How do decision makers prefer to have gains and losses framed for them? Do they prefer to have gains segregated and losses integrated as the theory predicts? This was tested in what we will refer to as Experiment 1. Subjects were asked to compare pairs of scenarios, four of which are presented in Table 1. In each case two events occur to Mr. A and a single event occurs to Mr. B. The subjects were asked to judge whether Mr. A or Mr. B was happier

TABLE 1 Experiment 1, from Thaler (1985)

Instructions: Below you will find four pairs of scenarios. In each case two events occur in Mr. A's life and one event occurs in Mr. B's life. You are asked to judge whether Mr. A or Mr. B is happier. Would most people rather be A or B? If you think the scenarios are emotionally equivalent, check "no difference." In all cases the events are intended to be financially equivalent.

1. Mr. A was given tickets to two lotteries involving the World Series. He won $50 in one lottery and $25 in the other. Mr. B was given a ticket to a single, larger World Series lottery. He won $75. Who was happier?

   A: 64%   B: 18%   No difference: 17% $N = 87$

2. Mr. A received a letter from the IRS saying that he made a minor arithmetical mistake on his tax return and owed $100. He received a similar letter the same day from his state income tax authority saying he owed $50. There were no other repercussions from either mistake. Mr. B received a letter from the IRS saying that he made a minor arithmetical mistake on his tax return and owed $150. There were no other repercussions from his mistake. Who was more upset?

   A: 75%   B: 16%   No difference: 8% $N = 87$

3. Mr. A's car was damaged in a parking lot. He had to spend $200 to repair the damage. The same day the car was damaged, he won $25 in the office football pool. Mr. B's car was damaged in a parking lot. He had to spend $175 to repair the damage. Who was more upset?

   A: 25%   B: 70%   No difference: 5% $N = 87$

4. Mr. A bought his first New York State lottery ticket and won $100. Also, in a freak accident, he damaged the rug in his apartment and had to pay the landlord $80. Mr. B bought his first New York State lottery ticket and won $20. Who was happier?

   A: 29%   B: 72%   No difference: 6% $N = 87$

(or more upset in the case of losses). The results of the experiment supported the hedonic framing principles in that a majority of subjects selected the frame predicted by the theory.

Notice that while the results of Experiment 1 were consistent with principles 1–4 above, this experiment is not a test of the hedonic editing hypothesis. In Experiment 1 subjects simply judged which frame they preferred. The hedonic editing hypothesis is a conjecture that subjects *actively* reframe events and outcomes in a systematic way. Indeed, Experiment 1 suggests additional limits on the hedonic editing hypothesis. If subjects in this study believed that the events would be reframed in a hedonically optimal manner, then they would judge all the pairs of scenarios as equivalent since Mr. A could reframe his situation to be that of Mr. B and vice versa. Another limitation is suggested by the following thought experiment. Imagine you had just received a unexpected gain of $50. This could be hedonically reframed into two gains of $25, but why stop there? Why not 50 gains of $1? Obviously there are some limits to self-deception, and these limits impose constraints on the way events are encoded. The limits of hedonic editing are further explored below.

3.2. A Test Based on Temporal Spacing

To test the hedonic editing hypothesis we need to ask subjects to make choices that reflect their preferences about the framing of events. One way to do this is by giving subjects a choice about the timing of events. For the next experiment, we assumed that the process of segregating a pair of events is facilitated by having the events occur on different days, and conversely that integrating events is easier if the events occur on the same day. We therefore presented another set of subjects with pairs of events and asked them whether they preferred that the events occur "on the same day" or "a week or two apart." The items we used were the same as those used in Experiment 1, plus some additional new items. The items and the results are presented in Table 2.

If the premise that temporal separation facilitates segregation is correct (it does seem reasonable), then the hedonic editing hypothesis implies that subjects will choose to have the events occur "apart" when segregation would be preferred, and "together" when integration would be hedonically optimal. As the results show, this prediction was only partly confirmed.

The responses to question 1 reveal that for pairs of gains subjects did respond in the way suggested by the hedonic editing hypothesis. Subjects preferred to spread out the arrival of pleasant events, presumably to help segregate the pleasures experienced. Using the same logic, subjects should prefer to have pairs of losses occur on the same day, to facilitate their integration. However, subjects did not express this preference. Rather, in questions 2 and 3 subjects indicated that they prefer to experience the losses separately. We have obtained this result repeatedly, for small or large losses, for non-monetary as well as monetary losses, and for unrelated and related pairs of events. This result is a severe blow to the hedonic editing hypothesis. By expressing a strict preference for experiencing pairs of losses on different days, the majority of subjects said two things: (1) they do not intend to integrate the second loss of the day with the first one; and (2) the second loss

TABLE 2 Experiment 2: Hedonic Editing: Temporal Spacing

Instructions: Below you will find three pairs of events. In each case the same events occur, either on the same day (for A) or two weeks apart (for B). You are asked to judge whether A or B is happier, or in the event of two negative events, who is more unhappy. Would most people rather be A or B? If you think the alternatives are emotionally equivalent, check "no difference." In all cases the events are intended to be financially equivalent. (Note: Having the events occur together does not imply that they occur sooner or later than if they were apart. That is not the question. You are only asked to judge whether it is better to have the events separately or together.)

1. The events are:
   (a) Win $25 in an office lottery.
   (b) Win $50 in an office lottery.

   Who is happier?

   A: 25%   B: 63%   No difference: 12% $N = 65$

2. The events are:
   (a) Receive a letter from the federal income tax authority saying that due to an arithmetical mistake $100 must be paid.
   (b) Receive a letter from the state income tax authority saying that due to an arithmetical mistake $50 must be paid.

   Who is more unhappy?

   A: 57%   B: 34%   No difference: 9% $N = 65$

3. The events are:
   (a) Receive a $20 parking ticket.
   (b) Receive a bill for $25 from the registrar because a form was filled in improperly.

   Who is more unhappy?

   A: 75%   B: 17%   No difference: 7% $N = 65$

will actually "hurt" more after the first than it would if experienced alone (if this were not true the subjects would be indifferent between the two options).[3]

3.3. Further Tests of the Failure to Integrate Losses

The failure to actively integrate losses is explored further in Experiment 3. Subjects were asked questions such as: when does losing $9 upset you more, when it occurs by itself, or directly after losing $30? Questions 1–3 were originally administered to a group of Cornell undergraduate psychology students. These questions plus items 4 and 5 were then given to a group of Cornell MBA students. Questions 6–10 were given to a different group of Cornell MBAs (see Table 3).

Question 1 investigates whether losses can be integrated with prior gains as hedonic editing entails. Subjects report that the *incremental* effect of losing $9 is less after a gain of $30 than by itself, consistent with hedonic editing.

In contrast, question 2 yields results inconsistent with hedonic editing principle 2 (integrate losses). A large majority of subjects say that losing $9 hurts more after losing $30 than alone. As in Experiment 2, the responses are clearly inconsistent with active integration of losses (as long as the loss function is convex), yet subjects do not answer as if they were ignoring the initial loss, as pure segregation would imply. Rather, this situation appears to provoke a complex reaction in which the initial loss increases the loss aversion associated with subsequent losses.

It is instructive to compare the responses to question 2 with those for questions 3 and 4. Here a small majority say that the $9 hurts less after the large $250 (or $1,000) loss than alone. These results rule out one alternative explanation of the responses to question 2, i.e., that the subjects misunderstood the instructions. If subjects incorrectly responded by choosing the option based on an evaluation of total utilities instead of the incremental utility of the $9, then they would have overwhelmingly picked (b) on questions 3 and 4. Questions 5 and 10 are particularly interesting. Together they suggest that the effect of a prior loss on the disutility of a subsequent loss is a function with an inverted U shape. The loss of $9 hurts more after a $36 loss than after a $9, but less after $1000 loss than after a $30. A tentative interpretation of this set of results is that while a small to moderate loss may sensitize the individual to

---

[3]Kahneman and Snell (forthcoming) also report anomalous results regarding the loss function. Subjects were asked whether some stimulus (such as a severe headache) was getting better or worse over several days. Most subjects thought the headache was getting worse, i.e., that the "loss function" for headaches was escalating. For such a loss function, subjects should be risk averse. However, most subjects gave risk-seeking responses to choices involving the same stimuli. Kahneman and Snell stress the difference between "experience utility" and "decision utility." The difference between 2 or 4 days of headaches may sound greater than the difference between 8 and 10, even though the experience of the extra two days of headaches would be worse in the latter instance. The relationship between their results and ours deserves attention.

TABLE 3 Experiment 3: Subjective Reactions to Losses

Consider the following two events: (a) you lose $x. (b) you lose $x after gaining $y. We are interested in the emotional impact of the loss of $x in both cases. Are you more upset about the loss of money when it occurs alone (a), or when it occurs directly after a gain (b)? Of course you are happier in total in (b), but we are interested only in the incremental impact of the loss. Below you will find several questions of this type. In each case please compare the incremental effect of the event described. If you feel there is no difference you may check that, but please express a preference if you have one.

PART A
1. (a) You lose $9.
   (b) You lose $9 after having gained $30.
   The loss of $9 hurts more in:
Cornell Undergrads $N = 137$ (a) 84%   (b) 10%   No difference: 6%
Cornell MBAs $N = 87$ (a) 70%   (b) 9%   No difference: 21%

2. (a) You lose $9.
   (b) You lose $9 after having lost $30.
   The loss of $9 hurts more in:
Cornell Undergrads $N = 137$ (a) 22%   (b) 75%   No difference: 3%
Cornell MBAs $N = 87$ (a) 13%   (b) 55%   No difference: 31%

3. (a) You lose $9.
   (b) You lose $9 after having lost $250.
   The loss of $9 hurts more in:
Cornell Undergrads $N = 137$ (a) 54%   (b) 37%   No difference: 9%
Cornell MBAs $N = 87$ (a) 39%   (b) 38%   No difference: 23%

PART B: Cornell MBAs $N = 87$
4. (a) You lose $9.
   (b) You lose $9 after suffering a loss of $1,000.
   The loss of $9 hurts more in:
   (a) 50%   (b) 33%   No difference: 17%

5. (a) You lose $9 after suffering a loss of $30.
   (b) You lose $9 after suffering a loss of $1,000.
   The loss of $9 hurts more in:
   (a) 51%   (b) 38%   No difference: 21%

PART C: Cornell MBAs $N = 81$
6. (a) You lose $9.
   (b) You lose $9 after suffering a loss of $9.
   The loss of $9 hurts more in:
   (a) 7%   (b) 64%   No difference: 28%

7. (a) You lose $9.
   (b) You lose $9 after suffering a loss of $18.
   The loss of $9 hurts more in:
   (a) 11%   (b) 65%   No difference: 23%

TABLE 3   Experiment 3: Subjective Reactions to Losses (*continued*)

8. (a) You lose $9.
   (b) You lose $9 after suffering a loss of $36.
   The loss of $9 hurts more in:
   (a) 12%   (b) 62%   No difference: 26%

9. (a) You lose $9.
   (b) You lose $9 after suffering a loss of $45.
   The loss of $9 hurts more in:
   (a) 14%   (b) 65%   No difference: 21%

10. (a) You lose $9 after suffering a loss of $9.
    (b) You lose $9 after suffering a loss of $36.
    The loss of $9 hurts more in:
    (a) 7%   (b) 68%   No difference: 25%

---

further losses of roughly the same magnitude, a large loss may numb the individual to additional small losses.[4]

Items 6–10 are used for a parametric exploration of these effects, manipulating the amount of the prior loss. The results suggest that the responses are not very sensitive to the exact value of the prior loss, as long as it is of the same magnitude as the subsequent loss. None of the differences among items 6–10 are significant, nor are these items significantly different from question 2.

To summarize, Experiments 2 and 3 present mixed evidence on the hedonic editing hypothesis. While subjects do seem to actively segregate gains, and cancel losses against larger gains, they do not appear to integrate losses. Also, subjects do not actively reframe the problems presented in Experiment 1 to make them all equivalent, suggesting that presentation mode plays an important role in the final editing of outcomes. In light of these results, we propose another editing rule consistent with what we have observed.

3.4. Quasi-Hedonic Editing Hypothesis

The results of Experiments 2 and 3 refute the hedonic editing hypothesis on two accounts. First, the hypothesis provides too active a characterization of the editing process. This suggests that to generate a more accurate description of the editing process, the hypothesis should be modified to make it closer to the concreteness editing rule in which no active rewriting is done by decision makers. Specifically, we propose that when subjects are presented choices in

---

[4]The large prior loss also produces a contrast effect which makes the subsequent small loss seem smaller.

the one-stage format (e.g., choose between a sure gain of $30 and a 50–50 chance to win $39 or $21), they do not actively segregate the sure gain.

Second, both experiments reveal that subjects have difficulty integrating losses. Therefore, we propose that when faced with a two-stage gamble involving a prior loss, subjects will not integrate subsequent losses with the initial loss. (However, after prior gains, subsequent losses *will* be integrated with [cancelled against] the prior gain.)

We call this the *quasi-hedonic* editing hypothesis because it follows the hedonic editing rules only part of the time. According to the quasi-hedonic editing hypothesis, the two-stage version of the gamble described above will be rewritten as:

$$\pi(.5)[v(30) + v(9)] + \pi(.5)v(21).^5 \tag{7}$$

In words this reads: "I have a 50 percent chance to win $30 and win $9, and a 50 percent chance to win just $21." The one-stage version will yield the same coding used in the concreteness formulation; that is, equation (5).

Consider now the same gamble with the exception that the $30 prior gain is replaced with a $30 prior *loss*. The quasi-hedonic editing hypothesis predicts that the two-stage version of this gamble will be encoded as:

$$\pi(.5)[v(-30) + v(-9)] + \pi(.5)[v(-30) + v(9)]. \tag{8}$$

Notice that here both the gain and the loss are segregated from the prior loss. Once again the one-stage version yields a concreteness encoding.

4. EDITING RULES
AND RISKY CHOICE

The tests of the hedonic editing hypothesis presented in section 3 were useful in establishing the ways in which the actual editing diverges from the hedonic ideal. The quasi-hedonic editing hypothesis represents our own initial effort at a descriptive theory of editing. However, this hypothesis and the others we have presented should really be evaluated in the domain of risky choice, the ultimate topic of interest.

---

[5] As we have indicated above, the results of Experiments 2 and 3 indicate that subjects not only segregate losses which follow prior losses, but that the subsequent losses are actually more painful than they would be in the absence of the prior loss. This could be accommodated in the theory by indexing the value function on prior losses. If $v(-x|-y)$ denotes the value of a loss of x following a loss of y then the prior results suggest that $v(-x|-y) < v(-x)$. Modifying the theory in this way complicates the notation somewhat and only strengthens the results discussed below, so we have retained the simpler formulation.

We use two methods to test the editing rules. First, some of the rules imply that the presentation format will not influence choices. These rules are tested by doing between-subject comparisons of responses to alternative representations of the same problem. Second, the various editing hypotheses make different predictions about the role of prior outcomes on risky choice. Some rules, for example, predict that (relatively small) prior outcomes will have no effect on choice, as in SEU theory. To test these implications, we conduct within-subject comparisons by asking subjects to make contingent choices for each of several possible initial outcomes.

The next section describes the experimental procedures, with the following section evaluating the results in terms of the editing rules.

4.1. Experimental Design

Investigating the influence of prior gains and losses of subsequent risky choice presents certain methodological problems. The ideal experiment is one in which subjects make actual choices for real money. However, an experiment in which subjects can lose money creates some ethical dilemmas. We have dealt with this issue as follows. Subjects were invited to participate in an experiment in which they would make several choices (no more than eight), each with a prior gain or loss (e.g., "you have won/lost X, now choose between gamble A and a sure outcome B). Only one of the choices presented to the subjects would actually be played, and the chances that any one problem would be selected varied such that the most attractive choices (i.e., those with large prior gains) were the most likely to be selected. Participation was always voluntary. This procedure allowed us to expose subjects to actual potential losses, even though few would actually lose money.

Our initial efforts using this design met with mixed success. Only about a third of the subjects agreed to participate in the experiment for real money (the others answered the questions on a hypothetical basis), and these real-money subjects proved to have extremely risk-seeking preferences. Since the goal of our study is to examine the effect of prior outcomes on risky choice, the subjects who agreed to play for real money were not very interesting since they tended to take the risk-seeking choice at almost every opportunity.

Learning from these experiences, we designed Experiment 4 in an attempt to elicit almost complete participation from a large undergraduate class. Our experience suggested two reasons why subjects were unwilling to participate: First, fear of losing money (even though the expected value of the game was significantly positive), and second, confusion—the experiment is complicated, and subjects were worried that they might not understand exactly what was going to happen. In addition, we observed that the participation rate for female subjects was much lower than for males. In light of these factors we designed Experiment 4 with the following changes:

1. The chances of having to play a gamble in which the subject could lose money was drastically reduced to .04.
2. The stakes in the gambles involving losses were reduced.
3. Subjects were told that if they did lose money, they could perform clerical work to pay off their debt at the rate of $5.00 per hour.
4. Two $100 bonuses were promised, one to be paid to one of the ten subjects selected to play out their gambles, and another to be paid to someone who agreed to play but was not selected as one of the ten.
5. In addition to careful written instructions, the experimenter also gave extended verbal instructions. (The instructions are available from the authors.)
6. Students who did not wish to participate for real money did not get to participate at all.
7. The experimenter was female.

While it is impossible to know which of these changes were important, the package worked extremely well. The experiment was conducted in a large introductory economics class at Cornell, and virtually every student (roughly 98 percent) agreed to participate.

The result of this experiment largely replicated the results we had obtained previously for the subjects who answered hypothetical questions (either as a subset of subjects who declined to play for real money, or as participants in an experiment in which everyone answered just hypothetical questions). The results of Experiment 4 are reported in Table 4, and the results of similar items from previous experiments using hypothetical questions are reported in Table 5. (The items in Table 5 differ by a factor of either 2 or 4 from the items shown in Table 4.)

In Experiment 4, and most of the other experiments reported in Table 5, half the subjects received questions in a two-stage version while the other half received questions in a one-stage format. Two types of gambles were used. In the first, subjects were offered a fair 50–50 gamble (a 50 percent chance to win $x and a 50 percent chance to lose $x) versus the status quo. The second gamble offered a choice between a sure gain of $x and a one-third chance to win $3x (and a 2/3 chance to win nothing).[6] Each of these gambles was combined with four levels of initial outcomes (in Experiment 4 these were: +$15, $0, −$2.25, −$7.50).

---

[6]Experience indicates that there is an advantage to using only choices that offer equal expected values. Especially when subjects must make a series of choices, if gambles differ on expected value some subjects will adopt a maximize expected value strategy for answering the questions. When expected values are equal, subjects are forced to think more deeply about the questions and decide what they really prefer.

4.2. Evaluating the Editing Rules

Before we examine the results of Experiment 4 in detail, it is useful to notice the prominent features of the data. It is obvious that both presentation format and prior outcomes influence choice. Consider, for example, Problems 1 and 4. There is more than a 30 percent shift in preferences between the one-stage and two-stage versions of each problem. The framing manipulation also has a dramatic influence on choice in Problem 7. Similarly, the prior outcomes clearly influence choices, particularly in the two-stage versions of the problems. (Compare Problems 1 and 3 with 2 and 4, and compare Problem 7 with 5, 6, and 8.)

The result that presentation format matters allows us to reject two of the editing rules: prospect theory with memory and hedonic editing. For the class

TABLE 4 Experiment 4

Two-Stage Format			Percent Risk-Seeking		One-Stage Format	
Initial	*Choices*		*N = 95*	*N = 111*	*Choices*	
Outcome	*Payoff*	*Prob.*	*Two-Stage*	*One-Stage*	*Payoff*	*Prob.*
1. +$15	$0	1			$15	1
	$4.50	.5	77	44	$19.50	.5
	−$4.50	.5			$10.50	.5
2. +$0	$0	1			$0	1
	$2.25	.5	41	50	$2.25	.5
	−$2.25				−$2.25	.5
3. −$2.25	$0	1			−$2.25	1
	$2.25	.5	69	87	$0	.5
	−$2.25	.5			−$4.50	.5
4. −$7.50	$0	1			−$7.50	1
	$2.25	.5	40	77	−$5.25	.5
	−$2.25	.5			−$9.75	.5
5. +$15	$5	1			$20	1
	$15	.33	72	68	$30	.33
	$0	.67			$15	.67
6. +$0	$5	1			$5	1
	$15	.33	61	71	$15	.33
	$0	.67			$0	.67
7. −$4.50	$5	1			+$0.50	1
	$15	.33	32	57	$10.50	.33
	$0	.67			−$4.50	.67
8. −$7.50	$2.50	1			−$5.00	1
	$7.50	.33	71	70	$0	.33
	$0	.67			−$7.50	.67

TABLE 5

Problem Number	Format Type	Initial Outcome	Sure Outcome	Gamble	Sample	% Risk-Seeking
1.	2-stage	$30.00	$ 0.00	($9, .5; −$9, .5)	C-MBA N = 44	70
		30.00	0.00	($9, .5; −$9, .5)	C-MBA N = 75	82
		7.50	0.00	($2.25, 5, −$2.25, 5)	C-BA N = 117	81
		7.50	0.00	($2.25, 5, −$2.25, 5)	UBC-BA N = 68	72
	1-stage	—	30.00	($39, .5; $21, .5)	C-MBA N = 46	43
		—	30.00	($39, .5; $21, .5)	C-MBA N = 46	44
4.	2-stage	−30.00	0.00	($9, .5; −$9, .5)	C-MBA N = 75	40
		−30.00	0.00	($9, .5; −$9, .5)	C-MBA N = 122	36
		−7.50	0.00	($2.25, .5; −$2.25, .5)	C-BA N = 117	33
		−7.50	0.00	($2.25, .5; −$2.25, .5)	UBC-BA N = 69	33
	1-stage	—	−30.00	(−$39, .5; −$21, .5)	C-MBA N = 46	72
		—	−30.00	(−$39, .5; −$21, .5)	C-MBA N = 70	69
3.	2-stage	−9.00	0.00	($9, .5; −$9, .5)	C-MBA N = 75	63
			0.00	($9, .5; −$9, .5)	C-MBA N = 122	57
	1-stage	—	−9.00	(0, .5; $18, .5)	C-MBA N = 70	71
7.	2-stage	−9.00	10.00	($30, .33; 0, .67)	C-MBA N = 122	34
		−9.00	10.00	($30, .33; 0, .67)	C-MBA N = 117	39
8.	2-stage	−30.00	10.00	($30, .33; 0, .67)	C-MBA N = 122	60
			10.00	($30, .33; 0, .67)	C-MBA N = 117	54

NOTES: C-MBA indicates Cornell MBA students. C-BA indicates Cornell undergraduate students. UBC-BA indicates University of British Columbia undergraduate students.

of problems considered here, these editing rules imply that decision makers adopt the same frame regardless of the presentation format, contrary to what we observe.

The fact that prior outcomes influence choices in the two-stage versions of Problems 1–4 is counter to the predictions of the no-memory version of prospect theory and of the concreteness hypothesis. Both these editing rules imply that the initial outcome is ignored and so predict risk averse choices for all four problems because of loss aversion; that is, because $v(x) < -v(-x)$.

Thus the first four editing rules are explicitly refuted by the data presented in Table 4. The quasi-hedonic editing hypothesis does much better. None of the results is directly inconsistent with quasi-hedonic editing, and many are predicted by the hypothesis. Unfortunately, the predictions of quasi-hedonic editing are often ambiguous, making direct testing difficult. For example, consider Problems 1 and 4. Quasi-hedonic editing and prospect theory make the same predictions for the one-stage version of the problem, namely risk seeking for losses and risk aversion for gains. For the two-stage problems the theories diverge. For Problem 4, with the prior loss, the quasi-hedonic editing hypothesis predicts that risky choice will be less attractive in the two-stage formulation since

$$\pi(.5)[v(-7.50) + v(-2.25)] + \pi(.5)[v(-7.50) + v(2.25)]$$
$$< \pi(.5)\,v(-9.75) + \pi(.5)v(-5.25).$$

To see this, cancel the π terms and rearrange to obtain:

$$v(-2.25) + v(+2.25) < v(-9.75) + v(-5.25) - 2v(-7.50).$$

Note that the left-hand side is negative (loss aversion) and the right-hand side is positive since v is convex in losses. Thus the shift toward risk aversion in the two-stage formulation compared to the one-stage is predicted by quasi-hedonic editing.[7]

For the two-stage prior gain (Problem 1), again it is possible to show that the shift toward risk seeking when we move from the one-stage version to the two-stage version is predicted by quasi-hedonic editing. We must show that

$$\pi(.5)[v(15) + v(4.50)] + \pi(.5)v(11.50) > \pi(.5)v(19.50) + \pi(.5)v(11.50),$$

which is obviously true because of the concavity of v in the domain of gains.[8]

---

[7]Does asymmetric editing predict actual risk aversion for this problem? To show that, we need to have $\pi(.5)[v(-7.50) + v(-2.25)] + \pi(.5)[v(-7.50) + v(2.25)] < v(-7.50)$, or rearranging terms, we need $\pi(.5)[v(2.25) + v(-2.25)] < v(-7.50) - 2\pi(.5)v(-7.50)$. This will be true if $2\pi(.5) \approx 1.0$, which seems plausible.

[8]Again, the prediction as to whether actual risk seeking will be observed depends on the proximity of the π function to the identity line at $p = .5$. To show that decision makers will prefer the risky choice we need to show that $\pi(.5)[v(15)+v(4.50)] + \pi(.5)v(11.50) > v(15)$. This is true so long as $[v(4.50) + v(11.50)]/v(15) > [1 - \pi(.5)]/\pi(.5)$, which will be true if $\pi(.5) \approx .5$, the same condition needed in the previous footnote.

In evaluating the implications of Experiment 4 for the editing rules we must stress that this experiment was not designed as a test of the quasi-hedonic editing rules. Rather, the quasi-hedonic editing rule emerged as an attempt to formalize the results of Experiments 2 and 3, and to construct an editing-based explanation of the results of Experiment 4 and the earlier experiments reported in Table 5. We do not claim that it is the only model consistent with these data. This caveat notwithstanding, the data have interest whether or not we have the correct theory to explain them. The next section examines the results in more detail.

5. CHOICE IN THE PRESENCE OF PRIOR LOSSES

In addition to providing a basis for evaluating potential editing rules, Experiment 4 reveals three empirical results worthy of direct attention. These are (1) risk aversion after prior (two-stage) losses; (2) risk seeking after prior (two-stage) gains; and (3) changes in risk-taking behavior when one outcome (certain or risky) can allow decision makers to "break even." This section addresses each of these results in turn.

5.1. Prior Losses

The convex shape of the loss function in prospect theory predicts that people will generally be risk-seeking in the domain of losses (for simple prospects). This prediction is repeatedly found in the empirical work reported by Kahneman and Tversky and others (e.g., Hershey and Schoemaker, 1980; Hershey, Kunreuther, and Schoemaker, 1982; Payne, Laughhunn, and Crum, 1980; and Slovic, Fischhoff, and Lichtenstein, 1982). If prior losses were facilely integrated with subsequent outcomes, we would expect decision makers to be risk-seeking for complex losses, just as they are for simple prospects involving losses. The quasi-hedonic editing hypothesis suggests something different. Because integration is not automatic, an initial loss might cause an increase in risk aversion, particularly when the second choice does not offer the opportunity to break even. Indeed, the results of Experiments 2 and 3 suggest that a prior loss might even sensitize people to subsequent losses of a similar magnitude. (Recall that subjects reported that the loss of $9 would hurt more after an initial loss of $30 than if it had occurred by itself.) This increase in loss aversion would tend to produce risk aversion for gambles that risk additional losses.

To investigate this question we used Problem 4. In Experiment 4, 60 percent of the subjects chose the risk averse option on this problem, and 60–67 percent of the subjects in the other experiments chose likewise. (In fact, even a majority of the real money subjects in the previous experiments were risk averse on this particular problem.)

5.2. Prior Gains: The House Money Effect

According to the quasi-hedonic editing hypothesis, risk aversion can be observed after prior losses because subsequent losses are not integrated with the prior outcome. In the case of prior gains, the opposite effect is predicted. After a gain, subsequent losses that are smaller than the original gain can be integrated with the prior gain, mitigating the influence of loss aversion and facilitating risk-seeking. The intuition behind this effect is captured by the expression in gambling parlance, "playing with the house money." Gamblers often use this phrase to express the feeling of gambling while ahead. The essence of the idea is that until the winnings are completely depleted, losses are coded as reductions in a gain, as if losing some of "their money" doesn't hurt as much as losing one's own cash. As in the case of prior losses, the one-stage formulation does not create this same sense of being ahead in the mental account, so for the one-stage version, the risk aversion prediction of prospect theory is expected.

The results for Problem 1 are consistent with these predictions. In the two-stage version of the question, 77 percent of the subjects in Experiment 4 were risk-seeking, while only 44 percent were risk-seeking when given the one-stage presentation. Similar results were obtained in the previous experiments using hypothetical questions. In the two-stage version 70–82 percent of the subjects were risk-seeking while only 43–44 percent of the subjects were risk-seeking in the one-stage case.

A recent study by Battalio, Kagel, and Komain (1988) provides an independent replication of the house money effect. In their experiments, any subject who was offered a gamble involving losses was endowed with $30 at the beginning of the experiment. This is equivalent to our subjects being "ahead $30." One of the gambles offered a 50 percent chance to win $10 and a 50 percent chance to lose $10. This problem is virtually identical to our Problem 1, with the stakes multiplied by a factor of two as they were in some of our earlier experiments reported in Table 5. They found that 21 of 35 subjects (60 percent) accepted this gamble. Interestingly, only 15 of the 35 subjects accepted a 50–50 chance to bet $20, suggesting that the house money effect may diminish as the size of the potential loss approaches the initial stake.[9]

---

[9]In another item, Battalio et al. asked their subjects to choose between gamble A which offered a 70 percent chance to lose $6 and a 30 percent chance to win $14, or gamble B which offered a 70 percent chance to lose $3 and a 50 percent chance to win $6. Of the subjects choosing for real money (who had been endowed with $30), 61 percent chose A, while only 42 percent of the subjects making hypothetical choices (who had not been told anything about an initial endowment) selected A. Battalio et al. also observed the risk-seeking for gambles offering only positive outcomes and a large probability of gain. For example, when asked to choose between a sure $17, and a gamble offering a 70 percent chance to win $10 and a 30 percent chance to win $30, 26 of 32 subjects (81 percent) chose the gamble. These subjects had previously been endowed with $5. These results may also be produced by a type of house money effect, though not necessarily related to the initial endowment.

5.3. Break-Even Effects

In their original formulation of prospect theory, Kahneman and Tversky (1979) address the question of how initial losses will affect subsequent choices:

> A change of reference point alters the preference order for prospects. In particular, the present theory implies that a negative translation of a choice problem, such as arises from incomplete adaptation to recent losses, increases risk seeking in some situations. Specifically, if a risky prospect $(x, p; -y, 1 - p)$ is just acceptable, then $(x - z, p; -y-z, 1 - p)$ is preferred over $(-z)$ for $x,y,z > 0$, with $x > z$. The well-known observation that the tendency to bet on long shots increases in the course of the betting day provides some support for the hypothesis that a failure to adapt to losses or to attain an expected gain induces risk-seeking. (pp. 286–287)

As we have seen, a prior loss does not always induce risk seeking. The empirical demonstrations of risk-seeking in the presence of losses provided by Kahneman and Tversky were always accompanied by an opportunity to get back to the original reference or "break-even" point. We believe that this is very important. Thus, while an initial loss may induce risk aversion for some gambles, other gambles, which offer the opportunity to break even, will be found acceptable.

In analyzing the influence of break-even effects, the race track example cited by Kahneman and Tversky is quite instructive. Notice that neither a shift toward risk-seeking nor the failure to adapt to losses is sufficient to explain the preference toward betting on long shots at the end of the betting day. A risk-seeking bettor who is behind by (say) $30 could bet $30 on an even money favorite as a method of getting even. However, the increased loss aversion produced by prior losses may render this strategy unappealing. A $2 bet on a 15-1 long shot offers a more attractive chance at breaking even because it does not risk losing significantly more money.

More generally, we expect that when prior losses are present, gambles which offer the prospect of changing the sign of the status of the current account will be treated differently from those which do not. There are several reasons, a priori, to expect options which offer the opportunity to "break even" to be different. First, these gambles allow the decision maker to cancel, or ignore, part of the outcomes. As Kahneman and Tversky (1979) argue, cancellation supplies decision makers with an appealing way of reducing problem complexity. When breaking even is possible, integration is facilitated; thus, risk seeking in the domain of losses should occur. Also, the ease of integration should reduce the effect of framing manipulations, yielding similar choices in either presentation format. To test these ideas, consider Problems 3, 7, and 8 in Tables 4 and 5.

In Problem 3, risk-seeking now predominates, and the differences between the behavior observed in the two versions of the problem are smaller. Subjects in the two-stage condition selected the risk-seeking option 69 percent of the time, while 87 percent of the subjects in the one-stage condition selected this choice. Thus, it appears that when outcomes allow decision makers to break even, a different frame, possibly encouraged by cancellation, is adopted.

Problems 7 and 8 show the importance of the break-even point. In Problem 7, where the certain outcome yields a small net gain, the risk averse choice receives about a two-thirds preference for the subjects receiving the two-stage version. In contrast, 57 percent of the subjects in the one-stage condition selected the risk-seeking choice. The editing interpretation of these results is that the sure outcome in the two-stage case is particularly attractive because it *eliminates* a loss as well as yielding a trivial gain $[-v(-\$5) + v(\$0.50)]$.

In Problem 8, where it is necessary to gamble to break even, about 70 percent of the subjects selected the risk-seeking alternative in either frame. Again the possibility of cancellation suggests that the alternative frames will be coded the same way.

6. DISCUSSION

6.1. Alternative Explanations

There are at least two other plausible explanations for why we obtain the result that people are risk averse for some gambles when they have had a segregated prior loss and risk-seeking after a segregated prior gain. First, the initial loss could create a negative affect, the initial gain a positive mood. Isen and her colleagues (1982) have demonstrated quite strong effects of mood upon risk-taking behavior. Second, the initial loss could possibly induce a negative "hot hand" effect (Gilovich, Valone, and Tversky, 1985). Subjects might feel that they aren't very lucky that day, and that their actual chance of winning is lower than the stated probability. We admit to finding both of these potential explanations appealing. However, a telling argument against these (and many other) alternative explanations is that they do not adequately explain the reversals we observe when the problems are reframed. While one might argue that hot-hand or mood effects are not as strong in the one-stage formulaton, the marked change seems supportive of the quasi-hedonic editing interpretation.

6.2. Applications

There is a large literature describing the effect of sunk costs on choice behavior (e.g., Arkes and Blumer, 1985; Staw, 1981; Thaler, 1980). For example, in an investment context, subjects seem more willing to invest in a faltering venture when they have previously committed funds to it (Staw, 1976). Our work suggests several circumstances under which the impact of sunk costs could be either minimized or exacerbated. Specifically, the observed effects might be substantially altered by reframing the options in two-stage or one-stage formats. Also, when options present the opportunity to "break even," tendencies toward risk-seeking in the domain of losses might be enhanced. Thus, we would expect investments in failing enterprises to be particularly prevalent when there is a hope, however dim, that one outcome might eradicate existing losses. However, the current analysis also suggests an important converse. Managers of profitable enterprises, flush with initial successes, will be more risk seeking. We know of no empirical investigations of this house-money hypothesis, but it represents an interesting research opportunity.[10]

Another potential domain for applying this research is in the study of investor behavior. The break-even effect suggests that individuals are averse to closing an account that shows a loss. This aversion can produce a reluctance to sell securities that have declined in value. Such a reluctance is observed in trading behavior. Shefrin and Statman (1985), Lakonishok and Smidt (1986), and Ferris, Haugen, and Makhija (1988) have all documented that volume for shares that have declined in value is lower than for shares that have increased in value. This result is particularly notable because the tax code provides investors with an incentive to sell losers and hold winners. (Investors can use losses to offset gains and reduce their taxes, while they have to pay capital gains taxes on winners.)

6.3. Conclusions

The results presented in this paper raise interesting issues concerning conditions when integration and segregation occur. While we have shown that integration is not always spontaneous, we have also indicated that it does occur in special cases, such as when losses can be offset against larger gains, and more generally whenever cancellation is possible. We believe that a variety of interesting factors affect integration, and subsequently, choice. For example, the importance of cancellation suggests that when the equivalence of outcomes is transparent, integration might occur. Factors such as compatibility in the nature of outcomes may also affect the impact of prior outcomes. For example, a prior outcome is less likely to have an effect if it were expressed in a different currency than the current decision.

Extensions to multiattribute choices also raise interesting issues. A prior outcome that is coded in a different mental account is less likely to influence a choice (see the theater ticket example in Kahneman and Tversky, 1984). It seems plausible that the failure to integrate losses observed in our experiments would be even stronger across attributes. That is, a loss in one domain will increase the loss aversion felt with respect to other domains. (Which hurts

---

[10]It is possible to interpret Roll's (1986) "hubris" hypothesis of corporate takeovers as consistent with the house money effect.

more: a toothache alone, or a toothache after being rejected for a new job?) If this is true, then in negotiations it will be particularly difficult to obtain concessions from a side that has already agreed to accept a loss.

Perhaps the most important conclusion to be reached from this research is that making generalizations about risk-taking preferences is difficult. General tendencies can be reversed by a simple reframing of options. This result points out how difficult it is to predict behavior. The question that has yet to be answered is: How do people spontaneously frame options they face in the world? One method, tried by Fischhoff (1983), is to pose alternative frames to subjects and ask them which feel more natural. However, as Fischhoff notes, this approach has some problems. Additional research paradigms are needed to investigate this important issue.

REFERENCES

The authors wish to acknowledge the financial support of the Alfred P. Sloan Foundation, the Russell Sage Foundation, and the Engineering Psychology Programs of the Office of Naval Research. Helpful comments have been made at all stages of this prolonged research effort by Daniel Kahneman and Amos Tversky, who should not in any way be held responsible for any remaining errors.

Arkes, H. R., and C. Blumer. "The Psychology of Sunk Costs." *Organizational Behavior and Human Decision Processes* 35, 1 (1985): 124–140.

Battalio, R. C.; J. H. Kagel; and J. Komain. "Testing Between Alternative Models of Choice under Uncertainty: Some Initial Results." Forthcoming, *Journal of Risk and Uncertainty*.

Ferris, S. P.; R. A. Haugen; and A. K. Makhija. "Predicting Contemporary Volume with Historic Volume at Differential Price Levels: Evidence Supporting the Disposition Effect." *Journal of Finance* 43 (1988): 677–697.

Fischhoff, B. "Predicting Frames." *Journal of Experimental Psychology: Learning, Memory and Cognition* 9 (1983): 103–116.

Gilovich, T.; R. Vallone; and A. Tversky. "The Hot Hand in Basketball: On the Misperception of Random Sequences." *Cognitive Psychology* 17 (1985): 295–314.

Hershey, J. C., and P. J. H. Schoemaker. "Risk Taking and Problem Context in the Domain of Losses: An Expected-utility Analysis." *Journal of Risk and Insurance* 47 (1980): 111–132.

Hershey, J. C.; H. C. Kunreuther; and P. J. H. Schoemaker. "Sources of Bias in Assessment Procedures for Utility Functions." *Management Science* 28 (1982): 936–954.

Isen, A. M.; B. Means; R. Patrick; and G. P. Nowicki. "Positive Affect and Decision Making." In M. S. Clark and S. Fiske, eds. *Affect and Cognition*, Hillsdale, NJ: Erlbaum, 1982.

Kahneman, D., and J. Snell. "Predicting Utility." Forthcoming in R. Hogarth, *Insights in Decision Making*. Chicago: University of Chicago Press.

Kahneman, D., and A. Tversky. "Prospect Theory: An Analysis of Decisions Under Risk." *Econometrica* 47 (1979): 263–291.

———. "Choices, Values, and Frames." *American Psychologist* 39 (1984): 341–350.

Lakonishok, Josef, and Seymour Smidt. "Capital Gain Taxation and Volume of Trading." *Journal of Finance* 41 (1986): 951–974.

Laughhunn, D. J., and J. W. Payne. "The Impact of Sunk Outcomes on Risky Choice Behavior." *INFOR (Canadian Journal of Operational Research and Information Processing)* 22 (1984): 151–181.

Payne, J. W.; D. J. Laughhunn; and R. Crum. "Translation of Gambles and Aspiration Level Effects in Risky Choice Behavior." *Management Science* 26 (1980): 1039–1060.

Roll, R. "The Hubris Hypothesis of Corporate Takeovers." *Journal of Business* 59 (1986): 197–216.

Shefrin, H., and M. Statman. "The Disposition to Sell Winners Too Early and Ride Losers Too Long: Theory and Evidence." The *Journal of Finance* 40, 3 (1985): 777–790.

Slovic, P. "From Shakespeare to Simon: Speculations—and some Evidence—About Man's Ability to Process Information." Oregon Research Institute Research Bulletin (April 1972).

Slovic, P.; B. Fischhoff; and S. Lichtenstein. "Response, Mode, Framing, and Information-Processing Effects in Risk Assessment." In R. Hogarth, ed. *New Directions for Methodology of Social and Behavioral Science: Question Framing and Response Consistency.* San Francisco: Jossey-Bass, 1982, pp. 21–36.

Staw, B. M., "Knee-deep in the Big Muddy: A Study of Escalating Commitment to a Chosen Alternative." *Organizational Behavior and Human Performance* 16 (1976): 27–44.

———. "The Escalation of Commitment to a Course of Action." *Academy of Management Review* 6, 4 (1981): 577–587.

Thaler, R. H. "Toward a Positive Theory of Consumer Choice." *Journal of Economic Behavior and Organization* 1 (March 1980): 39–60.

———. "Mental Accounting and Consumer Choice." Marketing Science 4, 3 (1985): 199–214.

Tversky, A., and D. Kahneman. "The Framing of Decisions and the Psychology of Choice." *Science* 211 (1981): 453–458.

Part Two

SELF-CONTROL AND INTERTEMPORAL CHOICE

4

AN ECONOMIC THEORY
OF SELF-CONTROL

Richard H. Thaler and H. M. Shefrin

The concept of self-control is incorporated in a theory of individual intertemporal choice by modeling the individual as an organization. The individual at a point in time is assumed to be both a farsighted *planner* and a myopic *doer*. The resulting conflict is seen to be fundamentally similar to the agency conflict between the owners and managers of a firm. Both individuals and firms use the same techniques to mitigate the problems which the conflicts create. This paper stresses the implications of this agency model and discusses as applications the effect of pensions on saving, saving and the timing of income flows, and individual discount rates.

For many years Christmas clubs paid no interest. Members deposited money each week but could only withdraw the money on December 1. The clubs were very popular, although they seemed to be dominated by simply depositing money in an interest-bearing savings account.

Passbook loans do still exist. These loans allow an individual with $5,000 in a savings account earning 5 percent interest to borrow at 9 percent using the balance as collateral, instead of at 10 percent with no collateral. Obviously the individual could simply withdraw the money from his savings account at an (opportunity) cost of only 5 percent.

Smoking clinics are a new and thriving business. A smoking clinic will help people who want to stop smoking—for a fee of several hundred dollars.

What does economic theory have to say about these institutions? George J. Stigler provides the following analysis:

> One can of course explain the participation in a Christmas fund by introducing another item of preference: a desire of people to protect themselves against a future lack of willpower. . . . If we stopped the analysis with this explanation,

Reprinted with permission from *Journal of Political Economy* 89,2 (April 1981): 392–406.

we would turn utility into a tautology: a reason, we would be saying, can always be found for whatever we observe a man to do. In order to preserve the predictive power of the utility theory, we must continue our Christmas fund analysis as follows. The foregone cost of putting money in a Christmas fund is the interest one could earn by putting the same money in a savings account. If interest rates on savings accounts rise, the cost of buying protection against a loss of willpower rises and less of it ought to be bought. (Stigler, 1966, p. 57)

We agree with the remarks above and therefore offer a model that says more about these institutions than the fact that the demand for their services will be negatively related to price. We do so by proposing a simple extension of orthodox models, using orthodox tools, that permits such behavior to be viewed as rational. This rationalization is based on an analysis of the technology of self-control using the theory of agency rather than reliance on ad hoc explanations in which transaction costs, taxes, and income effects play a major role. Our model can predict, in a nontautological way, the circumstances in which these kinds of behavior will be observed. In particular, our new theory of intertemporal choice has important implications for theories of saving behavior. In the last section of the paper we discuss some of these implications and offer empirical evidence in support of our ideas.

1. THE MODEL

The idea of self-control is paradoxical unless it is assumed that the psyche contains more than one energy system, and that these energy systems have some degree of independence from each other. (Donald McIntosh, 1969)

Why individuals would impose constraints on their future behavior is a problem that has received attention from economists since Strotz's (1955–56) classic paper.[1] Strotz and those who have followed him (Pollak, 1968; Blackorby et al., 1973; Peleg and Yaari, 1973; Hammond, 1976; and Yaari, 1977) have analyzed the phenomenon as one of *changing tastes*. In Strotz's formulation a conflict occurs between today's preferences and tomorrow's preferences if the discount function used today is not exponential with a constant exponent.

Our framework differs from the changing tastes literature in that we model man as having two sets of preferences that are in conflict at a single point in time. This idea is certainly not new. Adam Smith used a two-self model much like ours in his *Theory of Moral Sentiments* (1759). More recently Schelling (1960, 1978) and Buchanan (1975) have recognized the importance of simultaneous conflict in understanding self-control problems. Outside economics the idea is

---

[1]Two important contributions by noneconomists are Ainslee (1975) and Elster (1977).

commonplace, with the writings of Freud (1958) and Berlin (1969) deserving special mention.

Nonetheless, to the best of our knowledge our work is the first systematic, formal treatment of a two-self economic man. We have adopted a two-self model because, as McIntosh says above, the notion of self-control is paradoxical without it. Furthermore, we utilize an organizational analogy that leads to both insights into human behavior and a rich explanatory model. We will briefly describe the model here. We do so in order to make explicit the nature of our two-self conceptualization. The model also leads to specific predictions about behavior, which are discussed in Section 3 below.

Our model is cast in discrete time. Consider an individual with a fixed income stream $y = (y_1, y_2, \ldots, y_T)$. Think of period T as retirement and let $y_T = 0$. Let the individual choose a nonnegative level of consumption c_t in t. Call $c = (c_1, c_2, \ldots, c_T)$ a consumption plan. The conflict between short-run and long-run preferences is introduced by viewing the individual as an organization. At any point in time the organization consists of a planner and a doer. The planner is concerned with lifetime utility, while the doer exists only for one period and is completely selfish, or myopic. The period t doer is assumed to have direct control over period t consumption rate c_t. The doer's utility function is given by $Z_t(\cdot)$; Z_t is taken to be independent of all components of c except c_t.[2] Furthermore, suppose initially that Z_t is strictly increasing and concave in c_t.

In our model the planner does not actually consume but, rather, derives utility from the consumption of the doers. Therefore the planner's utility function is given by $V(Z_1, Z_2, \ldots, Z_T)$. Observe that a plan which maximizes V subject to the present value budget constraint, $\sum_{t=1}^{T} c_t \leq \sum_{t=1}^{T} y_t = Y$, is considered optimal from the planner's point of view. However, without some method to control the doer's actions, this plan cannot be implemented. Indeed, under the assumptions above, the actual consumption stream chosen would have total lifetime income consumed during the first period, when the period-one doer would borrow $Y - y_1$ on the "perfect" capital market. In order to prevent this from occurring, the planner requires some psychic technology capable of affecting the doer's behavior. Two main techniques are available for this: (1) The doer can be given *discretion* in which case either his *preferences* must be modified or his *incentives* must be altered, or (2) the doer's set of choices may instead be limited by imposing *rules* that change the constraints the doer faces.

We begin by analyzing the case in which no rules are used. We refer to this case as *pure discretion*. While we do not believe that the pure discretion case is empirically important (most people appear to use at least some kinds of rules), it provides a useful foundation for our model, to which rules are easily added.

---

[2] The extreme assumption that doers do not care at all about past or future doers is adopted just for expositional simplicity. Other arguments of Z_t could easily be added.

Furthermore, since this case corresponds closely to that usually considered in economics, it highlights the differences between our model and the standard framework.

Recall that $Z_t(\cdot)$ was assumed to be unbounded. We now specify that Z_t depends on a preference modification parameter θ_t selected by the planner. The choice of θ_t allows the planner to alter Z_t such that it possesses an internal maximum. By appropriately selecting θ_t, any desired c_t may be obtained; however, the lower the desired c_t is, the more modification will be required. Furthermore, $\delta Z_t / \delta \theta_t$ is negative; that is, modification reduces short-run utility and is therefore costly. Finally, we assume that the marginal cost of modification increases with θ. Thus successive reductions in c_t require increasing reductions in Z_t.

If the planner could exercise direct control over the choice of a consumption plan, θ_t would be set equal to zero for all t (because modification is costly) and c would be selected to maximize V subject to the budget constraint. Since under pure discretion this is assumed to be infeasible, the planner must instead choose $\theta = (\theta_1, \theta_2, \ldots, \theta_T)$ to maximize V. Essentially, modification is increased until the marginal utility derived from additional consumption in retirement (period T) equals the marginal loss in utility in earlier periods due to modification.

In the more general case when both rules and preference modification are permitted, the planner may also alter the budget constraint facing each doer. This allows the planner to reduce c_t without incurring modification costs. However, since available rules are imperfect (see next section), the planner will have to trade off modification costs with the opportunity costs associated with using second-best-type rules.

2. TECHNIQUES TO REDUCE CONFLICTS IN INDIVIDUALS AND ORGANIZATIONS

We have characterized self-control as an internal conflict resembling the principal-agent conflict between the owner and manager of a firm (see Ross, 1973; Jensen and Meckling, 1976). In this section we describe the actual techniques used by individuals and firms to mitigate these conflicts. The techniques fall into the two categories highlighted in the model: rules and incentives. We provide many illustrations of the methods individuals use because these are in essence part of our model. When individuals use rules it is impossible to characterize their behavior simply with first-order conditions. The limits on the kinds of rules which individuals will find feasible lead to the specific predictions about saving behavior discussed in Section 3. In this section we also compare the techniques individuals use with those used in firms. The close correspondence we find lends intuitive support to our principal-agent model.

2.1. Methods to Alter Incentives

Individuals use three basic techniques to alter the doer's incentives. First, the doer's preferences can be modified directly. Some individuals consider saving a good in and of itself.[3] In this case doer myopia does not inhibit saving. Second, inputs to a saving or dieting program can be explicitly monitored via weekly budgets or calorie counting (customers of diet clinics and credit counselors are advised to do this). Simply keeping track seems to act as a tax on any behavior which the planner views as deviant. Third, incentives can be explicitly altered: Alcoholics take the drug Antabuse which makes them ill if they take a drink; academics agree to give a paper at a conference to provide a proximate incentive to write it.

Firms use the same three methods. First, profit-sharing plans are quite popular even though they offer only trivial financial incentives to all but the highest executives. We believe firms adopt them because they help create an atmosphere in which the employees' preferences are more similar to those of the owner. Second, firms monitor departmental inputs through cost account-ing and then tie compensation to these input measures. Third, departmental profits are measured and used as performance measures for managers.

2.2. Methods to Alter Opportunities: Rules

If the costs of monitoring and persuasion are high, individuals will resort to rules that restrict the doer's opportunities. In the extreme, all doer discretion can be eliminated using what Strotz referred to as the strategy of precommit-ment. Such behavior is rational in our model if the rule can approximate the choices that the planner would select. Market precommitment institutions are observed, as we would predict, in such areas as saving and dieting. For example, people pay to go to "fat farms" which essentially are resorts that promise not to feed their customers.

Less extreme rules can limit the *range* of doer discretion, usually through the use of self-imposed rules of thumb. In the savings context several such rules appear to be commonly used. These rules alter the budget constraint faced by the doer in much the same way as credit limits imposed by lenders do.[4] A simple first departure from pure discretion is a ban on borrowing, the so-called debt ethic. A somewhat weaker rule which seems common is to prohibit borrowing except for specific purchases, like houses and automobiles. Another rule of thumb is a prohibition on dissaving combined with limits on

---

[3]This idea has been suggested by Scitovsky (1976). The importance of norms in controlling individual behavior is also stressed heavily by Adam Smith (1759, p. 326) and by Irving Fisher (1930).

[4]While it is difficult to document the extent to which these precise rules are used, 85 percent of Cagan's (1965) sample of Consumers Union members reported using one of these or similar rules to determine monthly saving.

borrowing. Using this rule of thumb, a person might borrow and lend simultaneously in spite of a substantial difference in the interest rates, as in the case of the passbook loan. The loan allows him to transfer consumption across time periods while it provides a regimented repayment scheme.

Rules can also eliminate discretion over a specific *class* of decisions for which the conflict is particularly acute. Dieters try not to keep cheesecake in the refrigerator and will refuse invitations to lavish dinner parties; problem gamblers avoid Las Vegas. Also, many smokers pay more for their cigarettes by buying them by the pack instead of the carton—it helps enforce a self-imposed ration such as one pack a day.

Again, the same types of rules are observed in organizations.[5] "Pure" rules are observed most often in bureaucratic organizations because the costs of monitoring output are so high. Rules that limit managerial discretion over a particular range are frequently in the form of guidelines (e.g., a plant manager can adapt any investment that exceeds some stated rate of return). Similarly, rules may prohibit discretion over a specific class of decisions; loan officers, for example, might need approval for loans to relatives or friends.

We wish to make three other points about internal rules of thumb. First, it is useful to consider these rules as learned as much as chosen. Rules like the debt ethic are learned from parents and other models, which suggests that there will be differences in the use of rules depending on social class, education, and age. Second, rules of thumb are likely to become habits. By establishing a routine, the doer decision process can be avoided. Third, to the extent that the rules do become habits, there will be rigidities built into the individual's behavior.[6] The implications of these observations are discussed in the next section.

3. IMPLICATIONS

We now turn to a discussion of the implications of the planner-doer model. What predictions about behavior can be made with our model that are inconsistent with the standard model? Some of these predictions are obvious. We predict that people will rationally choose to impose constraints on their own behavior. Furthermore, we predict that such precommitments will occur

---

[5]For a discussion of firms imposing constraints on their future financial policies, see Myers (1977).
[6]Habits can be formally introduced in two stages. At first stage Z_t can also be made a function of θ_s, $s < t$, to reflect the fact that self-control at the early dates renders self-control at later dates less costly. At the second stage, Z_t can also be parameterized on the adopted rule. In this case the function Z_t could exhibit an internal maximum in c_t when $\theta_t = 0$. It is interesting to note that modification would now be required in order to break the rule. This would tend to explain miserliness, for instance.

primarily for those goods whose benefits and costs occur at different dates. We present here some less obvious predictions based on our model.

Because our framework is richer than the standard theory, variables that the standard theory treats as irrelevant differences in form we model as differences in substance. In Sections 3.1 and 3.2 we consider how differences in the form of payment (holding the level constant) affect saving decisions, and in Section 3.3 we present variables other than borrowing and lending rates that determine individual marginal rates of time preference.

3.1. Pensions and Saving

Consider two identical individuals with the same total income and wealth. Assume that they both save some fraction s of their income. Now give one a mandatory pension plan that forces him to save $p < s$. What will happen to total saving? Though it is difficult to get a specific prediction from the standard model (see Feldstein, 1977), a first-order prediction would be that total saving is unaffected. Other forms of saving should fall by the approximate amount of the pension.

Our model has a different prediction: The pension plan produces saving at no psychic cost. Modification costs occur only when saving is voluntarily withheld. This is what we call "discretionary saving." Thus since the marginal cost of saving is lower at the old saving level, we expect total saving to go up. (In other words, the offset in other saving will be less than the size of the pension.)

Furthermore, in two cases the offset will be essentially zero: (1) The individual uses a saving rule such as "save s percent of disposable income" which is not changed when the pension is introduced (total saving increases by $[1 - s]py_t$), and (2) the individual uses discretion but treats saving as a good for its own sake rather than as a transfer to future consumption. In this case discretionary saving and retirement saving are not perfect substitutes as in the standard model; in fact, their cross-elasticities of demand could be zero.

The effect of pensions on saving has been investigated with individual data by Cagan (1965), Katona (1965), and Munnell (1974, 1976). All obtained similar results. Cagan used a sample of Consumer Union members. He found that for those members with a mandatory pension plan, other saving actually was higher than for those without pensions (see Cagan, 1965, p. 21). Munnell (1974) replicated Cagan's study using the same data source. She used a different measure of saving, replaced before-tax income with after-tax income, and restricted her analysis to a subset of observations she thought to be more reliable. She then regressed the nonpension saving to income ratio on several variables including a pension dummy. Her basic result was that the pension had no effect on other saving (i.e., a zero offset). The coefficient of the pension dummy was never significant. Its highest t value occurred for the 55–65 age group ($t = 1.2$), for which those with pensions saved 3 percent less than those without pensions. Though other explanations (such as selectivity bias) have been offered for these results, we find that they lend support to our model.

3.2. Saving and the Timing of Income Flows

The importance of current disposable income (as opposed to permanent income) yields another prediction from our model that differs from the standard theory. Consider two identical individuals, S and B; S receives a salary of $12,000 per year paid in 12 monthly installments of $1,000, while B receives a salary of $10,000 per year paid in monthly installments plus a guaranteed bonus of $2,000 paid in March each year. Standard theories of saving behavior would predict that these two individuals would save the same amount. Our model predicts that, on average, B will save more.

Although we know of no test of this hypothesis,[7] there is one bit of circumstantial evidence. In Japan, where there is a very high saving rate, bonus schemes are quite common. We think this is no coincidence. A test would be possible, given the right data. We predict that individuals who are paid a portion of their salary via a lump-sum bonus will have higher saving rates than those who receive their compensation in a smooth pattern. How does this follow from the model?

We have characterized saving behavior primarily as a set of self-imposed rules of thumb and externally enforced saving plans. For an individual like B, those rules and plans will be based on his regular monthly income. Contributions to pension plans, payments on whole life insurance policies, mortgage payments, and so forth must be made on a regular basis. Furthermore, most individuals prefer to have their monthly inflows and outflows roughly balance.[8] For B to act like S, he could deposit the bonus in the bank and draw it down gradually during the year (as if his salary were $12,000), or he could borrow the $2,000 over the course of the year and repay the loan when the bonus is paid. However, we feel that neither of these behavior patterns is likely to be widely observed. Notice that they violate either the ban on borrowing or the ban on dissaving. To the extent that these rules of thumb are used, imitating the behavior of S will be difficult. We believe that for the typical individual much of the bonus will end up being saved, especially through the purchase of durable goods. This amounts to the use of an auxiliary rule regarding the disposition of bonuses received. We expect that total saving for B will exceed that for S because of the technology of self-control. By paying the bonus the firm is acting as an external self-control device (much like parents

---

[7]However, a related issue is investigated by Landsberger (1966).

[8]This explains why many teachers sacrifice interest by electing to receive their academic-year salary paid in 12 monthly installments (September–August) rather than 10 (September–June).

who tell children that money gifts at Christmas must go into a savings account). Temptations to spend during the year will be overcome because the smaller monthly salary will make them seem beyond the individual's means. This technology seems to have been recognized by the millions of taxpayers each year who claim too few exemptions in order to assure a tax refund.[9] Obviously some self-deception (doer deception) is necessary for this device to work, but doers can apparently be deceived quite easily. How else can one explain the not uncommon practice of knowingly setting one's watch a few minutes ahead ("in order to get to places on time")?

As the analysis in this section suggests, the shape of the income stream will affect the type of saving strategy adopted. Those individuals with variable and uncertain incomes will find a discretionary rule such as saving *s* percent each month difficult to enforce in the low-income months. Without a mandatory saving plan, they would have to adopt some more complex strategy to save effectively. Similarly, those individuals whose incomes are expected to decline (such as professional athletes) would prefer to save a large proportion of their high current incomes and a smaller (perhaps negative) proportion of their lower future incomes. For both, a mandatory pension plan is particularly likely to increase total saving. A more sophisticated analysis of the effect of pensions on saving might detect differences of this sort.

The case of athletes points up the extreme difficulties in behavior that self-control can produce. Their declining income stream creates a difficult self-control problem in the high-income years. Some athletes hire agents to invest their incomes and limit their current spending, and many of them become rich. Others rely on discretionary strategies and end up bankrupt. Both types of behavior are possible in our model, depending on the degree of planner control and the types of precommitment strategies available. The best predictors of which individuals will fall into which groups are probably related to family background, since the family is the most likely place for the individual to learn (or not learn) the rules and norms necessary to overcome the self-control problems.[10]

3.3. Individual Marginal Rates of Time Preference

The orthodox theory of intertemporal choice as formulated by Irving Fisher produces a very strong result. Each person should equate his marginal rate of

[9]E.g., in 1969, 55 million taxpayers received refunds while 18 million owed taxes. In dollars, overpayments exceeded underpayments by 39 percent.

[10]The last two paragraphs were prompted by a suggestion from Sam Peltzman. Irving Fisher also discussed some of these issues. He notes that some individuals spend their weekly paycheck at the "grog house." (Others, we believe, avoid the grog house precisely on those days.) He attributes much of the observed differences in behavior to social class. Our differences with Fisher are discussed in the next section.

time preference (MRTP) with the relevant after-tax interest rate.[11] Thus the theory predicts that all individuals who face the same after-tax interest rate will make the same marginal intertemporal choices: Specifically, they will act as if they used the after-tax interest rate as their discount rate. This follows because individuals are assumed to use capital markets to arbitrage away any difference between what Fisher called their "rate of impatience" and the interest rate. It should be noted, however, that this result can fail to hold if capital markets impose quantity constraints on borrowers (capital rationing). In this case borrowers may be forced to stop borrowing even though their rate of impatience exceeds the interest rate.

In exactly the same fashion, self-imposed borrowing constraints such as those discussed in Section 2.2. prevent the complete internal arbitrage from taking place. Thus in our model, in which such constraints play an important role, the presumption that individual MRTPs will equal the interest rate no longer holds. Indeed, we expect to observe behavior that implies an MRTP greater than the interest rate and at the same time an unwillingness to engage in additional borrowing. Two points need to be raised about this implication. First, once rules are incorporated into the analysis, the failure to equate the MRTP to the interest rate may not violate an optimality condition. If rules are used it is because they lead to higher levels of utility than pure discretion would. The inequality created is costly, but the cost arises from the necessity of using a second-best technology. Because rules by nature must be simple, rules that select the precisely correct consumption bundle in every situation are infeasible. Second, notice that if a quantity constraint is binding, whether internally or externally imposed, observed MRTPs will be equal to or greater than the interest rate.

Attempts to measure individual MRTPs appear in studies by Kurz, Spiegelman, and West (1973) and Hausman (1979). Hausman studied families' purchases of room air conditioners. The trade-off between initial outlay and operating costs permitted him to estimate implicit MRTPs. The mean MRTP in his sample was about 25 percent, clearly above any relevant interest rate. Kurz et al. obtained similar results by asking hypothetical questions of participants in the Seattle and Denver Income Maintenance Experiments. They asked a sample of participants a series of questions of the following sort: What size bonus would you demand today rather than collect a bonus of $100 in 1 year? Several different forms of this type of question were asked, and the results were striking. For whites the mean rate of time preference implied by their answers varied between 36 and 76 percent. For blacks the rates varied between 40 and 122 percent. Of particular interest for present purposes is the fact that this sample included only those respondents who said they could

---

[11]We define the MRTP to be the marginal rate of substitution between tomorrow's consumption and today's consumption minus one.

TABLE 1 Estimated Discount Rates Using Mean Population Estimates

Income Class ($/yr)	Observations (N)	Implied Discount Rate (%)
600	6	89
10,000	15	39
15,000	16	27
25,000	17	17
35,000	8	8.9
50,000	3	5.1

SOURCE: Hausman, 1979.

borrow either $500 to make an installment purchase or $1,000 in cash. Furthermore, 81.3 percent of this subsample reported that they would not borrow $1,000 at current interest rates. (The mean perceived rate was generally less than 20 percent.) This strongly suggests the use of self-imposed borrowing constraints.

Once individual differences in MRTPs are anticipated, it becomes interesting to ask what factors determine those differences. A detailed examination is beyond the scope of this paper, but the model predicts that those factors determining individual rates of impatience will (for the reasons stated above) also affect observed MRTPs. These factors are discussed at length by Fisher (who draws on the writings of John Rae and Eugen Böhm-Bawerk). Fisher believed that age, income, and marital status affect the rate of impatience (in obvious directions). He felt that the shape of the income stream as well as the level was important; if income were expected to rise, the rate of impatience would be higher. Six "personal characteristics" were also deemed to be important: foresight, self-control, habit, expectation of life, concern for the lives of other persons, and fashion.[12]

In principle, the planner-doer model can be tested against the standard model quite simply. Observe some intertemporal choice that implies a discount rate (such as Hausman's study of air conditioners). Then regress the implied discount rate on the factors above *and* the individual's borrowing rate. The standard framework implies that only the borrowing rate will be a significant predictor. Our model implies that the other factors will also be important. Hausman did test one such variable. The implied rate of discount was computed for six income classes. His results appear in Table 1. Clearly the variation in discount rates cannot be attributed solely to variations in borrowing rates.

We would also expect age and social class to be important in predicting individual intertemporal choices. The young behave impatiently in part

[12]Fisher, 1930, p. 81. On this topic also see Maital and Maital (1977).

because they have yet to master the techniques of self-control. To the extent that these techniques are learned from parents, class differences will be observed. Most important, our model stresses the theoretical admissibility of these variables. Only further empirical work can establish their relative explanatory power.

4. SUMMARY AND CONCLUSION

We now briefly recapitulate our argument. We have investigated intertemporal choice as a problem in the economic theory of self-control. As the quotation at the beginning of Section 1 states, the concept of self-control is paradoxical unless some kind of multiself model of man is adopted. We have introduced self-control into a formal model of intertemporal choice by modeling man as an organization with a planner and many doers. Conflict occurs because the doers are myopic (i.e., selfish). This conflict is fundamentally similar to the agency relationship between the employer and the employee, and individuals use many of the same strategies that organizations adopt to deal with their "conflicts of interest." These strategies can involve doer/employee discretion while their incentives have somehow been altered, or they may entail the implementation of precommitment (a rule) to avoid the doer/employee decision process altogether.

The close correspondence between the solutions to control problems adopted by organizations and individuals provides strong support for our model. Although our model is nontraditional, our tools are strictly traditional. Formally, our model closely resembles that used by Ross (1973) in his study of the theory of agency. Finally, we note that ours is a theory of rational behavior, just as Ross's theory is of profit-maximizing behavior.

Many applications of the model are possible, and we have discussed a few briefly. The most important applications are in the study of individual saving behavior. Our hypotheses are quite different in spirit from the permanent income and life-cycle hypotheses that currently dominate the literature. On the basis of the evidence presented here, we feel these theories of saving should be reevaluated.

REFERENCES

This paper was written while Thaler was a visiting scholar at the National Bureau of Economic Research at Stanford, California. While there he received financial support from the Kaiser Family Foundation and the Robert Wood Johnson Foundation. Helpful comments on earlier drafts were provided by George Ainslee, James Buchanan, Tom Russell, and numerous other friends and colleagues. We thank them all.

Ainslee, George. "Specious Reward: A Behavioral Theory of Impulsiveness and Impulse Control." *Psychological Bull* 82 (July 1975): 463–496.

Berlin, Isaiah. "Two Concepts of Liberty." *Four Essays on Liberty*. New York: Oxford University Press, 1969.

Blackorby, Charles; David Nissen; Daniel Primont; and R. Robert Russell. "Consistent Intertemporal Decision Making." *Rev. Econ. Studies* 40 (April 1973): 239–248.

Buchanan, James. "The Samaritan's Dilemma." In *Altruism, Morality, and Economic Theory*. ed. Edmund S. Phelps. New York: Russell Sage Foundation 1975.

Cagan, Philip. *The Effect of Pension Plans on Aggregate Saving: Evidence from a Sample Survey*. New York: Columbia University Press (for NBER), 1965.

Elster, Jon. "Ulysses and the Sirens: A Theory of Imperfect Rationality." *Soc. Sci. Information* 16 (October 1977): 469–526.

Feldstein, Martin. "Do Private Pensions Increase National Saving?" Working paper no. 186. Cambridge, MA: NBER, 1977.

Fisher, Irving. *The Theory of Interest*. London: Macmillan, 1930.

Freud, Sigmund. "Beyond the Pleasure Principle." In *The Standard Edition of the Complete Psychological Works of Sigmund Freud*. ed. James Strachey and Anna Freud. London: Hogarth, 1958.

Hammond, Peter J. "Changing Tastes and Coherent Dynamic Choice." *Rev. Econ. Studies* 43 (February 1976): 159–173.

Hausman, Jerry A. "Individual Discount Rates and the Purchase and Utilization of Energy-using Durables." *Bell J. Econ.* 10 (Spring 1979): 33–54.

Jensen, Michael C., and William H. Meckling. "Theory of the Firm: Managerial Behavior, Agency Costs, and Ownership Structure." *J. Financial Econ.* 3 (October 1976): 305–360.

Katona, George. *Private Pensions and Individual Saving*. Ann Arbor: Univ. Michigan Inst. Soc. Res., 1965.

Kurz, M.; R. Spiegelman; and R. West. "The Experimental Horizon and the Rate of Time Preference for the Seattle and Denver Income Maintenance Experiments: A Preliminary Study." Menlo Park, CA.: SRI Internat. Res. Memorandum no. 21, November 1973.

Landsberger, Michael. "Windfall Income and Consumption: Comment." *A.E.R.* 56 (June 1966): 534–540.

McIntosh, Donald. *The Foundations of Human Society*. Chicago: University of Chicago Press, 1969.

Maital, Schlomo, and Sharona Maital. "Time Preference, Delay of Gratification and the Intergenerational Transmission of Economic Inequality: A Behavioral Theory of Income Distribution." In *Essays in Labor Market Analysis: In Memory of Yochanan Peter Comay*. ed. Orley C. Ashenfelter and Wallace E. Oates. New York: Wiley, 1977.

Munnell, Alicia H. *The Effort of Social Security on Personal Saving*. Cambridge, MA: Ballinger, 1974.

————. "Private Pensions and Saving: New Evidence." *J.P.E.* 84, 5 (October 1976): 1013–1032.

Myers, Stewart C. "Determinants of Corporate Borrowing." *J. Financial Econ.* 5 (November 1977): 147–175.

Peleg, Bezalel, and Menahem E. Yaari. "On the Existence of a Consistent Course of Action When Tastes Are Changing." *Rev. Econ. Studies* 40 (July 1973): 391–401.

Pollak, Robert A. "Consistent Planning." *Rev. Econ. Studies* 35 (April 1968): 201–208.

Ross, Stephen A. "The Economic Theory of Agency: The Principal's Problem." *A.E.R. Papers and Proc.* 63 (May 1973): 134–139.

Schelling, Thomas C. *The Strategy of Conflict.* Cambridge, MA: Harvard University Press, 1960.

————. "Egonomics, or the Art of Self-Management." *A.E.R. Papers and Proc.* 68 (May 1978): 290–294.

Scitovsky, Tibor. *The Joyless Economy: An Inquiry into Human Satisfaction and Consumer Dissatisfaction.* New York: Oxford University Press, 1976.

Smith, Adam. *Theory of Moral Sentiments.* London: Millar, 1759.

Stigler, George J. *The Theory of Price.* 3d ed. New York: Macmillan, 1966.

Strotz, Robert H. "Myopia and Inconsistency in Dynamic Utility Maximization." *Rev. Econ. Studies* 23, 3 (1955–56): 165–180.

Thaler, Richard H. "Toward a Positive Theory of Consumer Choice." *J. Econ. Behavior and Org.* 1 (1980): 39–60.

Yaari, Menahem E. "How to Eat an Appetite-arousing Cake." Research Memorandum no. 26, Center Res. Math. Econ. and Game Theory, Hebrew University, June 1977.

5

THE BEHAVIORAL LIFE-CYCLE HYPOTHESIS

Hersh M. Shefrin and Richard H. Thaler

1. INTRODUCTION

Modigliani and Brumberg's life-cycle theory of saving (1954) (and the similar permanent income hypothesis of Milton Friedman (1957) are classic examples of economic theorizing. The life-cycle (LC) model makes some simplifying assumptions in order to be able to characterize a well-defined optimization problem which is then solved. The solution to that optimization problem provides the core of the theory.

Attempts to test the life-cycle hypothesis have met with mixed success. As summarized by Courant et al. (1984), "But for all its elegance and rationality, the life-cycle model has not tested out very well. . . . Nor have efforts to test the life-cycle model with cross-sectional microdata worked out very successfully" (p. 279–280). Various alterations to the theory have been proposed to help it accommodate the data: add a bequest motive; hypothesize capital market imperfections; assume that the utility function for consumption changes over time; or specify a particular form of expectations regarding future income. These modifications often appear to be ad hoc, since different assumptions are necessary to explain each anomalous empirical result. In this paper, we suggest that the data can be explained in a parsimonious manner by making modifications to the life-cycle theory that are quite different in spirit from those cited above, namely modifications aimed at making the theory more behaviorally realistic. We call our enriched model the Behavioral Life Cycle (BLC) Hypothesis.

We are aware, of course, that criticizing the realism of the assumptions of an economic theory is hardly novel. It is trite to point out that few consumers are capable of making the present value calculations implicit in the theory. This

Reprinted with permission from *Economic Inquiry* 26 (October 1988): 609–643.

remark, while accurate, does little to help formulate a better theory. Perhaps, as Milton Friedman might argue, households save *as if* they knew how to calculate the (after-tax) annuity value of a windfall gain. Therefore, in an effort to get beyond this sort of general critique, we suggest that the life-cycle model can be enriched by incorporating three important behavioral features that are usually missing in economic analyses. (1) *Self-control:* We recognize that self-control is costly, and that economic agents will use various devices such as pension plans and rules-of-thumb to deal with the difficulties of postponing a significant portion of their consumption until retirement. We also incorporate temptation into the analysis since some situations are less conducive to saving than others. (2) *Mental accounting:* Most households act as if they used a system of mental accounts which violate the principle of fungibility. Specifically, some mental accounts, those which are considered "wealth," are less tempting than those which are considered "income." (3) *Framing:* An implication of the differential temptation of various mental accounts is that the saving rate can be affected by the way in which increments to wealth are "framed" or described. Our model predicts that income paid in the form of a lump sum bonus will be treated differently from regular income even if the bonus is completely anticipated. Building upon the research done on these topics by psychologists and other social scientists (see, e.g., Ainslie, 1975 and Mischel, 1981), we are able to make specific predictions about how actual household saving behavior will differ from the idealized LC model.

The plan of the paper is to first present the model and to use it to derive propositions about saving behavior that can distinguish it from the standard life-cycle hypothesis. We then present the evidence we have been able to compile from existing studies on each of the propositions.

2. THE MODEL

Self-Control and Temptation: The Problem

In the *Theory of Interest* Irving Fisher bases his explanation of personal saving upon five characteristics: foresight, self-control, habits, expectation of life, and love for posterity. We concentrate here on the first three factors, and the relationships among them. Foresight is important since retirement saving requires long-term planning. Self-control is necessary because immediate consumption is always an attractive alternative to retirement saving. Successfully dealing with self-control problems requires the cultivation of good habits. In presenting our model we begin with the concept of self-control.

How does self-control differ from ordinary choice? The distinguished psychologist William James says that the key attribute of self-control choices is the "feeling of effort" that is present.

Effort of attention is thus the essential phenomenon of will. Every reader must know by his own experience that this is so, for every reader must have felt some fiery passion's grasp. What constitutes the difficulty for a man laboring under an unwise passion of acting as if the passion were wise? Certainly there is no physical difficulty. It is as easy physically to avoid a fight as to begin one, to pocket one's money as to squander it on one's cupidities, to walk away from as towards a coquette's door. The difficulty is mental: it is that of getting the idea of the wise action to stay before our mind at all. (James [1890] 1981, p. 1167)

Incorporating the effort that is present in self-control contexts involves three elements normally excluded from economic analyses: internal conflict, temptation, and willpower. The very term "self-control" implies that the trade-offs between immediate gratification and long-run benefits entail a conflict that is not present in a choice between a white shirt and a blue one. When modeling choice under such circumstances the concept of temptation must be incorporated because of the obvious fact that some situations are more tempting than others. A model of saving that omits temptation is misspecified. The term willpower represents the real psychic costs of resisting temptation. The behavioral life cycle hypothesis modifies the standard life cycle model to incorporate these features. To capture formally the notion of internal conflict between the rational and emotional aspects of an individual's personality, we employ a dual preference structure. Individuals are assumed to behave *as if* they have two sets of coexisting and mutually inconsistent preferences: one concerned with the long run, and the other with the short run.[1] We refer to the former as the planner and the latter as the doer.[2] To place the preceding concepts into a formal structure consider an individual whose lifetime extends over T periods, with the final period representing retirement. The lifetime income stream is given by $y = (y_1, \ldots, y_T)$. For simplicity we assume a perfect capital market and zero real rate of interest. Let retirement income y_T be zero Then lifetime wealth is defined as $LW = \Sigma_t^T = 1 y_t$. Let the consumption stream be denoted by $c = (c_1, \ldots, c_T)$. The lifetime budget constraint is then $\Sigma c_t = LW$.

---

[1] Several other scholars have tried to model intertemporal choice taking self-control into account. All rely on some type of two-self formulation, though the models differ in how the two selves interact. See Elster (1979), Margolis (1982), Schelling (1984), and Winston (1980).

[2] While the planner-doer framework is in the tradition of "as if" economic models, our economic theory of choice is roughly consistent with the scientific literature on brain function. This literature deals with the organizational structure of the brain and its associated division into functional subcomponents. The *prefrontal cortex* has been called the "executive of the brain" (Fuster, 1980) and has been identified as the location of rational thought and planning. The planner in our model represents the prefrontal cortex. The prefrontal cortex continually interfaces with the *limbic system*, which is responsible for the generation of emotions (Numan, 1978). The doer in our model represents the limbic system. It is well known that self-control phenomena center on the interaction between the prefrontal cortex and the limbic system (Restak, 1984).

The conflict associated with self-control is captured by the contrasting time horizons of the planner and the doer. The doer is assumed to be pathologically myopic, concerned only with current period consumption. At date t the doer is assumed to possess a subutility function $U_t(c_t)$. We assume *diminishing marginal utility* ($U_t(\cdot)$ is concave in c_t), and also *nonsatiation* (U_t is strictly increasing in c_t). In contrast, the planner is concerned with maximizing a function of lifetime doer utilities.

Since temptation depends on immediate consumption opportunities, we define an opportunity set X_t to represent the feasible choices for consumption at date t. If free to choose from this set, the myopic doer would select the maximum feasible value of c_t (since that would maximize U_t on X_t). The planner would usually prefer a smaller c_t. Suppose the planner wants to reduce consumption by exerting willpower. We assume that if exercise of willpower does diminish c_t, there must be some psychic cost. If this were not the case, then exerting willpower would be effortless, and self-control problems such as overeating and overspending would not occur. The psychic cost of using willpower is represented by the symbol W_t. W_t may be thought of as a negative sensation (corresponding roughly to guilt) which diminishes the positive sensations associated with U_t. Total doer utility, denoted as Z_t, is then the sum of the pleasure and the pain:

$$Z_t = U_t + W_t \qquad (1)$$

The doer is assumed to exercise direct control over the consumption choice, and, being myopic, chooses c_t in order to maximize Z_t on X_t. This choice reflects the combined influence of both planner and doer. Willpower effort is effective if the maximizing values for Z_t and U_t (on X_t) are not the same.

Willpower effort can be applied in varying degrees. Therefore we define a *willpower effort variable*, denoted θ_t, to represent the amount of willpower exerted at date t. The function $\theta_t^*(c_t, X_t)$ gives the degree θ_t of willpower effort required to induce the individual to select consumption level c_t when opportunity set X_t is being faced. The following assumptions characterize the significant features about willpower effort.

1. An increase in willpower effort is necessary to reduce consumption; that is, θ_t^* is decreasing in c_t.
2. Increased willpower effort is painful in the sense that reductions in consumption resulting from willpower are accompanied by reductions in Z_t. Specifically, $\partial Z_t / \partial \theta_t$ is negative, which together with the previous assumption implies:

$$\frac{\partial Z_t}{\partial \theta_t} \cdot \frac{\partial \theta_t^*}{\partial c_t} > 0 \qquad (2)$$

3. Increased willpower effort is not only painful, but becomes increasingly more painful as additional willpower is applied. Specifically:

$$\partial / \partial c_t \left\{ \frac{\partial Z_t}{\partial \theta_t} \cdot \frac{\partial \theta_t^*}{\partial c_t} \right\} < 0 \tag{3}$$

To represent the idea that the planner corresponds to the rational part of the individual's personality, we associate a neoclassical utility function $V(\cdot)$ to the planner, with the arguments of V being the subutility levels Z_1 through Z_T. Since $\partial Z_t / \partial \theta_t$ is negative, willpower costs are incorporated in the planner's choice problem.

Since willpower is costly, the planner may seek other techniques for achieving self-control. These techniques are the subject of the following section.

Rules and Mental Accounting: The Solution

One solution to the conflict between planner and doer preferences is for the planner to restrict future choices by imposing constraints which alter X_t. For example, placing funds into a pension plan which disallows withdrawals reduces disposable income and thus shrinks the doer's choice set. We refer to any precommitment device of the above type as a rule.[3] Suppose that the planner were able to choose a rule that completely precommitted future consumption to a particular path. Since the doers would have no choices to make, no willpower effort would be required. In this situation, the planner would choose c to maximize V subject to the budget constraint, while leaving $\theta = 0$. Denote this optimal choice of c by c^p. The path c^p is a first-best solution to the planner's problem and corresponds precisely to the life-cycle consumption path. Therefore, LC hypothesis can be interpreted as a special case of the BLC model in which either willpower effort costs are zero, or a first-best rule is available to the planner. The predictions of the two models diverge because neither of these conditions is likely to be met. The person with zero willpower costs is obviously a rarity, and first-best rules are generally unavailable. While pension plans and other saving vehicles are marketed, there is a limited selection available, and they do not completely determine a consumption plan.

---

[3] It needs to be emphasized that in our model, the planner can actually implement any budget feasible consumption plan by selecting θ appropriately. The only issue is at what cost. Precommitment offers the possibility of implementing a given consumption plan at reduced willpower cost.

Uncertainty about both income flows and spending needs renders such plans impractical.[4]

When the precommitment enforcement mechanism is accomplished primarily by an outside agency, as with a pension plan, we refer to the rule as being *external*. Another class of rules, *internal* rules, are self-enforced and require greater willpower effort. An example of such a rule is a self-imposed prohibition on borrowing to finance current consumption. Again, it is natural to ask whether a system of internal rules can be used to achieve a first-best (life-cycle) outcome. The answer is no, because willpower is needed to enforce the rule. Formally, this feature is captured by assuming that the marginal utility decrease attributable to less consumption per se is less than the corresponding utility loss when willpower effort is used: i.e.,

$$D = \partial Z_t / \partial \theta_t \cdot \partial \theta_t^* / \partial c_t - \partial Z_t / \partial c_t > 0. \tag{4}$$

where $\partial Z_t / \partial c_t$ is evaluated at $\theta = 0$. The difference D can be regarded as the net marginal cost of using willpower. We make the additional assumption that willpower effort is especially costly at low consumption levels, but essentially costless at high levels. In other words, D decreases with c_t, and approaches zero for c_t sufficiently large.

There are limits on the type of rules which can be enforced at low willpower costs. A reading of the psychology literature on impulse control (e.g., Ainslie, 1975) suggests that effective rules must have the following characteristics. First, a habitual rule must exhibit simplicity, since complex responses seem to require conscious thinking, whereas habitual responses are subconsciously guided. Second, exceptions must be well defined and rare, again in order to avoid the need for conscious responses. Third, the rule must be dynamically stable: habits are not easily altered. Both internal and external rules then are second-best; therefore, descriptive models of saving behavior must reflect the second-best solutions that are adopted by real savers. While households' internal rules are idiosyncratic and context specific, there appear to be enough common elements to generate useful aggregation predictions. One of the most important elements concerns the decomposition of household wealth into a series of *mental accounts*.[5] One simple and stylized version of a mental

---

[4]M. King (1985) has criticized our characterization of the conflict between the planner and the doer as an agency problem on the grounds that there is no information asymmetry present. This criticism is misplaced. While in standard principal-agent models of the firm, it is the information asymmetry that prevents the principal from achieving a first-best outcome, an agency problem can exist without information asymmetry if the principal has limited *control* over the agents actions. That is the case we consider, for the reasons just described. The alternative bargaining formulation King suggests fails to capture some essential features of the problem such as the asymmetry between the strategies employed by the two parties. The planner precommits, the doer does not. The doer in our model generally does not engage in strategic behavior.

[5]For more on mental accounting, see Thaler (1985) and Kahneman and Tversky (1984).

accounting system divides wealth into three components: current spendable income (I); current assets (A); and future income (F). In the BLC, the marginal propensity to consume wealth is assumed to be account specific. This contrasts sharply with the traditional life cycle model which treats the labeling of wealth as irrelevant because wealth is regarded as completely fungible in a perfect capital market. Specifically, traditional theory postulates that the marginal propensity to consume is the same for the following four events: a $1,000 bonus received at work; a $1,000 lottery windfall; a $1,000 increase in the value of the household's home; and an inheritance, to be received with certainty in 10 years, with a present value of $1,000. In contrast, our behavioral enrichment of the life-cycle model assumes that households code various components of wealth into different mental accounts, some of which are more "tempting" to invade than others.

As explained below, the BLC theory postulates a specific set of inequalities in connection with the marginal propensity to consume from the preceding four wealth descriptions. The direction of these inequalities is not arbitrary, and we hypothesize that they evolved as a means of helping individuals to save. The decomposition of wealth into mental accounts constitutes an example of *framing*; see Kahneman and Tversky (1982). In treating wealth as fungible, traditional life-cycle theory makes an implicit frame invariance assumption. The BLC model assumes frame dependence.

To illustrate how the three account formulation works, consider a household that uses a pension rule which at each date deducts a fraction s of income, and prohibits access to accumulated funds before retirement. The mental account balances at date $t < T$ are as follows:

1. The current income account, $I = (1 - s)y_t$.
2. The current wealth account A (corresponding to cumulative discretionary (i.e., nonpension) savings through date $t - 1$) is:

$$\sum_{\tau=1}^{t-1} [(1 - s)y_\tau - c_\tau] \tag{5}$$

3. The balance in the future wealth account is the sum of future income (after pension withdrawals have been made) and pension wealth sY.

Of course, this three account formulation is a great simplification of actual mental accounting rules. In general, a more realistic model would break up the A account into a series of subaccounts, appropriately labeled. Some households may have a children's education account, which would be treated as being similar to a future income account until the children reached college age. Also, there is some ambiguity in how households treat various changes to their wealth. Asset income, for example, is generally kept in the A account, except perhaps dividend payments which may be treated as current income.[6] Small windfalls are likely to be coded as current income, while larger windfalls are placed into A. We assume that pension wealth is framed as future retirement income, although some households might treat it more like current assets. Similarly, there will be variation in the way in which households treat home equity; some will treat home equity as if it were part of F (and will not take out home equity loans), others as if it were part of A. We expect differences among households in the way they treat various accounts, and the model we present here can be considered a description of the representative household.

While the mental accounting system described above may seem bizarre to economists, it is remarkably similar to the accounting systems used by most private universities. A typical private university will distinguish between money in the "current" account which can be spent immediately, and money in the endowment. From the endowment, only income (somehow defined) can be spent while the principal must remain intact. The rules for allocation gifts to the different accounts are of interest. For example, small gifts from alumni that are part of the annual giving campaign are normally treated as "income," spendable immediately. Larger gifts, and those that are received as part of a "capital campaign" are put into the endowment account. Finally, a gift that is pledged, but only payable at the time of the donor's death, is generally not acknowledged in either the income or endowment accounts, and will therefore create no increase in current spending.

Suppose next that the individual wants to save more than the maximum pension deduction rate offered to him, that is, he wants to engage in what we term "discretionary" saving. Then it is necessary to use some willpower effort in order to generate the associated additional savings, avoid depleting those savings before retirement, and refrain from borrowing against future earnings. The magnitude of the associated willpower effort costs is assumed to depend inversely on the temptation to spend. Some situations are more tempting than others. Irving Fisher associated great temptation with payday, since individuals are flush with cash. In our model we assume that the temptation to spend a (marginal) dollar of wealth depends on the location of that dollar in the mental accounting system, with current income being the most tempting, followed by current assets, and then future wealth.

Technically, we take the doer utility function Z_t to be parameterized by the underlying mental accounting structure.[7] Recall that marginal doer utility is given by

$$\partial Z_t / \partial \theta_t \cdot \partial \theta_t^* / \partial c_t \qquad (6)$$

and reflects the cost of willpower effort at the margin. Figure 1 below depicts

---

[6]See Shefrin and Statman (1984).

[7]Formally, Z_t is parameterized by the choice set X_t where X_t specifies the account balances l_t, A_t, and F_t.

the graph of $Z_t(c_t, \theta_t^*, X_t)$ against c_t for a given mental accounting structure and account balances. It reflects the essential structure which we impose on the model. Consider the effects on Z_t due to increments in c_t. We take the first marginal unit of consumption to be financed out of the I account, with (4) reflecting the marginal utility of consumption. As consumption increases, the reduction in willpower effort contributes to higher utility, but in accordance with (3) at a diminishing rate. When the entire balance in the I account is consumed, no willpower effort need be applied to this account. The next marginal unit of consumption is then financed out of the A account.

We model the A account as being less tempting than the I account by assuming that as long as consumption from A is zero, the self-control technology requires no willpower effort in connection with this account. However, any positive consumption from A produces a fixed disutility penalty (representing an entry fee for invading the A account). Consequently, the first unit consumed from A is especially costly. Additional consumption from A results in additional utility as willpower effort is reduced. Again this occurs at a diminishing rate. Similar remarks apply when the F account is invaded.

To indicate how differential willpower effort costs for the various mental

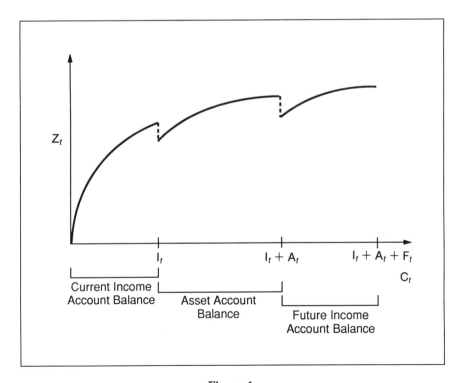

Figure 1.

account balances can be incorporated into the model, we focus attention on the current income account, and denote its balance at the outset of date t by the symbol m_t. When contemplating financing consumption from the current income account, m_t measures the amount of temptation to be faced. We postulate that the greater the temptation, the greater the willpower effort required to choose any given consumption level $c_t < m_t$. Formally, we assume that at any given level of c_t, increased temptation will make the doer worse off, in the sense that:

$$\partial Z_t/\partial m_t = \partial W_t/\partial m_t + \partial W_t/\partial\theta_t \cdot \partial\theta_t^*/\partial m_t < 0 \tag{7}$$

and

$$\partial/\partial m_t\{\partial Z_t/\partial\theta_t \cdot \partial\theta_t^*/\partial c_t\} < 0 \tag{8}$$

For example, consider an individual who plans to spend \$1,200 of his regular monthly take home pay of \$1,500. The preceding inequalities suggest that were his take home pay \$2,000, then stopping at \$1,200 would require greater willpower effort (cost). However, we also postulate that:

$$\partial^2 Z_t/\partial m_t^2 > 0 \tag{9}$$

so that successive unit increments in the income account produce less of a negative impact. That is, given the intention to consume \$1,200 out of the income account, the impact on temptation of additional take home pay of \$500 (from \$2,000 to \$2,500) involves less additional willpower effort than the \$500 increase from \$1,500 to \$2,000.[8]

Further details about the model and about the first-order conditions used to derive the predictions discussed below are presented in the appendix. In many ways, however, the key property of the model is the relaxation of the fungibility assumption of the LC model, and the introduction of the assumption that the marginal propensity to consume additions to wealth depend on the form in which this wealth is received. At a given date, the marginal propensity to consume is typically highest out of income (I), lowest out of future wealth (F), and somewhere in between for current assets (A). This implies that the BLC aggregate consumption function must incorporate at least three different income or wealth measures corresponding to the three mental accounts. That is, C = f(I,A,F), where I, A, and F now stand for their aggregate counterparts. The model suggests that:

$$1 \approx \partial C/\partial I > \partial C/\partial A > \partial C/\partial F \approx 0 \tag{10}$$

---

[8]We make the stronger assumption that the left-hand-side of (8) goes to zero monotonically as m_t approaches infinity.

This set of inequalities and the other features of the model yield a series of testable predictions. It is those predictions to which we now turn.

3. THE DIFFERENTIAL MPC HYPOTHESIS

Unfortunately, we know of no complete test of the hypothesis that the marginal propensity to consume differs across the three accounts in the way we suggest. We have therefore conducted a small survey as a direct test of the hypothesis.[9] A group of evening MBA students at Santa Clara University (most of whom work full-time) was recruited to fill out a questionnaire. The questions are reproduced in Table 1. Each question asks the respondent to estimate the marginal propensity to consume a windfall with an (approximate) present value of $2,400. In Question 1, the windfall comes in increments of $200 a month, and is most likely to be coded as regular income. In Question 2, the windfall comes in a $2,400 lump sum, which we hypothesize is large enough to be placed in the assets account, and should thus have a lower MPC. For Question 3 the windfall is not payable for 5 years, and, as it will be coded in the future income account, should yield a very low MPC. The results support the differential MPC hypothesis. The median annual MPCs for the three questions are $1,200, $785, and $0 respectively. These medians were the same for the whole sample as well as for the subset of 93 subjects that reported having at least $5,000 in liquid assets, so liquidity constraints are not an issue.

While we find these intuitions of MBA students compelling, it is important to obtain evidence based on actual behavior. While there is no other direct test of the differential MPC hypothesis, there is some partial evidence. Courant, Gramlich, and Laitner (1986) distinguish between two types of wealth: current and future. Current wealth includes current income. They report being astonished by the difference in the estimated marginal propensities to consume from these two accounts, since no difference is expected in the LC framework. They estimated the MPC out of current assets to be very high, implying that households consume approximately 25 percent of their existing assets every year. They point out that this suggests a high positive subjective rate of time discount. Yet the MPC out of future wealth was found to be considerably lower, in fact suggesting a *negative* discount rate (p. 302).

In an earlier study, Holbrook and Stafford (1971) used a permanent income model which differentiates among different sources of income (labor income, capital income, transfer payments, etc.). However, the permanent income framework employed treated the timing of wealth as irrelevant

---

[9]A similar study was conducted by Simon and Barnes (1971). Their results also support the differential MPC hypothesis.

(holding the present value constant). Consequently, the Holbrook-Stafford analysis did not distinguish among wealth which has been accumulated in the past, arrives as current income, or will arrive as part of future income. In our theory we assume that different sources of income are encoded into different mental accounts. Specifically, labor income is encoded into current income (I), while capital income, with the possible exception of dividend income (see Shefrin and Statman, 1984), is encoded into the A account upon arrival. Therefore we predict that the marginal propensity to consume from capital income is less than from labor income. This is what Holbrook and Stafford found. The estimated MPC out of labor income was approximately 0.9, while the estimated MPC out of capital income was 0.7. Interestingly, the MPC out of transfer payments received by members of the household other than the head is approximately 30 percent, indicating that such income tends to be saved, rather than consumed. (p. 16).

TABLE 1 Saving Questionnaire

For each of the following scenarios, please think about how you would actually behave. There are no right or wrong answers. Your responses are anonymous and confidential. If you are employed, please answer these questions as if the events described occurred this week. If you are a full-time student, please answer as you think you would behave if you were employed full-time. Thank you very much for your cooperation.

1. You have been given a special bonus at work. The bonus will be paid monthly over the course of a year, and will increase your *take home pay* by $200 per month for 12 months.

   By how much would you expect your monthly consumption to increase during the year? _____ dollars per month. Median = $100
   Total Consumption = $1,200

2. You have been given a special bonus at work. It will be paid in a lump sum of $2,400 (after tax) this month.

   By how much would you expect your consumption to increase in the following month? _____ dollars per month. Median = $400

   By how much would you expect your monthly consumption to increase during the rest of the following year? _____ dollars per month.
   Median = $35   Total Consumption = $785

3. You have been told that a distant relative has left you a small inheritance which has an after tax value of $2,400. You will not receive the money for five years. During that time the money will invested in an interest bearing account. After the five years you will definitely receive the $2,400 plus interest.

   By how much would you expect your consumption to rise *this* year as a result of this gift? _____ dollars per month. Median = $0

SAMPLE: Santa Clara University part-time MBA students. $N = 122$.

Evaluation

While there is no complete test of the differential MPC hypothesis, the evidence that does exist is strongly supportive.

4. PENSIONS AND SAVING

Consider an individual who saves 10 percent of his yearly income for retirement. Suppose that total saving consists of 6 percent that is required to be put into a pension plan and 4 percent "discretionary" savings. What will happen to total saving if the individual is forced to increase the pension component from 6 percent to 7 percent? Putting aside issues of bequests, liquidity constraints, tax rates, vesting, and induced retirement, the LC prediction is that total saving will be unaffected. Discretionary saving should fall by the amount of the increase in the pension contribution, in order to preserve the choice of lifetime consumption plan C. Let PS be pension saving and DS be discretionary saving. Then the LC prediction is that dDS/dPS = −1.0.

The corresponding prediction of the BLC model is:

PREDICTION 1. *The change in discretionary saving with respect to a change in pension saving is less (in absolute value) than 1.0. and, for the young, will approach zero.*

The intuitive explanation behind this statement is easily described. The representative household in our theory has a marginal propensity to consume from its income (I) account of nearly 1.0, but a marginal propensity to consume from its future wealth (F) account of 0. Therefore, when the pension plan transfers one dollar from I to F, total saving rises by almost one dollar. Since expenditures are usually adjusted to be consistent with disposable income, the payroll deduction reduces the money readily available to spend. Then, once the pension contribution becomes pension wealth, it is off-limits to current consumption. The formal argument is more involved, and is summarized in the appendix.

Prediction 1 illustrates the quasi rational or second-best nature of our model. Our representative savers are not fools. They have genuine human weaknesses that act as constraints on the planner's maximization problem. People who join Christmas clubs, for example, probably know that they are giving up interest, convenience, and liquidity in return for external enforcement of willpower. They may judge that trade sensible if the perceived alternative is to have too little money for Christmas presents. But what would be downright stupid would be to join a Christmas club and then borrow against the subsequent payout. We believe few people are that silly. Similarly for pensions, we believe that people allow themselves to think of a pension contribution as a reduction in income so that they do not defeat its primary purpose—the provision of income for retirement.

Our model also predicts a positive relationship between wealth (income) and the magnitude of the offset. Specifically:

PREDICTION 2. *The change in discretionary saving with respect to a change in pension saving increases (in absolute value) with income or wealth.*

This prediction arises because the cost of exercising willpower is taken to decline with income.[10] Willpower becomes increasingly difficult to exercise when income (and therefore consumption) diminishes. Within the model, the prediction can be derived from the assumption that willpower is especially costly at low consumption levels combined with inequality (8). Together these imply that the impact of a change in the account balance on the marginal utility of consumption falls as the account balance increases. Think about an individual who selects the maximum deduction rate s*, and augments his pension savings with additional discretionary saving (so that $c_r(s) < l_r$). Inequality (8) suggests that he will be less impacted by the last marginal increment Δs than corresponding individuals with zero or minimal discretionary saving.

Evidence

The evidence pertaining to Proposition 1 is substantial. The first work on this question was done over twenty years ago by Philip Cagan (1965) and George Katona (1965). Cagan used a sample of respondents to an extensive survey of its members conducted by the Consumers Union. Saving was defined as the family's change in net worth over the year. Saving was then broken down into discretionary saving (DS), pension saving (PS), and other contractual saving. He obtained the surprising result that membership in a pension plan *increased* other forms of saving, i.e., dDS/dPS > 0. He attributed this result to what he called the recognition effect. Membership in a pension plan was thought to increase the awareness of the need to save for retirement and thus encourage other saving. Katona's study was much like Cagan's, and obtained similar results.

Cagan's study has been criticized in the literature, especially by Alicia Munnell (1974). The most troublesome problem is one of which Cagan was aware: selectivity bias. Put simply, people with a taste for saving may be more likely to work for firms which offer a pension plan. This is discussed below. Munnell also criticized Cagan on other grounds and replicated his study using the same data. She used a different measure of saving, replaced before-tax income with after-tax income, and restricted her analysis to a subset of the observations that she thought were more reliable. She then regressed the non-pension saving rate on several variables including a pension dummy.

---

[10]See also Section 6 below on non-proportionality, a closely related issue.

While she did not obtain the positive coefficients found by Cagan, none of the coefficients was significantly negative.[11]

Two more recent papers on this issue have appeared in the *Economic Journal*. Francis Green (1981) used two British samples, the 1953 Oxford Saving Survey and a 1969 Family Expenditure Survey. Both data sets represent an improvement over those reported earlier since the magnitude of pension saving was available (rather than just a dummy variable for membership). However, the size of employer contributions was not available. Green used three definitions of "other saving": (1) total saving minus pension saving, (2) other long-term saving, and (3) total saving plus durable purchases minus pension saving. Each was regressed on wealth, age, and pension saving. Once again the anomalous but ubiquitous positive coefficients were obtained. Breaking up the samples into homogeneous groups based on age or income had no effect.

Green also investigated the possible selectivity bias issue raised by Munnell. Before discussing his results, consider the logic of the selectivity bias argument. Suppose the true value of dDS/dPS is -1.0. How could selectivity bias yield estimates of (essentially) zero? The mean marginal propensity to save of those without pensions must exceed the mean marginal propensity to save of those with pensions by the average level of pension contributions. This seems implausible but possible. Now consider the range of pension benefits offered by various employers. It is even more implausible to think that these match up precisely with the average savings propensities of their employees. So, Green re-estimated his equations restricting his sample to those families with pensions. Again, all estimates of dDS/dPS were positive.

M. A. King and L.D.L. Dicks-Mireaux (1982) estimated the effect of pensions on wealth as part of a larger study. They used a 1976 Canadian data set. The estimated offset to saving resulting from an additional dollar of pension wealth (evaluated at the mean values for the sample) was either $-.10$ or $-.24$, depending on the definition of wealth used.[12] While these estimates are of the "right" sign, they are clearly much smaller (in absolute value) than -1.0. King and Dicks-Mireaux also report that the magnitude of the offset increases with wealth, and this supports our second proposition. Specifically, they state:

---

[11]Another study by Munnell (1976) finds larger offsets. However, this study has some data limitations. The amount saved via pensions is unknown so a pension dummy must be used exclusively. More important, the results are not robust. The estimates reported for two different times differ greatly. The estimate for the latter period implies that those having pensions reduce their other saving by an amount three times the average value of pension contributions in the U.S. in that year. Also, the results change dramatically when an alternative specification is used. These problems make it difficult to interpret the findings.

[12]See also Dicks-Mireaux and King (1984). Using the same data set as in their earlier paper, they investigate the sensitivity of the pension and Social Security displacement effects to prior beliefs. They conclude that the estimates are relatively robust.

The estimated offset is an increasing function of wealth and at the mean values for the top decile group of the distribution of net worth the reduction in saving per additional dollar of pension wealth is estimated to be $1.00 for Social Security and $0.40 for private pensions. [p. 265]

The last two studies we will mention utilize the most comprehensive data sets yet analyzed. Mordecai Kurz (1981) used the 1979 survey conducted by the President's Commission on Pension Policy. This data set has very good information (by survey standards) on pension wealth, including the value of employers' contributions. Kurz estimated the pension wealth offset to total wealth for three subsamples: male heads, female heads, and two-head families. The marginal effect was calculated at three different ages (30, 50, and 60) using two different measures of permanent income or wealth. He estimated the total offset to be between .39 and .47, again substantially different from the 100% predicted by the LC model.

Finally, Peter Diamond and Jerry Hausman (1984) used the National Longitudinal Survey, done between 1966 and 1976. Their estimates are not directly comparable to the others since they calculated the elasticity of the saving to permanent income ratio with respect to the pension benefits to permanent income ratio (rather than dDS/dPS). This turned out to be $-.14$, where a complete offset would again have produced an estimate of -1.0.

There is also a large related literature pertaining to the effect of Social Security wealth on saving. We will make no attempt to survey those studies,[13] but we do want to make one point about the debate between Robert Barro and Martin Feldstein. Barro has argued that individuals will not reduce their saving in response to an increase in Social Security benefits because they will want to increase their bequests to compensate their heirs for future tax increases. Whether or not this argument is plausible, notice that no similar argument applies for fully funded pensions. Even unfunded pensions have intergenerational side effects only to the extent that pensions are imperfect substitutes for other bequeathable assets. Thus the fact that people do not offset increases in pension wealth suggests that similar findings in the Social Security arena are due to self-control reasons rather than intergenerational transfers. We thus feel Barro is likely to be proven empirically right, though for the wrong reasons.

Evaluation

The papers reported here used data sets spanning three decades and three countries. While the estimates of the offset vary between mildly positive (i.e., wrong sign) to nearly $-.5$, in no case is the estimated offset close to minus one.

---

[13]See Robert Barro (1978) which contains a reply by Feldstein.

While selectivity bias could explain these results, we find that argument unconvincing, especially in light of Green's results using only pension recipients. (One could control for selectivity bias by studying the saving behavior of the continuing employees in a firm that changed pension benefits.) Other rationalizations of offsets less than unity have been made, but it is difficult to explain a zero (much less positive) offset within any neoclassical framework. We judge this particular set of results quite supportive of the BLC model.

5. SAVING ADEQUACY

The essence of the life-cycle hypothesis is the idea of consumption smoothing. As stated earlier, if a time-dependent utility function is allowed, then virtually any intertemporal pattern of consumption can be reconciled with the life-cycle hypothesis and the theory becomes irrefutable. Operationally, the theory amounts to the prediction of a smooth consumption profile, so retirement consumption should equal preretirement consumption. Alternatively put, consumption in every period should equal the annuity value of lifetime wealth. The BLC prediction is the following:

PREDICTION 3. *In the absence of sufficiently large Social Security and pension programs, retirement consumption will be less than preretirement consumption.*

Prediction 3 is derived from the model using inequality (4) which is the formal representation of the principle that temptation induces impatience. The steeper the marginal utility of consumption function is at date t, the lower the resulting choice of c_T. If the Z_t function is the same at all dates, then the absence of entry fees into A and F (meaning the opportunity to borrow against future wealth) guarantees that the individual would choose $c_T < c_t$. Pensions and Social Security serve two functions. They reduce the temptation to spend out of income, and they protect a portion of lifetime wealth which is earmarked for retirement. Of course if mandatory pensions plus Social Security were sufficient to keep retirement consumption up to preretirement levels then self-control problems are unlikely to be important. Thus the size of the pension/saving offset discussed above becomes crucial to the interpretation of saving adequacy.

Before reviewing the evidence on this issue it is instructive to begin with some simple facts. Nearly all retirement saving is done through some routinized program. The most important vehicles are: Social Security, private pensions, home equity, and whole life insurance. The amount of discretionary saving done is qualitatively quite small. Diamond and Hausman (1984) found that half of the NLS sample of men aged 45–69 had wealth to income ratios of less than 1.6 if Social Security and pension wealth were excluded. Moreover, 30 percent had essentially zero non-pension wealth. Similar findings are reported by Kotlikoff, Spivak, and Summers (1982). Just the fact that so much of retirement saving is achieved through institutionalized mechanisms can be regarded as support for our framework (since the recognition of self-control problems can be viewed as the reason why people want such institutions), but the high rates of institutionalized saving also make it difficult to interpret the results.

Several authors have addressed the saving adequacy issue directly, with a wide variety of methods and data. Blinder, Gordon, and Wise (1983) used the 1971 Retirement History Survey. Their analysis can be summarized (and simplified) as follows. Let $w = W_t/W_T$ be the ratio of current wealth at age t to total lifetime wealth, where t is between age 60 and 65. Let $c = C_t/C_T$ be the ratio of the family's expected future person years of consumption at age t to the expected total when the head entered the labor market. Then the ratio $\gamma = w/c$ should be equal to unity if retirement saving is adequate. They estimated γ to be .45.

Courant, Gramlich, and Laitner (1984) used the Panel Study of Income Dynamics to analyze families' consumption profiles. They found that real consumption increases over time until retirement, then decreases. They interpret this within the life-cycle model as implying negative subjective rates of time preference while young. Our interpretation is quite different. Consumption rises while young because real income (and thus temptation) is also rising. Consumption falls during retirement because (a) real income falls since most pension benefits are not indexed; (b) the elderly grow to realize that their resources are inadequate and gradually adapt to a reduced standard of living.[14]

Kotlikoff, Spivak, and Summers (1982) dealt with saving adequacy directly. Using the 1969–1973 Retirement History Surveys, they calculated the ratio $RA = c_{oa}/c_{ya}$ where c_{oa} is the level annuity that can be purchased when old, given the present expected value of old age resources, and c_{ya} is the level annuity that can be purchased when young, based on the present expected value of lifetime resources. (They also calculated a similar ratio R based on simple present values without annuities.) At first glance their results seem to support the life-cycle model. Over 90 percent of the sample had values of R or RA of at least .8, many have ratios of unity or higher. However, it turns out that nearly all the wealth the elderly possess is in Social Security, pensions, and home equity.

---

[14]In the absence of annuities, uncertainty about the length of life can also induce consumption to fall during retirement. Yet much of wealth *is* in the form of Social Security and pension annuities. Uncertainty about the length of life can also affect the level of wealth at retirement, but the direction is ambiguous. Two risks must be weighed: The risk of dying sooner than expected (and thus having saved too much ex post), and the risk of dying later than expected (and thus having saved too little). Our intuition suggests that most people will be more concerned with the former than the latter, and thus Blinder et al. should find $\gamma > 1$ if people are risk averse life-cycle savers.

Slightly more than one-third of couples reported levels of net worth that represent less than 10 percent of their total future resources. In addition, 67 percent of married couples hold less than 10 percent of their future resources in liquid wealth. Of these couples, 21 percent had no liquid wealth whatsoever. (Kotlikoff, Spivak, and Summers, 1982, p. 1065)

The test of the life-cycle model then depends crucially on the pension and Social Security offsets. If these offsets are less than complete, then the saving adequacy cannot be attributed to rational saving behavior. The authors investigated this question and concluded that "in the absence of Social Security and private pensions, consumption in old age relative to lifetime consumption would be about 40 percent lower for the average person" (p. 1067).

Hamermesh (1983) also addressed the saving adequacy issue, but he used a different approach from Kotlikoff et al. He analyzed the spending patterns of retired households using the Retirement History Survey linked to Social Security records for information on income. The question Hamermesh asked was whether the elderly have sufficient income to sustain the levels of consumption they maintain early in retirement. He computed the ratio of consumption to annuitized income to answer this question. He found that consumption on average is not sustainable. In 1973, 54 percent of the retired households had consumption to income ratios exceeding 1.1. Since Social Security benefits represent nearly half of retirement income in his sample, Hamermesh also computed what the consumption to income ratio would be for various assumptions about the size of the saving/Social Security offset. If the offset is 50 percent then the average consumption to income ratio is around 1.5. If the offset is zero then the values climb to well over 2.0. Similar results would hold for pensions which are about another 30 percent of retirement income. Finally, Hamermesh found that between 1973 and 1975 the elderly reduced their real consumption by about 5 percent per year. This is a result similar to that obtained by Courant et al. The elderly respond to inadequate saving by reducing real consumption.

In comparing his measure of savings adequacy with Kotlikoff et al., Hamermesh made the point that consumption follows the inverted J-shaped age-earning profiles. "It may thus be more sensible to evaluate the adequacy of Social Security [and saving generally] by comparing its ability to sustain consumption during retirement to consumption just before retirement rather than to average lifetime consumption" (p. 7). Clearly by this standard, saving is inadequate.

Evaluation

The saving adequacy issue is much more difficult to evaluate than the effect of pensions on saving. Some authors; i.e., Blinder, Gordon, and Wise, and

Hamermesh, judge saving to be inadequate, while others, i.e., Kotlikoff, Spivak, and Summers, judge saving to be adequate. To the extent that saving is adequate, Social Security and pensions appear to be largely responsible. The fact that consumption seems to decline during retirement is consistent with the interpretation that saving has been inadequate, but it is also consistent with the fact that the expected age of death increases with age. Again it would be possible (in principle) to test the competing theories cleanly by studying the saving behavior of individuals who do not have access to pensions and Social Security, or for whom those institutions would be inadequate. An interesting case in point is professional athletes who earn high salaries for a short and uncertain period. We speculate that the typical 24-year-old superstar spends more than the annuity value of his expected lifetime wealth.

6. NON-PROPORTIONALITY

Wealth theories of saving are blind to levels of wealth. Consumption is smoothed, no matter what the level of permanent income happens to be. Friedman called this the proportionality principle. In contrast, our model predicts the following:

PREDICTION 4. *The saving rate increases with permanent income.*

We are not alone in rejecting the proportionality principle. In fact, our position was stated very well by Irving Fisher.

> In general, it may be said that, other things being equal, the smaller the income, the higher the preference for present over future income. . . . It is true, of course, that a permanently small income implies a keen appreciation of future wants as well as of immediate wants. . . . This result is partly rational, because of the importance of supplying present needs in order to keep up the continuity of life and the ability to cope with the future; and partly irrational, because the presence of present needs blinds one to the needs of the future. (Fisher, 1930, p. 72)

Our model simply formalizes and rationalizes Fisher's intuition. In our model the marginal cost of exercising willpower is very high at low consumption levels, but falls off as consumption increases. Therefore, willpower costs fall off as income (and therefore consumption) increases. To the poor, saving is a luxury.

The evidence on the proportionality issue as of 1972 was reported in the very thorough and insightful survey by Thomas Mayer (1972). Mayer also conducted five tests of his own. We will just reproduce his conclusion:

> There are many tests which disconfirm the proportionality hypothesis. What is even more persuasive, of all the many tests which have been undertaken by

friends of the hypothesis, *not a single one supports it.* I therefore conclude that the proportionality hypothesis is definitely invalidated. (Mayer, 1972, p. 348)

When Friedman investigated proportionality, he found that it was violated, but argued that the observed behavior could be explained by measurement error. Those with high incomes might save more, he hypothesized, because their incomes have a large (positive) transitory component. Diamond and Hausman (1984) investigated this explanation using modem panel data. They regressed the saving to permanent income ratio on permanent income in a piecewise linear form. The results implied that for incomes less than $4,770, each extra $1,000 of permanent income raises the ratio by 3.3 percent; beyond $4,770 it rises by 5.7 percent for each extra $1,000, and beyond $12,076 it rises by 14.2 percent. The differences are all statistically significant (p. 108).

Evaluation

The evidence against the proportionality principle is very strong. While the self-control hypothesis is only one of many possible explanations for the observed rising saving rate, the results on the interaction between income and the pension saving offset (Prediction 2) lend some support to our self-control based explanation.

7. HYPERSENSITIVITY

One of the simple, elegant features of the LC model is the way in which variability in income is handled. In each period (year) the consumer should consume the annuity value of his expected wealth. This statement applies whether or not the variability in income is deterministic or stochastic. Consumers are either implicitly or explicitly assumed to have some type of rational expectations, so permanent increases in income produce much larger responses in consumption than transitory increases because they lead to larger increases in wealth. Many factors are ruled irrelevant, for example the timing of the income across years and within a year (as long as there are efficient capital markets) and the form of the wealth (say human capital versus home equity).

Our model yields three propositions that are significantly in conflict with the LC hypothesis in this general area. In this section we will discuss the sensitivity of consumption to income generally. The following two sections concern the special cases of bonuses and windfalls.

PREDICTION 5. *Holding wealth constant, consumption tracks income.*

This prediction applies whether or not the variability is known (as with the age-earning profile) or unknown (as with a windfall). Formally the prediction is a consequence of the character of the planner's maximization problem. Recall that willpower effort costs are reduced by having consumption financed only out of the income account, with savings allocated directly to the asset accounts. In the first-best plan the entire income account is consumed at each date. In a second-best setting, this feature might still hold, even though some of the fluctuations in the income stream get transmitted to the consumption stream. It is just suboptimal to invade the asset accounts in order to smooth out consumption fluctuations which are not too large.

To evaluate the hypersensitivity issue it is instructive to compare some new evidence with some old evidence. Recall that Courant et al. found that consumption tends to follow the same hump-shaped pattern as the age-earnings profile. They rationalize this by attributing negative rates of subjective time preference (ρ) to the young. This rationalization seems implausible on the surface, and more to the point, inconsistent with other evidence about individual discount rates. Friedman (1957) estimated ρ to be .4 (though he tended to use .33). Holbrook (1966) reestimated ρ and found it to be closer to .5 than to .33. This implies a two-year horizon in the permanent income model. Holbrook concluded:

> . . . the shorter the horizon, the better is permanent income approximated by current income. When permanent income equals current income, the only significant special assumption of the PIH remaining is that of unitary-income elasticity of consumption. Therefore, the shorter the horizon, the smaller is the distinction between the PIH and what might be called the "current income hypothesis." In this sense, the evidence may be taken to indicate that it makes little difference which hypothesis is true, nearly the same conclusions follow from both. (1966, p. 754)

Other authors who have tried to estimate ρ in other contexts have also found rates in excess of market interest rates (e.g., Hausman, 1979; Gately, 1980; Thaler, 1981). Together these results yield an inconsistency for the wealth model. Friedman's empirical results can only be consistent with a wealth model if people have very high discount rates, while the observed consumption patterns are only consistent with wealth theories if people have negative discount rates before retirement.

Recently, the hypersensitivity issue was examined by Robert Hall and Fredrick Mishkin (1982). Hall and Mishkin derived the first truly rational expectations based model of consumption. They separated household income into three components: a deterministic component y_{Dt} which rises with age until just before retirement; a stochastic component y_{Lt} which fluctuates as lifetime prospects change and is specified as a random walk; and a stationary stochastic component y_{st} which fluctuates according to transitory influences and is described by a moving average time series process.

Hall and Mishkin were particularly interested in the parameter β_t which is

TABLE 2

		For Real Interest Rate Per Year Equal To			
		.05	.10	.20	.30
For Remaining	20 yrs	.095	.105	.170	.232
Lifetime	30 yrs	.071	.093	.167	.231

SOURCE: Hall and Mishkin, 1982.

the marginal propensity to consume out of transitory income y_{st}. The model predicts that β_t should be equal to the yearly annuity value of a dollar of transitory income. Therefore, β_t is determined by the expected remaining years of life and the interest rate. Hall and Mishkin gave some illustrative values for β_t which are reproduced in Table 2. However, when they estimated β_t for food consumption using the Panel Study of Income Dynamics from 1969–1975 the estimated value for β_t turned out to be .29. This is consistent with the model only at interest rates higher than those given in the table.[15] We take this to be a reconfirmation of the earlier Friedman-Holbrook estimates of discount rates in the .33–.50 range. It is noteworthy that they obtain this result in spite of the use of food consumption as the dependent variable. Food consumption would seem to be less volatile than some other components of consumption. The high estimate for β_t surprised Hall and Mishkin, and this led them to consider whether other factors were at work. Upon closer examination they found that 20 percent of all (food) consumption is not explained by the LC model, and in consequence hypothesized that it is "set to a fraction of current income instead of following the more complicated optimal rule." This led them to point out that they "are unable to distinguish this symptom of inability (or unwillingness) to borrow and lend from the type of behavior characteristic of consumers who simply face high interest rates."

In our earlier paper (Thaler and Shefrin, 1981) we pointed out that marginal rates of time preference greater than market rates of interest are consistent with our model if a self-imposed prohibition against borrowing (except to finance homes and other durables) is in effect. This hypothesized aversion to borrowing yields the same predicted behavior as the market imposed credit rationing suggested by Hall and Mishkin in the passage just quoted. How then can the two hypotheses be distinguished? A data set with detailed financial information would allow the credit rationing hypothesis to be tested. First of all, capital market constraints cannot be binding for any family with significant

---

[15] An alternative lagged formulation yields a lower value of β_t. Recently an alternative view of these results has been offered by Deaton (1986), Campbell (forthcoming), and Campbell and Deaton (1987). They argue that consumption is actually too smooth, rather than hypersensitive. Space limitations prevent us from discussing these interesting papers here.

liquid assets. Similarly, many families have equity in their homes or cash value in life insurance policies. These present easy credit sources. Finally, almost anyone with a steady job can qualify for some credit from banks and credit card companies. Any family that has not utilized these sources can be presumed to be unconstrained by the capital market. If the credit rationing hypothesis is correct, then the subset of families for whom the hypothesis can be ruled out should not display hypersensitivity. In the absence of such tests, one can only guess at the relative importance of the two hypotheses. There is some evidence that individuals have unused credit sources. For example, Mark Warshawsky (1987) finds that many life insurance policy holders fail to take advantage of the possibility of borrowing against their insurance policy, even when the interest rate is lower than the rate at which the individual could invest. We think that it is unlikely that the average consumer is borrowed to the limit.

Do the Retired Dissave Enough?

An interesting special case that has attracted considerable attention in the literature is the saving behavior of the retired. The LC model predicts that the retired will draw down on their wealth over time, that is, dissave. The BLC prediction is more complicated. Our model predicts that since annuity income is placed in the current income account, it will be spent more freely than the annuity value of other assets. Even though it makes sense for the retired to relax their rules that restrict access to savings, many households appear to have trouble making this transition.[16] Thus, we predict that households will draw down non-annuity wealth more slowly than the LC prediction.

Most studies of this issue do not support the LC prediction. Indeed, investigators using cross-sectional data have found the puzzling result that the retired actually continue to save (see, for example, Davies (1981), Mirer (1979), and the literature review in Bernheim (1987). This result has been taken as strong evidence of a bequest motive. However, in a recent paper, Hurd (1987) criticized these cross-sectional studies[17] and presented new evidence from the Longitudinal Retirement History Survey. Hurd found little support for a bequest motive since the behavior of households with living children was indistinguishable from childless households. He also found that retired households do dissave. However, a question remains whether they dissave fast enough to be consistent with the LC model. A key question in evaluating this is how to treat housing wealth. Hurd found that retired households dissaved

---

[16]To paraphrase a well-known expression, it is hard to teach an old household new rules.
[17]The most important source of bias in the cross section, according to Hurd, is due to differential rates of survivorship. For example, the rich tend to live longer than the poor, so the older age groups have disproportionate numbers of the rich.

13.9 percent of their total bequeathable (that is, non-annuity) wealth over the period 1969–1979, and 27.3 percent of their bequeathable wealth excluding housing wealth. The former figure is clearly too low (by LC standards) while the latter figure might be considered reasonable. Hurd argued that excluding housing wealth was appropriate because of the costs of changing housing consumption levels. We are not convinced by this argument. While it is true that moving is costly, housing wealth can be reduced by borrowing. Typical retired homeowning households have no mortgage,[18] and thus could draw down on their housing wealth using the credit market. Their failure to do so must be considered at least partially a self-imposed borrowing constraint rather than credit rationing. Indeed, "reverse mortgages"[19] have been offered in some areas with very little consumer response. Some direct evidence that retired households voluntarily maintain the equity in their homes is provided by Venti and Wise (1987). They report that for the elderly who sell one house and buy another, they are as likely to increase as to decrease housing equity, and conclude that the typical elderly person who moves is not liquidity constrained. The elderly appear reluctant to consume out of their "home equity" account, even during retirement.

Evaluation

Individuals behave as if they had excessively high rates of discount. Nevertheless, much of lifetime consumption is successfully postponed. While credit markets do not permit massive borrowing against future income, we judge the hypersensitivity observed by Friedman and by Hall and Mishkin more plausibly explained by self-imposed borrowing prohibitions than by market-imposed quantity constraints. Similarly, the elderly appear to spend money from their income account more readily than they draw down their assets, especially their housing wealth. Again this appears to represent voluntary behavior rather than capital market imperfections.

8. BONUSES

Define a bonus as a fully anticipated temporary increase in income. Our model then yields the following prediction.

---

[18]For example, Hogarth (1986) contains information on a subsample of 770 respondents in the RHS selected as having a head of household who was working in 1969, retired in 1971, and survived through 1979. For this group, the median mortgage was zero. See also Sherman (1976), who states: "The overwhelming majority of homeowners older than 65 are without mortgage debt—apparently because they paid it off before retiring" (p. 72).

[19]With a reverse mortgage, the (usually) retired home owner uses collateral in the house to borrow money from a bank. The proceeds of the loan are typically paid to the borrower in monthly payments. When the borrower dies or decides to sell the house, the loan is repaid.

PREDICTION 6. *The marginal propensity to consume bonus income is lower than the marginal propensity to consume regular income.*

This prediction reflects the combination of an assumption and a principle. The assumption is that bonus income, because it arrives as a large lump sum, is allocated to the A account, not the I account. The principle discussed in the theory section is that the marginal propensity to consume out of the income account exceeds that of the asset account.

The pooling of income into a lump-sum bonus increases saving in two ways. First, by lowering regular monthly income (relative to spreading out the bonus) the temptation to spend each month is reduced. Regular monthly expenditures tend to be geared to regular monthly income. To set a higher level of monthly expenditures would require the individual either to borrow against the future bonus or draw down on the saved bonus during the year, each of which would violate typical mental accounting rules. Second, when the bonus does arrive, a considerable binge can occur and still permit an increase in the saving rate relative to normal. Also, if the binge is spent on durables then some saving occurs in that way.

Bonuses are a nice illustration of a framing effect. In a standard economic model, a completely anticipated bonus is simply income with another name. Thus the distribution of earnings into income and bonus would be considered irrelevant. Our model offers the potential for increased explanatory power by considering variables, such as bonuses, about which the standard theories are silent.

The only evidence we have been able to find regarding bonuses comes from Japan. In Japan, most workers receive semiannual bonuses. Ishikawa and Ueda (1984) have studied the saving behavior of the Japanese and estimate the significance of the bonuses. Using a pooled cross-section time series approach, they estimated the marginal propensities to consume out of regular and bonus income respectively. Tests suggested pooling what they called normal years 1969–73, 1977–78, and treating the two recession-oil shock periods 1974–76 and 1979–80 separately. For the normal years they could reject the hypothesis that households treat the two sources of income equivalently. The marginal propensity to consume bonus income was estimated to be .437 while the corresponding figure for non-bonus income was .685. The difference is significant. The difference holds with durable expenditures included or excluded from consumption, though as should be expected, expenditures on durables respond much more to bonus income than to other parts of income. During 1974–76 the MPC out of bonuses jumped to over 1.0. This suggests that households used bonuses in bad years to smooth out consumption. The last period studied, 1979–80, returns to the pattern of a lower MPC out of bonus income.

Could the low MPC out of bonus income be explained by the permanent income hypothesis if bonuses are treated as transitory income? This explanation is dubious since the bonuses are fairly well anticipated. As one Japanese observer has put it:

> The trouble, however, lies in the interpretation of "transitory" income. Although they are called bonuses, they are fully institutionalized and workers expect bonuses as an intrinsic part of their normal income. Furthermore, workers can anticipate fairly well the level of bonus payments and thus a rational worker will treat them as permanent, rather than transitory, components of his income. (Shiba, 1979, p. 207)

Nevertheless, Ishikawa and Ueda investigated this possibility directly using actual expectations data on bonus income. They used a sample of roughly 5,000 workers who were asked to estimate 6 months in advance how large their next bonus would be. Later, actual bonuses received and consumption data were also collected. The authors then tested to see whether the respondents had rational expectations and whether they responded differently to permanent and transitory components of bonus income. The results indicated that expectations were not rational (bonuses were underestimated), but the MPC out of the transitory component of bonus income was approximately the same as the MPC out of the permanent component. Both were estimated to be .46.

The authors' conclusion about their findings is the same as ours. "First, the permanent income-life cycle hypothesis does not seem to apply to Japanese worker households. . . [and second] Households distinguish bonus earnings from the rest of their income" (p. 2).

Evaluation

The results on bonuses are probably the hardest to rationalize within the LC framework. Similar tests would be possible in the United States if a sample of workers with and without bonuses were collected. Unfortunately, most data sets do not distinguish bonus income from normal wages and salaries.

9. WINDFALLS

Predictions 5 and 6 together imply the following:
PREDICTION 7. *(a) For (non-negligible) windfalls, the marginal propensity to consume is less than the marginal propensity to consume regular income but greater than the annuity value of the windfall. (b) The marginal propensity to consume out of windfall income declines as the size of the windfall increases.*

The explanation of the first feature is basically identical to the argument for bonuses. The only difference is that the marginal propensity to consume from the windfall income is higher than for bonuses if the windfall is truly unexpected. This is because the individual has no opportunity to adjust his earlier saving in anticipation of the windfall. The explanation of the second feature is based on mental accounting. People tend to consume from income and leave perceived "wealth" alone. The larger a windfall is, the more wealth-like it becomes, and the more likely it will be included in the less tempting Assets account. A corollary is that changes in perceived wealth (such as increases in the value of home equity) are saved at a greater rate than windfalls considered "income."

The best study we have found regarding actual windfalls was done by Michael Landsberger (1966). He studied the consumption behavior of Israeli recipients of German restitution payments after World War II. What makes the study particularly useful for our purposes is that there is substantial variation in the size of the windfall within the sample. His sample of 297 was divided into five groups based on the windfall as a percent of family income. The family incomes and MPC out of total income were about the same for each group. However, as our theory predicts, the MPC out of windfall income increased sharply as the size of the windfall decreased. For the group with the largest windfalls (about 66 percent of annual income) the MPC was about 23 percent, while the group receiving the smallest windfalls (about 7 percent of annual income) had MPC's in excess of 2.0. Small windfalls were spent twice!

Evaluation

Windfalls ironically facilitate both splurges and saving. Windfalls are not treated as simple increments to wealth. Temptation matters.

10. POLICY IMPLICATIONS

The theory and evidence we have presented here suggest quite novel considerations for national policies regarding personal saving. Normally, when a government wants to alter the saving rate, it concentrates on changing either the level of income or the after-tax rate of return to saving. If the desire is to increase saving, then our analysis suggests that other seemingly irrelevant changes be considered. For example:

1. A tax cut not accompanied by (complete) changes in withholding rates should increase saving more than an equivalent tax cut fully reflected in withholding. This follows because the underwithholding will yield refunds that (like bonuses) should produce high saving rates.
2. Since pensions increase saving, firms could be encouraged to offer mandatory (or even discretionary) pension plans. Requiring firms to have pension plans would have the additional benefit that future demands on the Social

Security system might be reduced as the elderly begin to have substantial pension wealth.
3. Similarly, firms could be encouraged to use Japanese-style bonuses as part of their compensation scheme. This form of payment is no more costly to firms (it might even be cheaper on a present value basis) and would, according to our analysis, increase saving.

11. CONCLUSION

The LC model is clearly in the mainstream tradition of microeconomic theory. It is typical of the general approach in microeconomics, which is to use a normative-based maximizing model for descriptive purposes. The recent papers by Hall and Mishkin and Courant et al. are really advances in the LC tradition.

Our model is quite different in spirit. First of all, our agents have very human limitations, and they use simple rules of thumb that are, by nature, second-best. While the LC model is a special case of our model (when either a first-best rule exists or there is no self-control problem), our model was developed specifically to describe actual behavior, not to characterize rational behavior. It differs from a standard approach in three important ways.

1. It is consistent with behavior that cannot be reconciled with a single utility function.
2. It permits "irrelevant" factors (i.e., those other than age and wealth) to affect consumption. Even the form of payment can matter.
3. Actual choices can be strictly within the budget set (as a Christmas club).

The relationship between the self-control model and the LC model is similar to the relationship between Daniel Kahneman and Amos Tversky's (1979) prospect theory and expected utility theory. Expected utility theory is a well-established standard for rational choice under uncertainty. Its failure to describe individual behavior has led to the development of other models (such as prospect theory) that appear to do a better job at the tasks of description and prediction. The superiority of prospect theory as a predictive model, of course, in no way weakens expected utility theory's value as a prescriptive norm. Similarly, since we view the LC model as capturing the preferences of our planner, we do not wish to question its value to prescriptive economic theory. The LC model has also served an enormously useful role in providing the theory against which empirical evidence can be judged. For example, the one-to-one pension offset was a result derived from the LC model (without bequests), and the numerous studies we cite were no doubt stimulated by the opportunity to test this prediction. Saving adequacy even more directly requires a life cycle criterion of appropriate saving with which actual saving can be compared.

At times we have argued that the use of ad hoc assumptions, added to the theory after the anomalous empirical evidence has been brought forward, renders the LC model untestable. It is reasonable to ask whether our model is testable. We think that it is. Every one of the propositions we examined in this paper represents a test our model might have failed. For example, if the estimated pension offsets were mostly close to -1.0 instead of mostly close to zero, we would have taken that as evidence that self-control problems are empirically unimportant. Similarly, the effects of bonuses on saving could have been negligible, implying that mental accounting has little to add.

Other tests are also possible. Our theory suggests the following additional propositions.

PREDICTION 8. *Holding lifetime income constant, home ownership will increase retirement wealth.*

PREDICTION 9. *The marginal propensity to consume inheritance income will depend on the form in which the inheritance is received.*

The more the inheritance resembles "income" rather than "wealth," the greater will be the MPC. Thus the MPC will be greater for cash than for stocks, and greater for stocks than for real estate.

PREDICTION 10. *The marginal propensity to consume dividend income is greater than the marginal propensity to consume increases in the value of stock holdings.*

We have not investigated the empirical validity of these propositions. We hope others who are skeptical of our theory will do so. Nevertheless, while we think that neither our theory nor the LC theory is empty, refutation is probably not the most useful way of thinking about the task at hand. It is easy to demonstrate that any theory in social science is wrong. (We do not believe that individuals literally have planners and doers, for example.) Negative results and counterexamples must be only a first step. We intend this paper to be constructive rather than destructive. We hope to have shown that the consideration of self-control problems enables us to identify variables that are usually ignored in economic analyses but which have an important influence on behavior.

REFERENCES

Professor, Department of Economics, Santa Clara University, and Professor, Johnson Graduate School of Management, Cornell University. We wish to thank Franco Modigliani for providing many thoughtful comments on a previous draft of this paper. Thaler would also like to thank the Behavioral Economics Program at the Sloan Foundation for financial support.

Ainslie, George. "Specious Reward: A Behavioral Theory of Impulsiveness and Impulse Control." *Psychological Bulletin* 82 (1975): 463–496.

Barro, Robert. *The Impact of Social Security on Private Saving.* Washington, DC: American Enterprise Institute, 1978.

Bernheim, B. Douglas. "Dissaving After Retirement: Testing the Pure Life Cycle Hypothesis." in *Issues in Pension Economics.* ed. Zvi Bodie; John B. Shoven; and David Wise. Chicago: University of Chicago Press, 1987.

Blinder, Alan; Roger Hall Gordon; and Donald Wise. "Social Security, Bequests, and the Life Cycle Theory of Saving: Cross Sectional Tests." in *The Determinants of National Saving and Wealth.* ed. R. Hemming and F. Modigliani. International Economic Association, 1983.

Blumenthal, Tuvia. *Saving in Postwar Japan.* Cambridge, MA: Harvard East Asian Monographs, 1970.

Bodkin, Ronald. "Windfall Income and Consumption: Reply." *American Economic Review* 56 (1966): 540–545.

Cagan, Philip. *The Effect of Pension Plans on Aggregate Savings.* New York: National Bureau of Economic Research, 1965.

Campbell, John Y. "Does Saving Anticipate Declining Labor Income? An Alternative Test of the Permanent Income Hypothesis." Forthcoming, *Econometrica.*

———, and Angus Deaton. "Is Consumption Too Smooth?" Mimeo, Princeton University, January 1987.

Courant, Paul; Edward Gramlich; and John Laitner. "A Dynamic Micro Estimate of the Life Cycle Model." in *Retirement and Economic Behavior.* ed. Henry G. Aaron and Gary Burtless. Washington, DC: Brookings Institution, 1986.

Davies, James B. "Uncertain Lifetime, Consumption, and Dissaving in Retirement." *Journal of Political Economy* 89 (June 1981): 561–577.

Deaton, Angus S. "Life-Cycle Models of Consumption: Is the Evidence Consistent with the Theory?" National Bureau of Economic Research Working Paper No. 1910, 1986.

Diamond, Peter, and Jerry Hausman. "Individual Retirement and Saving Behavior." *Journal of Public Economics* 23 (1984): 81–114.

Dicks-Mireaux, Louis, and Mervyn King. "Pension Wealth and Household Savings: Tests of Robustness." *Journal of Public Economics* 23 (1984): 115–139.

Elster, Jon. *Ulysses and the Sirens.* Cambridge: Cambridge University Press, 1979.

Fisher, Irving. *The Theory of Interest.* London: Macmillan, 1930.

Friedman, Milton. *A Theory of the Consumption Function.* Princeton, NJ: Princeton University Press, 1957.

Fuster, Joaquin M. *The Prefrontal Cortex.* New York: Raven Press, 1980.

Gately, Dermot. "Individual Discount Rates and the Purchase and Utilization of Energy-Using Durables: Comment." *Bell Journal of Economics* 11 (1980): 373–374.

Green, Francis. "The Effect of Occupational Pension Schemes on Saving in the United Kingdom: A Test of the Life Cycle Hypothesis." *Economic Journal* 91 (March 1981): 136–144.

Hall, Robert, and Fredrick Mishkin. "The Sensitivity of Consumption to Transitory Income: Estimates from Panel Data on Households." *Econometrica* 50 (1982): 461–481.

Hamermesh, Daniel. "Consumption During Retirement: The Missing Link in the Life Cycle." Michigan State University, 1983.

Hausman, Jerry. "Individual Discount Rates and the Purchase and Utilization of Energy-Using Durables." *The Bell Journal of Economics* 10 (1979): 33–54.

Hogarth, Jeanne M. "Changes in Financial Resources During Retirement: A Descriptive Study." Ithaca, NY: Cornell University, Department of Consumer Economics and Housing, 1986.

Holbrook, Robert. "Windfall Income and Consumption: Comment." *American Economic Review* 56 (1966): 534–540.

Holbrook, Robert, and Frank Stafford. "The Propensity to Consume Separate Types of Income: A Generalized Permanent Income Hypothesis." *Econometrica* 39 (January 1971): 1–21.

Hurd, Michael D. "Savings of the Elderly and Desired Bequests." *American Economic Review* 77, 3 (1987): 298–312.

Ishikawa, Tsuneo, and Kazuo Ueda. "The Bonus Payment System and Japanese Personal Savings." in Aoki Masahiko, ed. *The Economic Analysis of the Japanese Firm*. New York: North-Holland, 1984.

James, William. *The Principles of Psychology*. 2 vols. New York: Holt, 1890.

Kahneman, Daniel, and Amos Tversky. "Prospect Theory: An Analysis of Decision Under Risk," *Econometrica* 47 (1979): 262–291.

———. "Choices, Values, and Frames." *The American Psychologist* 39 (1984): 341–350.

Katona, George. *Private Pensions and Individual Saving*. Ann Arbor: University of Michigan, 1965.

King, Mervyn A. "The Economics of Saving: A Survey of Recent Contributions." In Kenneth Arrow and S. Hankapohja, eds. *Frontiers of Economics*. Oxford: Basil Blackwell, 1985.

King, Mervyn A., and L.D.L. Dicks-Mireaux. "Asset Holdings and the Life Cycle." *Economic Journal* 92 (June 1982): 247–267.

Kotlikoff, Lawrence; Avfa Spivak; and Lawrence Summers. "The Adequacy of Savings." *American Economic Review* 72 (1982): 1056–1069.

Kurz, Mordecai. "The Life-Cycle Hypothesis and the Effects of Social Security and Private Pensions on Family Savings." Technical Report #335, Institute for Mathematical Studies in the Social Sciences, Stanford University, 1981.

Landsberger, Michael. "Windfall Income and Consumption: Comment." *American Economic Review* 56 (June 1966): 534–539.

Margolis, Howard. *Selfishness, Altruism and Rationality*. Cambridge: Cambridge University Press, 1982.

Mayer, Thomas. *Permanent Income, Wealth and Consumption*. Berkeley: University of California, 1972.

Mirer, Thad W. "The Wealth-Age Relationship Among the Aged." *American Economic Review* 69 (1979): 435–443.

Mischel, Walter. "Metacognition and the Rules of Delay." In J.H. Flavell and L. Ross, eds. *Social Cognitive Development Frontiers and Possible Futures*. New York: Cambridge University Press, 1981.

Modigliani, Franco, and Richard Brumberg. "Utility Analysis and the Consumption Function: An Interpretation of Cross-Section Data." In K.K. Kurihara, ed. *Post Keynesian Economics*. New Brunswick, NJ: Rutgers University Press, 1954.

Munnell, Alicia. *The Effect of Social Security on Personal Saving*. Cambridge, MA: Ballinger, 1974.

———. "Private Pensions and Saving: New Evidence." *Journal of Political Economy* 84 (October 1976).

Numan, Robert A. "Cortical-Limbic Mechanisms and Response Control: A Theoretical Review." *Physiological Psychology* 6 (1978): 445–470.

Restak, Richard. *The Brain*. New York: Bantam, 1984.

Schelling, Thomas. "Self Command in Practice, in Policy and in a Theory of Rational Choice." *American Economic Review* (May 1984): 1–11.

Shefrin, H.M., and Meir Statman. "Explaining Investor Preference for Cash Dividends." *Journal of Financial Economics* 13 (June 1984): 253–282.

Sherman, Sally R. "Assets at the Threshold of Retirement." in *Almost 65: Baseline Data from the Retirement History Study*. Social Security Administration, 1976.

Shiba, Tsunemasa. "The Personal Savings Functions of Urban Worker Households in Japan." *Review of Economics and Statics* (1979): 206–213.

Simon, Julian, and Carl Barnes. "The Middle-Class U.S. Consumption Function: A Hypothetical Question Study of Expected Consumption Behavior." *Oxford University Institute of Economics and Statistics Bulletin* 33 (1971): 73–80.

Thaler, Richard. "Some Empirical Evidence on Dynamic Inconsistency." *Economic Letters* 8 (1981):101–107.

———. "Mental Accounting and Consumer Choice." *Marketing Science* (Summer 1985).

———, and H.M. Shefrin. "An Economic Theory of Self-Control." *Journal of Political Economy* 89 (1981): 392–406.

Venti, Steven F., and David A. Wise. "Aging, Moving, and Housing Wealth." National Bureau of Economic Research Working Paper, 1987.

Warshawsky, Mark. "The Sensitivity Market Incentives: The Case of Policy Loans." *Quarterly Journal of Economics* LXIX, 2 (1987): 286–295.

Winston, Gordon. "Addiction and Backsliding." *Journal of Economic Behavior and Organization* 1 (1980): 295–324.

APPENDIX

The model in Section II features three mental accounts—current income I, the asset balance A, and future income F. For ease of exposition we have described the structure of the account balances in Section II as if the F account is never used to finance current consumption. This is why pension wealth (sLW), against which borrowing is prohibited, can be placed into the F account without requiring an account of its own. In the discussion below, we allow the possibility that the F account may be invaded, but implicitly assume that the entry penalty attached to F is sufficiently high so as to deter frequent entry. We also assume that the entry penalty into the F account is larger than the entry penalty into the A account. Therefore, the individual would never wish to borrow from the F account while the A account has a positive balance. A more complex mental accounting formulation is required to model the issue of simultaneous borrowing and holding of liquid assets which we address in Thaler and Shefrin (1981). For instance, some households take out automobile loans, despite having a positive balance in a saving account earmarked for their children's education.

As in Section II the income account balance at any nonterminal date $t<T$ is defined as $I_t = (1-s)y_t$. Although we defined the asset balance by (5) in the text, a technical qualification is required when the F account is invaded, since the value of (5) is negative in this case. When the asset account is empty at date t, then we wish to have $A_t = 0$, with any further borrowing being financed out of the F account. In this regard, denote the value of (5) by B_t. Then A_t is formally defined as $\max\{B_t, 0\}$. A similar qualification is required for F_t. We define F_t as:

$$\sum_{\tau=t+1}^{T-1} (1-s)y_\tau + sLW + \min\{B_t, 0\}$$

where the $\min\{B_t, 0\}$ term reflects eventual required repayment on past borrowing.

The propositions which underlie the empirical portion of the paper follow from the optimality conditions that characterize the planner's choice of c and s. The first-order conditions associated with c concern the marginal utility to the planner from an additional unit of c_t. This is given by:

$$\partial V/\partial Z_t \cdot \partial Z_t/\partial\theta_t \cdot \partial\theta_t^*/\partial c_t - \Sigma_{\tau=t+1}^T \partial V/\partial Z_\tau\{\partial Z_\tau/\partial m_\tau + \partial Z_\tau/\partial\theta_\tau \cdot \partial\theta_t^*/\partial m_\tau\}\alpha_\tau(c_\tau) \quad (11)$$

with $\alpha_\tau c_\tau$ equal to 1 if the A account has been invaded at date t, and zero otherwise. While the first term in the above sum is the direct utility associated with c_t, the second term reflects the reduced temptation effect associated with future consumption from the A account prior to T. This marginal utility is to be compared with the marginal utility of retirement consumption.

$$\partial V/\partial Z_T \cdot \partial Z_T/\partial c_T \quad (12)$$

The optimality conditions require that when (12) exceeds (11), consumption at t be reduced and transferred to T through increased discretionary saving. However, if (11) exceeds (12) we need to consider two cases. In the first case the account being used to finance c_t has not been drawn down to zero. Then c_t should be increased. If the financing account has been drawn down to zero, then attention needs to be paid to whether invading the next account becomes worthwhile. If not, then (11) will exceed (12) at the optimum. We refer to the condition (11) = (12) as the Fisher condition (equalization of marginal utilities) and (11) > (12) as the generalized Fisher condition. The second type of optimality condition is associated with the selection of the pension deduction rate s. With c given, the impact of a marginal change in s is through the temptation effect. When $c_t < l_t$, the net benefit at t from a marginal increment Δs in s is:

$$- \partial V/\partial Z_t \, \{\partial Z_t/\partial m_t + \partial Z_t/\partial \theta_t \, \partial \theta_t^*/\partial m_t\} \, y_t \qquad (13)$$

When c_t is financed out of the A_t account, there is also a temptation impact due to the amount of willpower effort needed in connection with c_t. It has the same general form as (13). However, this effect is small compared to the discrete effect which occurs when the increment Δs forces the invasion of the A (and/or F) account since this entails the entry penalty. Consequently, the choice of s will essentially balance off the lowered temptation costs in the I account against the additional entry penalties for invading the A (and/or F) account.

An implication of the model is that an increase in the pension saving rate will increase retirement savings. Consider the formal argument for this statement. Begin with the case in which no pension plan is available (so that the maximum deduction rate s^* is zero), and let a small pension plan be made available ($\Delta s^* > 0$). Let the household contemplate increasing its deduction rate by Δs. Consider how total saving in our model is impacted by the marginal increase Δs. Let $c(s)$ be the planner's optimal choice of c, given s. If the pension deduction does not cause the household to become liquidity constrained, then the LC prediction is that $c(s)$ is invariant to the choice of s. Suppose that the increment Δs does not alter the account used to finance the representative household's marginal (i.e., last) unit of consumption at any date. For instance, if at date t the individual was consuming only out of one (prior to Δs), then it will continue to do so after Δs. Recall that the increment Δs in s shifts wealth into the F account from the I account. Suppose that $c_t(s) < l_t$ so that date t consumption is financed solely from the income account. Observe that inequality (8) implies that the impact of Δs is to cause a decrease in the marginal temptation to consume at level $c_t(s)$. However, the marginal utility of retirement consumption $c_T(s)$ remains unchanged. Therefore Δs causes the marginal utility of $c_t(s)$ to fall below its retirement counterpart, thereby leading date t consumption to be decreased in response. Consequently unlike the LC prediction, $c(s)$ is nonconstant in s. If date t is typical then lifetime saving c_T rises with s. We regard this as the representative case.

There are other cases to be considered as well.

1. If consumption $c_t(s) = 1_t$ (and we continue to consider the case when Δs does not induce the invasion of A), then date t consumption falls simply because 1_t falls with Δs.
2. When $c_t(s)$ is financed out of the A account, then the marginal temptation hypothesis applied to $1_t + A_t$ implies that c_t declines with Δs.
3. However, when the $c_t(s) = 1_t$ and the individual is indifferent to invading A_t, then the increment Δs actually induces an increase in c_t as A_t gets invaded. This situation is typical for choices of s which are greater than optimal.

Under the hypothesis that the pension deduction rate begins below the optimal levels, so that Δs is considered an improvement, we predict that lifetime saving (meaning retirement consumption c_T) rises with Δs.

6

SOME EMPIRICAL EVIDENCE ON DYNAMIC INCONSISTENCY

Richard H. Thaler

Individual discount rates are estimated from survey evidence. For gains, they are found to vary inversely with the size of the reward and the length of time to be waited. Rates are found to be much smaller for losses than for gains.

1. INTRODUCTION

The economic theory of intertemporal choice, as formulated by Irving Fisher, is both simple and elegant. In the case of perfect capital markets, everyone behaves the same way at the margin since firms and individuals borrow or lend until their marginal rate of substitution between consumption today and consumption tomorrow is equal to the interest rate. This, like all economic theory of the consumer, is normatively based. It is easy to show that if a consumer failed to act as the theory predicts, there would be some way to rearrange his consumption plan to make him better off. Yet do individuals really act this way? Economists at least since the time of Böhm–Bawerk have been skeptical. Both Böhm–Bawerk (1981) and Strotz (1955–1956) have speculated that people act as if their discount rates (the rate at which they trade-off consumption increments at different points in time) vary with the length of time to be waited. Strotz (1955–1956, p. 177), for example, states:

> Special attention should be given, I feel, to a discount function . . . which differs from a logarithmically linear one in that it "over values" the more proximate satisfaction relative to the more distant ones. . . . My own supposition is that most of us are "born" with [such] discount functions.

Reprinted with permission from *Economic Letters* 8 (1981): 201–207. © North-Holland Publishing Company.

It is this discount function which leads to Strotz's famous dynamic inconsistency. It can be illustrated with the following simple example:

A. Choose between: (A.1) One apple today.
                     (A.2) Two apples tomorrow.
B. Choose between: (B.1) One apple in one year.
                     (B.2) Two apples in one year plus one day.

While some people may be tempted to select (A.1) no one would select (B.1). Yet if the rate of discount is constant (as it "should be") then the choices are formally identical. (Dynamic inconsistency arises if (B.2) is selected now and when the choice is reconsidered in 364 days (B.1) is selected.)

This latter describes an initial step in an attempt to discover whether individuals do choose in the manner in which Strotz suggested. Specifically the hypothesis to be tested is that the discount rate implicit in choices will vary inversely with the length of time to be waited.

In addition, another hypothesis, suggested by the model in Thaler and Shefrin (1981) will be tested. This hypothesis is that the discount rate will vary inversely with the size of the reward for which the individual must wait. This hypothesis is derived from viewing intertemporal choice as problem in self-control. Waiting for a reward requires some mental effort. If this effort does not increase proportionally with the size of the rewards (if there are some fixed psychic costs to waiting) then the hypothesized result will be present. A third hypothesis can be put simply: losses are different than gains. According to economic theory a person should be willing to pay the same amount to receive $100 a month sooner or to postpone paying $100 for a month. Yet it was not expected that this would be empirically validated. While I did not know exactly how preferences would differ for losses rather than gains one result was expected: The implicit discount rate for losses will be lower than for gains. Even someone who appears very impatient to receive a gain may nevertheless take a "let's get it over with" attitude toward losses.

2. METHOD

As a preliminary method of investigating these hypotheses a set of questionnaires was prepared. Four different forms were used: three for gains and one for losses.

Space does not permit reproducing the instructions here, but they can be summarized as follows. For gains the subjects were told that they had won some money in a lottery held by their bank. They could take the money now or wait until later. They were asked how much they would require to make waiting just as attractive as getting the money now. Each subject received a

3 × 3 table to fill in with amounts varied in one dimension and length of time to wait in the other. The cover story for the fines involved a traffic ticket that could be paid now or later. In all cases subjects were instructed to assume that there was no risk of not getting the reward (or of avoiding the fine) if they waited. All amounts would be received (or paid) by mail.

The sizes of the prizes (fines) and the length of time to be waited was varied among the forms. The figures used are given in Table 1.

3. RESULTS

The subjects were students at the University of Oregon who answered an advertisement in the newspaper. This was one of several tests they were asked to complete. About twenty usable responses were obtained for each form. (A few subjects did not understand the task and their responses were omitted from the analysis.)

The results are summarized in Table 2 which resembles those the subjects were asked to fill in. I have reported the median responses (there was wide variation among subjects). The numbers in parentheses are the continuously compounded discount rates implicit in the answers.

The first thing one notices in these tables is that the implicit discount rates are very large. While this may to some extent be a reflection of the hypothetical nature of the questions and the youth of the subjects, Hausman (1979) in his study of air conditioner purchases also found very high discount rates. Furthermore, the absolute magnitudes are less important than the relative variation within each table. As the tables show, these variations are quite dramatic and systematic. For the three forms using gains, both of the hypothesized effects are observed.

The implicit discount rates drop sharply as the size of the prize or the length of time increases. The only exception to this occurs for the middle column of form (B) where the rates for 12 months are higher than for 6 months. This result seems to have occurred because some subjects just doubled their 6 month responses in the 12 month column. In spite of this anomaly, however, the overall pattern is hard to ignore.

TABLE 1

Form	Amounts	Time to Wait
(1)	$15, $250, $3,000	3 mo. 1 yr. 3 yrs.
(2)	75, 250, 1,200	6 mo. 1 yr. 5 yrs.
(3)	15, 250, 3,000	1 mo. 1 yr. 10 yrs.
(4)	−15, −100, −250	3 mo. 1 yr. 3 yrs.

Form (D) produced qualitatively different results. The discount rates implicit in the answers here are much lower, as was expected. The tendency for the rates to decline with increases in the size of the fine is also observed, but the effect of the length of time is not present. The essential result is that losses are very different from gains.

4. DISCUSSION

Clearly if the results of this preliminary investigation are taken seriously, they cast considerable doubt on the descriptive validity of the standard theory of intertemporal choice. The standard theory would predict that the discount rates in each cell of each table would be equal for any given person, and differences among persons would only reflect differences in borrowing or lending rates. Instead we observe that the discount rates vary systematically across cells and the differences among individuals are much greater than variation in interest rates could possibly explain. Why? Consider each effect in turn.

**TABLE 2 Median Responses
and Continuously Compounded Discount Rates (in percent)**

	Amount of Early Prize	*Later Prize Paid In*		
		3 Months	*1 Year*	*3 Years*
(A)	$15	$ 30 (277)	$ 60 (139)	$ 100 (63)
	$250	$ 300 (73)	$ 350 (34)	$ 500 (23)
	$3,000	$3,500 (62)	$4,000 (29)	$ 6,000 (23)
		6 Months	*1 Year*	*5 Years*
(B)	$75	$ 100 (58)	$ 200 (98)	$ 500 (38)
	$250	$ 300 (36)	$ 500 (69)	$ 1,000 (28)
	$1,200	$1,500 (45)	$2,400 (69)	$ 5,000 (29)
		1 Month	*1 Year*	*10 Years*
(C)	$15	$ 20 (345)	$ 50 (120)	$ 100 (19)
	$250	$ 300 (219)	$ 400 (120)	$ 1,000 (19)
	$3,000	$3,100 (39)	$4,000 (29)	$10,000 (12)
	Amount of Early Fine	*Later Fine Due In*		
		3 Months	*1 Year*	*3 Years*
(D)	$15	$ 16 (26)	$ 20 (29)	$ 28 (20)
	$100	$ 102 (6)	$ 118 (16)	$ 155 (15)
		$ 251 (1)	$ 270 (8)	$ 310 (7)

Length of time Responses imply that the subjects have a discount *function* which is nonexponential. Put simply, the relative marginal price of waiting for rewards appears to decline as the time necessary to wait increases. Two related explanations are intuitively appealing. First, the psychophysics of time suggests that the difference between today and tomorrow will seem greater than the difference between a year from now and a year plus one day. Yet an exponential discount rate requires that these differences be perceived to be equal. Second, for the longer time periods (3 years or more) arithmetic errors may help create the effect. A person who wanted to give the "correct" answer would first figure his opportunity cost (depending on whether he was a borrower or lender) and then calculate the future value of the stated prize. To do this he would have to estimate an exponential growth function. Other researchers (Wagenaar and Sagaria, 1975) have found that individuals tend to underestimate such functions. However, I do not believe this explanation should be overly stressed. It surely cannot explain the results for less than three years, and I believe only has a pronounced impact on the 10 year column in form (C).

Size effects As the size of the reward increases, the implicit discount rate falls. This result has an attractive self-control explanation. Waiting for a reward requires effort. For small rewards ($15) a substantial (proportional) return may be required to make the wait worthwhile. Subjects may be thinking along the following lines: $15 is a dinner, $250 is a new stereo component or a trip to San Francisco, $3,000 is a good used car. When they are asked how much they would have to receive to wait 3 months [form (A)] their responses are roughly "an extra dinner," "a new cartridge," or "an extra night in San Francisco," and "a fancy model of the same car." Put in this way the answers seem at least somewhat more reasonable. The psychophysical concept of the just noticeable difference also seems to come into play here. For small amounts, the rate of return must be substantial before the gain seems worth the wait. A similar result for search theory is discussed in Thaler (1980).

An interesting side effect of this result is that subjects' actions are closer to the normative model, the larger are the stakes. This is consistent with the usual economists view that people get the big decisions right.

It should be noted that both the time and size effects can be "explained" by introducing a "fixed cost to waiting." Yet the scenario used made the actual costs minimal. Thus if it is a fixed cost which yields these results, it is clearly a fixed *psychic* cost rather than some transactions cost.

Sign effects That behavior is qualitatively different for gains and losses comes as no surprise. As I have argued elsewhere (Thaler, 1980) opportunity costs are generally *not* equated to out-of-pocket costs. Specifically, opportunity costs tend to be underweighted relative to out-of-product costs. (The same result appears in Kahneman and Tversky's "Prospect Theory," 1979.) Since failure to wait for a reward creates an opportunity cost while postponing a loss incurs an out-of-pocket cost it should be expected that implicit discount rates will be higher for gains, as we observe.

5. CONCLUSION

Economists are generally suspect of hypothetical questions, perhaps for good reasons. Nonetheless, recent studies by Grether and Plott (1979) and Grether (1980) have found no difference between the behavior of subjects who were playing for real money and those playing for hypothetical stakes. This seems to argue that the results reported here should not be dismissed out-of-hand. My colleague Baruch Fischhoff and I have done extensive further testing with hypothetical questions and have obtained similar results. Real money experiments would be interesting but seem to present enormous tactical problems. (Would subjects believe they would get paid in five years?) Also, to use the stakes described here would be prohibitively expensive. Perhaps the most feasible research strategy is Hausman's technique of studying the implicit discount rates in consumers' actual decisions. Until more such studies are conducted, however, it would seem prudent to allow for the possibility that individual discount rates are not necessarily equal to the interest rate, and tend to vary with the size and sign of the reward and the length of the delay.

REFERENCES

The author wishes to thank Baruch Fischhoff and Paul Slovic of Decision Research in Eugene, Oregon, for helping design and administer the questionnaires used herein.

Bôhm-Bawerk, E. *The Positive Theory of Capital*. Trans. W. Smart (London: Macmillan, 1981).

Grether, D. "Bayes Rule as a Descriptive Model: The Representativeness Heuristic." *Quarterly Journal of Economics* (November 1980): 537–557.

Grether, D., and C. Plott. "Economic Theory of Choice and the Preference Reversal Phenomenon." *American Economic Review* 69 (September 1979): 623–638.

Hausman, J. "Individual Discount Rates and the Purchase and Utilization of Energy-using Durables." *Bell Journal of Economics* 10 (Spring 1979): 33–54.

Kahneman, D., and A. Tversky. "Prospect Theory: An Analysis of Decision Under Risk." *Econometrica* 47 (March 1979): 263–292.

Strotz, R. "Myopia and Inconsistency in Dynamic Utility Maximization." *Review of Economic Studies* 23 (1955–1956): 165–180.

Thaler, R. "Toward a Positive Theory of Consumer Choice." *Journal of Economic Behavior and Organization* (1980): 39–60.

Thaler, R., and H. Shefrin. "An Economic Theory of Self-control." *Journal of Political Economy* 89, 2 (April 1981): 392–406.

Wagenaar, W., and S. Sagaria. "Misperception of Exponential Growth." *Perception and Psychophysics* 18 (1975): 416–422.

Part Three

EXPERIMENTAL ECONOMICS

7

THE PSYCHOLOGY OF CHOICE AND THE ASSUMPTIONS OF ECONOMICS

Richard H. Thaler

INTRODUCTION

Neoclassical economics is based on the premise that models that characterize rational, optimizing behavior also characterize actual human behavior. The same model is used as a normative definition of rational choice and a descriptive predictor of observed choice. Many of the advances in economic theory over the last 50 years have constituted clarifications of the normative model. One of the most significant of these advances was the normative theory of choice under uncertainty, expected utility theory, formulated by John von Neumann and Oskar Morgenstern (1947). Expected utility theory defined rational choice in the context of uncertainty. Because of the dual role economic theories are expected to play, expected utility theory also provided the basis for a new style of research pioneered by Maurice Allais (1953) and Daniel Ellsberg (1961). Allais and Ellsberg exploited the precision of the theory to construct crisp counterexamples to its descriptive predictions. Interestingly, both Allais and Ellsberg used similar methods to demonstrate the force of their counterexamples. Some prominent economists and statisticians were presented with problems to which most gave answers inconsistent with the theory. Inducing Savage to violate one of his own axioms was taken to be sufficient proof that a genuine effect had been discovered. When Savage was confronted with the inconsistency of his choices and his axioms, he responded

Reprinted with permission from Alvin Roth, ed. *Laboratory Experiments in Economics: Six Points of View*. New York: Cambridge University Press, 1987.

137

that he had made a mistake, and wished to change his choices! This reaction is very instructive. Savage readily admitted that the choices he made were intuitively attractive, but not so attractive that he wished to abandon his axioms as the appropriate standard to characterize rational choice.

While this original work was done by economists, the continued research on individual decision making has been conducted primarily by psychologists. In the last two decades a new field has emerged which may perhaps be called behavioral decision research (BDR).[1] The research in BDR has combined the tradition of Allais and Ellsberg's counterexamples with Savage's respect for the normative theory. The BDR approach to the study of human decision making has been similar to (and strongly influenced by) the psychological approach to the study of perception. Much can be learned about visual processes by studying powerful optical illusions. Counterexamples such as those of Allais and Ellsberg have the force of an illusion to many and have provided similar insights into decision processes. It goes without saying that the existence of an optical illusion that causes us to see one of two equal lines as longer than the other should not reduce the value we place on accurate measurement. On the contrary, illusions demonstrate the need for rulers! Similarly, a demonstration that human choices often violate the axioms of rationality does not necessarily imply any criticism of the axioms of rational choice *as* a normative ideal. Rather, the research is simply intended to show that for descriptive purposes, alternative models are sometimes necessary.

Expected utility theory has not been the only source for counterexamples in BDR. BDR has exploited other aspects of the normative theory of rational choice to construct insightful counterexamples. The hypotheses that individuals make choices and judgments that are consistent with the principles of optimization and the laws of probability yield additional specific predictions that can be tested. In summarizing the research in this area I have selected fifteen specific principles of rationality that are used by economists to describe actual choices. Each of these tenets is widely (though not universally) accepted as a normative principle. Yet for each, there is evidence that the tenet is descriptively inappropriate. (While each tenet makes a somewhat different point about actual behavior, the tenets are not meant to be independent.)

The plan of the paper is as follows. Section 1 offers a brief and selective review of the studies of individual decision making, and the observed conflicts with the tenets of rational choice. Section 2 discusses some methodological issues, specifically the role of learning and incentives. Finally, Section 3 concerns some of the implications of BDR for economics.

---

[1] A more common term for the field is behavioral decision theory (BDT). BDR seems more accurate than BDT for two reasons: the field is as much empirical as it is theoretical, and there is more than one theory.

1. CHOICE

1.1 Decision Weights

The following principle, formalized as the substitution axiom by von Neumann and Morgenstern (1947), the extended sure-thing principle by Savage (1954), and the independence axiom by Luce and Krantz (1971), can be informally stated as Tenet 1.

TENET 1. *Cancellation. The choice between two options depends only on the states in which those options yield different outcomes.*

There are various techniques used to construct counterexamples. One technique is to devise a pair of problems to which subjects give inconsistent answers. Allais (1953) used this technique to demonstrate a violation of the independence axiom. Allais's problem pair was:

Problem 1. Choose between:
A. $1 million with certainty.
B. $5 million with probability .1, $1 million with probability .89, and $0 with probability .01.

Problem 2. Choose between:
C. $1 million with probability .11, and $0 with probability .89.
D. $5 million with probability .10, and $0 with probability .90.

The common responses, including those of Allais' famous subjects, are A and D. These violate the independence axiom. More recently Kahneman and Tversky (1979) replicated Allais' findings with another problem pair. This pair demonstrates that the enormous amounts of money in the original formulation are not essential.

Problem 3. Choose between:
A. $2,500 with probability .33   (18%)
   $2,400 with probability .66
   0 with probability   .01
B. $2,400 with certainty   (82%)

Problem 4. Choose between:
A. $2,500 with probability .33   (83%)
   0 with probability   .67
B. $2,400 with probability .34   (17%)
   0 with probability   .66

[Source: Kahneman and Tversky, 1979]

The number of subjects who chose each option is indicated in parentheses. Since Problem 4 is obtained from Problem 3 by eliminating a .66 chance of winning 2,400, the combined choices violate the independence axiom. Problems 3 and 4 illustrate what Kahneman and Tversky call the *certainty effect*. The reversals in both Allais's problem and this pair are explained by the apparent overweighting of certainty relative to probabilities less than unity.

Allais's parodox has stimulated numerous attempts to provide alternative theories that are consistent with the observed choices. One class of alternative models (for example, Chew, 1983; Fishburn, 1983; and Machina, 1982) are attempts to make the theory more descriptively valid by relaxing the cancellation principle in a minimal fashion. So, for example, the Allais paradox can be handled by replacing the independence axiom with a more general representation. In prospect theory Kahneman and Tversky (1979) have taken a different approach. Prospect theory is explicitly a *descriptive* theory, with no normative pretensions. As such, it was developed inductively, starting with the results of experimental research, rather than deductively from a set of axioms. It is an attempt to make sense of many different kinds of anomalies, some, as we shall see, even more damaging to the rational modeling tradition than the counterexamples discussed so far.

There are two central features of prospect theory: a decision weighting function, $\pi(p)$, which translates subjective probabilities into decision weights; and a value function, $v(\cdot)$, which serves the role of the traditional utility function and which will be discussed below. The π function is a monotonic function of p, but is not a probability; π does not satisfy either tenet 1 or 2. It has the following properties. First, while the scale is normalized so that $\pi(0) = 0$ and $\pi(1) = 1$, the function is not well behaved near the end points. Second, for low probabilities $\pi(p) > p$, but $\pi(p) + \pi(1 - p) \leq 1$. Thus low probabilities are overweighted, moderate and high probabilities are underweighted, and the latter effect is less pronounced than the former. Third, $\pi(pr)/\pi(p) < \pi(prq)/\pi(pq)$ for all $0 < p, q, r \leq 1$. That is, for any fixed probability ratio q, the ratio of decision weights is closer to unity when the probabilities are lower than when they are higher, e.g., $\pi(.1)/\pi(.2) > \pi(.4)/\pi(.8)$. An illustrative π function is shown in Figure 1.

TENET 2. *Expectation. The utility of an outcome is weighted by its probability. Decision weights do not depend on the origin of the uncertainty.*
Another way to create a violation of rational choice is to induce subjects to exhibit a strict preference between two alternatives that are normatively equivalent. Ellsberg discovered that people are sensitive to attributes of prospects that are not captured in the standard formulation. The simplest version of Ellsberg's problem is as follows.

Problem 5. There are two urns containing a large number of red and black balls. Urn A is known to have 50 percent red balls and 50 percent black balls.

Urn B has red and black balls in unknown proportions. You will win $100 if you draw the color ball of your choice from an urn. From which urn would you rather choose a ball?

Most subjects express a strict preference for Urn A with the known proportion rather than the "ambiguous" Urn B. Subjects readily admit that they would be indifferent about trying for a red or black ball from the ambiguous urn, thereby indicating that their subjective probabilities of each are the same and presumably equal to 1/2, which is the known proportion in Urn A. Nevertheless, most subjects feel that the ambiguous urn is in some sense riskier. This preference for the known urn violates Tenet 2.

Dealing with ambiguity in a theoretical model of choice is more complicated than dealing with violations of the cancellation principle. The prospect theory decision weights, for example, are defined over stated probabilities, and are thus undefined in ambiguous situations. A further complication is that preferences about ambiguity appear to depend on both the sign and magnitude

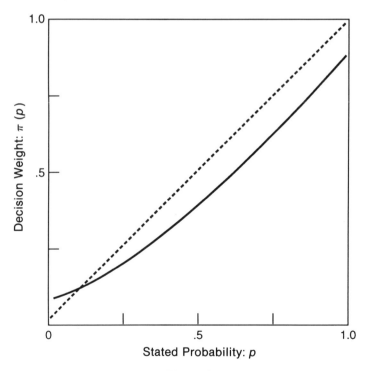

Figure 1.

of the outcomes, so a complete description would necessitate abandoning the independence between the decision weights and the outcomes.[2]

1.2. Values

Tenet 3. *Risk Aversion. The utility function for wealth is concave (risk averse).*
While risk aversion is neither an axiom of rationality nor a necessary component of economic analysis, the assumption of diminishing marginal utility has a tradition in the study of choice behavior that dates back to Bernoulli and is widely used in economics today. The popularity of gambling has long been recognized as a potential problem for the assumption of risk aversion, but gambling is (I think reasonably) generally considered to be a special case explained in large part by the utility of the activity rather than the utility of the outcomes. (It is also explained, in part, by the overweighting of small probabilities.) Problem 6 demonstrates a violation of risk aversion that is more troubling than the popularity of gambling.

Problem 6. Choose between:
   A. An 80% chance to lose $4,000, or   (92%)
   B. A certain loss of $3,000.   (8%)

[Source: Kahneman and Tversky, 1979]

Problem 6 illustrates a common preference for risk-seeking in the domain of losses that is generally observed and opposite to the usual preference in the domain of gains. This suggests a reformulation of the utility function that depends on the sign of the perceived changes in wealth, in violation of the following tenet.

Tenet 4. *Asset Integration. The domain of the utility function is final states.*
In expected utility theory wealth is the carrier of value. To successfully describe behavior, Tenet 4 must be relaxed. Consider the following pair of problems.

Problem 7. Assume yourself richer by $300 than you are today. You are offered a choice between:
   A. A sure gain of $100, or   (72%)
   B. A 50% chance to gain $200 and a 50% chance to gain nothing.   (28%)

---

[2]For example, ambiguity may be preferred for small gains or for losses. For one recent approach to the study of ambiguity, see Einhorn and Hogarth (1985).

Problem 8. Assume yourself richer by $500 than you are today. You are offered a choice between:
    A. A sure loss of $100, or   (36%)
    B. A 50% chance to lose $200 and a 50% chance to lose nothing.   (64%)

[Source: Tversky and Kahneman, 1986]

Since the problems are identical in terms of final asset positions, the inconsistency between the choices demonstrates that subjects tend to evaluate prospects in terms of *gains and losses* relative to some reference point, rather than final states. As in Problem 6, subjects choose the risky choice in Problem 8 (which is characterized in terms of losses) while selecting the risk-averse choice in Problem 7 (which is described in terms of gains). Both of these phenomena (attention to gains and losses and risk seeking in the domain of losses) are captured in the *value function* in Kahneman and Tversky's prospect theory (Kahneman and Tversky, 1979).

The formulation of the value function was intended to incorporate three important behavioral regularities observed in the study of both perception and choice. First, people seem to respond to perceived gains or losses rather than to their hypothetical final end states (wealth positions) as assumed by expected utility theory. Second, there is diminishing marginal sensitivity to changes, irrespective of the sign of the change. Third, losses loom larger than gains. The corresponding features of the value function are: (1) the value function explicitly adopts *changes* as the carriers of value; (2) the value function is assumed to be concave for gains and convex for losses, $v''(x) < 0$, $x > 0$; $v''(x) > 0$, $x < 0$; (3) the function is steeper for losses than gains, that is, $v(x) < -v(-x)$, $x > 0$. This last feature is called *loss aversion*. A typical value function is illustrated in Figure 2.

In many contexts, the concept of loss aversion, the sharp disutility associated with perceived losses, is more useful than the concept of risk aversion. Behavior often considered motivated by risk aversion, such as an unwillingness to accept low-stakes gambles at better than fair odds, is more accurately characterized as loss aversion.

1.3. Framing

TENET 5. *Preference Ordering. Preferences are independent of the method used to elicit them.*
The existence of a well-defined preference ordering is one of many assumptions that are often taken for granted. If a preference ordering exists, then it should be recoverable in any number of alternative elicitation procedures. Dramatic violations of Tenet 5 were discovered in a series of experiments conducted by psychologists Sarah Lichtenstein and Paul Slovic (1971).

Lichtenstein and Slovic asked subjects first to choose between two bets. One bet, called the "p bet," offered a high probability of winning a small amount of money (e.g., a 35/36 chance to win $4.00). The other bet, called the "$ bet," offered a smaller chance of winning a larger amount of money (e.g., a 11/36 chance to win $16). The expected value of the two bets was about the same. Subjects were also asked to value each bet by stating the minimum amount they would accept to sell each of the bets if they owned the right to play them (or, alternatively, the maximum amount they would pay to buy the gamble). Surprisingly, a large proportion of the subjects who preferred the p bet in the choice task assigned a larger value to the $ bet in the judgment task. Thus, in violation of Tenet 5, preferences depend on the method of elicitation. This result, called the *preference reversal effect*, has been replicated with real money on the floor of a Las Vegas casino (Lichtenstein and Slovic, 1973) and by economists David Grether and Charles Plott (1979).[3]

Tenet 6. *Invariance. Choices between options are independent of their representation or description.*

Like the existence of a preference ordering, the invariance principle is so basic to rational choice that it is usually tacitly assumed in the characterization of options rather than explicitly assumed as an axiom of choice. Moreover, while cancellation and expectation may be considered by some to be expendable features of rational choice, invariance is essential. Nevertheless, numerous experiments have shown that choice depends on the way the problem is formulated or *framed*. One example of this is the Problem pair 6 and 7 shown above, in which reframing the outcomes altered choices. The following three problems demonstrate that the framing of contingencies can also influence choice.

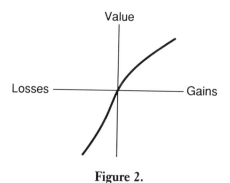

Figure 2.

[3]For a recent review, see Slovic and Lichtenstein, 1983.

Problem 9. Which of the following options do you prefer?
A. A sure win of $30   (78%)
B. An 80% chance to win $45   (22%)

Problem 10. Consider the following two-stage game. In the first stage, there is a 75% chance to end the game without winning anything, and a 25% chance to move into the second stage. If you reach the second stage you have a choice between:
C. A sure win of $30   (74%)
D. An 80% chance to win $45   (26%)

Your choice must be made before the game starts, i.e., before the outcome of the first stage game is known. Please indicate the option you prefer.

Problem 11. Which of the following options do you prefer?
E. A 25% chance to win $30   (42%)
F. A 20% chance to win $45   (58%)

[Source: Tversky and Kahneman, 1981]

Since Problems 10 and 11 are identical in terms of probabilities and outcomes they should produce consistent responses. However, subjects appear to treat Problem 10 as equivalent to Problem 9 rather than Problem 11. The attraction of option A in Problem 9 is explained by the certainty effect. In Problem 10, the attractiveness of option C is due to the illusion of certainty created by the two stage formulation. Tversky and Kahneman (1981) call this the *pseudocertainty effect*. When the framing of a contingency suggests certainty, the option will acquire the same attractiveness accorded to a genuinely certain event.
Another essential principle of rational choice is dominance.

TENET 7. *Dominance. If option A is better than option B in every respect, then A is preferred to B.*
The following set of problems illustrates how both invariance and dominance can be violated.

Problem 12. Imagine that you face the following pair of concurrent decisions. First examine both decisions, then indicate the options you prefer:

Decision (i) Choose between:
A. A sure gain of $240   (84%)
B. 25% chance to gain $1,000 and 75% to gain nothing.   (16%)

Decision (ii) Choose between:
- C. A sure loss of $750   (13%)
- D. 75% chance to lose $1,000 and 25% chance to lose nothing   (87%)

[Source: Tversky and Kahneman, 1981]

The majority choices indicate the usual pattern of risk aversion in the domain of gains and risk seeking in the domain of losses. A total of 73 percent of the subjects chose the portfolio A&D while only 3 percent picked the combination B&C. This pattern is of interest because the combination B&C actually dominates A&D. This becomes obvious when the problem is reformulated.

Problem 13. Choose between:
- E. (=A&D): 25% chance to win $240 and 75% chance to lose $760.   (0%)
- F. (=B&C): 25% chance to win $250 and 75% chance to lose $750.   (100%)

[Source: Tversky and Kahneman, 1981]

The violations of invariance and dominance illustrated by Problems 12 and 13 raise two important points. First, since invariance and dominance are fundamental to any rational model of choice, no hybrid, nearly rational model can possibly capture this type of behavior. Second, the problems illustrate the useful distinction between *transparent* and *opaque* choices. All subjects choose the dominant option in Problem 13 because the dominance is so easy to detect. In contrast, the dominance is not transparent in Problem 12, and so most subjects go astray. If all real life problems were transparent, BDR would have much less relevance to economics. Expected utility theory is often an accurate representation of choices in transparent problems. Alas, the world appears to be opaque.

1.4. Deterministic Choice

The psychology of choice applies to deterministic choice, as well as decisions under uncertainty. Here the basic principles of economic analysis provide the tenets that can be questioned by counterexamples. One of the first lessons in Economics 101 is the concept of opportunity costs.

Tenet 8. *Opportunity Costs. Willingness to pay equals willingness to sell (disregarding income effects and transactions costs); opportunity costs and out-of-pocket costs are equivalent.*
Willingness to pay and willingness to accept compensation are two measures of the value a person places on something. In the absence of transactions costs

these two measures should differ only by an income effect, which in most cases is small. I first noticed a large discrepancy between these measures when doing research on the value of saving lives. Subjects were asked two questions: (1) How much would you pay to reduce your risk of death by .001? (2) How much would you have to be paid to take a risk of death of .001? Responses for Question 2 typically exceeded those for Question 1 by more than an order of magnitude![4] In less dramatic contexts, people often act as if they wouldn't sell an item in their endowment for $x, but if the item were lost or stolen, they wouldn't replace it at a cost of less than $x. In Thaler (1980), I called this the *endowment effect*, and pointed out that the behavior is partly explained by loss aversion.

The disparity between buying and selling prices has been demonstrated in an elegantly simple experiment run by Knetsch and Sinden (1984). Knetsch and Sinden gave half their subjects tickets to a lottery and the other half of the subjects three dollars. Then the first group was given the opportunity to sell their tickets for three dollars and the second group was permitted to buy tickets for three dollars. Again, a large disparity was observed. Of the people given a ticket, 82 percent (31 of 38) kept them, whereas only 38 percent of the other group (15 out of 39) opted to buy a ticket. Notice that this experiment used real stakes and had no income effects confounding the results. This disparity between buying and selling prices raises serious problems for practitioners of cost benefit analysis who must try to put monetary values on goods that are not traded in markets.

Another basic principle of microeconomics is that of marginal analysis.

TENET 9. *Marginal Analysis. Choices are made to equate marginal costs with marginal benefits.*

One application of marginal analysis is optimal search. Search for the lowest price should continue until the expected marginal gain equals the value of the search costs. This is likely to be violated if the context of the search influences the perception of the value of the savings. Thaler (1980) argued that individuals were more likely to spend 20 minutes to save $5 on the purchase of a clock radio than to save the same amount on the purchase of a $500 television.[5] This intuition was confirmed in the following example.

---

[4]While the disparity is in the same direction as a potential income effect, the disparity is much too large to be plausibly explained in this way.

[5]Savage commented on the same behavioral regularity. "A man buying a car for $2,134.56 is tempted to order it with a radio installed, which will bring the total price to $2,228.41, feeling that the difference is trifling. But, when he reflects that, if he already had the car, he certainly would not spend $93.85 for a radio for it, he realizes that he has made an error." [Savage, 1954, p. 103] Of course, many people may not do the second part of Savage's analysis; or, even if they do, they may nevertheless feel that the purchase of the radio really hurts less when bought together with the car.

Problem 14. Imagine that you are about to purchase a jacket for ($125) [$15], and a calculator for ($15) [$125]. The calculator salesman informs you that the calculator you wish to buy is on sale for ($10) [$120] at the other branch of the store, located a 20-minute drive away. Would you make the trip to the other store?

[Source: Tversky and Kahneman, 1981]

The responses to the two versions of this problem were quite different. When the calculator cost $125 only 29% of the subjects said they would make the trip, whereas 68% said they would go when the calculator cost only $15.

Economics students often make mistakes in applying Tenet 9 by confusing average and marginal costs. A recent experiment by Gottfries and Hylton (1983) shows that even MIT students are not immune to this error. Students on the MIT dining plan pay for meals according to a schedule in which the price per meal falls considerably after a certain number of meals have been purchased. Gottfries and Hylton asked students on this meal plan whether they would switch to another dining hall or restaurant for two weeks. The price of the alternative was above the marginal cost of the meal plan but below the average cost. Among those students for whom the lower marginal cost was relevant, 68 percent said they would switch and gave as their reason "to save money."

Of the tenets presented in this paper, the following may be violated most often.

TENET 10. *Sunk Costs. Fixed, historical, and other sunk costs do not influence decisions.*
A classic sunk cost situation is illustrated by the following example.

Problem 15. You have tickets to a basketball game in a city 60 miles from your home. The day of the game there is a major snowstorm, and the roads are very bad. Holding constant the value you place on going to the game, are you more likely to go to the game: (a) if you paid $20 each for the tickets, or (b) if you got the tickets for free?

[Source: Thaler, 1980]

The lure of the sunk cost is so strong in this problem that, when it is presented to subjects untrained in economics, substantial explanations must be given to convince subjects that the economic analysis is sensible.

Numerous studies have documented the failure of subjects to ignore sunk costs (e.g., Staw, 1976; Teger, 1980; Laughhunn and Payne, 1984; and Thaler and Johnson, 1986), but one particularly clean demonstration in a natural setting was done by Arkes and Blumer (1985). In their experiment, customers who purchased season tickets to a campus theater group were assigned randomly to either one of two experimental groups or a control group. The experimental groups received refunds of $2.00 or $7.00 from the normal $15 price of the tickets, while the control group received no refund. The season consisted of ten plays. The authors analyzed the attendance to the first five plays separately from the last five. Over the first five plays, the sunk cost had a significant effect. Those who paid full price attended significantly more plays than those who received a discount. This effect was not significant for the second half of the season, suggesting that sunk costs may become less relevant with time.

Households and individuals behave as if they had an implicit mental accounting system. One reason why sunk costs are not ignored is that costs that have not been "mentally amortized" are coded as losses. Mental accounting also influences choices when either sources or uses of funds are placed in particular accounts. Choices influenced in this way violate Tenet 11.

TENET 11. *Fungibility. Money is spent on its highest valued use. Money has no labels.* The following problems show how the relevance of sunk costs can be influenced by the mental accounting system.

Problem 16. Imagine that you have decided to see a play where admission is $10 per ticket. As you enter the theater you discover that you have lost a $10 bill. Would you still pay $10 for a ticket to the play?

Yes: 88%   No: 12%

Problem 17. Imagine that you have decided to see a play and paid the admission price of $10 per ticket. As you enter the theater you discover that you have lost your ticket. The seat was not marked and the ticket cannot be recovered. Would you pay $10 for another ticket?

Yes: 46%   No: 54%

[Source: Tversky and Kahneman, 1981]

In Problems 16 and 17 the loss of the $10 affects the choice of whether to buy a ticket only when it is coded in the same account.

A key question in the investigation of mental accounting systems is the relationship between costs and losses. In the context of the prospect theory loss function, when is a cost a loss? One way in which a portion of a cost may be coded as a loss is if the cost is considered to be excessive by the customer. This coding can lead to violations of the following tenet.

TENET 12. *Domain of Utility. Willingness to pay for a good depends only on the characteristics of the good and not on the perceived merits of the deal.*
The potential importance of the reference price (the price a consumer expects to have to pay in a particular context) is illustrated by the following pair of questionnaires. (One group of subjects received the information in parentheses and the other received the information in brackets.)

Problem 18. You are lying on the beach on a hot day. All you have to drink is ice water. For the last hour you have been thinking about how much you would enjoy a nice cold bottle of your favorite brand of beer. A companion gets up to go make a phone call and offers to bring back a beer from the only nearby place where beer is sold (a fancy resort hotel) [a small, run-down grocery store]. He says that the beer may be expensive and so asks how much you are willing to pay for the beer. He says that he will buy the beer if it costs as much or less than the price you state, but if it costs more than the price you state he will not buy it. You trust your friend and there is no possibility of bargaining with (the bartender) [the store owner].

[Source: Thaler, 1985]

When this questionnaire was administered to the participants in an executive education program, the median responses were $2.65 in the hotel version and $1.50 in the grocery store version. This disparity occurs even though the question is incentive compatible, and there is no "atmosphere" consumed in either version. This result violates Tenet 12.

In contrast to Tenet 12, I have suggested that consumers consider the value of the "deal" (a function of the difference between the price paid and the reference price), as well as the utility of the item being purchased, in evaluating a potential transaction (Thaler, 1985). The beer on the beach example illustrates that when consumers feel that they are being treated unfairly they will be unwilling to make a purchase that would otherwise make them better off. Conversely, if a good is perceived as a sufficiently attractive bargain, it may be purchased even if its value is less than its price.

The last tenet of this section is implicit in most economic analyses.

TENET 13. *Economic Opportunities. All legal economic opportunities for gains will be exploited.*
While Tenet 13 may seem reasonable at first, clearly there are some limits to what constitutes an economic opportunity. If you observe someone drop his wallet on the bus, does this constitute an economic opportunity? To what extent is behavior governed by social norms? A related question concerns implicit contracts. To what extent is enforceability necessary for implicit contracts to operate? In collaboration with Daniel Kahneman and Jack Knetsch, I have been involved with a research project investigating these

issues with a new (to BDR) methodology (Kahneman, Knetsch, and Thaler, 1986a,b). Residents of Toronto and Vancouver were contacted by telephone and asked questions regarding their perceptions of fairness. I will report here the responses to a question about an unenforceable implicit contract, namely, tipping in strange restaurants.

Problem 19. If the service is satisfactory, how much of a tip do you think most people leave after ordering a meal costing $10 in a restaurant that they visit frequently?
    Mean response: $1.28

Problem 20. If the service is satisfactory, how much of a tip do you think most people leave after ordering a meal costing $10 in a restaurant that they do not expect to visit again?
    Mean response: $1.27

Our panel evidently does not treat the possibility of enforcement as a significant factor in the control of tipping.

1.5. Judgment

The principles of rationality and maximization are used by economists not just to describe people's choices but also their judgments. Thus the following tenet, while associated with a specific modern branch of macroeconomics, is really in keeping with, rather than a radical departure from, the general principles of economic theory.

TENET 14. *Rational Expectations. Probabilistic judgments are consistent and unbiased.*
When John Muth (1961) coined the term *rational expectations* he believed he was merely applying standard techniques to the problem of expectations. This is clear from his definition of rational expectations: ". . . the same as the predictions of the relevant economic theory" (p. 316). It is instructive to note that in Steven Sheffrin's (1983) recent review of the rational expectations literature he finds little empirical support for the notion that actual expectations satisfy the criteria that define rational expectations. In reviewing several studies using the Livingston data set (a collection of published professional inflation forecasts) Sheffrin concludes: "The results of the extensive research on the Livingston data are, at best, mixed. The verdict on Muth rationality for the aggregate series depends on the time period examined, the econometric techniques, and the aggregation procedure. The one study on the individual responses clearly rejected the rationality hypothesis" (p. 21). Since rational expectations models are intended to be positive theories, one might think that

the lack of empirical support for the hypothesis would be considered damaging. However, some advocates of the hypothesis have continued to use it apparently on the grounds that there is no alternative.

> The rational expectations assumption may be excessively strong . . . but it is a more persuasive starting point than the alternative of using a rule of thumb for expectations formation that is independent of the stochastic properties of the time path of the variable about which expectations are formed. A fundamental difficulty with theories of expectations that are not based on the predictions of the relevant economic model . . . is that they require a theory of systematic mistakes. (Barro and Fisher, 1976, p. 163)

To provide a theory of systematic mistakes, one must become more concerned with the actual processes used to make judgments (and choices). This point was stressed in the pioneering work of Herbert Simon (e.g., 1955). Simon's interest in artificial intelligence gave him not only great respect for the human mind, but also considerable appreciation for the mind's limitations. He stressed that because of the mind's limited information processing and storage capabilities, humans must use simple rules of thumb and heuristics to help make decisions and solve problems. Simon coined the terms "bounded rationality" and "satisficing" to describe man's limited mental abilities and decision making strategies respectively.

Kahneman and Tversky took the next step in developing a theory of systematic mistakes by identifying three specific heuristics people use in making judgments of magnitudes, frequencies, or probabilities: the *availability*, *representativeness*, and *anchoring and adjustment* heuristics. Each of the heuristics is a useful way of making judgments, but the use of each leads to predictable, systematic errors. When using the availability heuristic (Tversky and Kahneman, 1973) people estimate the frequency of a class by the ease with which they can recall specific instances in that class. Thus "John" is judged to be a common name (by English speakers) since it is easy to think of many people with that name. Biases are generated when the frequency of the event in question is not perfectly correlated with its ease of recall. This is illustrated by the following problems:

Problem 21. In four pages of a novel (about 2,000 words), how many words would you expect to find that have the form _ _ _ _ i n g (seven letter words that end with "ing")? Indicate your best estimate by circling one of the values below:

0   1–2   3–4   5–7   8–10   11–15   16+   median = 13.4

Problem 22. In four pages of a novel (about 2,000 words), how many words would you expect to find that have the form _ _ _ _ _ n _ (seven letter words that have the letter n in the sixth position)? Indicate your best estimate by circling one of the values below:

0   1–2   3–4   5–7   8–10   11–15   16+   median = 4.7

[Source: Tversky and Kahneman, 1983]

Subjects here estimate that there are many more words ending with "ing" because it is easier to retrieve instances of that type. This judgment violates the conjunction rule of probability: the probability of a conjunction P(A&B) cannot exceed the probability of either of its constituents, P(A) and P(B).

The bias in Problems 21 and 22 is caused by the nature of the memory retrieval system. In other cases a bias can be induced by external factors. When asked whether suicide or homicide is more common, most people guess homicide since it receives greater press coverage, though in fact suicide is more common. Slovic, Fischhoff, and Lichtenstein (1979) have found that generally people overestimate the frequency of highly publicized causes of death (such as accidents and floods) and underestimate the frequencies of quieter fatalities (such as diabetes and stroke).

The representativeness heuristic (Kahneman and Tversky, 1972, 1973) is used to estimate the likelihood that a particular event or case belongs to a certain class. The representativeness heuristic judges such a frequency by comparing the similarity of the case with the image or stereotype of the class. Here a bias is generated when frequency and similarity are not well correlated. This is illustrated by the next problem.

Problem 23. Consider a regular six-sided die with four green faces and two red faces. The die will be rolled 20 times and the sequence of greens (G) and reds (R) will be recorded. You are asked to select one sequence, from a set of three, and you will win $25 if the sequence you choose appears on successive rolls of the die. Please check the sequence of greens and reds on which you prefer to bet.
  A. RGRRR
  B. GRGRRR
  C. GRRRRR

[Source: Tversky and Kahneman, 1983]

Notice that sequence A is simply sequence B with the first G deleted. Thus A must be more probable than B. However, sequence B may appear more "representative" of the die than sequence A because it has two Gs rather than one. The latter consideration is evidently quite powerful since about 63 percent of the subjects chose B with only 35 percent choosing A (the rest taking C). Once again the use of a heuristic leads to a violation of the conjunction rule and thus Tenet 13. In this case the majority choice also violates stochastic dominance.

The final tenet is a common assumption in both theoretical and applied economics research.

Tenet 15. *Bayesian Learning. Probabilistic judgments are updated by the appropriate use of Bayes's rule.*
One of the biases that can be introduced by using the representativeness heuristic is the violation of Bayes's rule. Empirical research (Kahneman and Tversky, 1972, 1973) indicates that subjects tend to give too little weight to prior or base rate information and too much weight to new information. For example, in one experiment subjects were given a description of a man and were asked to guess whether he was a lawyer or an engineer. Subjects' answers were insensitive to whether they had been told the descriptions came from a sample containing 70 percent lawyers or 30 percent lawyers (Kahneman and Tversky, 1973). Perhaps because Tenet 15 is so commonly used in economics research, David Grether (1980) replicated the Kahneman and Tversky findings with a clever new experimental design.

Subjects were shown two bingo cages, one of which (cage X) had three balls marked "N" and three marked "G" while the other (cage Y) had four Ns and two Gs. One of the cages was selected by a random process (a draw from a third bingo cage). The prior probabilities of selecting either cage were transparent to the subjects. A sample of six draws with replacement was taken from the selected cage, and the subjects' task was to guess which cage had been selected.

Grether's design allowed him to estimate a logit model in which the dependent variable was the cage selected and the independent variables were the prior odds and likelihood ratio (in multiplicative form). If subjects made judgments as if they were using Bayes's rule, the estimated coefficients for the two independent variables would both be 1.0. Instead, the estimated coefficient for the likelihood ratio was significantly higher than the coefficient for the prior, indicating that subjects were giving insufficient weight to the prior, as predicted by the representativeness heuristic. Significantly, and of considerable surprise to Grether, subjects who were given financial incentives to respond accurately did no better than those without financial incentives.

One manifestation of the use of the representativeness heuristic is that predictions tend to be non-regressive. For example, when one group of subjects are asked to *evaluate* a high school student's record, and another group is asked to *predict* (on the basis of the same record) how well the student will do in college, the groups tend to give equally extreme judgments, whereas, of course, the latter judgments should be much less extreme. In a dynamic world, such behavior will produce *overreaction* to new information. As noted by Kenneth Arrow (1982), the price movements in financial markets seem to display precisely this type of behavior. Arrow cites the work of Shiller (1981), which shows that stock prices are excessively volatile. Dreman (1982) uses the same argument to explain the observed excess return to firms with low price earnings ratios, and De Bondt and Thaler (1985) were able to predict similar excess returns to firms that have previously had large negative excess returns. Arrow concludes:

> I hope to have made a case for the proposition that an important class of intertemporal markets shows systematic deviations from individual rational behavior and that these deviations are consonant with evidence from very different sources collected by psychologists. (Arrow, 1982, p. 8)

2. METHODOLOGICAL ISSUES

The research described above is characterized by three general traits: (1) short questions appealing to subjects' intuitions; (2) little or no monetary incentives; (3) no opportunity for learning. The latter two characteristics have received some criticism and, therefore, deserve attention.

2.1. Incentives

The issue of monetary incentives can be addressed at two levels. (1) Is the purely hypothetical nature of many of the experiments a matter of concern? Would even small monetary incentives eliminate the observed anomalies? (2) Are the differences between the stakes in the laboratory and real world sufficiently large that *all* laboratory experiments are of questionable value in assessing actual choice behavior? I will discuss each point in turn.

For some kinds of problems it is a simple matter to make the payments to subjects depend on the quality of their decisions. To see whether the addition of monetary incentives would improve decision making, numerous researchers, both psychologists and economists, have run parallel experiments with and without incentives (e.g., Grether, 1980; Grether and Plott, 1979; Knetsch and Sinden, 1984; Lichtenstein and Slovic, 1971, 1973; Lichtenstein, Fischhoff, and Phillips, 1977; Pommerehne, Schneider, and Zweifel, 1982; Reilly, 1982; Tversky and Kahneman, 1981, 1983). These methodological experiments have produced two basic conclusions. First, monetary incentives do induce the subjects to pay a little more attention, so the data generated with incentives tend to have less noise. Second, the violations of rationality observed tend to be somewhat *stronger* in the incentive condition (see, for example, Grether and Plott, 1979). This result, while of considerable surprise to the economists who have obtained it, is not really counterintuitive. If the effects under study are real, then the presence of monetary incentives simply acts to magnify the effect by inducing the subjects to be attentive.

The expectations of some economists on this issue have been that, without incentives, subjects will lie about their true preferences and beliefs, perhaps using some clever strategic ploy, and/or subjects will not bother to think carefully about the problems posed and will respond in an offhand fashion. Subjects are portrayed as devious, cognitive misers. There is little, if any, empirical evidence for this characterization. Nevertheless, I do not wish to give the impression that the studies cited validate the use of hypothetical questions in all types of research. Hypothetical questions appear to work well when subjects have access to their intuitions and have no particular incentive to lie. When strangers are asked for the time of day, few intentionally lie. However, it would be naive to expect truthful answers to questions about cheating on exams or income taxes.

That monetary incentives have proven to be irrelevant in many cases should be considered good news. Asking purely hypothetical questions is inexpensive, fast, and convenient. This means that many more experiments can be run with much larger samples than is possible in a monetary incentives methodology. (The experiments described in this paper often have used over a hundred subjects to answer each of several versions of the questions.) Also, in some cases the use of real money is impossible. It is not practical to use real stakes to investigate subjects' preferences regarding large amounts of money, and it is difficult to expose subjects to actual losses of even moderate amounts.[6]

Since even real money experiments are played for relatively small stakes, a different sort of critique is that the incentives in the real world are greater, and thus rationality may obtain "when it counts."[7] This critique is related to the "cognitive miser" hypothesis: the failings that have been observed are rational reactions to the "cost of thinking." I find the hypothesis implausible. There is no evidence to suggest that thinking longer or harder about cognitive illusions makes them go away, anymore than there is reason to think that staring more intently at mirages makes them disappear. Furthermore, people do not appear to be particularly rational in making the really important decisions in life. The

---

[6]Thaler and Johnson (1986) have run some real money choice experiments involving losses by allowing subjects to select themselves into real money and hypothetical conditions. This procedure has some potential merit, but it has the problem that the real money subjects tend to be much more risk seeking than those in the hypothetical condition, making comparisons across conditions difficult.

[7]This critique applies with equal force to any experimental markets that fail to obtain a rational equilibrium, e.g., Plott and Sunder (1983). A true believer can interpret an experiment that does obtain a rational equilibrium (such as Plott and Sunder's earlier paper, 1982) as evidence that markets work while dismissing the latter paper as irrelevant because the stakes are too small or the traders too inexperienced. Such a bias, if reflected in the choice of papers to be published, could considerably distort the impression generated by experimental economics about the robustness of the predictions of economic theory.

high failure rate of new businesses is a case in point. It is hard to reconcile this datum with both rational expectations and risk aversion. Furthermore, while it would be possible for people to hire consultants to help them overcome their cognitive failings in important situations, this is rarely observed. Even for the purchase of a house, the single largest financial decision most people make, few people get any decision-making help, aside from that received from a real estate agent, a person more likely to initiate biases than to eliminate them.

2.2. Learning

When a subject is given a single opportunity to make a particular choice or judgment and makes a mistake, it is natural to ask whether the subject wouldn't do better if there were opportunities for learning. While it is indisputable that people can and do learn, it is not clear what is the best way of finding out how people choose outside the lab. Suppose a subject is given a problem to solve, and the subject makes a mistake. Suppose the subject is then given considerable practice on the same task with highly structured, constructive feedback. What should be concluded if the subject eventually learns to avoid the mistake? Should we conclude that the mistake will not be made in the real world? Not necessarily.

What does it mean to say that a subject has learned a task? All teachers are familiar with the frustration of seeing how badly students can perform on last month's concept when incorporated into this month's test. Does any statistics teacher suffer the delusion that the students who successfully answered a problem on Bayes's rule in June will apply the concept correctly, out of context, in July, much less several years later? The reason for conducting one-shot decision-making experiments is to try to discover the intuitions that subjects bring with them to the lab. Those intuitions do not include the proper use of Bayes's rule, nor the proper use of the (implicit) concepts of sunk costs and opportunity costs. There is every reason to believe that an initial response in the lab will be the one that is most like the response a subject will make in a similar real life problem. The response after several learning trials may be no more general than the response students give on exam questions.

Although the subjects in BDR experiments may not have learned to solve the problems posed by the experimenters, perhaps they have learned to deal with their own problems successfully. Is there any reason to believe that the real world teaches people to choose and judge rationally? Unfortunately, one must be skeptical about this prospect. First, many decisions are made infrequently. Particularly for major decisions, most people get too few trials to receive much training. We marry, choose careers, and take jobs at most a few times.

Second, even for repeated decisions, the quality of the learning depends crucially on the quality of the feedback. As Einhorn and Hogarth (1978) have shown, many routine situations are structured in a way that the feedback is not conducive to learning. In some tasks, confidence in one's judgment ability can increase with experience, regardless of the actual quality of the judgments being made (for example, admissions directors at selective colleges with a low dropout rate). Feedback is often delayed, and even when failure is recognized there are usually multiple explanations for it. Hindsight biases (Fischhoff, 1975) also interfere with proper *ex post* evaluations. Particularly in stochastic environments, learning about the quality of the decisions being made simply from the outcomes being observed is very difficult.

Third, even studies of expert decision making have found numerous biases. A study by McNeil, et al. (1982) illustrates this point in dramatic (and disturbing) fashion. Three large groups of subjects were given a question regarding a choice between surgery and radiation treatments for lung cancer. The subjects were patients, physicians, and graduate students of business. Two versions of the problem were given, one with the outcomes framed as survival probabilities, the other with the outcomes framed as mortality probabilities. There was a large discrepancy between the answers to this problem across the two frames for all three groups of subjects. (The attractiveness of surgery increased when the data were presented as probabilities of living.) Of interest here is the fact that the framing manipulation had the greatest effect on the sample of physicians. Thus, rather than being immune to framing, the doctors turned out to be particularly susceptible. This result was obtained despite the fact that the decision they faced was quite realistic, and one for which they had considerable experience.

In at least one case, a class of experts has learned to avoid a bias that most other individuals exhibit, namely, overconfidence. In studies of *calibration* (see Lichtenstein, Fischhoff, and Phillips, 1977) subjects are given a factual statement (e.g., Albany is the capital of New York State) and are then asked to state the probability they assign to the statement being true. The general result of overconfidence is reflected in the finding that when subjects say they are "sure" the statement is true (i.e., $p = 1.0$), the statement is false about 20 percent of the time. The one group of experts studied that does not exhibit overconfidence (and, in fact, is nearly perfectly calibrated) is meteorologists. When the weatherman says that there is an 80 percent chance of rain, it will rain about 80 percent of the time. This high degree of calibration is to be expected (in spite of a bad reputation), since practicing meterologists receive quick, precise, and repeated feedback, exactly the conditions that facilitate learning. Since most people do not get this type of feedback on the job, or in life generally, this result would seem to be the exception rather than the rule.

2.3. Markets, Evolution, and Ecological Validity

One way in which both learning and incentives are sometimes brought into the analysis is to argue that competitive markets will somehow force individuals to behave rationally. The question to ask is how? The evolutionary analogy has been used to argue that firms that fail to maximize profits will be driven out of business by those firms that get things right (Alchian, 1950; Friedman, 1953; Winter, 1964). This argument has some merit, and we would certainly expect the decisions of General Motors and IBM to be more in keeping with economic theory than some of their less successful competitors. (Though even in these cases, one must be careful. Evolutionary processes tend to be fairly slow.) It is quite another matter, however, to apply this argument to individuals in their roles as employees, consumers, savers, and investors. Violations of transitivity or dominance are rarely life-threatening. Since concepts such as rational expectations, life-cycle saving, and optimal search are used to model individuals as well as firms, these assumptions should be confirmed empirically rather than on the basis of some evolutionary argument.

It is true that some highly efficient markets can render irrationality irrelevant. Someone who believes that pesos are better than dollars (since more is better than less) is generally protected by the efficiency of foreign exchange markets. In other markets, however, there is ample opportunity for bad decision making to matter (Russell and Thaler, 1985). The market does not automatically protect a consumer who buys an inefficient product because its advertisement was worded (framed) cleverly, nor is there protection for an unemployed worker who turns down offers for jobs because she mistakenly thinks that she can find another job at her old wage rate.

The issues raised in this section all relate to the question of ecological validity, an issue of concern to all experimentalists. Many experimental economics studies use repeated trials and monetary incentives on the grounds that these factors make the experiments more like real markets. The validity of this assertion is less obvious than it seems. Individuals interact with other market participants in many ways. Some offer opportunities for learning, but few if any offer the instantaneous feedback utilized in some market experiments. A provocative and useful illustration of these issues is provided by Coursey, Hovis, and Schulze (CHS) (forthcoming). CHS investigate the disparity between willingness to pay (WTP) and willingness to accept (WTA) as demonstrated by Knetsch and Sinden (1984). They note that Knetsch and Sinden's methodology "ignores much of the tradition and procedures developed in experimental economics" (p. 1). By employing a market mechanism CHS hoped to obtain what they regard as "true" values for WTP and WTA.

The commodity studied by CHS was SOA, a foul tasting but harmless liquid. Subjects either offered to taste one ounce of the stuff for twenty seconds for a fee (WTA), or agreed to pay to avoid tasting the liquid (WTP). A three stage process was used to solicit WTP and WTA. In the first stage subjects made purely hypothetical, uninformed offers without knowing how badly SOA tasted. In the second stage subjects tasted a few drops of SOA and then made new hypothetical bids. At this point the usual disparity was observed, namely WTA exceeded WTP by more than a plausible income effect. The experimenter then tried to systematically lower the WTAs and raise the WTPs. The method by which this was accomplished was not described. In the third stage, the subjects participated in groups of eight in a Vickrey auction. Four of the members of the group would have to taste the liquid. The results of this auction, however, were not binding unless, after the market clearing price was announced, the "winners" unanimously agreed to accept the outcome. Furthermore, even if unanimity was obtained in one of the first four trials, the process continued until trial five. The authors commented on their procedure as follows:

> Both the unanimity requirement and the nonbinding practice trials have been shown to be helpful in promoting learning, and, as a result, in revealing true values in induced value experiments. In particular, the unanimity requirement allows a "winner" who has made a mistake to reject the outcome and force another auction trial. (p. 6)

The most striking result of the experiment was that the disparity between WTP and WTA was greatly reduced n the latter trials of the auction, with all of the adjustment occurring in the WTAs. Taking this result at face value, what conclusions should be reached? One reasonable conclusion is that intensive practice and repetition can help subjects learn to equate opportunity costs and out-of-pocket costs. However, just as it would be a mistake to conclude from the earlier studies that there is always a buying-selling discrepancy, it would also be a mistake to conclude that CHS's results imply that there will be no discrepancy in market contexts.[8] It remains an open question what market contexts are similar to the conditions in the CHS experiments.

3. IMPLICATIONS

3.1. How Much Rationality Is Appropriate?

Consider the following problem and decide what answer you would give before going on:

> In the following exercise, you will represent Company A (the acquirer) which is currently considering acquiring Company T (the target) by means of a tender offer. You plan to tender in cash for 100% of Company T's shares but are unsure

---

[8]Both my work (Thaler, 1980, 1985) and that of Kahneman and Tversky (1984) have stressed the difference between costs and losses. The buying-selling discrepancy, to the extent it is caused by loss aversion rather than issues of legitimacy, will not occur for those who consider themselves "traders." A grocer does not consider the sale of a loaf of bread a loss. Even nontraders will behave differently when there is an active resale market. See Kahneman, Knetsch, and Thaler (1986).

how high a price to offer. The main complication is this: the value of the company depends directly on the outcome of a major oil exploration project it is currently undertaking.

The very viability of Company T depends on the exploration outcome. In the worst case (if the exploration fails completely), the company under current management will be worth nothing—$0/share. In the best case (a complete success), the value under current management could be as high as $100/share. Given the range of exploration outcomes, *all share values between $0 and $100 per share are considered equally likely*. By all estimates the company will be worth considerably more in the hands of Company A than under current management. In fact, whatever the value under current management, *the company will be worth 50% more under the management of Company A than under Company T*.

The board of directors of Company A has asked you to determine the price they should offer for Company T's shares. This offer must be made *now*, *before* the outcome of the drilling project is known. . . . *Thus, you (Company A) will not know the results of the exploration project when submitting your offer, but Company T will know the results when deciding whether or not to accept your offer. In addition, Company T is expected to accept any offer by Company A that is greater than or equal to the (per share) value of the company under its own management.*

As the representative of Company A, you are deliberating over price offers in the range $0/share to $150/share. What offer per share would you tender?

[Source: Samuelson and Bazerman, 1985]

A typical subject's analysis of this problem is as follows. The expected value of the firm to the current owner is $50. It is worth 50 percent more to me. Therefore, I should bid something in the interval between $50 and $75. Nearly all subjects (114 out of 123) made positive bids, mostly in the $50–$75 range. Nevertheless, it is fairly straightforward to show that the optimal bid in this problem is zero. The key to the correct analysis is that there is asymmetric information. Since the owner knows the firm's true value, she will sell only if you bid more than that amount. Thus if you bid, say, $60, she will accept only if the value to her is less than $60. The expected value of the firm to her, contingent on her acceptance of your bid, is therefore just $30, or only $45 to you. So a bid of $60 has a negative expected profit, as does any positive bid.

As the results of Samuelson and Bazerman's experiment demonstrated, the above analysis is far from transparent (Daniel Kahneman and I replicated their results with a group of faculty and doctoral students: 20 of 24 subjects made positive bids, and two of those who bid zero later admitted that they did the right thing only out of cowardice). To get the right answer requires appreciating the role of asymmetric information, a subtle point. Now suppose a firm was being sold under the conditions specified in the problem. What should we predict will be the winning bid? The standard economic prediction of the winning bid would be $0. Since optimal behavior requires only zero bids, that is what the theory must predict. Notice that the theory implicitly assumes that the problem is transparent *to every potential bidder*. If even one person fails to get the analysis right, then the winning bid will be positive.

The characterization of the relevant economic theory for this problem is not simply hypothetical. Samuelson and Bazerman's problem corresponds exactly to George Akerlof's (1970) classic model of the market for lemons in which there is no equilibrium at a positive price. Again, his analysis depends on the implicit assumption that all potential used car buyers understand the implications of the asymmetry in information. If some potential buyers do not appreciate the lemons problem, then there is a positive equilibrium price. There is a paradox here. Akerlof's analysis assumes that an idea that had not been previously understood by other economists is nevertheless transparent to all the participants in his model.

The obvious question to resolve is how best to try to describe the behavior of economic agents in complex environments. Perhaps in the market for used cars a healthy dose of skepticism on the part of buyers will lead them to behave as if they understood the subtleties of asymmetric information. Whether this happens is an empirical question. In the absence of empirical evidence it might be sensible to extend Akerlof's analysis by investigating the operation of models with both asymmetric information and limited rationality.

CONCLUSION

Most economists believe that their subject is the strongest of the social sciences because it has a theoretical foundation, making it closer to the acknowledged king of sciences, physics. The theory, they believe, is a tool which gives them an inherent advantage in explaining human behavior compared with their weaker social science cousins. While the power of economic theory is surely unsurpassed in social science, I believe that in some cases this tool becomes a handicap, weighting economists down rather than giving them an edge. The tool becomes a handicap when economists restrict their investigations to those explanations consistent with the paradigm, to the exclusion of simpler and more reasonable hypotheses. For example, in commenting on the size effect anomaly in financial markets (small firms appear to earn excess returns, most of which occur the first week in January), an editor of the *Journal of Financial Economics* commented: "To successfully explain the 'size effect,' new theory must be developed that is consistent with rational maximizing behavior on the part of *all* actors in the model" (Schwert, 1983, p. 10, emphasis added). Isn't it possible that the explanation for the excess return to small firms in January is based, at least in part, on some of the agents behaving less than fully rationally

Many economists continue to assume rationality because they think they have no alternative. Robert Lucas has said this explicitly.

> The attempt to discover a competitive equilibrium account of the business cycle may appear merely eccentric, or at best, an aesthetically motivated theoretical exercise. On the contrary, it is in fact motivated entirely by practical considerations. The problem of quantitatively assessing hypothetical countercyclical policies (say, a monetary growth rule or a fiscal stabilizer) involves imagining how agents will behave in a situation which has never been observed. To do this successfully, one must have some understanding of the way agents' decisions have been made in the past *and* some method of determining how these decisions would be altered by the hypothetical change in policy. In so far as our descriptions of past behavior rely on arbitrary mechanical rules of thumb, adjustment rules, illusions, and unspecified institutional barriers, this task will be made difficult, or impossible. Who knows how "illusions" will be affected by an investment tax credit? (Lucas, 1981, p. 180)

Two comments on this quotation seem in order. First, there is no guarantee that the models based solely on rational behavior are correct. This is an empirical question to be addressed by macroeconomists. Certainly not everyone shares Lucas's explanation for apparent involuntary unemployment. Second, while the task of incorporating less than fully rational agents into economic models may be difficult, as Lucas states, the research summarized in this paper suggests that the task of producing a theory of systematic error is not impossible.

REFERENCES

Akerlof, George A. "The Market for 'Lemons': Quality Uncertainty and the Market Mechanism." *Quarterly Journal of Economics* 84 (August 1970): 488–500.

Alchian, Armen A. "Uncertainty, Evolution and Economic Theory." *Journal of Political Economy* 58 (June 1950): 211–221.

Allais, Maurice. "Le comportement de l'homme rationnel devant le risque: Critique des postulats et axiomes de l'ecole Américaine." *Econometrica* 21 (October 1953): 503–546.

Arkes, Hal R., and Catherine Blumer. "The Psychology of Sunk Cost." *Organizational Behavior and Human Decision Processes* 35 (1985): 124–140.

Arrow, Kenneth J. "Risk Perception in Psychology and Economics." *Economic Inquiry* 20 (January 1982): 1–9.

Barro, Robert, and Stanley Fisher. "Recent Developments in Monetary Theory." *Journal of Monetary Economics* (1976): 133–176.

Chew, Soo Hong. "A Generalization of the Quasilinear Mean with Applications to the Measurement of Income Inequality and Decision Theory Resolving the Allais Parodox." *Econometrica* 51 (July 1983): 1065–1092.

Coursey, Donald L.; John J. Hovis; and William D. Schulze. "On the Supposed Disparity Between Willingness to Accept and Willingness to Pay Measures of Value." Forthcoming, *Quarterly Journal of Economics*.

De Bondt, Werner F. M., and Richard Thaler. "Does the Stock Market Overreact?" *Journal of Finance* 60 (July 1985): 793–805.

Dreman, David. *The New Contrarian Investment Strategy*. New York: Random House, 1982.

Einhorn, Hillel J., and Robin M. Hogarth. "Confidence in Judgment: Persistence of the Illusion of Validity." *Psychological Review* 85 (September 1978): 395–416.

———. "Ambiguity and Uncertainty in Probabilistic Inference." *Psychological Review* 92 (October 1985): 433–461.

Ellsberg, Daniel. "Risk, Ambiguity and the Savage Axioms." *Quarterly Journal of Economics* 75 (November 1961): 643–669.

Fischhoff, Baruch. "Hindsight and Foresight: The Effect of Outcome Knowledge on Judgment Under Uncertainty." *Journal of Experimental Psychology: Human Perception and Performance* 1 (1975): 288–299.

Fishburn, Peter C. "Transitive Measurable Utility." *Journal of Economic Theory* 31 (December 1983): 293–317.

Friedman, Milton. "The Methodology of Positive Economics." In Milton Friedman, *Essays in Positive Economics*. Chicago: University of Chicago Press, 1953.

Gottfries, Nils, and Keith Hylton. "Are MIT Students Rational." Unpublished, March 1983.

Grether, David M. "Bayes Rule as a Descriptive Model: The Representativeness Heuristic." *Quarterly Journal of Economics* 95 (November 1980): 537–557.

Grether, David M., and Charles R. Plott. "Economic Theory of Choice and the Preference Reversal Phenomenon." *American Economic Review* 69 (September 1979): 623–638.

Haltiwanger, John, and Michael Waldman. "Rational Expectations and the Limits of Rationality: An Analysis of Heterogeneity." *American Economic Review* 75 (June 1985): 326–340.

Kahneman, Daniel, Jack Knetsch, and Richard Thaler. "Fairness and the Assumptions of Economics." *Journal of Business* (October 1986).

———. "Fairness as a Constraint of Profit Seeking: Entitlements in the Market." Unpublished, 1986.

Kahneman, Daniel, and Amos Tversky. "Subjective Probability: A Judgment of Representativeness." *Cognitive Psychology* 3 (1972): 430–454.

———. "On the Psychology of Prediction." *Psychological Review* 80 (1973): 237–251.

———. "Prospect Theory: An Analysis of Decision Under Risk." *Econometrica* 47 (March 1979): 263–291.

———. "Choices, Values and Frames." *American Psychologist* 39 (April 1984): 341–350.

Knetsch, Jack L., and John A. Sinden. "Willingness to Pay and Compensation Demanded: Experimental Evidence of an Unexpected Disparity in Measures of Value." *Quarterly Journal of Economics* 99 (August 1984): 507–521.

Laughhunn, D. J., and John W. Payne. "The Impact of Sunk Outcomes on Risky Choice Behavior." *INFOR (Canadian Journal of Operations Research and Information Processing)* 22 (1984): 151–181.

Lichtenstein, Sarah, and Paul Slovic. "Reversals of Preference Between Bids and Choices in Gambling Decisions." *Journal of Experimental Psychology* 89 (January 1971): 46–55.

———. "Response-Induced Reversals of Preference in Gambling: An Extended Replication in Las Vegas." *Journal of Experimental Psychology* 101 (November 1973): 16–20.

Lichtenstein, Sarah; Baruch Fischhoff; and Lawrence D. Phillips. "Calibration of Probabilities: The State of the Art." In H. Jungerman and G. deZeeuw, eds. *Decision Making and Change in Human Affairs*. Amsterdam: D. Reidel, 1977.

Lucas, Robert E. *Studies in Business-Cycle Theory* Cambridge, MA: MIT Press, 1981.

Luce, R. Duncan, and David H. Krantz. "Conditional Expected Utility." *Econometrica* 39 (March 1971): 253–271.

Machina, Mark J. " 'Expected Utility' Analysis Without the Independence Axiom." *Econometrica* 50 (March 1982): 277–323.

McNeil, Barbara J.; Stephen G. Pauker; Harold C. Sox; and Amos Tversky. "On the Elicitation of Preferences for Alternative Therapies." *New England Journal of Medicine* 306 (May 27, 1982): 1259–1262.

Muth, John F. "Rational Expectations and the Theory of Price Movements." *Econometrica* 29 (1961): 315–335.

Plott, Charles, and Shyam Sunder. "Rational Expectations and the Aggregation of Diverse Information in Laboratory Security Markets." California Institute of Technology, Department of Social Sciences, Working Paper No. 934, 1983.

———. "Efficiency of Experimental Security Markets with Insider Information: An Application of Rational Expectation Models." *Journal of Political Economy* 90 (August 1982): 663–698.

Pommerehne, Werner W.; Friedrich Schneider; and Peter Zweifel. "Economic Theory of Choice and the Preference Reversal Phenomenon: A Reexamination." *American Economic Review* 72 (June 1982): 569–574.

Reilly, Robert J. "Preference Reversal: Further Evidence and Some Suggested Modifications in Experimental Design." *American Economic Review* 72 (June 1982): 576–584.

Russell, Thomas, and Richard H. Thaler. "The Relevance of Quasi Rationality in Competitive Markets." *American Economic Review* 75 (December 1985): 1071–1082.

Samuelson, William F., and Max H. Bazerman. "The Winner's Curse in Bilateral Negotiations." In Vernon L. Smith, ed. *Research in Experimental Economics*, Vol. 3. Greenwich, CT: JAI Press, 1985, pp 105–137.

Savage, Leonard J. *The Foundations of Statistics*. New York: Wiley, 1954.

Schwert, George W. "Size and Stock Returns, and Other Empirical Regularities." *Journal of Financial Economics* 12 (July 1983): 3–12.

Sheffrin, Steven M. *Rational Expectations*. New York: Cambridge University Press, 1983.

Shiller, Robert J. "Do Stock Prices Move Too Much to be Justified by Subsequent Changes in Dividends." *American Economic Review* 71 (June 1981): 421–436.

Simon, Herbert A. "A Behavioral Model of Rational Choice." *Quarterly Journal of Economics* 69 (February 1955): 99–118.

Slovic, Paul; Baruch Fischhoff; and Sarah Lichtenstein. "Rating the Risks." *Environment* 21 (1979): 14–20, 36–39.

Slovic, Paul, and Sarah Lichtenstein. "Preference Reversals: A Broader Perspective." *American Economic Review* 73 (September 1983): 596–605.

Staw, Barry M. "Knee-deep in the Big Muddy: A Study of Escalating Commitment to a Chosen Course of Action." *Organizational Behavior and Human Performance* 16 (1976): 27–44.

Teger, A. I. *Too Much Invested to Quit*. New York: Pergamon, 1980.

Thaler, Richard H. "Toward a Positive Theory of Consumer Choice." *Journal of Economic Behavior and Organization* 1 (March 1980): 39–60.

———. "Mental Accounting and Consumer Choice." *Marketing Science* 4 (Summer 1985): 199–214.

Thaler, Richard, and Eric Johnson. "Hedonic Framing and the Break-Even Effect." Cornell University, Johnson Graduate School of Management Working Paper, 1986.

Tversky, Amos, and Daniel Kahneman. "Availability: A Heuristic for Judging Frequency and Probability." *Cognitive Psychology* 5 (1973): 207–232.

———. "The Framing of Decisions and the Psychology of Choice." *Science* 211 (January 30, 1981): 453–458.

———. "Extensional Versus Intuitive Reasoning: The Conjunction Fallacy in Probability Judgment." *Psychological Review* 90 (October 1983): 293–315.

———. "Rational Choice and the Framing of Decisions." *Journal of Business* (October 1986), Forthcoming.

von Neumann, John, and Oskar Morgenstern. *Theory of Games and Economic Behavior*. Princeton, NJ: Princeton University Press, 1947.

Winter, Sidney G., Jr. "Economic 'Natural Selection' and the Theory of the Firm." *Yale Economic Essays* 4 (Spring 1964): 225–272.

8

EXPERIMENTAL TESTS OF THE ENDOWMENT EFFECT AND THE COASE THEOREM

Daniel Kahneman, Jack L. Knetsch, and Richard H. Thaler

1. INTRODUCTION

The standard assumptions of economic theory imply that when income effects are small differences between an individual's maximum willingness to pay for a good (WTP) and minimum compensation demanded for the same entitlement (willingness to accept or WTA) should be negligible (Willig, 1976). Thus, indifference curves are drawn without reference to current endowments; any difference between equivalent and compensating variation assessments of welfare changes are in practice ignored[1]; and there is wide acceptance of the Coase theorem assertion that, subject to income effects, the allocation of resources will be independent of the assignment of property rights when costless trades are possible.

The assumption that entitlements do not affect value contrasts sharply with empirical observations of significantly higher selling than buying prices. For example, Thaler (1980) found that the minimal compensation demanded for accepting a .001 risk of sudden death was higher by one or two orders of magnitude than the amount people were willing to pay to eliminate an identical existing risk. Other examples of similar reported findings are summarized in Table 1. The disparities observed in these examples are clearly too large to be explained plausibly by income effects.

Reprinted with permission from *Journal of Political Economy* 98, 6 (1990): 1325–1348.

[1] For example, the conventional prescription for assessing environmental and other losses is that, "practically speaking, it does not appear to make much difference which definition is accepted" (Freeman, 1979, p. 3).

167

Several factors probably contribute to the discrepancies between the evaluations of buyers and sellers which are documented in Table 1. The perceived illegitimacy of the transaction may, for example, contribute to the extraordinary high demand for personal compensation for agreeing to the loss of a public good (e.g., Rowe et al., 1980). Standard bargaining habits may also contribute to a discrepancy between the stated reservation prices of buyers and sellers. Sellers are often rewarded for overstating their true value, and buyers for understating theirs (Knez, Smith, and Williams, 1985). By force of habit

TABLE 1 Summary of Past Tests of Evaluation Disparity

	Means			Medians		
Study and Entitlement	WTP	WTA	Ratio	WTP	WTA	Ratio
HYPOTHETICAL SURVEYS						
Hammack and Brown (1974)						
Marshes	$247	$1,044	4.2	NA	NA	NA
Sinclair (1976)						
Fishing	NA	NA	NA	35	100	2.9
Banford et al. (1979)						
Fishing Pier	43	120	2.8	47	129	2.7
Postal service	22	93	4.2	22	106	4.8
Bishop and Heberlein (1979)						
Goose-hunting permits	21	101	4.8	NA	NA	NA
Rowe et al. (1980)						
Visibility	1.33	3.49	2.6	NA	NA	NA
Brookshire et al. (1980)						
Elk hunting[a]	54	143	2.6	NA	NA	NA
Heberlein and Bishop (1985)						
Deer hunting	31	513	16.5	NA	NA	NA
REAL EXCHANGE EXPERIMENTS						
Knetsch and Sinden (1984)						
Lottery tickets	1.28	5.18	4.0	NA	NA	NA
Heberlein and Bishop (1985)						
Deer hunting	25	172	6.9	NA	NA	NA
Coursey et al. (1987)						
Taste SOA[b]	3.45	4.71	1.4	1.33	3.49	2.6
Brookshire and Coursey (1987)						
Park trees[b,c]	10.12	56.60	5.6	6.30	12.96	2.1

[a] Middle level change of several used in study.
[b] Final values after multiple iterations.
[c] Average of two levels of tree plantings.

they misrepresent their true valuations even when such misrepresentation confers no advantage, as in answering hypothetical questions or one-shot or single transactions. In such situations the buying-selling discrepancy is simply a strategic mistake, which experienced traders will learn to avoid (Coursey, Hovis, and Schultz, 1987; Brookshire and Coursey, 1987).

The hypothesis of interest here is that many discrepancies between WTA and WTP, far from being a mistake, reflect a genuine effect of reference positions on preferences. Thaler (1980) labeled the increased value of a good to an individual when the good becomes part of the individual's endowment the *endowment effect*. This effect is a manifestation of *loss aversion*, the generalization that losses are weighted substantially more than objectively commensurate gains in the evaluation of prospects and trades (Kahneman and Tversky, 1979; Tversky and Kahneman, 1989). An implication of this asymmetry is that if a good is evaluated as a loss when it is given up, and as a gain when it is acquired, loss aversion will, on average, induce a higher dollar value for owners than for potential buyers, reducing the set of mutually acceptable trades.

There are some cases when no endowment effect would be expected, such as when goods are purchased primarily for resale rather than for utilization. A particularly clear case of a good held exclusively for resale is the notional token typically traded in experimental markets commonly used to test the efficiency of market institutions (Smith, 1982; Plott, 1982). Such experiments employ the *induced value technique* in which the objects of trade are tokens to which private redemption values that vary among individual participants have been assigned by the experimenter (Smith, 1976). Subjects can obtain the prescribed value assigned for the tokens when redeeming them at the end of the trading period; the tokens are otherwise worthless.

No endowment effect would be expected for such tokens as they have a value to the participants that is exactly prescribed by the experimenter, and traders are unlikely to place any value on the tokens themselves. Thus, buyers and sellers should both value tokens at the induced value that they have been given. Making use of this equality, markets using induced value tokens can be used as control experiments to determine whether evaluation disparities observed in markets for real goods could be attributable to transactions costs, misunderstandings, or the use of bargaining strategies. Any discrepancy between the buying and selling values can be isolated in an experiment by comparing the outcomes of markets for real goods with those of otherwise identical markets for induced value tokens. If no differences in values are observed for the induced value tokens, then economic theory predicts that no differences between buying and selling values will be observed for consumption goods evaluated and traded under the same conditions.

The results from a series of experiments involving real exchanges of tokens and of various consumption goods are reported in this paper. In each case, a random allocation design was used to test for the presence of an endowment effect. Half of the subjects were endowed with a good and became potential sellers in each market; the other half of the subjects were potential buyers. Conventional economic analysis yields the simple prediction that one half of the goods should be traded in voluntary exchanges. If value is unaffected by ownership, then the distribution of values in the two groups should be the same except for sampling variation. The supply and demand curves should therefore be mirror images of each other, intersecting at their common median. The null hypothesis is, therefore, that half of the goods provided should change hands. Label this predicted volume V*. If there is an endowment effect, the value of the good will be higher for sellers than for buyers, and observed volume V will be less than V*. The ratio V/V* provides a unit-free measure of the undertrading that is produced by the effect of ownership on value. To test the hypothesis that market experience eliminates undertrading, the markets were repeated several times.

A test for the possibility that observed undertrading was due to transaction costs was provided by a comparison of the results from a series of induced value markets with those from the subsequent goods markets carried out with identical trading rules. Notice that this comparison can also be used to eliminate numerous other possible explanations for the observed undertrading. For example, if the instructions to the subjects are confusing or misleading, the effects should show up in both the induced value markets and the experimental markets for real goods. Section 2 describes studies of trading volume in induced value markets and in consumption goods markets. Section 3 provides a further test for strategic behavior, and demonstrates that the disparity findings are not likely due to this cause. Section 4 investigates the extent to which the undertrading of goods is produced by reluctance to buy and reluctance to sell. Section 5 examines undertrading in bilateral negotiations and provides a test of the Coase Theorem. Section 6 describes an experiment that rules out income effects and a trophy effect as explanations of the observed valuation disparity. Implications of the observed effects are discussed in Section 7.

2. REPEATED MARKET EXPERIMENTS

In Experiment 1, 44 students in an advanced undergraduate Law and Economics class at Cornell University received a packet of general instructions plus 11 forms, one for each of the markets that were conducted in the experiment. The first three markets were for induced value tokens. Sellers received the following instructions (with differences for buyers in brackets):

> In this market the objects being traded are tokens. You are an owner, so you now own a token [You are a buyer, so you have an opportunity to buy a token] which

has a value to you of $x. It has this value to you because the experimenter will give you this much money for it. The value of the token is different for different individuals. A price for the tokens will be determined later. For each of the prices listed below, please indicate whether you prefer to: (1) Sell your token at this price, and receive the market price. [Buy a token at this price and cash it in for the sum of money indicated above.] (2) Keep your token and cash it in for the sum of money indicated above. [Not buy a token at this price.] For each price indicate your decision by marking an X in the appropriate column.

Part of the response form for sellers follows:
  At a price of $8.75 I will sell _____   I will not sell _____
  At a price of $8.25 I will sell _____   I will not sell _____

The same rectangular distribution of values—ranging from $0.25 to $8.75 in steps of 50 cents—was prepared for both buyers and sellers. Because not all the forms were actually distributed, however, the induced supply and demand curves were not always precisely symmetrical. Subjects alternated between the buyer and seller role in the three successive markets, and were assigned a different individual redemption value in each trial.

Experimenters collected the forms from all participants after each market period, and immediately calculated and announced the market-clearing price,[2] the number of trades, and whether or not there was excess demand or supply at the market-clearing price.[3] Three buyers and three sellers were selected at random after each of the induced markets and were paid off according to the preferences stated on their forms and the market-clearing price for that period.

Immediately after the three induced value markets, subjects on alternating seats were given Cornell coffee mugs, which sell for $6.00 each at the bookstore. The experimenter asked all participants to examine a mug, either their own or their neighbor's. The experimenter then informed the subjects that four markets for mugs would be conducted using the same procedures as the prior induced markets with two exceptions: (1) One of the four market trials would subsequently be selected at random and only the trades in this trial would be executed, and (2) In the binding market trial, *all* subjects' actions would be implemented, rather than just the three buyers and sellers in the

---

[2] The instructions stated "*It is in your best interest to answer these questions truthfully.* For any question, treat the price as fixed. (In economics jargon, you should act as 'price takers'.)" All the subjects were junior and senior economics majors so they were familiar with the terms used. If subjects asked how the market prices were determined they were told, truthfully, that the market price was the point at which the elicited supply and demand curves intersected. The uniformity of the results across many different experiments suggests that this information had no discernible effect on behavior. Furthermore, the responses of the subjects in the induced value portion of the experiments indicate that nearly all understood and accepted their role as price takers. See also Experiment 5 in which a random price procedure was used.
[3] When this occurred, a random draw determined which buyers and sellers were accommodated.

induced value markets.[4] The initial assignment of buyer and seller roles was maintained for all four trading periods. The clearing price and the number of trades were announced after each period. The market that "counted" was indicated after the fourth period, and transactions were executed immediately—all sellers who had indicated that they would give up their mug for sums at the market-clearing price exchanged their mugs for cash, and successful buyers paid this same price and received their mug. This design was used to permit learning to take place over successive trials and yet make each trial potentially binding. The same procedure was then followed for four more successive markets using boxed ball-point pens with a visible bookstore price tag of $3.98, which were distributed to the subjects who had been buyers in the mug markets.

For each goods market subjects completed a form similar to that used for the induced value tokens, with the following instructions:

> You now own the object in your possession. [You do not own the object that you see in the possession of some of your neighbors.] You have the option of selling it [buying one] if a price, which will be determined later, is acceptable to you. For each of the possible prices below indicate whether you wish to: (1) Sell your object and receive this price (pay this price and receive an object to take home with you), or (2) Keep your object and take it home with you [not buy an object at this price]. For each price indicate your decision by marking an X in the appropriate column.

The buyers and sellers in the consumption goods markets faced the same incentives as they had experienced in the induced value markets. Buyers maximized their potential gain by agreeing to buy at all prices below the value they ascribed to the good, and sellers maximized their welfare by agreeing to sell at all prices above the good's worth to them. As in the induced value markets, it was in the best interest of the participants to act as price takers.

As shown in Table 2, the markets for induced value tokens and consumption goods yielded sharply different results. In the induced value markets, as expected, the median buying and selling prices were identical. The ratio of actual to predicted volume (V/V*) was 1.0, aggregating over the three periods. In contrast, median selling prices in the mug and pen markets were more than twice median buying prices, and the V/V* ratio was only .20 for mugs and .41 for pens. Observed volume did not increase over successive periods in either the mug or pen markets, providing no indication that subjects learned to adopt equal buying and selling prices.

---

[4]The experimental design was intended to give the markets for consumption goods every possible chance to be efficient. While in the induced value markets not everyone was paid, in the consumption goods markets everyone was paid. Also, the consumption goods markets were conducted after the induced value markets, and were repeated 4 times each, to allow the subjects the maximum opportunity for learning.

The results of the first and last markets for coffee mugs are also displayed in Figure 1. There are four features to notice in this figure.

1. Both buyers and sellers display a wide range of values, indicating that in the absence of an endowment effect there would be enough rents to produce gains from trade. Indeed the range of values is similar to that used in the induced value markets which had near perfect market efficiency.
2. The payment of a small commission for trading, such as $0.25 per trade, would not significantly alter the results.
3. The mugs were desirable. Every subject assigned a positive value to the mug, and the lowest value assigned by a seller was $2.25.
4. Neither the demand or supply curve changes very much between the first and last market.

Experiment 2 was conducted in an undergraduate microeconomics class at Cornell ($N = 38$). The procedure was identical to that of Experiment 1, except that the second consumption good was a pair of folding binoculars in a cardboard frame, available at the bookstore for $4. The results are reported in Table 3.

TABLE 2 Results of Experiment 1

| | | Induced Value Markets | | |
Trial	Actual Trades	Expected Trades	Price	Expected Price
1.	12	11	$3.75	3.75
2.	11	11	4.75	4.75
3.	10	11	4.25	4.25

Trial	Trades	Price	Median Buyer Reservation Price	Median Seller Reservation Price
MUGS (EXPECTED TRADES = 11)				
4.	4	$4.25	2.75	5.25
5.	1	4.75	2.25	5.25
6.	2	4.50	2.25	5.25
7.	2	4.25	2.25	5.25
PENS (EXPECTED TRADES = 11)				
8.	4	1.25	.75	2.50
9.	5	1.25	.75	1.75
10.	4	1.25	.75	2.25
11.	5	1.25	.75	1.75

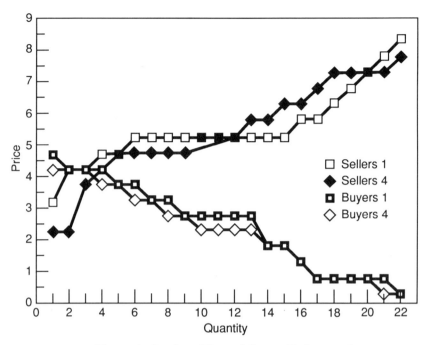

Figure 1. *Supply and Demand Curves, Markets 1 and 4*

TABLE 3 **Results of Experiment 2**

| | | Induced Value Markets | | |
Trial	Actual Trades	Expected Trades	Price	Expected Price
1.	10	10	$3.75	$4.25
2.	9	10	4.75	4.25
3.	7	8	4.25	4.75

Trial	Trades	Price	Median Buyer Reservation Price	Median Seller Reservation Price
MUGS (EXPECTED TRADES = 9.5)				
4.	3	$3.75	$1.75	$4.75
5.	3	3.25	2.25	4.75
6.	2	3.25	2.25	4.75
7.	2	3.25	2.25	4.25
BINOCULARS (EXPECTED TRADES = 9.5)				
8.	4	$1.25	$ .75	$1.25
9.	4	.75	.75	1.25
10.	3	.75	.75	1.75
11.	3	.75	.75	1.75

In Experiments 3 and 4, conducted in Simon Fraser University undergraduate economics classes, the subjects were asked to provide minimum selling prices or maximum buying prices rather than answer the series of "yes or no" questions used in Experiments 1 and 2. The induced value markets were done with no monetary payoffs, and were followed by four markets for pens in Experiment 3 and five markets for mugs in Experiment 4. In Experiment 3 subjects were told that the first three markets for pens would be for practice, so only the fourth and final market would be binding. In Experiment 4, one of the five markets was selected at random to count, as in Experiments 1 and 2. Other procedures were unchanged. The results are shown in Table 4.

Experiments 2–4 all yielded results similar to those obtained in Experiment 1. Summing over the induced value markets in all four experiments, the V/V* index was .91. This excellent performance was achieved without participants having the benefit of experience with the trading rules, with limited monetary incentives in Experiments 1 and 2, and with no monetary incentives in Experiments 3 and 4. In the markets for consumption goods, with all participants facing monetary incentives and having gained experience with the market rules from the induced value markets, V/V* averaged .31, and median selling prices were more than double the corresponding buying prices. Trading procedures were precisely identical in markets for goods and for induced value tokens. The high volume of trade in money tokens therefore eliminates transaction costs (or any other feature that was present in both types of markets) as an explanation of the observed undertrading of consumption goods.

TABLE 4 Results of Experiments 3 and 4

Trial	N	Object	Actual Trades	Expected Trades	Ratio of Seller MV to Buyer MV
EXPERIMENT 3					
1	26	Induced	5	6.5	NA
2	26	Pen	2	6.5	6.0
3	26	Pen	2	6.5	6.0
4	26	Pen	2	6.5	5.0
5	26	Pen	1	6.5	5.0
EXPERIMENT 4					
1	74	Induced	15	18.5	NA
2	74	Induced	16	18.5	NA
3	74	Mug	6	18.5	3.8
4	74	Mug	4	18.5	2.8
5	72	Mug	4	18	2.2
6	73	Mug	8	18	1.8
7	74	Mug	8	18.5	1.8

It should be noted that subjects in the position of buyers were not given money to use for purchases, but rather had to make transactions using their own money. (Subjects were told to bring money to class, and that credit and change would be available if necessary. Some subjects borrowed from friends to make payments.) The aim was to study transactions in a realistic setting. While the present design makes potential sellers slightly wealthier, at least in the first market, the magnitude of the possible income effect is trivial. In one of the markets the equilibrium price was only 75 cents, and the prices in other markets were never above a few dollars. Also, as shown in Experiments 7, 8, and 9 below, equal undertrading was found in designs that completely eliminated the possibility of an income effect or cash constraint.

As shown in Tables 2–4, subjects showed almost no undertrading even on their first trial in an induced value market. Evidently neither bargaining habits nor any transaction costs impede trading in money tokens. On the other hand, there is no indication that participants in the markets for goods learned to make valuations independent of their entitlements. The discrepant evaluations of buyers and sellers remained stable over four, and in one case five, successive markets for the same good, and did not change systematically over repeated markets for successive goods.

A difference in procedure probably explains the apparent conflict between these results and the conclusion reached in some other studies, that the WTA-WTP discrepancy is greatly reduced by market experience. The studies that reported a disciplinary effect of market experience assessed this effect by comparing the responses of buyers and sellers in preliminary hypothetical questions or nonbinding market trials to their behavior in a subsequent binding trial with real monetary payoffs (Knez et al., 1985; Coursey et al., 1987; Brookshire and Coursey, 1987). In the present experiments, the markets for consumption goods were real and potentially binding from the first trial, and the WTA-WTP discrepancy was found to be stable over a series of such binding trials.

It should be stressed that previous research did not actually demonstrate that the discrepancy between buyers and sellers is eliminated in markets. Although the discrepancy between the final selling and buying prices in the SOA experiment of Coursey et al. (1987) was not statistically significant, the ratio of median prices of sellers and buyers was still 2.6.[5] If the buyers and sellers had been allowed to trade according to their final bids, a total of 9 advantageous exchanges would have occurred between the two groups, compared to the theoretical expectation of 16 trades (for details see Knetsch and Sinden, 1987). This V/V* ratio of .56 is quite similar to the ratios observed

---

[5]The ratio of the mean selling and buying prices is 1.4 if all subjects are included. However, if one buyer and one seller with extreme valuations are excluded the ratio is 1.9. These numbers were reported in an earlier version of Coursey et al. (1987).

in Experiments 1 through 4. In the study by Brookshire and Coursey (1987), the ratio of mean prices was indeed reduced by experience, from a high of 77 for initial hypothetical survey responses, to 6.1 in the first potentially binding auction conducted in a laboratory. However, the ratio remained at 5.6 in the final auction.

3. TESTING FOR MISREPRESENTATION

As previously stated, subjects faced identical incentives in the induced value and consumption goods phases of Experiments 1–4. Therefore, it seems safe to attribute the difference in observed trading to the endowment effect. However, some readers of earlier drafts of this paper have suggested that because of the way market prices were determined, subjects might have felt they had an incentive to misstate their true values in order to influence the price, and perhaps this incentive was perceived to be greater in the consumption goods markets. To eliminate this possible interpretation of the previous results Experiment 5 was carried out in a manner similar to the first four experiments, except that subjects were told that the price would be selected at random. As is well known, this is an incentive compatible procedure for eliciting values (see Becker, DeGroot, and Marshak, 1964).

Each participant received instructions that read in part (with appropriate alternative wording in the buyers' forms):

> After you have finished, one of the prices listed below will be selected at random and any exchanges will take place at that price. If you have indicated you will sell at this price you will receive this amount of money and will give up the mug; if you have indicated that you will keep the mug at this price then no exchange will be made and you can take the mug home with you.

> Your decision can have no effect on the price actually used because the price will be selected at random.

The experiment was conducted in a series of six tutorial groups of a business statistics class at Simon Fraser University. The use of small groups helped assure complete understanding of the instructions, and the exercises were conducted over the course of a single day to minimize opportunities for communication between participants. Each group was divided equally and half the subjects were designated as sellers by random selection, the other half became buyers. A total of 59 people took part.

Two induced value markets for hypothetical payoffs and a subsequent third real exchange market for money and mugs were conducted with identical trading rules used in all three. All participants maintained the same role as either buyers or sellers for the three markets. As in Experiments 1 and 2, the prices that individuals chose to buy or to sell were selected from possible prices ranging from $0 to $9.50 listed by 50-cent increments.

The results of this experiment were nearly identical to the earlier ones in which the actual exchanges were based on the market-clearing price. Even though possibly less motivating hypothetical values were used in the two induced value markets, nearly all participants pursued a profit maximizing selection of prices to buy or sell the assets. Fourteen exchanges at a price of $4.75 were expected in the first induced value market on the basis of the randomly distributed values written on the forms. Thirteen trades at this price were indicated by the prices actually selected by the participants. The results of the second hypothetical induced value market were equally convincing with 16 of the 17 expected exchanges made at the expected price of $5.75. The procedures and incentives were apparently well understood by the participants.

Mugs comparable to those used in other experiments were distributed to the potential sellers after the induced value markets were completed. A mug was also shown to all of the potential buyers. The following form with instructions, nearly identical to the ones used in the induced value markets, was then distributed (with the alternative wording for buyers in brackets).

You now [do not] have and own a mug which you can keep and take home. You also have the option of selling it and receiving [buying one to take home by paying] money for it.

For each of the possible prices listed below, please indicate whether you wish to:

(1) Receive [pay] that amount of money and sell your [buy a] mug, or

(2) Not sell your [buy a] mug at this price.

After you have finished, one of the prices listed below will be selected at random and any exchanges will take place at that price. If you have indicated you will sell [buy] at this price you will receive this amount of money [a mug] and will give up the mug [pay this amount of money]; if you have indicated that you will keep the [not buy a] mug at this price then no exchange will be made and you can take the mug home with you [do not pay anything].

Notice the following two things: (1) Your decision can have no effect on the price actually used because the price will be selected at random. (2) It is in your interest to indicate your true preferences at each of the possible prices listed below.

For each price indicate your decision by marking an X in the appropriate column.

	I Will Sell [Buy]	I Will Keep [Not Buy] the Mug
If the price is $0	————	————
If the price is $0.50	————	————
....		
If the price is $9.50	————	————

After the instructions were read, reviewed by the experimenter, and questions answered, participants completed the forms indicating either their lowest selling price or highest buying price. A random price, from among the list from $0 to $9.50, was then drawn and exchanges based on this price were completed.

The results again showed a large and significant endowment effect. Given the 29 potential buyers, 30 potential sellers, and the random distribution of the mugs, 14.5 exchanges would be expected if entitlements did not influence valuations. Instead, only 6 were indicated on the basis of the values actually selected by the potential buyers and sellers ($V/V^* = .41$). The median selling price of $5.75 was over twice the median buying price of $2.25, and the means were $5.78 and $2.21 respectively.

4. RELUCTANCE TO BUY VERSUS RELUCTANCE TO SELL

Exchanges of money and a good (or between two goods) offer the possibilities of four comparisons: a choice between gaining either the good or money; a choice between losing one or the other; buying (giving up money for the good); and selling (giving up the good for money) (Tversky and Kahneman, 1989). The endowment effect results from a difference between the relative preferences for the good and money. The comparison of buying and selling to simple choices between gains permits an analysis of the discrepancy between WTA and WTP into two components: reluctance to sell (exchanging the good for money) and reluctance to buy (exchanging money for the good).

Experiments 6 and 7 were carried out to assess the weight of reluctance to buy and reluctance to sell in undertrading of a good similar to the goods used in the earlier experiments. The subjects in Experiment 6 were 77 Simon Fraser students, randomly assigned to three groups. Members of one group, designated Sellers, were given a coffee mug, and were asked to indicate whether or not they would sell the mug at a series of prices ranging from $0 to $9.25. A group of Buyers indicated whether they were willing to buy a mug at each of these prices. Finally, Choosers were asked to choose, for each of the possible prices, between receiving a mug or cash.

The results again reveal substantial undertrading: While 12.5 trades were expected between Buyers and Sellers, only three trades took place ($V/V^* = 0.24$). The median valuations were: Sellers, $7.12; Choosers, $3.12; and Buyers, $2.87. The close similarity of results for Buyers and Choosers indicates that there was relatively little reluctance to pay for the mug.

Experiment 7 was carried out with 117 students at the University of British Columbia. It used an identical design except that price tags were left on the mugs. The results were fully consistent with those in Experiment 6. Nineteen trades were expected on the basis of valuation equivalence, but only one was concluded on the basis of actual valuations ($V/V^* = .05$). The median valuation of Sellers was $7.00, Choosers $3.50, and Buyers $2.00.

It is worth noting that these results eliminate any form of income effect as an explanation of the discrepant valuations since the wealth positions of the Sellers and Choosers were identical. The allocation of a particular mug to each Seller evidently induced a sense of endowment that the Choosers did not share: the median value of the mug to the Sellers was more than double the value indicated by the Choosers even though their choices were objectively the same. The results imply that the observed undertrading of consumption goods may be largely due to a reluctance to part with entitlements.

5. BILATERAL BARGAINING AND THE COASE THEOREM

According to the Coase Theorem, the allocation of resources to individuals who can bargain and transact at no cost should be independent of initial property rights. However, if the marginal rate of substitution between one good and other is affected by endowment, then the individual who is assigned the property right to a good will be more likely to retain it. A bilateral bargaining experiment (Experiment 8) was carried out to test this implication of the endowment effect.

The subjects were 35 pairs of students in seven small tutorials at Simon Fraser University. The students were enrolled either in a beginning economics course or an English class. Each student was randomly paired with another student in the same tutorial group, with care taken to assure that students entering the tutorial together were not assigned as a pair. A game of Nim, a simple game easily explained, was played by each pair of participants. The winners of the game were each given a 400 gram Swiss chocolate bar and told it was theirs to keep.

An induced value bargaining session was then conducted. The member of each pair who did not win the Nim game, and therefore did not receive the chocolate bar, was given a ticket and an instruction sheet that indicated that the ticket was worth $3 because it could be redeemed for that sum. The ticket owners were also told they could sell the ticket to their partner if mutually agreeable terms could be reached. The partners (the chocolate bar owners) received instructions indicating that they could receive $5 for the ticket if they could successfully buy it from the owner. Thus there was a $2 surplus available to any pair completing a trade.

The pairs were then given an unlimited amount of time to bargain. Subjects were told that both credit and change were available from the experimenter. Results of the bargaining sessions were recorded on their instruction sheets.

Of the 35 pairs of participants, 29 agreed to an exchange ($V/V^* = .83$). The average price paid for the 29 tickets was $4.09, with 12 of the exchange prices being exactly $4. Payments of the redemption values of the tickets were made as soon as the exchanges were completed. These payments were made in single dollar bills to facilitate trading in the subsequent bargaining session. After the ticket exchanges were completed, owners of the chocolate bars were told they could sell them to their partners if a mutually agreeable price could be determined. The procedures used for the tickets were once again applied to these bargaining sessions.

An important effect of the preliminary induced value ticket bargains was to provide the ticket owners with some cash. The average gain to the ticket owners (including the six who did not sell their tickets) was $3.99. The average gain to their partners (the chocolate bar owners) was only $0.76. Thus the potential chocolate bar buyers were endowed with an average of $3.23 more than the owners, creating a small income effect toward the buyers. Also, to the extent that a windfall gain such as this is spent more causally by subjects than other money (for evidence on such a "house money effect," see Thaler and Johnson, forthcoming) trading of chocolate bars should be facilitated.

Results of the chocolate bar bargains once again suggest reluctance to trade. Rather than the 17.5 trades expected from the random allocations, only 7 were observed ($V/V^* = .4$). The average price paid in those exchanges that did occur was $2.69. (The actual prices were: $6.00, 3.10, 3.00, 2.75, 2.00, 1.00, and 1.00.) If the six pairs of subjects who did not successfully complete bargains in the first stage are omitted from the sample on the grounds that they did not understand the task or procedures, then 6 trades are observed where 14.5 would be expected ($V/V^* = .414$). Similarly, if two more pairs are dropped because the prices at which they exchanged tickets was outside the range $3.00–5.00, then the number of trades falls to 4, and V/V^* falls to .296. (No significant differences between the students in the English and economics classes were observed.[6])

To be sure that the chocolate bars were valued by the subjects, and that these valuations would vary enough to yield mutually beneficial trade, the same chocolate bars were distributed to half of the members of another class at Simon Fraser. Those who received chocolate bars were asked the minimum price they would accept to sell their bar, while those without the bars were asked the maximum price they would pay to acquire a bar. The valuations of the bars varied from $0.50 to $8.00. The average values ascribed by sellers was $3.98 while the buyers' average valuation was $1.25. (The median values were $3.50 and $1.25.)

---

[6]We conducted two similar bargaining experiments that yielded comparable results. Twenty-six pairs of subjects negotiated the sale of mugs and then envelopes containing an uncertain amount of money. Buyers had not been given any cash endowment. These sessions yielded 6 and 5 trades respectively, where 13 would be expected. Also, some induced value bilateral negotiation sessions were conducted in which only 50 cents of surplus was available. (The seller's valuation was $1.50 and the buyer's was $2.00.) Nevertheless, 21 of a possible 26 trades were completed.

6. THE ENDOWMENT EFFECT
IN CHOICES BETWEEN GOODS

The previous experiments documented undertrading in exchanges of money and consumption goods. Experiment 9 establishes the same effect in exchanges between two goods.

Participants in three undergraduate classes at the University of Victoria were offered a choice between the same two goods. All students in one class were given a coffee mug at the beginning of the session, as compensation for completing a short questionnaire. After answering the questions, which took less than five minutes, the experimenters showed the students a 400 gram Swiss chocolate bar and told them they could have one in exchange for the mug.[7] Those students wishing to exchange the mug for a chocolate bar wrote the word "Trade" on a card provided, and the experimenters immediately made the exchange. The students in another class were offered an opportunity to make the opposite exchange after first being given the chocolate bar. The students in a third class were simply offered a choice, at the beginning of the session, between a chocolate bar and a mug.

The proportion of students selecting the mug was 89 percent in the class originally endowed with mugs ($N = 76$), 56 percent in the class offered a choice ($N = 55$) and only 10 percent in the class originally endowed with chocolate bars ($N = 87$). For most participants a mug was more valuable than the chocolate when it had to be given up, but less valuable when the chocolate had to be given up. This experiment confirms that undertrading can occur even when income effects are ruled out. It also demonstrates an endowment effect for a good that was distributed to everyone in the class and, therefore, did not have the appeal of a prize or trophy.

7. DISCUSSION

The evidence presented in this paper supports what may be called an instant endowment effect: the value that an individual assigns to such objects as mugs, pens, binoculars, and chocolate bars appears to increase substantially as soon as that individual is given the object.[8] The apparently instantaneous nature of the reference point shift and consequent value change induced by giving a person possession of a good goes beyond previous discussions of the endow-

---

[7]Both goods were familiar to participants; the mugs were priced at $4.95 in the University bookstore, and the candy bars were available from many local shops for $6.

[8]The impression gained from informal pilot experiments is that the act of giving the participant physical possession of the good results in more consistent endowment effect. Assigning subjects a chance to receive a good, or a property right to a good to be received at a later time, seemed to produce weaker effects.

ment effect, which focused on goods that have been in the individual's possession for some time. While long-term endowment effects could be explained by sentimental attachment or by an improved technology of consumption in the Stigler-Becker (1977) sense, the differences in preference or taste demonstrated by the over 700 participants in the experiments reported in this paper cannot be explained in this fashion.

The endowment effect is one explanation for the systematic differences between buying and selling prices that has been observed so often in past work. One of the objectives of this study was to examine an alternative explanation for this buying-selling discrepancy, namely, that it reflects a general bargaining strategy (Knez and Smith, 1987) which would be eliminated by experience in the market (Coursey, Hovis, and Schulze, 1987; Brookshire and Coursey, 1987). Our results do not support this alternative view. The trading institution used in Experiments 1–7 encouraged participants to be price-takers (especially in Experiment 5), and the rules provided no incentive to conceal true preferences. Furthermore, the results of the induced value markets indicate that the subjects understood the demand revealing nature of the questions they were asked, and acted accordingly. Substantial undertrading was nevertheless observed in markets for consumption goods. As for learning and market discipline, there was no indication that buying and selling prices converged over repeated market trials, though full feedback was provided at the end of each trial. The undertrading observed in these experiments appears to reflect a true difference in preferences between the potential buyers and sellers. The recurrence of this result reduces the risk that the outcome is produced by an experimental artifact. In short, the present findings indicate that the endowment effect can persist in genuine market settings.

The contrast between the induced value markets and the consumption goods markets lends support to Heiner's (1985) conjecture that the results of induced value experiments may not generalize to all market settings. The defining characteristic of the induced value markets is that the values of the tokens are set by the experimenter, and are thus more clearly defined than the values of consumption goods. Preferences for consumption goods may exhibit *value ambiguity*, that is, consumers may not be able to assign a unique monetary value to an object. When objects have a well-defined monetary value, loss aversion is irrelevant because transactions are evaluated simply on the basis of net gain or loss. (If someone is offered six dollars for a five dollar bill, there is no sense of loss associated with accepting the trade.) In the presence of value ambiguity, this cancellation of the loss of the object against the dollars received is not possible because the good and money are not strictly commensurate. Of course, some markets may share the key features of the induced value markets, particularly when the conditions of pure arbitrage are approached. When these conditions are not met, then the outcomes may be altered by the existence of value ambiguity and loss aversion.

The results of the experimental demonstrations of the endowment effect have direct implications for economic theory and economic predictions. Contrary to the assumptions of standard economic theory that preferences are independent of entitlements,[9] the evidence presented here indicates that people's preferences depend on their reference positions. Consequently, preference orderings are not defined independently of endowments—good A may be preferred to B when A is part of an original endowment, but the reverse may be true when initial reference positions are changed. Indifference curves will have a kink at the endowment or reference point (see Tversky and Kahneman, 1989); and an indifference curve tracing acceptable trades in one direction may even cross another indifference curve which plots the acceptable exchanges in the opposite direction (Knetsch, 1989).

The existence of endowment effects reduces the gains from trade. In comparison to a world in which preferences are independent of endowment, the existence of loss aversion produces an inertia in the economy because potential traders are more reluctant to trade than is conventionally assumed. This is not to say that Pareto optimal trades will not take place. Rather, there are simply fewer mutually advantageous exchanges possible, and so the volume of trade is lower than it otherwise would be.

To assess the practical significance of the endowment effect it is important to first consider some necessary conditions for the effect to be observed. Experiments 6 and 7 suggest that the endowment effect is primarily a problem for sellers; we observed little reluctance to buy, but much reluctance to sell. Furthermore, not all sellers are afflicted by an endowment effect. The effect did not appear in the markets for money tokens, and there is no reason in general to expect reluctance to resell goods that are held especially for that purpose. An owner will not be reluctant to sell an item at a given price if a perfect substitute is readily available at a lower price. This reasoning suggests that endowment effects will almost certainly occur when owners are faced with an opportunity to sell an item purchased for use, which is not easily replaceable. Examples might include tickets to a sold-out event, hunting licenses in limited supply (Bishop and Heberlein), works of art, or a pleasant view.

While the conditions necessary for an endowment effect to be observed may appear to limit its applicability in economic settings, in fact these conditions are very often satisfied, and especially so in the bargaining contexts to which the Coase theorem is applied. For example, tickets to Wimbledon are allocated by means of a lottery. A standard Coasean analysis would imply that in the presence of an efficient ticket brokerage market, winners of the lottery would

---

[9]Although ownership can affect taste in the manner suggested by Stigler and Becker, in the absence of income effects it is traditional to assume that the indifference curves in Edgeworth Box diagram do not depend on the location of the endowment point.

be no more likely to attend the matches than other tennis fans who had won a similar cash prize in an unrelated lottery. In contrast, the experimental results presented in this paper predict that many winners of Wimbledon tickets will attend the event, turning down opportunities to sell their tickets which exceed their reservation price for buying them.

Endowment effects can also be observed for firms and other organizations. Endowment effects are predicted for property rights acquired by historic accident or fortuitous circumstances, such as government licenses, landing rights, or transferable pollution permits. Owing to endowment effects, firms will be reluctant to divest themselves of divisions, plants, and product lines even though they would never consider buying the same assets; indeed, stock prices often rise when firms do give them up. Again, the prediction is not an absence of trade, just a reduction in the volume of trade.

Isolating the influence of endowment effects from those of transaction costs as causes of low trading volume is, of course, difficult in actual market settings. For instances where transaction costs are low relative to the presumed gains from trade, otherwise inexplicably low trade volumes might then be attributable to endowment effects—and evidence of such outcomes might be found in some markets. This was—by design—the case in the experimental markets, where the efficiency of the induced value markets demonstrated the minimal effect of transaction costs or other impediments on exchange decisions, leaving the great reluctance to trade mugs and other goods to be attributable to endowment effects.

Endowment effects are not limited to cases involving physical goods or to legal entitlements. The reference position of individuals and firms often includes terms of previous transactions or expectations of continuation of present, often informal, arrangements. There is clear evidence of dramatically asymmetric reactions to improvements and deteriorations of these terms and a willingness to make sacrifices to avoid unfair treatment (Kahneman, Knetsch, and Thaler, 1986). The reluctance to sell at a loss, owing to a perceived entitlement to a formerly prevailing price, can explain two observations of apparent undertrading. The first pertains to housing markets. It is often observed that when housing prices fall, volume also falls. When house prices are falling, houses remain on the market for much longer than in periods when prices are rising. Similarly, the volume for stocks that have declined in price is lower than the volume for stocks that have increased in value (Shefin and Statman, 1985; Ferris, Haugen, and Makhija, 1988), although tax considerations would lead to the opposite prediction.

Another manifestation of loss aversion in the context of multiattribute negotiations is what might be termed "concession aversion"—a reluctance to accept a loss on any dimension of an agreement. A straightforward and common instance of this is the downward stickiness of wages. A somewhat more subtle implication of concession aversion is that it can produce inefficient contract terms owing to historic precedents. Old firms may have more inefficient arrangements than new ones, because new companies can negotiate without the reference positions created by prior agreements. Some airlines, for example, are required to carry three pilots on some planes while others— newer ones—operate with two.

Disputes in which both parties are viewed as incurring losses with any concession are likely to be more intractable than those in which one party is seen as incurring much less aversive foregone gains. Court decisions commonly follow such distinctions by according greater protection to "losses" than to "foregone gains," by favoring possessors of goods over other claimants, by limiting recovery of lost profits relative to compensation for actual expenditures, and failing to enforce most gratuitous promises that are coded as foregone gains to the injured party (Cohen and Knetsch, 1989).

To conclude, the evidence reported here offers no support for the contention that observations of loss aversion and the consequential evaluation disparities are artifacts, nor should they be interpreted as mistakes likely to be eliminated by experience, training or "market discipline." Instead, the findings support an alternative view of endowment effects and loss aversion as fundamental characteristics of preferences.

REFERENCES

Financial support was provided by Fisheries and Oceans Canada, the Ontario Ministry of the Environment, and the behavioral economics program of the Alfred P. Sloan Foundation. The authors wish to thank Vernon Smith for encouraging us to conduct these experiments and for providing extensive comments on earlier drafts. Of course, the usual disclaimer applies.

Banford, Nancy, Jack L. Knetsch, and Gary A. Mauser. "Feasibility Judgements and Alternative Measures of Benefits and Costs." *Journal of Business Administration* 11 (1979): 25–35.

Becker, G. M., M. H. DeGroot, and J. Marshak. "Measuring Utility by a Single-Response Sequential Method." *Behavioral Science* 9 (July 1964): 226–32.

Bishop, R. C., and Thomas A. Heberlein. "Measuring Values of Extra-Market Goods: Are Indirect Measures Biased?" *American Journal of Agricultural Economics* 61 (1979): 926–930.

Brookshire, David S., and Don L. Coursey. "Measuring the Value of a Public Good: An Empirical Comparison of Elicitation Procedures." *The American Economic Review* 77 (September 1987): 554–566.

Brookshire, David S., Alan Randall, and John R. Stoll. "Valuing Increments and Decrements in Natural Resource Service Flows." *American Journal of Agricultural Economics* 62 (1980): 478–488.

Cohen, David, and Jack L. Knetsch. "Judicial Choice and Disparities Between Measures of Economic Values." Simon Fraser University Working Paper, 1989.

Coursey, Don L., John J. Hovis, and William D. Schulze. "The Disparity Between Willingness to Accept and Willingness to Pay Measures of Value." *Quarterly Journal of Economics* CII (August 1987): 679–690.

Ferris, Stephen P., Robert A. Haugen, and Anil K. Makhija. "Predicting Contemporary Volume with Historic Volume at Differential Price Levels: Evidence Supporting the Disposition Effect." *Journal of Finance* 43 (1988): 677–697.

Freeman, A. Myrick. *The Benefits of Environmental Improvement.* Baltimore: Johns Hopkins Press, 1979.

Hammack, J., and G. Brown. *Waterfowl and Wetlands: Toward Bioeconomic Analysis.* Baltimore: Johns Hopkins Press, 1974.

Heberlein, Thomas A., and Richard C. Bishop. "Assessing the Validity of Contingent Valuation: Three Field Experiments." Paper presented at the International Conference on Man's Role in Changing the Global Environment, Italy, 1985.

Heiner, Ronald A. "Experimental Economics: Comment." *The American Economic Review* 75 (1985): 260–263.

Kahneman, Daniel, and Amos Tversky. "Prospect Theory: An Analysis of Decision Under Risk." *Econometrica* 47 (1979): 263–291.

Kahneman, Daniel, Jack L. Knetsch, and Richard Thaler. "Fairness as a Constraint on Profit-Seeking: Entitlements in the Market." *The American Economic Review* 76 (September 1986): 728–741.

Knetsch, Jack L. "The Endowment Effect and Evidence of Non-reversible Indifference Curves." *American Economic Review* 79 (December 1989): 1277–1288.

Knetsch, Jack L., and J. A. Sinden. "Willingness to Pay and Compensation Demanded: Experimental Evidence of an Unexpected Disparity in Measures of Value." *Quarterly Journal of Economics* XCIX (August 1984): 507–521.

———. "The Persistence of the Valuation Disparity." *Quarterly Journal of Economics* CII (August 1987): 691–695.

Knez, Marc, and Vernon L. Smith. "Hypothetical Valuations and Preference Reversals in the Context of Asset Trading." In Alvin Roth, ed., *Laboratory Experiments in Economics: Six Points of View.* Cambridge: Cambridge University Press, 1987.

Knez, Peter, Vernon L. Smith, and Arlington W. Williams. "Individual Rationality, Market Rationality, and Value Estimation." *The American Economic Review* 75 (May 1985): 397–402.

Plott, Charles. "Industrial Organization Theory and Experimental Economics." *Journal of Economic Literature* 20 (1982): 1485–1527.

Rowe, Robert D., Ralph C. d'Arge, and David S. Brookshire. "An Experiment on the Economic Value of Visibility." *Journal of Environmental Economics and Management* 8 (1980): 1–19.

Sinclair, William F. *The Economic and Social Impact of Kemano II Hydroelectric Project on British Columbia's Fisheries Resources.* Vancouver: Department of Fisheries and Oceans, 1978.

Smith, Vernon L. "Experimental Economics: Induced Value Theory." *The American Economic Review* 66 (1976): 274–279.

——. "Microeconomic Systems as an Experimental Science." *The American Economic Review* 72 (1982): 923–955.

Stigler, George J., and Gary S. Becker. "De Gustibus Non Est Disputandum." *The American Economic Review* 67 (1977): 76–90.

Thaler, Richard. "Toward a Positive Theory of Consumer Choice." *Journal of Economic Behavior and Organization* 1 (March 1980): 39–60.

Thaler, Richard, and Eric J. Johnson. "Gambling with the House Money and Trying to Break Even: The Effects of Prior Outcomes on Risky Choice." *Management Science*, Forthcoming.

Tversky, Amos, and Daniel Kahneman. "Loss Aversion and Risky Choice." Unpublished Working Paper, Stanford University, 1989.

Willig, R.D. "Consumer's Surplus Without Apology." *The American Economic Review* 66 (1976): 589–597.

9

THE PSYCHOLOGY AND ECONOMICS CONFERENCE HANDBOOK

Richard H. Thaler

1. GUIDE TO DISCUSSANTS

While most of George Stigler's articles have received the attention they deserve, there is one piece that I think has been neglected, though its potential contribution to the knowledge transmitted at a conference like this one is enormous. The article I refer to is titled "The Conference Handbook" (Stigler 1977). In this incisive piece Stigler argues that conferences could be run much more efficiently if discussants could utilize a standard list of comments that could be called out by number, much as in the old story about the prisoners who told their jokes by number. Stigler offers several introductory remarks and 32 specific comments. For example, introductory remark F could be used nicely at an interdisciplinary conference like this one: "It is good to have a nonspecialist looking at our problem. There is always a chance of a fresh viewpoint, although usually, as in this case, the advantages of the division of labor are reaffirmed." The specific comments begin with the classic 1: "Adam Smith said that." Two others that might come in handy at this conference are 23: "The motivation of the agents in this theory is so narrowly egotistic that it cannot possibly explain the behavior of real people"; and 24: "The flabby economic actor in this impressionistic model should be replaced by the utility-maximizing individual" (pp. 442, 443).

While Stigler's comments are insightful and quite versatile, I have found that conferences that combine psychologists and economists present a special set of problems to discussant and attendee alike, and so I am taking this

Reprinted with permission from *Journal of Business* 59, 4, Part 2 (1986): S279–S284. © The University of Chicago Press.

opportunity to provide a customized list of comments that can be used in these situations. The comments I will mention are those that are most frequently offered by economists when discussing the work of psychologists. For the sake of fairness, a subject in which I have recently become interested, I will also offer brief responses.

1. If the stakes are large enough, people will get it right. This comment is usually offered to rebut a demonstration of embarrassing inconsistency on the part of a group of undergraduate students participating in an experiment at one of our leading universities. Many such demonstrations have offered the subjects little or no incentive to think hard or to get the "right" answer, so it is reasonable to ask whether financial incentives might not eliminate less than fully rational answers. This, of course, is an empirical question. Do people tend to make better decisions when the stakes are high? There is little evidence that they do.

Some investigators have tested to see whether the introduction of moderate-sized financial incentives will eliminate irrational behavior. For example, Grether and Plott (1979) replicated Lichtenstein and Slovic's (1971) demonstration of the preference reversal phenomenon with and without financial incentives. They discovered to their surprise that the preference reversals were somewhat stronger when financial incentives were used. Of course, no one has received enough financial support to replicate preference reversal phenomena at very large stakes, but the assertion that systematic mistakes will always disappear if the stakes are large enough should be recognized for what it is—an assertion unsupported by any data.

2. In the real world people will learn to get it right. This comment, as is the first one, is derived from a reasonable concern that many experiments have not offered the subjects much if any opportunity to learn. The validity of the assertion again comes down to an empirical question. Do real world environments facilitate learning? Unfortunately, there is little reason to be optimistic. Accurate learning takes place only when the individual receives timely and organized feedback. As Einhorn and Hogarth (1978) have shown, many repetitive decision-making tasks do not provide this type of learning opportunity. For example, a common, well-documented decision-making failing is overconfidence. Subjects in many contexts have been shown to display this trait. Einhorn and Hogarth have shown that in decision-making tasks in which the decision maker usually succeeds, such as selecting students for admission into a highly selective college with a very attractive applicant pool, experience will tend to increase confidence regardless of the ability of the decision maker to discriminate good from bad applicants. Thus experience does not necessarily lead to learning.

3. In the aggregate, errors will cancel. This remark should be used with caution since the errors that have been discovered by the psychologists studying decision making are systematic. Similarly, the statement, If it is not rational, it is random and thus unpredictable, is incorrect. Behavior can be (and is often shown in the laboratory to be) purposeful, regular, and yet systematically different from the axioms of economic theory. I like the term "quasi rational" to describe such behavior. Someone who systematically overreacts to new information in violation of Bayes's rule is predictable yet only quasi rational.

4. In markets, arbitrage and competition will eliminate the effects of irrational agents. Markets can provide a unique context for agents to choose in an environment with both monetary incentives and learning opportunities. Moreover, the existence of other agents, ready to exploit the slightest slip, could create a situation in which mistakes are quickly eliminated. Under what circumstances will arbitrage and competition render the choices of quasi-rational agents irrelevant? This question is addressed in my recent paper with Tom Russell (Russell and Thaler, 1985). We investigate the operation of competitive markets in which some agents are fully rational and others are quasi rational. We then find the conditions that are sufficient to guarantee that such markets will yield rational equilibria, that is, the equilibria that would obtain if all the agents were rational. We find that these conditions are quite restrictive and are unlikely to occur in any but the most efficient of financial markets. In goods markets, a mistake by one individual will generally not create an arbitrage or profit opportunity for someone else. In these circumstances, mistakes can persist. While it is wrong to assume that behavior discovered in the psychologist's lab will necessarily survive in real world markets, it is also wrong to assume that markets will always eliminate such behavior.

5. Where is the theory? The original contributions to what is now referred to as behavioral decision theory were simply empirical anomalies, such as those discovered by Allais and by Ellsberg. Even without theories, however, these results were very useful in showing where the existing theory (expected utility theory) made predictions about behavior that were systematically wrong. The papers presented in this session by Tversky and Kahneman (1986) and by Einhorn and Hogarth (1986) have taken these original anomalies and tried to develop descriptive theories that can account for the observed behavior. These explicitly descriptive theories cannot be derived from normative axioms. Nevertheless, they are theories, and they seem to do a good job of predicting behavior.

6. Economic theory has done very well so far, and if it is not broken . . . . How successful is economic theory? The answer to this question depends on what constitutes a test. I propose the following ground rules. A test can be used as supporting evidence by the proponents of a theory if and only if the same test would have been accepted as a refutation had it come out the other way. Let me illustrate by example. If you look through a typical microeconomics textbook you will find few if any "tests" of the theory. However, there is one frequently reported test by Ray Battalio, John Kagel, and their colleagues, who perform experimental studies using animal subjects. (See, e.g., Kagel et al., 1975.) These studies have demonstrated that rats and pigeons have downward-sloping demand curves and upward-sloping labor supply curves. Such results are cited as supporting the theory. However, if rats were found to violate the substitution axiom, would that count as a refutation of expected utility theory? If rat markets failed to clear, would we abandon the efficient market hypothesis in finance?

More productive than the selective citing of supporting evidence by both sides would be the adoption of the research procedure recommended by the Dutch psychologist Willem Hofstee. Hofstee (1984) recommends that scientists engage in reputational bets. Suppose that X thinks that rational models predict well and that Y thinks otherwise. Then X and Y must stipulate an experiment or other empirical investigation on which they agree in advance to disagree about their predictions of the outcome of the experiment. Hofstee has developed an incentive compatible method for eliciting probabilistic forecasts from each scientist about the outcomes of the experiment. Once the bets are made, a third scientist is brought in to run the experiment, and the three publish the results. A new bureau would be necessary to keep track of each scientist's rating, as is done in chess. Perhaps a rule could be adopted that in order to maintain "grand master" status a bet has to be made every so often.

Economists and psychologists who genuinely made an effort to find some propositions to bet on might discover that there is less disagreement than was suspected. Perhaps economists do not really believe their models are descriptively accurate or psychologists do not believe their laboratory experiments would generalize to the market. Let us find out! My betting parlor in Ithaca is now open for business.

2. POSITIVE STEPS

Many of the results that have created the stimulation for this conference have been negative—counterexamples to the received theory. What positive steps can be taken? In many cases economic theory imposes restrictions on models by specifying variables that should not enter the analysis. For example, marginal analysis, the heart of microeconomic theory, specifies that only marginal costs and benefits should alter decisions. Historical or sunk costs should be irrelevant. Yet anyone who has tried to teach this concept knows that ignoring sunk costs does not come naturally to the uninitiated. Therefore it should not be surprising to discover that sunk costs often influence choices (Thaler, 1980; Arkes and Blumer, 1985). Positive theories of choice, then, will relax the restriction that sunk costs are irrelevant and will investigate the role they may play in actual decision making. The size of the first part of a two-part pricing scheme, for example, might affect utilization at the margin. (If I paid for it, I am going to use it!) The three papers presented in this session (Einhorn and Hogarth; Simon; and Tversky and Kahneman, 1986) provide other examples of opportunities for improving the descriptive validity of economic theories by relaxing the restrictions.

Herb Simon has stressed for years the importance of cognitive limitations on human decision making. One example of the way his twin concepts of bounded rationality and "satisficing" can be used to enrich economic theory is to incorporate task complexity into descriptive models. Research has demonstrated that, as tasks become more complex, individuals adopt simplifying decision-making strategies (Payne, 1976; Russo and Dosher, 1983). Economic theorists usually leave task complexity out of their models by assuming that any decision-making problem, no matter how complex, will be solved optimally. Descriptive validity would be increased by assuming that the use of simplifying rules and heuristics (with their accompanying biases) will be used more often in complex situations (even when the stakes are high).

Einhorn and Hogarth (1986) suggest relaxing the assumption that perceived ambiguity is irrelevant to choice. Since ambiguity is aversive in many (though not all) situations, the inclusion of ambiguity in a model of individual decision making under uncertainty may help enrich models of insurance purchases (see, e.g., Hogarth and Kunreuther, 1985).

Kahneman and Tversky's research has demonstrated repeatedly that even the most innocuous of assumptions, such as the invariance of choice to problem formulation, may need to be relaxed. Here the possibilities for enriching the economic model are endless. What are the comparative effects on consumption of a "temporary tax increase" compared to an equally large "temporary tax surcharge"? Can we be sure, without any empirical evidence, that the two are identical?

3. TWO FALSE STATEMENTS

I will end my remarks with the following two false statements.

1. Rational models are useless.
2. All behavior is rational.

I have offered these false statements because both sides in the debate that will be taking place at this conference and at similar conferences in the future have a tendency to misstate the other side's views. If everyone would agree that these statements are false, then no one would have to waste any time repudiating them.

REFERENCES

This chapter was originally presented as commentary on papers by Hillel Einhorn and Robin Hogarth, Herbert Simon, and Daniel Kahneman and Amos Tversky at a conference on "The Behavioral Foundations of Economic Theory."

Allais, Maurice. "Le comportement de l'homme rationnel devant le risque: Critique des postulats et axiomes de l'Ecole Américane." *Econometrica* 21 (October 1953): 503–546.

Arkes, H. R., and C. Blumer. "The Psychology of Sunk Cost." *Organizational Behavior and Human Decision Process* 35 (1985): 124–140.

Einhorn, H., and Hogarth, R. 1978. Confidence in judgment: Persistence in the illusion of validity. *Psychological Review* 85, no. 5: 395–416.

———. "Decision Making Under Ambiguity." *Journal of Business* 59 (October 1986): S225–250.

Ellsberg, D. "Risk, Ambiguity, and the Savage Axioms." *Quarterly Journal of Economics* 75 (November 1961): 643–669.

Grether, D., and C. Plott. "Economic Theory and the Preference Reversal Phenomenon." *American Economic Review* 69 (1979): 623–638.

Hofstee, W. K. B. "Methodological Decision Rules as Research Policies: A Betting Reconstruction of Empirical Research." *Acta Psychologica* 56 (1984): 93–109.

Hogarth, R., and H. Kunreuther. "Risk, Ambiguity and Insurance." Working paper. Chicago: University of Chicago, Graduate School of Business, Center for Decision Research, 1985.

Kagel, J.; H. Rachlin; L. Green; R. C. Battalio; R. L. Basmann; and W. R. Klemm. "Experimental Studies of Consumer Demand Using Laboratory Animals." *Economic Inquiry* 13 (March 1975): 22–38.

Lichtenstein, S., and P. Slovic. "Reversal of Preferences Between Bids and Choices in Gambling Decision." *Journal of Experimental Psychology* 89 (1971): 46–55.

Payne, J. "Task Complexity and Contingent Processing in Decision Making: An Informational Search and Protocol Analysis." *Organizational Behavior and Human Performance* 26 (1976): 366–387.

Russell, T., and R. Thaler. "The Relevance of Quasi Rationality and Competitive Markets." *American Economic Review* 75, 5 (December 1985): 1071–1082.

Russo, J. E., and B. Dosher. "Strategies for Multiattribute Choice." *Journal of Experimental Psychology: Memory, Learning and Cognition* 9 (1983): 676–696.

Simon, Herbert A. "Rationality in Psychology and Economics." *Journal of Business* 59 (October 1986): S209–224.

Stigler, G. J. "The Conference Handbook." *Journal of Political Economy* 85, 2 (1977): 441–443.

Thaler, R. "Toward a Positive Theory of Consumer Choice." *Journal of Economic Behavior and Organization* 1 (March 1980): 39–60.

Tversky, Amos, and Daniel Kahneman. "Rational Choice and the Framing of Decisions." *Journal of Business* 59 (October 1986): S251–278.

Part Four

FAIRNESS

10

FAIRNESS AS A CONSTRAINT ON PROFIT SEEKING: ENTITLEMENTS IN THE MARKET

Daniel Kahneman, Jack L. Knetsch, and Richard H. Thaler

Community standards of fairness for the setting of prices and wages were elicited by telephone surveys. In customer or labor markets, it is acceptable for a firm to raise prices (or cut wages) when profits are theatened and to maintain prices when costs diminish. It is unfair to exploit shifts in demand by raising prices or cutting wages. Several market anomalies are explained by assuming that these standards of fairness influence the behavior of firms.

Just as it is often useful to neglect friction in elementary mechanics, there may be good reasons to assume that firms seek their maximal profit as if they were subject only to legal and budgetary constraints. However, the patterns of sluggish or incomplete adjustment often observed in markets suggest that some additional constraints are operative. Several authors have used a notion of fairness to explain why many employers do not cut wages during periods of high unemployment (George Akerlof, 1979; Robert Solow, 1980). Arthur Okun (1981) went further in arguing that fairness also alters the outcomes in what he called customer markets—characterized by suppliers who are perceived as making their own pricing decisions, have some monopoly power (if only because search is costly), and often have repeat business with their clientele. Like labor markets, customer markets also sometimes fail to clear:

> . . . firms in the sports and entertainment industries offer their customers tickets at standard prices for events that clearly generate excess demand. Popular new

Reprinted with permission from *American Economic Review* 76, 4 (1986): 728–741.

models of automobiles may have waiting lists that extend for months. Similarly, manufacturers in a number of industries operate with backlogs in booms and allocate shipments when they obviously could raise prices and reduce the queue. [p. 170]

Okun explained these observations by the hostile reaction of customers to price increases that are not justified by increased costs and are therefore viewed as unfair. He also noted that customers appear willing to accept "fair" price increases even when demand is slack, and commented that ". . . in practice, observed pricing behavior is a vast distance from do-it-yourself auctioneering" (p. 170).

The argument used by these authors to account for apparent deviations from the simple model of a profit-maximizing firm is that fair behavior is instrumental to the maximization of long-run profits. In Okun's model, customers who suspect that a supplier treats them unfairly are likely to start searching for alternatives; Akerlof (1980, 1982) suggested that firms invest in their reputation to produce goodwill among their customers and high morale among their employees; and Arrow argued that trusted suppliers may be able to operate in markets that are otherwise devastated by the "lemons" problem (Akerlof, 1970; Kenneth Arrow, 1973). In these approaches, the rules of fairness define the terms of an enforceable implicit contract: Firms that behave unfairly are punished in the long run. A more radical assumption is that some firms apply fair policies even in situations that preclude enforcement—this is the view of the lay public, as shown in a later section of this paper.

If considerations of fairness do restrict the actions of profit-seeking firms, economic models might be enriched by a more detailed analysis of this constraint. Specifically, the rules that govern public perceptions of fairness should identify situations in which some firms will fail to exploit apparent opportunities to increase their profits. Near-rationality theory (Akerlof and Janet Yellen, 1985) suggests that such failures to maximize by a significant number of firms in a market can have large aggregate effects even in the presence of other firms that seek to take advantage of all available opportunities. Rules of fairness can also have significant economic effects through the medium of regulation. Indeed, Edward Zajac (1985) has inferred general rules of fairness from public reactions to the behavior of regulated utilities.

The present research uses household surveys of public opinions to infer rules of fairness for conduct in the market from evaluations of particular actions by hypothetical firms.[1] The study has two main objectives: (1) to

---

[1] Data were collected between May 1984 and July 1985 in telephone surveys of randomly selected residents of two Canadian metropolitan areas: Toronto and Vancouver. Equal numbers of adult female and male respondents were interviewed for about ten minutes in calls made during evening hours. No more than five questions concerned with fairness were included in any interview, and contrasting questions that were to be compared were never put to the same respondents.

identify community standards of fairness that apply to price, rent, and wage setting by firms in varied circumstances; and (2) to consider the possible implications of the rules of fairness for market outcomes.

The study was concerned with scenarios in which a *firm* (merchant, landlord, or employer) makes a pricing or wage-setting decision that affects the outcomes of one or more *transactors* (customers, tenants, or employees). The scenario was read to the participants, who evaluated the fairness of the action as in the following example:

Question 1. A hardware store has been selling snow shovels for $15. The morning after a large snowstorm, the store raises the price to $20. Please rate this action as:
Completely Fair——— Acceptable——— Unfair——— Very Unfair———

The two favorable and the two unfavorable categories are grouped in this report to indicate the proportions of respondents who judged the action acceptable or unfair. In this example, 82 percent of respondents ($N = 107$) considered it unfair for the hardware store to take advantage of the short-run increase in demand associated with a blizzard.

The approach of the present study is purely descriptive. Normative status is not claimed for the generalizations that are described as "rules of fairness," and the phrase, "it is fair," is simply an abbreviation for "a substantial majority of the population studied thinks it fair." The paper considers in turn three determinants of fairness judgments: the reference transaction, the outcomes to the firm and to the transactors, and the occasion for the action of the firm. The final sections are concerned with the enforcement of fairness and with economic phenomena that the rules of fairness may help explain.

1. REFERENCE TRANSACTIONS

A central concept in analyzing the fairness of actions in which a firm sets the terms of future exchanges is the *reference transaction*, a relevant precedent that is characterized by a reference price or wage and by a positive reference profit to the firm. The treatment is restricted to cases in which the fairness of the reference transaction is not itself in question.

The main findings of this research can be summarized by a principle of *dual entitlement*, which governs community standards of fairness: Transactors have an entitlement to the terms of the reference transaction, and firms are entitled to their reference profit. A firm is not allowed to increase its profits by arbitrarily violating the entitlement of its transactors to the reference price, rent, or wage (Max Bazerman, 1985; Zajac, 1985). When the reference profit of a firm is threatened, however, it may set new terms that protect its profit at transactors' expense.

Market prices, posted prices, and the history of previous transactions between a firm and a transactor can serve as reference transactions. When there is a history of similar transactions between firm and transactor, the most recent price, wage, or rent will be adopted for reference unless the terms of the previous transaction were explicitly temporary. For new transactions, prevailing competitive prices or wages provide the natural reference. The role of prior history in wage transactions is illustrated by the following pair of questions:

Question 2A. A small photocopying shop has one employee who has worked in the shop for six months and earns $9 per hour. Business continues to be satisfactory, but a factory in the area has closed and unemployment has increased. Other small shops have now hired reliable workers at $7 an hour to perform jobs similar to those done by the photocopy shop employee. The owner of the photocopying shop reduces the employee's wage to $7.

(N = 98) Acceptable 17% Unfair 83%

Question 2B. A small photocopying shop has one employee [as in Question 2A]. The current employee leaves, and the owner decides to pay a replacement $7 an hour.

(N = 125) Acceptable 73% Unfair 27%

The current wage of an employee serves as reference for evaluating the fairness of future adjustments of that employee's wage—but not necessarily for evaluating the fairness of the wage paid to a replacement. The new worker does not have an entitlement to the former worker's wage rate. As the following question shows, the entitlement of an employee to a reference wage does not carry over to a new labor transaction, even with the same employer:

Question 3. A house painter employs two assistants and pays them $9 per hour. The painter decides to quit house painting and go into the business of providing landscape services, where the going wage is lower. He reduces the workers' wages to $7 per hour for the landscaping work.

(N = 94) Acceptable 63% Unfair 37%

Note that the same reduction in wages that is judged acceptable by most respondents in Question 3 was judged unfair by 83 percent of the respondents to Question 2A.

Parallel results were obtained in questions concerning residential tenancy. As in the case of wages, many respondents apply different rules to a new tenant and to a tenant renewing a lease. A rent increase that is judged fair for a new lease may be unfair for a renewal. However, the circumstances under which the rules of fairness require landlords to bear such opportunity costs are narrowly defined. Few respondents consider it unfair for the landlord to sell the accommodation to another landlord who intends to raise the rents of sitting tenants, and even fewer believe that a landlord should make price concessions in selling an accommodation to its occupant.

The relevant reference transaction is not always unique. Disagreements about fairness are most likely to arise when alternative reference transactions can be invoked, each leading to a different assessment of the participants' outcomes. Agreement on general principles of fairness therefore does not preclude disputes about specific cases (see also Zajac, 1985). When competitors change their price or wage, for example, the current terms set by the firm and the new terms set by competitors define alternative reference transactions. Some people will consider it unfair for a firm not to raise its wages when competitors are increasing theirs. On the other hand, price increases that are not justified by increasing costs are judged less objectionable when competitors have led the way.

It should perhaps be emphasized that the reference transaction provides a basis for fairness judgments because it is normal, not necessarily because it is just. Psychological studies of adaptation suggest that any stable state of affairs tends to become accepted eventually, at least in the sense that alternatives to it no longer readily come to mind. Terms of exchange that are initially seen as unfair may in time acquire the status of a reference transaction. Thus, the gap between the behavior that people consider fair and the behavior that they expect in the marketplace tends to be rather small. This was confirmed in several scenarios, where different samples of respondents answered the two questions: "What does fairness require?" and "What do you think the firm would do?" The similarity of the answers suggests that people expect a substantial level of conformity to community standards—and also that they adapt their views of fairness to the norms of actual behavior.

2. THE CODING OF OUTCOMES

It is a commonplace that the fairness of an action depends in large part on the signs of its outcomes for the agent and for the individuals affected by it. The cardinal rule of fair behavior is surely that one person should not achieve a gain by simply imposing an equivalent loss on another.

In the present framework, the outcomes to the firm and to its transactors are defined as gains and losses in relation to the reference transaction. The transactor's outcome is simply the difference between the new terms set by the firm and the reference price, rent, or wage. The outcome to the firm is evaluated with respect to the reference profit and incorporates the effect of exogenous shocks (for example, changes in wholesale prices), which alter the profit of the firm on a transaction at the reference terms. According to these definitions, the outcomes in the snow shovel example of Question 1 were a $5 gain to the firm and a $5 loss to the representative customer. However, had the same price increase been induced by a $5 increase in the wholesale price of snow shovels, the outcome to the firm would have been nil.

The issue of how to define relevant outcomes takes a similar form in studies of individuals' preferences and of judgments of fairness. In both domains, a descriptive analysis of people's judgments and choices involves rules of *naive accounting* that diverge in major ways from the standards of rationality assumed in economic analysis. People commonly evaluate outcomes as gains or losses relative to a neutral reference point rather than as endstates (Kahneman and Amos Tversky, 1979). In violation of normative standards, they are more sensitive to out-of-pocket costs than to opportunity costs and more sensitive to losses than to foregone gains (Kahneman and Tversky, 1984; Thaler, 1980). These characteristics of evaluation make preferences vulnerable to framing effects, in which inconsequential variations in the presentation of a choice problem affect the decision (Tversky and Kahneman, 1986).

The entitlements of firms and transactors induce similar asymmetries between gains and losses in fairness judgments. An action by a firm is more likely to be judged unfair if it causes a loss to its transactor than if it cancels or reduces a possible gain. Similarly, an action by a firm is more likely to be judged unfair if it achieves a gain to the firm than if it averts a loss. Different standards are applied to actions that are elicited by the threat of losses or by an opportunity to improve on a positive reference profit—a psychologically important distinction which is usually not represented in economic analysis.

Judgments of fairness are also susceptible to framing effects, in which form appears to overwhelm substance. One of these framing effects will be recognized as the money illusion, illustrated in the following questions:

Question 4A. A company is making a small profit. It is located in a community experiencing a recession with substantial unemployment but no inflation. There are many workers anxious to work at the company. The company decides to decrease wages and salaries 7 percent this year.
(N = 125) Acceptable 38% Unfair 62%

Question 4B . . . with substantial unemployment and inflation of 12 percent. . . . The company decides to increase salaries only 5 percent this year.
(N = 129) Acceptable 78% Unfair 22%

Although the real income change is approximately the same in the two problems, the judgments of fairness are strikingly different. A wage cut is coded as a loss and consequently judged unfair. A nominal raise which does not compensate for inflation is more acceptable because it is coded as a gain to the employee, relative to the reference wage.

Analyses of individual choice suggest that the disutility associated with an outcome that is coded as a loss may be greater than the disutility of the same objective outcome when coded as the elimination of a gain. Thus, there may be less resistance to the cancellation of a discount or bonus than to an equivalent price increase or wage cut. As illustrated by the following questions, the same rule applies as well to fairness judgments.

Question 5A. A shortage has developed for a popular model of automobile, and customers must now wait two months for delivery. A dealer has been selling these cars at list price. Now the dealer prices this model at $200 above list price.

$(N = 130)$ Acceptable 29% Unfair 71%

Question 5B. . . . A dealer has been selling these cars at a discount of $200 below list price. Now the dealer sells this model only at list price.

$(N = 123)$ Acceptable 58% Unfair 42%

The significant difference between the responses to Questions 5A and 5B (*chi*-squared $= 20.91$) indicates that the $200 price increase is not treated identically in the two problems. In Question 5A the increase is clearly coded as a loss relative to the unambiguous reference provided by the list price. In Question 5B the reference price is ambiguous, and the change can be coded either as a loss (if the reference price is the discounted price), or as the elimination of a gain (if the reference price is the list price). The relative leniency of judgments in Question 5B suggests that at least some respondents adopted the latter frame. The following questions illustrate the same effect in the case of wages:

Question 6A. A small company employs several people. The workers' incomes have been about average for the community. In recent months, business for the company has not increased as it had before. The owners reduce the workers' wages by 10 percent for the next year.

$(N = 100)$ Acceptable 39% Unfair 61%

Question 6B. A small company employs several people. The workers have been receiving a 10 percent annual bonus each year and their total incomes have been about average for the community. In recent months, business for the company has not increased as it had before. The owners eliminate the workers' bonus for the year.

$(N = 98)$ Acceptable 80% Unfair 20%

3. OCCASIONS
FOR PRICING DECISIONS

This section examines the rules of fairness that apply to three classes of occasions in which a firm may reconsider the terms that it sets for exchanges.

(*i*) *Profit reductions*, for example, by rising costs or decreased demand for the product of the firm. (*ii*) *Profit increases*, for example, by efficiency gains or reduced costs. (*iii*) *Increases in market power*, for example, by temporary excess demand for goods, accommodations or jobs.

Protecting Profit

A random sample of adults contains many more customers, tenants, and employees than merchants, landlords, or employers. Nevertheless, most participants in the surveys clearly consider the firm to be entitled to its reference profit: They would allow a firm threatened by a reduction of its profit below a positive reference level to pass on the entire loss to its transactors, without compromising or sharing the pain. By large majorities, respondents endorsed the fairness of passing on increases in wholesale costs, in operating costs, and in the costs associated with a rental accommodation. The following two questions illustrate the range of situations to which this rule was found to apply.

Question 7. Suppose that, due to a transportation mixup, there is a local shortage of lettuce and the wholesale price has increased. A local grocer has bought the usual quantity of lettuce at a price that is 30 cents per head higher than normal. The grocer raises the price of lettuce to customers by 30 cents per head.

$(N = 101)$ Acceptable 79% Unfair 21%

Question 8. A landlord owns and rents out a single small house to a tenant who is living on a fixed income. A higher rent would mean the tenant would have to move. Other small rental houses are available. The landlord's costs have increased substantially over the past year and the landlord raises the rent to cover the cost increases when the tenant's lease is due for renewal.

$(N = 151)$ Acceptable 75% Unfair 25%

The answers to the last question, in particular, indicate that it is acceptable for firms to protect themselves from losses even when their transactors suffer substantial inconvenience as a result. The rules of fairness that yield such judgments do not correspond to norms of charity and do not reflect distributional concerns.

The attitude that permits the firm to protect a positive reference profit at the transactors' expense applies to employers as well as to merchants and landlords. When the profit of the employer in the labor transaction falls below the reference level, reductions of even nominal wages become acceptable. The next questions illustrate the strong effect of this variable.

Question 9A. A small company employs several workers and has been paying them average wages. There is severe unemployment in the area and the company could easily replace its current employees with good workers at a lower wage. The company has been making money. The owners reduce the current workers' wages by 5 percent.

(N = 195) Acceptable 23% Unfair 77%

Question 9B. . . . The company has been losing money. The owners reduce the current workers' wages by 5 percent.

(N = 195) Acceptable 68% Unfair 32%

The effect of firm profitability was studied in greater detail in the context of a scenario in which Mr. Green, a gardener who employs two workers at $7 an hour, learns that other equally competent workers are willing to do the same work for $6 an hour. Some respondents were told that Mr. Green's business was doing well, others were told that it was doing poorly. The questions, presented in open format, required respondents to state "what is fair for Mr. Green to do in this situation," or "what is your best guess about what Mr. Green would do . . . ." The information about the current state of the business had a large effect. Replacing the employees or bargaining with them to achieve a lower wage was mentioned as fair by 67 percent of respondents when business was said to be poor, but only by 25 percent of respondents when business was good. The proportion guessing that Mr. Green would try to reduce his labor costs was 75 percent when he was said to be doing poorly, and 49 percent when he was said to be doing well. The differences were statistically reliable in both cases.

A firm is only allowed to protect itself at the transactor's expense against losses that pertain directly to the transaction at hand. Thus, it is unfair for a landlord to raise the rent on an accommodation to make up for the loss of another source of income. On the other hand, 62 percent of the respondents considered it acceptable for a landlord to charge a higher rent for apartments in one of two otherwise identical buildings, because a more costly foundation had been required in the construction of that building.

The assignment of costs to specific goods explains why it is generally unfair to raise the price of old stock when the price of new stock increases:

Question 10. A grocery store has several months' supply of peanut butter in stock which it has on the shelves and in the storeroom. The owner hears that the wholesale price of peanut butter has increased and immediately raises the price on the current stock of peanut butter.

(N = 147) Acceptable 21% Unfair 79%

The principles of naive accounting apparently include a FIFO method of inventory cost allocation.

The Allocation of Gains

The data of the preceding section could be interpreted as evidence for a cost-plus rule of fair pricing, in which the supplier is expected to act as a broker in passing on marked-up costs (Okun). A critical test of this possible rule arises when the supplier's costs diminish: A strict cost-plus rule would require prices to come down accordingly. In contrast, a dual-entitlement view suggests that the firm is only prohibited from increasing its profit by causing a loss to its transactors. Increasing profits by retaining cost reductions does not violate the transactors' entitlement and may therefore be acceptable.

The results of our companion study (1986, see Chapter 11) indicated that community standards of fairness do not in fact restrict firms to the reference profit when their costs diminish, as a cost-plus rule would require. The questions used in these surveys presented a scenario of a monopolist supplier of a particular kind of table, who faces a $20 reduction of costs on tables that have been selling for $150. The respondents were asked to indicate whether "fairness requires" the supplier to lower the price, and if so, by how much. About one-half of the survey respondents felt that it was acceptable for the supplier to retain the entire benefit, and less than one-third would require the supplier to reduce the price by $20, as a cost-plus rule dictates. Further, and somewhat surprisingly, judgments of fairness did not reliably discriminate between primary producers and middlemen, or between savings due to lower input prices and to improved efficiency.

The conclusion that the rules of fairness permit the seller to keep part or all of any cost reduction was confirmed with the simpler method employed in the present study.

Question 11A. A small factory produces tables and sells all that it can make at $200 each. Because of changes in the price of materials, the cost of making each table has recently decreased by $40. The factory reduces its price for the tables by $20.

$(N = 102)$ Acceptable 79% Unfair 21%

Question 11B. . . . the cost of making each table has recently decreased by $20. The factory does not change its price for the tables.

$(N = 100)$ Acceptable 53% Unfair 47%

The even division of opinions on Question 11B confirms the observations of the previous study. In conjunction with the results of the previous section, the findings support a dual-entitlement view: the rules of fairness permit a firm not to share in the losses that it imposes on its transactors, without imposing on it an unequivocal duty to share its gains with them.

Exploitation of Increased Market Power

The market power of a firm reflects the advantage to the transactor of the exchange which the firm offers, compared to the transactor's second-best alternative. For example, a blizzard increases the surplus associated with the purchase of a snow shovel at the regular price, compared to the alternatives of buying elsewhere or doing without a shovel. The respondents consider it unfair for the hardware store to capture any part of the increased surplus, because such an action would violate the customer's entitlement to the reference price. Similarly, it is unfair for a firm to exploit an excess in the supply of labor to cut wages (Question 2A), because this would violate the entitlement of employees to their reference wage.

As shown by the following routine example, the opposition to exploitation of shortages is not restricted to such extreme circumstances:

Question 12. A severe shortage of Red Delicious apples has developed in a community and none of the grocery stores or produce markets have any of this type of apple on their shelves. Other varieties of apples are plentiful in all of the stores. One grocer receives a single shipment of Red Delicious apples at the regular wholesale cost and raises the retail price of these Red Delicious apples by 25 percent over the regular price.

(N = 102) Acceptable 37% Unfair 63%

Raising prices in response to a shortage is unfair even when close substitutes are readily available. A similar aversion to price rationing held as well for luxury items. For example, a majority of respondents thought it unfair for a popular restaurant to impose a $5 surcharge for Saturday night reservations.

Conventional economic analyses assume as a matter of course that excess demand for a good creates an opportunity for suppliers to raise prices, and that such increases will indeed occur. The profit-seeking adjustments that clear the market are in this view as natural as water finding its level—and as ethically neutral. The lay public does not share this indifference. Community standards of fairness effectively require the firm to absorb an opportunity cost in the presence of excess demand, by charging less than the clearing price or paying more than the clearing wage.

As might be expected from this analysis, it is unfair for a firm to take advantage of an increase in its monopoly power. Respondents were nearly unanimous in condemning a store that raises prices when its sole competitor in a community is temporarily forced to close. As shown in the next question, even a rather mild exploitation of monopoly power is considered unfair.

Question 13. A grocery chain has stores in many communities. Most of them face competition from other groceries. In one community the chain has no competition. Although its costs and volume of sales are the same there as elsewhere, the chain sets prices that average 5 percent higher than in other communities.

(N = 101) Acceptable 24% Unfair 76%

Responses to this and two additional versions of this question specifying average price increases of 10 and 15 percent did not differ significantly. The respondents clearly viewed such pricing practices as unfair, but were insensitive to the extent of the unwarranted increase.

A monopolist might attempt to increase profits by charging different customers as much as they are willing to pay. In conventional theory, the constraints that prevent a monopolist from using perfect price discrimination to capture all the consumers' surplus are asymmetric information and difficulties in preventing resale. The survey results suggest the addition of a further restraint: some forms of price discrimination are outrageous.

Question 14. A landlord rents out a small house. When the lease is due for renewal, the landlord learns that the tenant has taken a job very close to the house and is therefore unlikely to move. The landlord raises the rent $40 per month more than he was planning to do.

(N = 157) Acceptable 9% Unfair 91%

The near unanimity of responses to this and similar questions indicates that an action that deliberately exploits the special dependence of a particular individual is exceptionally offensive.

The introduction of an explicit auction to allocate scarce goods or jobs would also enable the firm to gain at the expense of its transactors, and is consequently judged unfair.

Question 15. A store has been sold out of the popular Cabbage Patch dolls for a month. A week before Christmas a single doll is discovered in a storeroom. The managers know that many customers would like to buy the doll. They announce over the store's public address system that the doll will be sold by auction to the customer who offers to pay the most.

(N = 101) Acceptable 26% Unfair 74%

Question 16. A business in a community with high unemployment needs to hire a new computer operator. Four candidates are judged to be completely qualified for the job. The manager asks the candidates to state the lowest salary they would be willing to accept, and then hires the one who demands the lowest salary.

(N = 154) Acceptable 36% Unfair 64%

The auction is opposed in both cases, presumably because the competition among potential buyers or employees benefits the firm. The opposition can in some cases be mitigated by eliminating this benefit. For example, a sentence added to Question 15, indicating that "the proceeds will go to UNICEF" reduced the negative judgments of the doll auction from 74 to 21 percent.

The strong aversion to price rationing in these examples clearly does not extend to all uses of auctions. The individual who sells securities at twice the price paid for them a month ago is an object of admiration and envy—and is certainly not thought to be gouging. Why is it fair to sell a painting or a house at the market-clearing price, but not an apple, dinner reservation, job, or football game ticket? The rule of acceptability appears to be this: Goods for which an active resale market exists, and especially goods that serve as a store of value, can be sold freely by auction or other mechanisms allowing the seller to capture the maximum price. When resale is a realistic possibility, which is not the case for most consumer goods, the potential resale price reflects the higher value of the asset and the purchaser is therefore not perceived as sustaining a loss.

4. ENFORCEMENT

Several considerations may deter a firm from violating community standards of fairness. First, a history or reputation of unfair dealing may induce potential transactors to take their business elsewhere, because of the element of trust that is present in many transactions. Second, transactors may avoid exchanges with offending firms at some cost to themselves, even when trust is not an issue. Finally, the individuals who make decisions on behalf of firms may have a preference for acting fairly. The role of reputation effects is widely recognized. This section presents some indications that a willingness to resist and to punish unfairness and an intrinsic motivation to be fair could also contribute to fair behavior in the marketplace.

A willingness to pay to resist and to punish unfairness has been demonstrated in incentive compatible laboratory experiments. In the ultimatum game devised by Werner Guth, Rolf Schmittberger, and Bernd Schwarze (1982), the participants are designated as allocators or recipients. Each allocator anonymously proposes a division of a fixed amount of money between himself (herself) and a recipient. The recipient either accepts the offer or rejects it, in which case both players get nothing. The standard game theoretic solution is for the allocator to make a token offer and for the recipient to accept it, but Guth et al. observed that many allocators offer an equal division and that recipients sometimes turn down positive offers. In our more detailed study of resistance to unfairness (1986), recipients were asked to indicate in advance how they wished to respond to a range of possible allocations: A majority of participants were willing to forsake $2 rather than accept an unfair allocation of $10.

Willingness to punish unfair actors was observed in another experiment, in which subjects were given the opportunity to share a sum of money evenly with one of two anonymous strangers, identified only by the allocation they had proposed to someone else in a previous round. About three-quarters of the undergraduate participants in this experiment elected to share $10 evenly with a stranger who had been fair to someone else, when the alternative was to share $12 evenly with an unfair allocator.

A willingness to punish unfairness was also expressed in the telephone surveys. For example, 68 percent of respondents said they would switch their patronage to a drugstore five minutes further away if the one closer to them raised its prices when a competitor was temporarily forced to close; and, in a separate sample, 69 percent indicated they would switch if the more convenient store discriminated against its older workers.

The costs of enforcing fairness are small in these examples—but effective enforcement in the marketplace can often be achieved at little cost to transactors. Retailers will have a substantial incentive to behave fairly if a large number of customers are prepared to drive an extra five minutes to avoid doing business with an unfair firm. The threat of future punishment when competitors enter may also deter a temporary monopolist from fully exploiting short-term profit opportunities.

In traditional economic theory, compliance with contracts depends on enforcement. It is a mild embarrassment to the standard model that experimental studies often produce fair behavior even in the absence of enforcement (Elizabeth Hoffman and Matthew Spitzer, 1982, 1985; our paper, 1986; Alvin Roth, Michael Malouf, and J. Keith Murninghan, 1981; Reinhard Selten, 1978). These observations, however, merely confirm common sense views of human behavior. Survey results indicate a belief that unenforced compliance to the rules of fairness is common. This belief was examined in two contexts: tipping in restaurants and sharp practice in automobile repairs.

Question 17A. If the service is satisfactory, how much of a tip do you think most people leave after ordering a meal costing $10 in a restaurant that they visit frequently?

$(N = 122)$ Mean response = $1.28

Question 17B. . . . in a restaurant on a trip to another city that they do not expect to visit again?

$(N = 124)$ Mean response = $1.27

The respondents evidently do not treat the possibility of enforcement as a significant factor in the control of tipping. Their opinion is consistent with the widely observed adherence to a 15 percent tipping rule even by one-time customers who pay and tip by credit card, and have little reason to fear embarrassing retaliation by an irate server.

The common belief that tipping is controlled by intrinsic motivation can be accommodated with a standard microeconomic model by extending the utility function of individuals to include guilt and self-esteem. A more difficult question is whether firms, which the theory assumes to maximize profits, also fail to exploit some economic opportunities because of unenforced compliance with rules of fairness. The following questions elicited expectations about the behavior of a garage mechanic dealing with a regular customer or with a tourist.

Question 18A. [A man leaves his car with the mechanic at his regular / A tourist leaves his car at a] service station with instructions to replace an expensive part. After the [customer/tourist] leaves, the mechanic examines the car and discovers that it is not necessary to replace the part; it can be repaired cheaply. The mechanic would make much more money by replacing the part than by repairing it. Assuming the [customer/tourist] cannot be reached, what do you think the mechanic would do in this situation?
Make more money by replacing the part
> Customer: 60% Tourist: 63%

Save the customer money by repairing the part
> Customer: 40% Tourist: 37%

Question 18B. Of ten mechanics dealing with a [regular customer/tourist], how many would you expect to save the customer money by repairing the part?
Mean response
> Customer: 3.62 Tourist: 3.72

The respondents do not approach garages with wide-eyed naive faith. It is therefore all the more noteworthy that they expect a tourist and a regular customer to be treated alike, in spite of the obvious difference between the two cases in the potential for any kind of enforcement, including reputation effects.[2]

Here again, there is no evidence that the public considers enforcement a significant factor. The respondents believe that most mechanics (usually excluding their own) would be less than saintly in this situation. However, they also appear to believe that the substantial minority of mechanics who would treat their customers fairly are not motivated in each case by the anticipation of sanctions.

[2] Other respondents were asked to assess the probable behavior of their own garage under similar circumstances: 88 percent expressed a belief that their garage would act fairly toward a regular customer, and 86 percent stated that their garage would treat a tourist and a regular customer similarly.

5. ECONOMIC CONSEQUENCES

The findings of this study suggest that many actions that are both profitable in the short run and not obviously dishonest are likely to be perceived as unfair exploitations of market power.[3] Such perceptions can have significant consequences if they find expression in legislation or regulation (Zajac, 1978; 1985). Further, even in the absence of government intervention, the actions of firms that wish to avoid a reputation for unfairness will depart in significant ways from the standard model of economic behavior. The survey results suggest four propositions about the effects of fairness considerations on the behavior of firms in customer markets, and a parallel set of hypotheses about labor markets.

Fairness in Customer Markets

PROPOSITION 1: *When excess demand in a customer market is unaccompanied by increases in suppliers' costs, the market will fail to clear in the short run.*

Evidence supporting this proposition was described by Phillip Cagan (1979), who concluded from a review of the behavior of prices that, "Empirical studies have long found that short-run shifts in demand have small and often insignificant effects [on prices]" (p. 18). Other consistent evidence comes from studies of disasters, where prices are often maintained at their reference levels although supplies are short (Douglas Dacy and Howard Kunreuther, 1969).

A particularly well-documented illustration of the behavior predicted in Proposition 1 is provided by Alan Olmstead and Paul Rhode (1985). During the spring and summer of 1920 there was a severe gasoline shortage on the U.S. West Coast where Standard Oil of California (SOCal) was the dominant supplier. There were no government-imposed price controls, nor was there any threat of such controls, yet SOCal reacted by imposing allocation and rationing schemes while maintaining prices. Prices were actually higher in the East in the absence of any shortage. Significantly, Olmstead and Rhode note that the eastern firms had to purchase crude at higher prices while SOCal, being vertically integrated, had no such excuse for raising price. They conclude from confidential SOCal documents that SOCal officers ". . . were clearly concerned with their public image and tried to maintain the appearance of being 'fair' " (p. 1053).

PROPOSITION 2: *When a single supplier provides a family of goods for which there is differential demand without corresponding variation of input costs, shortages of the most valued items will occur.*

There is considerable support for this proposition in the pricing of sport and entertainment events, which are characterized by marked variation of demand

---

[3]This conclusion probably holds in social and cultural groups other than the Canadian urban samples studied here, although the detailed rules of fairness for economic transactions may vary.

for goods or services for which costs are about the same (Thaler, 1985). The survey responses suggest that charging the market-clearing price for the most popular goods would be judged unfair.

Proposition 2 applies to cases such as those of resort hotels that have in-season and out-of-season rates which correspond to predictable variations of demand. To the extent that constraints of fairness are operating, the price adjustments should be insufficient, with excess demand at the peak. Because naive accounting does not properly distinguish between marginal and average costs, customers and other observers are likely to adopt off-peak prices as a reference in evaluating the fairness of the price charged to peak customers. A revenue-maximizing (low) price in the off-season may suggest that the profits achievable at the peak are unfairly high. In spite of a substantial degree of within-season price variation in resort and ski hotels, it appears to be the rule that most of these establishments face excess demand during the peak weeks. One industry explanation is: "If you gouge them at Christmas, they won't be back in March."

PROPOSITION 3: *Price changes will be more responsive to variations of costs than to variations of demand, and more responsive to cost increases than to cost decreases.*

The high sensitivity of prices to short-run variations of costs is well documented (Cagan). The idea of asymmetric price rigidity has a history of controversy (Timur Kuran, 1983; Solow, 1980; George Stigler and James Kindahl, 1970), and the issue is still unsettled. Changes of currency values offer a potential test of the hypothesis that cost increases tend to be passed on quickly and completely, whereas cost decreases can be retained at least in part. When the rate of exchange between two currencies changes after a prolonged period of stability, the prediction from Proposition 3 is that upward adjustments of import prices in one country will occur faster than the downward adjustments expected in the other.

PROPOSITION 4: *Price decreases will often take the form of discounts rather than reductions in the list or posted price.*

This proposition is strongly supported by the data of Stigler and Kindahl. Casual observation confirms that temporary discounts are much more common than temporary surcharges. Discounts have the important advantage that their subsequent cancellation will elicit less resistance than an increase in posted price. A temporary surcharge is especially aversive because it does not have the prospect of becoming a reference price, and can only be coded as a loss.

Fairness in Labor Markets

A consistent finding of this study is the similarity of the rules of fairness that apply to prices, rents, and wages. The correspondence extends to the economic predictions that may be derived for the behavior of wages in labor markets and of prices in customer markets. The first proposition about prices asserted that resistance to the exploitation of short-term fluctuations of demand could prevent markets from clearing. The corresponding prediction for labor markets is that wages will be relatively insensitive to excess supply.

The existence of wage stickiness is not in doubt, and numerous explanations have been offered for it. An entitlement model of this effect invokes an implicit contract between the worker and the firm. Like other implicit contract theories, such a model predicts that wage changes in a firm will be more sensitive to recent firm profits than to local labor market conditions. However, unlike the implicit contract theories that emphasize risk shifting (Costas Azariadis, 1975; Martin Baily, 1974; Donald Gordon, 1974), explanations in terms of fairness (Akerlof, 1979, 1982; Okun, 1981; Solow, 1980) lead to predictions of wage stickiness even in occupations that offer no prospects for long-term employment and therefore provide little protection from risk. Okun noted that "Casual empiricism about the casual labor market suggests that the Keynesian wage floor nonetheless operates; the pay of car washers or stock clerks is seldom cut in a recession, even when it is well above any statutory minimum wage" (1981, p. 82), and he concluded that the employment relation is governed by an "invisible handshake," rather than by the invisible hand (p. 89).

The dual-entitlement model differs from a Keynesian model of sticky wages, in which nominal wage changes are always nonnegative. The survey findings suggest that nominal wage cuts by a firm that is losing money or threatened with bankruptcy do not violate community standards of fairness. This modification of the sticky nominal wage dictum is related to Proposition 3 for customer markets. Just as they may raise prices to do so, firms may also cut wages to protect a positive reference profit.

Proposition 2 for customer markets asserted that the dispersion of prices for similar goods that cost the same to produce but differ in demand will be insufficient to clear the market. An analogous case in the labor market involves positions that are similar in nominal duties but are occupied by individuals who have different values in the employment market. The prediction is that differences in income will be insufficient to eliminate the excess demand for the individuals considered most valuable, and the excess supply of those considered most dispensable. This prediction applies both within and among occupations.

Robert Frank (1985) found that the individuals in a university who already are the most highly paid in each department are also the most likely targets for raiding. Frank explains the observed behavior in terms of envy and status. An analysis of this phenomenon in terms of fairness is the same as for the seasonal pricing of resort rooms: Just as prices that clear the market at peak demand will be perceived as gouging if the resort can also afford to operate at off-peak rates, a firm that can afford to pay its most valuable employees their market value may appear to grossly underpay their less-valued colleagues. A related prediction is that variations among departments will also be insufficient to clear the market. Although salaries are higher in academic departments that compete with the private sector than in others, the ratio of job openings to applicants is still lower in classics than in accounting.

The present analysis also suggests that firms that frame a portion of their compensation package as bonuses or profit-sharing will encounter relatively little resistance to reductions of compensation during slack periods. This is the equivalent of Proposition 4. The relevant psychological principle is that losses are more aversive than objectively equivalent foregone gains. The same mechanism, combined with the money illusion, supports another prediction: Adjustments of real wages will be substantially greater in inflationary periods than in periods of stable prices, because the adjustments can then be achieved without making nominal cuts—which are always perceived as losses and are therefore strongly resisted. An unequal distribution of gains is more likely to appear fair than a reallocation in which there are losers.

This discussion has illustrated several ways in which the informal entitlements of customers or employees to the terms of reference transactions could enter an economic analysis. In cases such as the pricing of resort facilities, the concern of customers for fair pricing may permanently prevent the market from clearing. In other situations, the reluctance of firms to impose terms that can be perceived as unfair acts as a friction-like factor. The process of reaching equilibrium can be slowed down if no firm wants to be seen as a leader in moving to exploit changing market conditions. In some instances an initially unfair practice (for example, charging above list price for a popular car model) may spread slowly until it evolves into a new norm—and is no longer unfair. In all these cases, perceptions of transactors' entitlements affect the substantive outcomes of exchanges, altering or preventing the equilibria predicted by an analysis that omits fairness as a factor. In addition, considerations of fairness can affect the form rather than the substance of price or wage setting. Judgments of fairness are susceptible to substantial framing effects, and the present study gives reason to believe that firms have an incentive to frame the terms of exchanges so as to make them appear "fair."

REFERENCES

The research was carried out when Kahneman was at the University of British Columbia. It was supported by the Department of Fisheries and Oceans Canada. Kahneman and Thaler were also supported by the U.S. Office of Naval Research and the Alfred P. Sloan Foundation, respectively. Conversations with J. Brander, R. Frank, and A. Tversky were very helpful.

Akerlof, George A. "The Market for 'Lemons': Quality Uncertainty and the Market Mechanism." *Quarterly Journal of Economics* 84 (August 1970): 488–500.

———. "The Case against Conservative Macroeconomics: An Inaugural Lecture." *Economica* 46 (August 1979): 219–237.

———. "A Theory of Social Custom, of Which Unemployment May Be One Consequence." *Quarterly Journal of Economics* 94 (June 1980): 749–775.

———. "Labor Contracts as Partial Gift Exchange." *Quarterly Journal of Economics* 97 (November 1982): 543–569.

Akerlof, George A., and Janet L. Yellen. "Can Small Deviations from Rationality Make Significant Differences to Economic Equilibrium?" *American Economic Review* 75 (September 1985): 708–720.

Arrow, Kenneth. "Social Responsibility and Economic Efficiency." *Public Policy* 21 (Summer 1973): 303–317.

Azariadis, Costas. "Implicit Contracts and Unemployment Equilibria." *Journal of Political Economy* 83 (December 1975): 1183–1202.

Baily, Martin N. "Wages and Employment Under Uncertain Demand." *Review of Economic Studies* 41 (January 1974): 37–50.

Bazerman, Max H. "Norms of Distributive Justice in Interest Arbitration." *Industrial and Labor Relations Review* 38 (July 1985): 558–570.

Cagan, Phillip. *Persistent Inflation: Historical and Policy Essays.* New York: Columbia University Press, 1979.

Dacy, Douglas C., and Howard Kunreuther. *The Economics of Natural Disasters.* New York: Free Press, 1969.

Frank, Robert H. *Choosing the Right Pond; Human Behavior and the Quest for Status.* New York: Oxford University Press, 1985.

Gordon, Donald F. "A Neo-Classical Theory of Keynesian Unemployment." *Economic Inquiry* 12 (December 1974): 431–459.

Guth, Werner; Rolf Schmittberger; and Bernd Schwarze. "An Experimental Analysis of Ultimatum Bargaining." *Journal of Economic Behavior and Organization* 3 (1982): 367–388.

Hoffman, Elizabeth, and Matthew L. Spitzer. "The Coase Theorem: Some Experimental Tests." *Journal of Law and Economics* 25 (April 1982): 73–98.

———. "Entitlements, Rights, and Fairness: An Experimental Examination of Subjects' Concepts of Distributive Justice." *Journal of Legal Studies* 14 (June 1985): 259–297.

Kahneman, Daniel; Jack L. Knetsch; and Richard Thaler. "Fairness and the Assumptions of Economics." *Journal of Business* 9, 4, Part 2 (1986): S285–S300. See Chapter 11 in this book.

Kahneman, Daniel, and Amos Tversky. "Prospect Theory: An Analysis of Decision Under Risk." *Econometrica* 47 (March 1979): 263–291.

———. "Choices, Values, and Frames." *American Psychologist* 39 (April 1984): 341–350.

Kuran, Timur. "Asymmetric Price Rigidity and Inflationary Bias." *American Economic Review* 73 (June 1983): 378–382.

Okun, Arthur. *Prices and Quantities: A Macroeconomic Analysis.* Washington, DC: The Brookings Institution, 1981.

Olmstead, Alan L., and Paul Rhode. "Rationing Without Government: The West Coast Gas Famine of 1920." *American Economic Review* 75 (December 1985): 1044–1055.

Roth, Alvin; Michael Malouf; and J. Keith Murnighan. "Sociological Versus Strategic Factors in Bargaining." *Journal of Economic Behavior and Organization* 2 (June 1981): 153–177.

Selten, Reinhard. "The Equity Principle in Economic Behavior." In Hans W. Gottinger and Werner Leinfellner, eds., *Decision Theory and Social Ethics: Issues in Social Choice*, Dordrecht: D. Reidel, 1978, 289–301.

Solow, Robert M. "On Theories of Unemployment." *American Economic Review* 70 (March 1980): 1–11.

Stigler, George J., and James K. Kindahl. *The Behavior of Industrial Prices.* NBER, New York: Columbia University Press, 1970.

Thaler, Richard. "Toward a Positive Theory of Consumer Choice." *Journal of Economic Behavior and Organization* 1 (March 1980): 39–60. See Chapter 1 in this book.

———. "Mental Accounting and Consumer Choice." *Marketing Science* 4 (Summer 1985): 199–214. See Chapter 2 in this book.

Tversky, Amos, and Daniel Kahneman. "Rational Choice and the Framing of Decisions." *Journal of Business* 59 (October 1986): S251–S278.

Zajac, Edward E. *Fairness or Efficiency: An Introduction to Public Utility Pricing.* Cambridge, MA: Ballinger, 1978.

———. "Perceived Economic Justice: The example of Public Utility Regulation." In H. Peyton Young, ed., *Cost Allocation: Methods, Principles and Applications.* Amsterdam: North-Holland, 1985.

11

FAIRNESS
AND THE ASSUMPTIONS
OF ECONOMICS

Daniel Kahneman, Jack L. Knetsch, and Richard H. Thaler

The traditional assumption that fairness is irrelevant to economic analysis is questioned. Even profit-maximizing firms will have an incentive to act in a manner that is perceived as fair if the individuals with whom they deal are willing to resist unfair transactions and punish unfair firms at some cost to themselves. Three experiments demonstrated that willingness to enforce fairness is common. Community standards for actions affecting customers, tenants, and employees were studied in telephone surveys. The rules of fairness, some of which are not obvious, help explain some anomalous market phenomena.

The advantages and disadvantages of expanding the standard economic model by more realistic behavioral assumptions have received much attention. The issue raised in this article is whether it is useful to complicate—or perhaps to enrich—the model of the profit-seeking firm by considering the preferences that people have for being treated fairly and for treating others fairly.

The absence of considerations of fairness and loyalty from standard economic theory is one of the most striking contrasts between this body of theory and other social sciences—and also between economic theory and lay intuitions about human behavior. Actions in many domains commonly conform to standards of decency that are more restrictive than the legal ones: the institutions of tipping and lost-and-found offices rest on expectations of such actions. Nevertheless, the standard microeconomic model of the profit-maximizing firm assigns essentially no role to generosity and social conscience or even to good will or indignation. The economic agent is assumed to be law-abiding but not "fair"—if fairness implies that some legal

Reprinted with permission from *Journal of Business* 59, 4, Part 2 (1986): S285–S300. © The University of Chicago Press.

opportunities for gain are not exploited. This nonfairness assumption expresses a resistance to explanations of economic actions in moral terms that has deep roots in the history of the discipline. The central insight that gave rise to modern economics is that the common good is well served by the free actions of self-interested agents in a market.

Like the assumption of rationality, the assumption of nonfairness could take several forms, which may be ordered from "pure as-if" to "true believer." The as-if position is methodological rather than substantive. It assigns the entire burden of proof to anyone who would complicate the basic model and accepts as grounds for its revision only improved predictions of economic variables, not direct tests of its assumptions. A moderate true-believer position would be that the economic arena, like a boxing ring or a poker game, is an environment in which many of the rules that govern other human interactions are suspended. In the extreme true-believer position any appearance of concern for values of fairness or for the welfare of strangers is interpreted in terms of self-interest and strategic behavior.

Although not logically required for the pursuit of standard economic analyses, true belief in nonfairness appears to be common among economists. It is often viewed as an embarrassment to the basic theory that people vote, do not always free ride, and commonly allocate resources equitably to others and to themselves when they are free to do otherwise. There is a clear preference for treating apparent indications of fairness (or of irrationality) as isolated phenomena of little economic significance.

In opposition to the dominant trend several economists have invoked a notion of fairness in their interpretations of regulation (Zajac 1978, 1985) and of the market phenomena of price and wage stickiness (Hirschman, 1970; Arrow, 1973; Akerlof, 1979, 1982; Solow, 1980). Arthur Okun (1981) offered a notably detailed account of the demands of customers and employees for fair treatment and of the role of perceived unfairness in triggering a search for alternative suppliers. Okun made a strong case that many customer markets resemble labor markets more than they do pure auction models. Like labor markets, customer markets sometimes fail to clear, an observation that Okun explained by the hostility of customers to price increases that are not justified by increased costs.

The opposition to price rationing as a response to a shortage is easily documented. An example is provided by the following question, which was put to 191 adult residents of the Vancouver metropolitan region as part of a telephone survey.

> A football team normally sells some tickets on the day of their games. Recently, interest in the next game has increased greatly, and tickets are in great demand. The team owners can distribute the tickets in one of three ways. (1) By auction: the tickets are sold to the highest bidders. (2) By lottery: the tickets are sold to the people whose names are drawn. (3) By queue: the tickets are sold on a first-come

first-served basis. Rank these three in terms of which you feel is the most fair and which is the least fair—the auction, the lottery, and the queue.

The results for this question are given in Table 1.

In terms of economic efficiency, the three procedures are ranked from the auction, which would allocate the good to the customers willing to pay the most for it, down to the wasteful method of queueing. The inverse ordering obtains when the allocation procedures are ranked by their fairness.

In what ways could community standards of fairness deter firms from exploiting excess demand? A radical possibility, which corresponds to lay beliefs (Kahneman, Knetsch, and Thaler, 1986), is that there is a significant incidence of cases in which firms, like individuals, are motivated by concerns of fairness. The characteristic of these cases is that the firm behaves "fairly" in the absence of inducements such as the promise of future custom or the threat of regulation. An important example that appears to satisfy this criterion was documented by Olmstead and Rhode (1985) in their analysis of the behavior of a dominant supplier during the West Coast oil famine of 1920.

A less radical position is that actions that the public will perceive as unfair are deterred by the resistance of potential transactors. This resistance will be most effective if it is backed up by a willingness on the part of customers and employees to pay some cost to avoid unfair transactions and unfair firms. There are indications that such a willingness may exist.

The following pair of questions, reported in Thaler (1985), was administered to two groups of participants in an executive education program. One group received the version including the passages in brackets, while the other received the passages in parentheses.

You are lying on the beach on a hot day. All you have to drink is ice water. For the past hour you have been thinking about how much you would enjoy a nice cold bottle of your favorite brand of beer. A companion gets up to go make a phone call and offers to bring back a beer from the only nearby place where beer is sold [a fancy resort hotel] (a run-down grocery store). He says that the beer might be expensive and so asks how much you would be willing to pay for the beer. He says he will buy the beer if it costs as much or less than the price you state, but if it costs more than the price you state he will not buy it. You trust your friend, and there is no chance of bargaining with the [bartender] (store owner). What price do you state?

TABLE 1 Ranking of Allocation Methods

Allocation Method	Most Fair (%)	Least Fair (%)
Auction	4	75
Lottery	28	18
Queue	68	7

The median response for the fancy-hotel version was $2.65, while the median response for the grocery-store version was $1.50. Evidently, people are willing to pay different amounts for a beer to be consumed on the beach, depending on where it was purchased. Put another way, people would refuse to buy a beer from the grocery store at a price less than their reservation price rather than pay what they consider to be an excessive amount. Note that, because different prices are considered appropriate for the grocery and for the hotel, the two establishments face different demands for a physically identical good to be consumed under identical circumstances.

These introductory considerations lead to several questions. How prevalent is "fair" behavior in the absence of enforcement? Does resistance to unfair treatment occur in real as well as in hypothetical problems? Do people only resist unfair transactions in which they are directly involved, or are they willing to incur costs to punish unfair actors? What are the specific rules of fairness that apply to firms in their transactions? Could the inclusion of considerations of fairness improve the understanding of significant economic facts? We will now review three studies that dealt with these questions.

The first study includes three experiments that are concerned with the enforcement of fairness. The second study uses a survey of public opinion to investigate whether the public considers cost-plus markup the rule of fair pricing. The third study, which is only summarized here (Kahneman et al., 1986), consists of an extensive survey of rules of fairness that the public would apply to retailers, employers, and landlords.

Study 1: Resisting Unfairness

The behavior that we label resistance to unfairness was recently observed in experiments by Guth, Schmittberger, and Schwarz (1982) and by Binmore, Shaked, and Sutton (1985). The first of these experiments introduced the following ultimatum game. One player, A (allocator), is asked to propose a division of a sum of money, X, between himself or herself and an anonymous player, R (recipient). Player R may either accept A's proposal or reject it, in which case both players receive nothing. The game-theoretic solution to this problem is that A should offer R a token payment and that R should accept any positive offer. The results were not consistent with this presumption. Most allocators offered more than a token payment, and many offered an equal split. Also, some positive offers were declined by recipients, indicating a resistance to unfair allocations and a willingness to pay to avoid them. Guth et al. were not able to report much about this behavior because most offers in their experiment were obviously fair and occasions for resistance correspondingly rare. Experiment 1 was designed to elicit a response to unfair proposals from all participants.

The experiment was conducted in a psychology class and in a commerce (business administration) class at the University of British Columbia. Each participant was given a sheet that included instructions and a response form. An example of the instructions for the first part of the experiment is given below.

> In this experiment you are matched at random with a student in the class—call him or her X. You will not get to know who X is. A sum of $10 has been provisionally allocated to the two of you. Because our budget does not permit us to pay everybody, 20 pairs of students will be chosen in a random draw and will be paid according to their responses. In responding to this questionnaire you should assume that you will be among those who are paid. X will propose a division of the $10 between the two of you, by selecting one of the options listed below. You must decide now which options are acceptable to you and which, if any, are unacceptable. If the option actually proposed by X is one that you marked acceptable, the $10 will be paid out accordingly. If the option that X proposes is unacceptable to you, neither of you gets anything. To make sure you understand the rules, please answer the following two questions before continuing. (1) If X allocates you $3.00 and you marked that value acceptable, you get $_____, and X gets $_____. (2) If X allocates you $3.00 and you marked that value unacceptable, you get $_____, and X gets $_____.

The possible allocations ranged from $9.50 to X and $0.50 to the recipient to an even split of $5.00 each, in steps of $0.50. The participants were instructed to designate each offer as acceptable or unacceptable. Half the students in the psychology class were informed that they would be paired with an unknown undergraduate student in a commerce class. All the participants in the commerce class were informed that they would be paired with a psychology student.

After completing the first task the participants turned to the next page, which instructed them to allocate $10.00 to themselves or to "a student, Z (*not* the one whom we called X)." The rules were the same as they were for the first part. The answers to the second question were used to determine the payoffs as indicated. The verbal instructions to the subjects promised that all payoffs would be in sealed envelopes to protect their privacy. The main results are shown in Table 2.

Contrary to the game-theoretic prediction but in accordance with other experimental observations the actual allocations were quite generous (Selten, 1978; Guth et al., 1982; Hoffman and Spitzer, 1982; but see also Binmore et al., 1985; Hoffman and Spitzer, 1985).

Of greater interest here is the observation that a substantial proportion of participants were willing to reject positive offers. The results do not indicate whether these individuals were motivated by a reluctance to participate in an unfair transaction, or by a wish to punish an unfair allocator, or perhaps by both. In either case the resistance to unfairness exhibited in this experiment is of the type that might deter a profit-maximizing agent or firm from seeking to exploit some profit opportunities. A widespread readiness to resist unfair transactions or to punish unfair actors even at some cost could present a significant threat to firms in competitive environments.

Experiment 2 was designed to obtain an indication of the prevalence of unenforced fairness in anonymous transactions and to establish whether people are willing to incur a cost to reward fairness and to punish unfairness when the fair or unfair actions were directed at someone else. Subjects in this experiment were students in an undergraduate psychology class at Cornell University. In the first part of the experiment subjects were instructed to divide $20 with an anonymous student in the same class, with no possibility of rejection by the recipient. The allocation was made by choosing between two possibilities: $18 to self and $2.00 to the other, or $10 to each. The participants were informed that eight pairs (selected at random from 161 students) would actually be paid according to their responses. Precautions were taken to ensure the privacy of payoffs.

The second part of the experiment, introduced after the first was completed, is explained in the following instructions.

> This part of the experiment will be limited to those members of the class who were not selected to be paid in the first part. You will be matched at random with two other students, and you will get to share some money with one or both of them. If the two people made different decisions in the first stage (e.g., one of them took $10 and one took $18), then you must make a decision about how to allocate the money. Call the person who took $10 and gave the other one $10 student E (for even). Call the person who took $18 and gave the other one $2.00 student U (for uneven). Your choices are as follows: you may allocate $5.00 to yourself, $5.00 to student E, and nothing to student U; or you may allocate $6.00 to yourself, nothing to student E, and $6.00 to student U. If both the students with whom you are grouped made the same decision, then you will receive $6.00, and each of them will receive $3.00. For this stage 15 groups of students will actually be paid.

TABLE 2 Experiment 1 Results

	Class		
	Psychology/ Psychology	*Psychology/ Commerce*	*Commerce/ Psychology*
Mean Amount Offered ($)	4.76	4.47	4.21
Equal Split Offers (%)	81	78	63
Mean of Minimum Acceptable ($)	2.59	2.24	2.00
Demands > $1.50 (%)	58	59	51
Participants (N)	43	37	35

NOTE: Data presented are by subsample: the results do not include 22 subjects whose answers to the test questions indicated a misunderstanding of the instructions.

The results of the first part of the experiment show that fair allocations are observed even under conditions of complete anonymity and with no possibility of retaliation. Of the 161 students, 122 (76 percent) divided the $20 evenly. This is stronger evidence for the prevalence of fairness to strangers than was obtained in Experiment 1. A fair allocation in an ultimatum game could be explained by the allocator's fear, often justified, that the recipient might reject a small positive offer.

The second stage of the experiment was designed to see whether the subjects would pay $1.00 to punish an unfair allocator and simultaneously reward a fair one. A clear majority (74 percent) made that choice, indicating a preference to divide $10 evenly with a fair allocator rather than divide $12 with an unfair allocator. Not surprisingly, there was a substantial correlation between the choices made in the two stages. Of 122 subjects who took $10 in the first stage, 107 (88 percent) preferred to share with student E in the second stage. In contrast, of the 39 subjects who took $18, only 12 (31 percent) shared with student E.

A class in the Cornell School of Industrial and Labor Relations was used for Experiment 3, in which only the second part of Experiment 2 was administered. The subjects were told (truthfully) that they would be matched with members of another class that had participated in part 1 of the experiment but had not been selected to be paid. Unlike the previous experiments, all the participants in Experiment 3 were paid in accordance with their expressed preferences. These procedural differences did not affect the willingness to pay for justice: 26 of the 32 subjects (81 percent) preferred to share $10 with a fair allocator rather than share $12 with an unfair one.

Two hypotheses that were mentioned in the introduction could explain why firms might sometimes fail to exploit legal but "unfair" profit opportunities. The radical hypothesis is that the owners and managers of firms have a preference for acting fairly. The alternative hypothesis is that transactors may be willing to punish an offending firm by withholding their current and future business. The results of these experiments provide clear evidence for the willingness to punish invoked in the second hypothesis. The prevalence of unenforced fairness in Experiment 2 and in others reported in the literature lends some credence to the more radical possibility as well.

Study 2: Cost Plus Is Not the Rule of Fair Pricing

The second study was motivated by a hypothesis that turned out to be wrong: that the community standard for fair pricing is that the prices of goods should be determined by adding a markup to unit costs. The hypothesis had some initial support in the observation of cost-plus pricing as a routine procedure in firms (Cyert and March, 1963). Okun (1981, p. 153) noted that "many supplying firms present themselves to their customers as procurement agencies operating under a brokerage arrangement" in which "the broker receives a specified fraction of the total value of the transaction."

The critical test for the fairness hypothesis of cost-plus pricing arises when the supplier's costs decrease. Consider the simple example of a monopolist who sells a fixed supply of a particular kind of table for $150 each and now realizes a $20 reduction in costs for each table. By a cost-plus rule with constant profit per unit the supplier should lower the price of each table by $20. By brokerage rules with proportional markup the price should be reduced by more than $20. To test whether cost plus is the rule of fair pricing this basic scenario of a supplier facing decreased costs was presented to respondents in a telephone survey.

Additional hypotheses considered possible qualifications to a general cost-plus rule of pricing, which would link the notion of fair profit to the nature of the value added by the firm or to the source of the opportunity for increased profit. Specifically, the predictions were (1) that the cost-plus rule might apply strictly only to middlemen, not to producers, and (2) that the cost-plus rule might apply only to savings due to reduced input costs but not to savings achieved by increasing efficiency. The instructive result of the study was that all these hypotheses were either completely or partially contradicted by the data.

The surveys were included in telephone interviews with adult residents in the Toronto metropolitan area. One of eight different versions of the basic questionnaire was presented to each respondent. One of these versions is presented below in full.

> My first questions are about the behavior of people in business. Suppose a factory produces a particular table, which it sells to wholesalers. The factory has been selling all the tables it can produce for $150 each. Suppose that the factory has now found a supplier who charges $20 less for the materials needed to make each table. Does fairness require the factory to change its price from $150? [Respondents who answered "yes" were now asked, "What is a fair price that it could charge the wholesalers?"] [All respondents were then asked the following question.] Imagine instead that the factory saved $20 on each table not by getting less expensive supplies but by inventing a more efficient way of making the tables. Does fairness require the factory to change its price from $150 in this case? [Continued as above.]

Different groups of respondents were asked these questions about four kinds of firms: a factory, as in the example above; "a carpenter works alone in his workshop to make tables, which he sells directly to individual customers"; "a wholesaler is the only one that distributes a particular kind of table"; and "a furniture store is the only one that sells a particular kind of table." Four other versions were generated by asking the same two questions in the opposite order. A total of 975 responses were obtained, divided about equally among the eight versions. Table 3 shows the main results for the first question asked in each version.

The main hypothesis of this study is unequivocally rejected. Even in the cases that are the most favorable to a cost-plus pricing rule (a wholesaler or retailer facing reduced input costs) only about one-third of the respondents applied that rule in designating a fair price. Half the respondents stated that fairness does not require the firm to pass on any part of its savings. The standards of fairness that respondents applied were far more favorable to firms than was suggested by the cost-plus rule.

The other two hypotheses concerning the determinants of fair pricing fared no better. Although the carpenter working alone was favored significantly more than other firms, this effect appears due to the size of the firm rather than to its role as producer. The results for the furniture factory lend no support to the general hypothesis that a producer can fairly retain a larger share of an incremental profit than can a middleman.

Finally, the prediction concerning the source of the profit increment also finds no support in Table 3. The notion of a brokerage agreement suggested that it might be fair for a supplier to retain a profit increment that it obtains by increasing efficiency, although a similar increment due to decreased input costs should be passed on to customers. Contrary to this hypothesis, the proportion allowing the firm to maintain its price appeared to be slightly higher in the case of cheaper supplies than in the case of increased efficiency.

The results reported so far were all derived from comparisons between the responses to the first of the two questions that each respondent answered. The effect of the source of the profit increment could also be tested in a second way

TABLE 3 Results of Cost-Plus Questions

	Seller			
Source of Savings	*Store*	*Wholesaler*	*Carpenter*	*Factory*
Cheaper Supply:				
Cost-plus responses ($130 or less) (%)	34	31	19	20
No-price-change-required responses (%)	47	51	63	48
Means of fair prices ($)	141.11	142.32	144.12	142.97
Increased Efficiency:				
Cost-plus responses ($130 or less) (%)	31	23	13	40
No-price-change-required responses (%)	39	46	60	35
Means of fair prices ($)	141.73	142.19	145.54	140.15

because each respondent was asked to evaluate the two possibilities in immediate succession. The conclusion of this within-individual analysis is rather different from the conclusion reached by comparing the responses of different samples. Most respondents (67 percent) stated the same fair price for an efficiency gain and for a reduction of input costs. Among those who distinguished between the two cases, however, a majority (62 percent overall) stated a lower fair price in the case of a cost reduction than in the case of an efficiency gain. This result confirms the original hypothesis and is highly reliable ($p < .001$ by chi square test for correlated proportions).

The difference between these results and those of Table 3 could reflect the higher statistical power of within-individual comparisons. It may also reflect a more interesting distinction between levels of strength for factors or rules of fairness. We define a weak factor (or rule) as one that affects evaluations of contrasting cases only when these cases are judged in relation to each other, as is likely to happen with successive questions. The effects of stronger factors can be demonstrated without the benefit of such implicit comparisons. No comparison is required, for example, to evoke different evaluations of a hardware store that raises the price of snow shovels in a blizzard and of one that does not.

A determinant or rule of fairness can be both weak and clear. For an example from another domain consider two prizes: (1) a week in Paris and (2) a week in Paris and $1.00 in cash. Separate evaluations of the attractiveness of these prizes would surely be indistinguishable, although everyone will prefer the second to the first in a direct choice.

In these terms, the distinction between cost reduction and efficiency gains was shown by the within-respondent comparisons to have some validity as a rule of fairness. The rule was not clear, however, as the agreement between respondents was far from perfect. The between-respondent design showed it to have little or no strength. The proposed cost-plus rule failed a test of strength because respondents did not generally apply it to set a fair price in a particular case considered in isolation. It remains possible that respondents might follow a cost-plus rule if asked to consider together the appropriate price response to increases and to reductions of costs. The rule is at best weak, then, but it could still be valid and even clear. A rule that is weak by the present definition can be of much theoretical interest. When the task is to predict which actions of firms will be generally rejected as unfair, however, it is reasonable to start with the strongest rather than with the clearest rules.

The present analysis suggests a caution to theorists not to rely on the clarity of their own intuitions to estimate the strength of fairness rules. Any systematic speculation about rules of fairness inevitably involves explicit comparisons of contrasting cases. Intuitions derived from such comparisons may prove a poor guide to the relative importance of different factors in a between-respondent design. The methodological conclusions of this discussion are (1) that theoretical speculation about rules of fairness is not a substitute for observation of community standards, and (2) that between-respondent comparisons are necessary to measure the strength of rules rather than their clarity. These considerations led us to adopt a between-respondent design in subsequent surveys of rules of fairness.

Study 3: Rules of Fairness

The failure of the cost-plus hypothesis in Study 2 prompted a more extensive study of community standards of fairness for firms, which is described in detail elsewhere (Kahneman et al., 1986). Telephone surveys were conducted in the Vancouver and Toronto metropolitan areas, using a broader range of examples and a different question format than those used in Study 2. Most questions required the respondents to evaluate the fairness of an action in which a firm sets a price, rent, or wage that affects the outcomes of a transactor (customer, tenant, or employee) and deviates from a relevant precedent (the reference transaction). The following examples illustrate the method.

> A landlord owns and rents out a single small house to a tenant who is living on a fixed income. A higher rent would mean the tenant would have to move. Other small rental houses are available. The landlord's costs have increased substantially over the past year, and the landlord raises the rent to cover the cost increases when the tenant's lease is due for renewal.

> A small photocopying shop has one employee who has worked in the shop for 6 months and earns $9.00 per hour. Business continues to be satisfactory, but a factory in the area has closed, and unemployment has increased. Other small shops have now hired reliable workers at $7.00 per hour to perform jobs similar to those done by the photocopy-shop employee. The owner of the photocopying shop reduces the employee's wage to $7.00.

The results of these examples are shown in Table 4.

The examples illustrate two of the general rules that were found to govern fairness judgments in the surveys. (1) It is unfair for a firm to exploit an increase in its market power to alter the terms of the reference transaction at the direct expense of a customer, tenant, or employee. (2) It is acceptable for a

TABLE 4 Responses to Illustrative Survey Questions

Landlord Example	%	Photocopying Shop Example	%
Completely Fair	39	Completely Fair	4
Acceptable	36	Acceptable	13
Somewhat Unfair	18	Somewhat Unfair	34
Very Unfair	7	Very Unfair	49

firm to maintain its profit at the reference level by raising prices or rents or by cutting wages as necessary.

The rule against adjusting prices to changed market conditions implies that it is unfair for a firm to exploit excess supply of labor to cut the wages of its employees. In the context of consumer markets and rental housing the same rule implies that an increase in demand unaccompanied by an increase in costs is not an acceptable reason to raise prices or rents. The opposition to exploitation of market power also entails strong rejection of excessive monopoly gains (see also Zajac, 1985) and of price discrimination. The introduction of auctions as an instrument of rationing is also opposed: most respondents think, for example, that if a single Cabbage Patch doll is discovered in a storeroom, it would be quite unfair for the store to auction it to the highest bidder. The spirit of this rule is well expressed in Okun's sardonic remark (1981, p. 153): "No price announcement has ever explained to customers that the supplier has moved to a new position to capture a larger share of the surplus in the relation as a result of a stronger market."

An interpretation of the hostility of respondents to exploitations of excess demand is that transactors (customers, tenants, and employees) are considerd to have an entitlement to the terms of the reference transaction, which cannot be violated arbitrarily by firms to increase their profits (Bazerman, 1985; Zajac, 1985). The other side of the coin is that the public considers the firm entitled to its reference profit. In a conflict between the transactor's claim to the reference price (or wage) and the firm's claim to its reference profit, it is acceptable for the firm to impose its claim rather than compromise. As illustrated by the tenant example, respondents agreed that a firm may protect its profit by passing on a cost increase in its entirety, even when doing so causes considerable loss or inconvenience.

There is a notable asymmetry between the rules of fairness that apply when circumstances increase or decrease the profits of a firm. The rules of fairness evidently permit firms to pass on the entire amount of a cost increase, but, as was shown in Study 2 and further confirmed in Study 3, firms are allowed to retain most of the benefits of a cost reduction.

Fairness and Framing. The concepts that economists use in their analyses of transactions are not always apt for a descriptive treatment of individual choice or of fairness judgments. A descriptive treatment must sometimes ignore distinctions that are normatively essential or introduce distinctions that are normatively irrelevant. In particular, a descriptive analysis requires that the outcomes of participants in a transaction should be defined as changes relative to a reference state rather than in absolute and objective terms (Kahneman and Tversky, 1979). The determination of the reference level in a choice is subject to framing effects, which can yield inconsistent preferences for the same objective consequences (Tversky and Kahneman, 1986). Similarly, judgments of fairness cannot be understood without considering the factors that determine the selection of a reference transaction.

Reference transactions are often tied to a particular good. For example, most respondents believe that it is unfair for a store to mark up the jars of peanut butter in its stock when wholesale prices rise, apparently because they associate the cost to the individual jar. The reference transaction may also reflect the history of relations between the firm and a particular individual: different rules apply to a current employee or tenant and to their potential replacements.

The notion of a reference state defines the gains and losses of participants in a way that violates the logic of economic analysis. Consider, for example, the contrasting rules that govern what a firm may fairly do when its reference profit is threatened or when its market power increases. In an economic analysis a firm that does not exploit its market power incurs an opportunity cost, which is considered equivalent to a decreased profit. This is the case, for example, when an employer pays an employee more than the replacement wage. Community standards of fairness—at least as indicated by the Canadian respondents surveyed—require employers and landlords to absorb such opportunity costs, just as they require hardware stores to maintain their price for snow shovels after a spring blizzard. On the other hand, fairness rules allow firms complete recovery of actual cost increases without any requirement to share the pain. A theory that assumes the equivalence of opportunity costs and out-of-pocket losses cannot do justice to these strong intuitions.

A number of economic phenomena can be predicted on the assumption that the rules of fairness have some influence on the behavior of firms (Kahneman et al., 1986). The rules of fairness tend to induce stickiness in wages and asymmetric price rigidities. They also favor a much greater use of temporary discounts than of temporary surcharges in price adjustments. Where costs for a category of goods are similar, opposition to price rationing may lead to sellouts for the most desirable items (e.g., the main game on the football calendar or the Christmas week in a ski resort). There is some evidence for all these predictions, which represent anomalies in the standard model.

Discussion

The most striking aspect of the basic microeconomic model, and the one that distinguishes it most sharply from other social sciences, is its conceptual parsimony. The behavior of economic agents is attributed to a well-defined objective—for firms it is the maximization of profits—that is pursued with complete rationality within legal and budgetary constraints. The idea of maximizing agents, all endowed with complete information, interacting in a Walrasian auction, is used to obtain predictions of market outcomes from a minimal set of assumptions about individual participants. The model of the agents is so simple that their decisions become predictable from an objective description of the environment.

There is a similarity in the programs of economics and classical stimulus-response behaviorism: both approaches seek to predict behavior from a specification of its circumstances. The environment considered in elementary microeconomics is quite simple. It can be completely described in terms of specific opportunities to maximize the objective function, and it is assumed that all such opportunities are exploited.

There are two ways of enriching this basic model. They differ in their cost and in the resistance that they may arouse among many economists. An uncontroversial move is to adopt a more complex view of the environment and of the interactions among transacting agents. Many subtleties become evident when the assumption of perfect information is dropped, allowing ignorance and risk, and when the costs of searching and transacting are considered. Much current research in economics is in this vein.

A more controversial move is to complicate the model of the agent. This can be done by allowing market behavior to be affected by added motives besides buying cheap and selling dear or by abandoning the standard assumption of rational expectations. There are at least two good reasons to resist such moves. First, adding complexity to the model of the agent generally makes it more difficult to derive unequivocal predictions of behavior from a specification of the environment. Second, there is a threat of a slippery slope. It appears all too easy to lengthen the lists of noneconomic motives or cognitive errors that might affect economic behavior.

In spite of these cautions it is sometimes useful to enrich the model of economic agents by explicitly introducing a behavioral factor that is ignored in the standard theory. Such an effort is ultimately tested by whether it helps to resolve recognized anomalies and to identify new ones. Parsimony requires that a new behavioral assumption should be introduced only if it specifies conditions under which observations deviate significantly from the basic model and only if it predicts the direction of these deviations.

Norms of fairness may satisfy this test of usefulness if, as some evidence suggests, they have a significant effect on market phenomena. A conservative revision of the standard theory will retain the model of the profit-maximizing firm and alter only the model of the transactors with which the firm must deal by endowing them with explicit rules for the judgment of fairness and with a willingness to reject unfair transactions and to discriminate against unfair firms. These characteristics of transactors affect the environment in which profit-maximizing firms operate and alter the behavior of these firms in predictable ways. A more radical revision of the standard model would incorporate a preference for fairness in the objective function of at least some firms.

The contribution of the present study has been to identify some of the criteria that people use in their fairness judgments and to demonstrate the willingness of people to enforce fairness at some cost to themselves. A realistic description of transactors should include the following traits. (1) They care about being treated fairly and treating others fairly. (2) They are willing to resist unfair firms even at a positive cost. (3) They have systematic implicit rules that specify which actions of firms are considered unfair. Further, fairness rules are not describable by the standard economic model or by a simple cost-plus rule of thumb. Instead, judgments of fairness are influenced by framing and other factors considered irrelevant in most economic treatments. By incorporating these traits into an enriched model of customers, tenants, and employees, better predictions about the behavior of the firms with which they deal may be obtained.

Perhaps the most important lesson learned from these studies is that the rules of fairness cannot be inferred either from conventional economic principles or from intuition and introspection. In the words of Sherlock Holmes in "The Adventure of The Copper Beeches": "Data! Data! Data! I cannot make bricks without clay."

REFERENCES

The research for this paper was supported by the Department of Fisheries and Oceans Canada. Kahneman and Thaler were also supported, respectively, by the U.S. Office of Naval Research and by the Alfred P. Sloan Foundation. Conversations with J. Brander, R. Frank, and A. Tversky were very helpful. We also thank Leslie McPherson and Daniel Treisman for their assistance.

Akerlof, G. "The Case Against Conservative Macroeconomics: An Inaugural Lecture." *Economica* 46 (August 1979): 219–237.

———. "Labor Contracts as Partial Gift Exchange." *Quarterly Journal of Economics* 97 (November 1982): 543–569.

Arrow, K. "Social Responsibility and Economic Efficiency." *Public Policy* 21 (Summer 1973): 303–317.

Bazerman, M. H. "Norms of Distributive Justice in Interest Arbitration." *Industrial and Labor Relations* 38 (July 1985): 558–570.

Binmore, K.; A. Shaked; and J. Sutton. "Testing Noncooperative Bargaining Theory: A Preliminary Study." *American Economic Review* 75 (December 1985): 1178–1180.

Cyert, R. M., and J. G. March. *A Behavioral Theory of the Firm*. Englewood Cliffs, NJ: Prentice-Hall, 1963.

Guth, W.; R. Schmittberger; and B. Schwarz. "An Experimental Analysis of Ultimatum Bargaining." *Journal of Economic Behavior and Organization* 3 (1982): 367–388.

Hirschman, A. L. *Exit, Voice and Loyalty*. Cambridge, MA: Harvard University Press, 1970.

Hoffman, E., and M. L. Spitzer. "The Coase Theorem: Some Experimental Tests." *Journal of Law and Economics* 25 (1982): 73–98.

————. "Entitlements, Rights, and Fairness: An Experimental Examination of Subjects' Concepts of Distributive Justice." *Journal of Legal Studies* 14 (1985): 259–297.

Kahneman, D.; J. L. Knetsch, and R. H. Thaler. "Fairness as a Constraint on Profit Seeking: Entitlements in the Market." *American Economic Review* 76, 4 (1986): 728–741. See Chapter 10 in this book.

Kahneman, D., and A. Tversky. "Prospect Theory: An Analysis of Choice Under Risk." *Econometrica* 47 (March 1979): 263–291.

Okun, A. *Prices and Quantities: A Macroeconomic Analysis.* Washington, DC: Brookings Institution, 1981.

Olmstead, A. L., and P. Rhode. "Rationing Without Government: The West Coast Gas Famine of 1920." *American Economic Review* 15 (December 1985): 1044–1055.

Selten, R. "The Equity Principle in Economic Behavior." In Hans W. Gottinger and Werner Leinfellner, eds. *Decision Theory and Social Ethics: Issues in Social Choice.* Dordrecht: Reidel, 1978.

Solow, R. M. "On Theories of Unemployment." *American Economic Review* 70 (1980): 1–11.

Thaler, R. H. "Mental Accounting and Consumer Choice." *Marketing Science* (1985): 199–214. See Chapter 2 in this book.

Tversky, A., and D. Kahneman. "Rational Choice and the Framing of Decisions." *Journal of Business* 59 (October 1986): S251–S278.

Zajac, E. E. *Fairness or Efficiency: An Introduction to Public Utility Pricing.* Cambridge, MA: Ballinger, 1978.

————. "Perceived Economic Justice: The Example of Public Utility Regulation." In H. Peyton Young, ed. *Cost Allocation: Methods, Principles and Applications.* Amsterdam: North-Holland, 1985.

Part Five

FINANCIAL MARKETS

12

THE RELEVANCE OF QUASI RATIONALITY IN COMPETITIVE MARKETS

Thomas Russell and Richard H. Thaler

SMART

My dad gave me one dollar bill
'cause I'm his smartest son,
And I swapped it for two shiny quarters
'cause two is more than one!

And then I took the quarters
And traded them to Lou
For three dimes—I guess he don't know
That three is more than two!

Just then, along came old blind Bates
And just 'cause he can't see
He gave me four nickels for my three dimes
And four is more than three!

And I took the nickels to Hiram Coombs
Down at the seed-feed store,
And the fool gave me five pennies for them,
And five is more than four!

And then I went and showed my dad,
And he got red in the cheeks
And closed his eyes and shook his head—
Too proud of me to speak!

SHEL SILVERSTEIN
*Where the Sidewalk Ends**

*Copyright © 1974 by Snake Eye Music, Inc. New York: Harper & Row, 1974 (reproduced with permission of the publisher).

Economists generally attribute considerable rationality to the agents in their models. The recent popularity of rational expectations models is more an example of a general tendency than a radical departure. Since rationality is simply *assumed*, there is little in the literature to suggest what would happen if some agents were not rational. This is surprising in light of the accumulating

Reprinted with permission from D. Bell, H. Raiffa, and A. Tversky, eds. *Decision-Making: Descriptive, Normative and Prescriptive Interactions.* New York: Cambridge University Press, 1988.

evidence that supports Herbert Simon's view that man should be considered at most boundedly rational. In fact, Kenneth Arrow concludes his recent review of this evidence as follows: "I hope to have made a case for the proposition that an important class of intertemporal markets shows systematic deviations from individual rational behavior and that these deviations are consistent with evidence from very different sources" (1982, p. 8).

In this chapter we start to explore the implications of irrationality for economics. We begin by defining what we mean by rational, and what departures from rationality we think are most likely. We then consider what happens if rational and less than fully rational agents (whom we call quasi rational) interact in competitive markets. We show that the knee-jerk reaction of some economists that competition will render irrationality irrelevant is apt only in very special cases, probably rarely observed in the real world. Our analysis highlights the important roles played by arbitragers and entrepreneurs. We find that, perhaps counter to intuition, more competition can actually make things worse by leaving no possibility of a profit to an entrepreneur who offers education or information.

RATIONALITY, QUASI RATIONALITY, AND FRAMING

Suppose two individuals face the same budget set, but choose different consumption bundles. What could be the reason? Three distinctly different reasons can be identified: (1) the individuals have different tastes (utility functions); (2) the individuals have different information; (3) one of the individuals has made a mistake. In this chapter we are primarily concerned with behavior of the third type, so we need a method of modeling mistakes.

There is no place for mistakes in the conventional economics framework. In part, this is because of the difficulty of identifying nonrational (by which we mean nonutility-maximizing) behavior. Consider, for example, the observation of a single purchase. The prices that an agent faces determine a budget hyperplane, and any point on that hyperplane that the agent chooses supports some indifference surface. Thus any chosen point can be consistent with maximization.

Suppose we examine more than one expenditure. Is it possible, on the basis of a *series* of expenditures, to characterize these acts as rational or nonrational? Defining rational now to mean maximizing for a single,[1] increasing concave utility function, the answer is a qualified yes. If the actions contain within them a violation of the weak axiom of revealed preference (which is to say, that

[1]The word single is crucial, since if tastes are allowed to change, or if a taste for "variety" is permitted, then virtually any set of actions can be rationalized.

we observe both *a* chosen when *b* is affordable, and *b* chosen when *a* is affordable), then it can be concluded that no fixed increasing strictly concave function is being maximized. Typically economists have looked for violations of the weak axiom in the choices made by agents confronted with different budget sets. Unfortunately, as Hal Varian (1982) has shown, the price income data of the real world seldom oblige by providing other than nested budget sets, so much of the time violations of the weak axiom are simply not possible.

Another way in which, in principle, one could seek violations of the weak axiom is to present the agent with the same budget set, but presented in different ways. Then his choice must not change. This hypothetical test was first suggested by the inventor of the technique of revealed preference, Paul Samuelson (1983). Samuelson considered the following problems. Suppose that we confront an agent with an income-price vector (Y, p) and observe the choice x. Now confront the agent with the income-price vector (mY, mp) where m is a positive constant. Unless the consumer again chooses x, the weak axiom is being violated. The reason is simple. By multiplying both income and prices by m we do not change the budget set. Thus any choice $y = x$ at (mY, mp) violates the axiom.

The same approach has been used more recently by cognitive psychologists to demonstrate simple violations of rationality. In a remarkable series of experiments, Daniel Kahneman and Amos Tversky (1979, 1981) have shown that subjects presented with the same problem (budget set) described in different ways repeatedly change their responses. Kahneman and Tversky call such victories of form over substance "framing" effects.

The violations that Kahneman and Tversky find are not only prevalent, they are systematic. That is to say, depending on how the problem is framed, it can be predicted whether the agent will choose x or y. We propose calling any such regular yet nonrational behavior *quasi rational*. Quasi rational behavior will include some actions that can be considered mistakes in the classification scheme described above. To incorporate such mistakes in a model of a competitive market, an extra feature has to be added to the characterization of consumer behavior. The extra feature captures the consumer's process of translating raw information into a perceived budget set.

Suppose, then, that we think of agents as being given not budget sets but the ingredients from which they can construct a budget set. Call this the information set I. Assume that the individual constructs the budget set B from I using a mapping which we call F so that $B = F(I)$.[2] Once the agent has B, we know from standard duality theory that maximizing choices can be represented as the appropriate derivatives of an indirect utility function U defined

---

[2] The language used here promises more than it delivers. The use of such terms as mapping and information sets does not mean that we have a mathematically rigorous theory of this process, and is meant to be suggestive only.

on B. With the approach suggested here, U is actually defined on I so that we have $U(F(I))$ as the integral of the maximizing choices.

What is the nature of F? It may have subjective elements, but F is not entirely subjective. It should, for example, conform to the laws of mathematics. Thus, if I is a sample drawn from some population with replacement, then F should not depend on the order in which the observations are drawn or recorded. In some cases, the mapping from I to B will be so obvious that we would expect no one to get it wrong. Kahneman and Tversky call such mappings *transparent*. The cases of interest are those where the mapping is more complex or, as they say, *opaque*.

There is no shortage of evidence documenting human judgments which fail to satisfy rational objective standards. In many cases (see Kahneman, Paul Slovic, and Tversky, 1982) these lapses seem to be associated with the use of a rule of thumb (i.e., the representativeness heuristic, and the availability heuristic) in which the decision maker sometimes focuses on irrelevant aspects of the information set in constructing his budget set.

This suggests a useful distinction between correct and incorrect mappings. We label the correct (or set of correct)[3] mapping F^* and any incorrect mappings F'.[4] We now have the apparatus to characterize all three reasons referred to earlier why choices (under the same budget set) may diverge: (1) differences in I; (2) differences in U; or (3) differences in F. Those choices consistent with an indirect utility function $U(F^*(I))$ are considered rational while those based on any other mapping, F', are considered quasi rational. The term quasi rational has been chosen to capture both the rational maximizing that is suggested by the systematic regularities shown in the experimental data (subjects do not choose at random) and the inconsistencies with the axioms of rational choice.

The existence of the mapping F is not completely foreign to economics. In expected utility theory, for example, the agent has a preference function over consequences but chooses acts. A mapping F from acts to consequences is needed to construct the budget set. In a subcase of this, portfolio theory of the Markowitz mean-variance type, investors observe the prices of assets but have preferences over the mean and variance of returns. Again a mapping F is needed to construct the relevant budget set. Indeed in financial economics the implication of heterogeneity in F is an ongoing area of investigation (Joram Mayshar, 1983; Robert Jarrow, 1983). We are here assuming not just heterogeneity in F, but the existence of a correct and incorrect F. As we shall see, however, some of the structure is identical. Finally, even in decision making under certainty, the new economic theory of the consumer of Kelvin Lancaster

---

[3]We need not be concerned here with whether F^* is unique. It is sufficient for our analysis that we be able to identify some incorrect mapping F'.
[4]The mixture of subjectivity and required consistency appears also in the subjective theory of probability. It is discussed in very clear terms by Bruno de Finetti (1977).

(1966) and Gary Becker (1965), in which consumers have preferences over characteristics but purchase market goods, requires a mapping from goods to characteristics in order to construct the budget set.

The existence of the mapping F enables us to characterize *in principle* even a single choice as nonrational. Suppose we give a consumer information concerning two choices, x and y, and that, under the true mapping F^*, x and y are identical but y is cheaper. If an individual buys x, that is nonrational. Nevertheless, it is virtually impossible to classify an act as nonrational *in practice* because of the difficulty in controlling for differences in tastes $U(.)$, or in information I.

This suggests precisely the role of the laboratory experiment. By controlling for tastes and information it is possible to identify F, and in this way conclude that the behavior is indeed nonrational. It is true that, for every real world example of quasi rational behavior we can offer, rationality cannot be ruled out. This, however, in no way rules it in. At the present state of our knowledge, it seems we must allow the possibility that some behavior is quasi rational. Nevertheless, with few exceptions, economists have tended to ignore the work of the cognitive psychologists and have continued to investigate markets with only rational agents. Why is the experimental work given so little attention? Economists have generally been critical of these results for the following reasons:

1. "Much of the research is based on hypothetical questions. Thus respondents have little incentive to respond properly." This critique has been examined by David Grether and Charles Plott (1979) and by Grether (1980) in their replications of work by psychologists. In both studies the quasi rational behavior was at least as strong in a condition with monetary incentives as in a condition with purely hypothetical questions. Thus while skepticism of hypothetical questions may be reasonable, the evidence about quasi rationality cannot be attributed solely to this problem.

2. "The experiments are done in the laboratory." While this statement is true, there is other evidence of irrational behavior outside of the lab. For example, Howard Kunreuther et al. (1978) found irrational factors to be very important in determining who would buy government-subsidized flood insurance.

3. "In the real world, people will learn." There are two responses to this critique. First, the subjects have not yet learned to choose according to our normative theories, otherwise one would not obtain the reported experimental results. Secondly, as Hillel Einhorn and Robin Hogarth (1978) have emphasized, many situations will not provide feedback in a way that will facilitate learning. Without well-structured feedback, learning may be negligible.

4. "Economists are interested in aggregate behavior and these individual errors will wash out when we aggregate." Since the errors that have been

identified are systematic (i.e., in a predictable direction), this statement is just wrong. However, there is a more subtle version of this idea.

5. "Markets will eliminate the errors." While this statement is sometimes made, it is not clear by what mechanism markets will eradicate irrational choices. While it has been argued that evolution will eventually eliminate firms that choose improperly, there is no such process at work for individuals. So far as we know, quasi rationality is rarely fatal.

In summary, there is a large body of experimental evidence suggesting that humans make judgments and decisions in a way that can be characterized as quasi rational. This evidence cannot be dismissed easily. It therefore seems prudent to begin to inquire about the workings of markets in which some agents are quasi rational. Do the quasi rationals affect prices? Does a competitive market protect or exploit the quasi rational segment? What roles do arbitrageurs and entrepreneurs play? It is to these questions we now turn.

MARKETS WITH QUASI RATIONAL AGENTS

We will investigate competitive markets with two kinds of agents, rational and quasi rational. To capture the quasi rational behavior, we use an extended Lancastrian model of consumption. Consumers purchase goods in the market but derive utility from the characteristics the goods possess rather than from the goods per se. There is an objective mapping from goods to characteristics. The rational consumers perceive this mapping. The quasi rationals perceive a different incorrect mapping.[5]

Model 1: The Basic Model[6]

We begin by considering the simplest possible model which includes both rational and quasi rational agents and allows competitive behavior. We make the following assumptions:

Preferences. All individuals are assumed to have the same preferences[7] over two characteristics:

$$U = C_1^{1/2} + C_2. \tag{1}$$

---

[5] A similar notion is used in Douglas Auld (1972) and Claude Colantoni et al. (1976).

[6] This section has benefited from the helpful comments of Keith Berry.

[7] It might be thought that it would be easier to work this example with a Cobb-Douglas utility function. However, it is easy to show that, if we combine Cobb-Douglas preferences with the simple linear consumption technology we are about to introduce, the demand for goods is independent of the technical coefficients. This result is not robust so we work with a less common but more general class of utility function.

We concentrate our attention on characteristic 1, C_1, so that characteristic 2, C_2, should be thought of as an aggregate of all other characteristics. We assume that all individuals have the same income Y, and that this income is high enough for C_2 to be bought.

The objective characteristics technology. Characteristic 1 is contained in two goods, g_1 and g_2, and only in these goods. Characteristic 2 is contained in the aggregate good g_3 and only in g_3. By Walras' law we need only consider equilibria in the markets for g_1 and g_2. We assume

$$g_1 = C_1; \quad g_2 = \beta C_1 \tag{2}$$

is the true consumption technology relating quantities of characteristics to quantities of goods. Note that, by saying $g_2 = \beta C_1$, we mean that to obtain one unit of C_1 we must purchase β units of g_2.

The quasi rational mapping. Quasi rational agents believe that the relationship in (2) is actually

$$g_1 = C_1; \quad g_2 = \gamma C_1 \quad \gamma = \beta. \tag{3}$$

The number of agents. L agents are rational, M quasi rational.

Supply. There is a fixed supply of goods 1 and 2, g_1, g_2.

Demand. Let P_i = price of good i, $i = 1, 2, 3$. Let P_{Ci} = price of characteristic i, $i = 1, 2$. Normalize prices by setting $P_3 = P_{C2} = 1$. Then as a function of P_{C1}, the price of characteristic 1, demand for characteristic 1 can be written as

$$D_{C1} = \frac{1}{(2P_{C1})^2} \tag{4}$$

If good 1 is bought, the price per unit of characteristic 1 is $P_{C1} = P_1$. If good 2 is bought, $P_{C1} = P_2\beta$. Obviously buyers will buy C_1 at what seems to them to be the lower price. Thus rational demands D^R are given by

$$D_1^R = (1/(2P_1)^2, 0, t/(2P_1)^2)$$
$$D_2^R = (0, \beta/(2\beta P_2)^2, (1 - t)/(2P_1)^2)$$

as

$$P_1 < \beta P_2, P_1 > \beta P_2, P_1 = \beta P_2,$$

where t is an arbitrary scalar $0 \leq t \leq 1$. Quasi rational demands for goods 1 and 2 are the same with β replaced with γ.

Now we have

PROPOSITION 1: A *necessary condition for an equilibrium to be a rational equilibrium is that*

$$P_1^* = \beta P_2^*.$$

PROOF: Unless this condition is satisfied, rational individuals will not buy both goods. From this we may deduce

PROPOSITION 2: *Let* $\gamma < (>)\beta$. *Then a necessary condition for an equilibrium to be a rational equilibrium is that*

$$M/L \leq \gamma \bar{g}_2/\beta^2 \bar{g}_1 \quad (M/L \leq \bar{\beta} g_1/\bar{g}_2).$$

PROOF: Let $\gamma < \beta$. Then at any rational price pair $P_1 = P_2\beta$ quasi rationals will not buy good 1. Clear the market in good 2 using only quasi rational demand. Then

$$M\gamma/(2\gamma P_2^*)^2 = \bar{g}_2$$

so that

$$P_2^* = \sqrt{M/4\gamma \bar{g}_2}.$$

For rationality we must have

$$P_1^* = \beta P_2^* = \beta\sqrt{M/4\gamma \bar{g}_2}.$$

At this price total demand for good 1 is given by

$$L/(2\beta\sqrt{M/4\gamma \bar{g}_2})^2$$

We will fail to have a rational equilibrium if this is less than the total supply of good 1, i.e., if

$$L\gamma \bar{g}_2/\beta^2 M < \bar{g}_1,$$

from which the inequality in the proposition follows.

Now let $\gamma > \beta$. Then the quasi rationals will not buy good 2. Repeating the argument we see that we must have rational demand for good 2 greater than or equal to g_2, from which the inequality follows. QED.

Note that, in this example, when $\gamma < \beta$ the degree of error does enter the condition for rationality. On the other hand, when $\gamma > \beta$, the condition does not involve γ. Why is there this asymmetry?

In the model we have assumed that the quasi rationals make an error in evaluating only good 2. When they do not buy this good, as when $\gamma > \beta$, this error cannot affect the outcome. This result is quite general. When there are fewer characteristics than goods, errors in evaluating goods which are not bought cannot affect the outcome.

Note also that, although the quasi linear utility function is itself quite special, the presence of γ in the conditions for rationality does not depend in any vital way on the special nature of this function. In general when $\gamma < \beta$, proposition 2 will look like

$$L\beta P_2(M, y, \overline{g}_2, \gamma) \geq \overline{g}_1,$$

where P_2 is the price which clears the market for good 2 when only the quasi rationals buy it. Obviously P_2 in general depends on γ.

Proposition 2 states that a rational equilibrium will not obtain if there are "too many" quasi rational consumers. The next proposition follows directly.

PROPOSITION 3: *There exist equilibria which are not rational equilibria.*

This result demonstrates that the existence of markets is not sufficient to eliminate the effect of quasi rational behavior. This market, however, has two special features which help sustain the quasi rationality: (1) the only way to trade characteristics is to trade goods; (2) there are no short sales. Both of these features are important and are analyzed in turn.

Markets for Characteristics

One way in which characteristics could be traded directly is if they could be "stripped" from the goods and sold separately. This may or may not be feasible. For example, it is possible to disassemble an automobile and sell all of its parts, but it is not possible to disassemble and sell its relevant characteristics such as ride, handling, fuel economy, comfort, etc. An extreme case of interest is where characteristics can be decomposed costlessly.

PROPOSITION 4: *If characteristics can be decomposed and marketed costlessly, then a rational equilibrium will obtain.*

PROOF: Suppose $\gamma > \beta$. Then if equilibrium were not rational, $P_1 > P_2\beta$. But this would mean that P_{C1} to the quasi rationals who buy good 1 is greater than P_{C1} to the rationals who buy good 2. Thus the law of one price does not hold in characteristics, yielding an incentive for the rationals to buy good 2, strip it of its CX_1, repackage C_1 in good 1 and sell it at a profit. (There is likewise an apparent incentive for the quasi rationals to repackage in reverse, but we assume this will immediately reveal the true relationship between goods and characteristics, and so will not occur.) The action of the rationals will thus drive up the price until $P_1 = \beta P_2$.

In goods markets the cost of characteristics stripping is determined by production technology. In asset markets, however, characteristic stripping is not so much a matter of technology as it is the number of markets and cost of using the markets. For example,[8] with a low-cost futures market in Treasury bills, a six-month Treasury bill can be stripped of its three-month component by selling a three-month futures contract in the bill. This means that the price of three-month T-bills and the combination of one six-month T-bill and one three-month future T-bill cannot get far out of line, even if financial officers of corporations have a preference for simple contracts such as three-month bills and are willing to pay a premium for such contracts.

Costless characteristics repackaging de facto sets up a market in characteristics so that the law of one price in characteristics must hold. In the absence of this market, a market in goods is not, in general, a substitute for a market in characteristics.

Short Selling

In goods markets it is not generally feasible to take a short position. Markets are just not organized in a way that allows a speculator to borrow and sell Chrysler automobiles or Heinz ketchup in the expectation of a future drop in price. Short selling is permitted in some financial markets, however, and so to extend our analysis to include those markets we explore the ramifications of permitting short sales.

PROPOSITION 5: *Short selling will guarantee that the equilibrium is rational provided: (a) within the time space that g_1 and g_2 are traded, there exists a time T^* such that after T^* the true relationship between characteristics and goods is known to everyone; (b) only the rationals sell short.*

PROOF: Again assume $\gamma > \beta$. Then, if the equilibrium is not rational, $P_1 > P_2\beta$. But, at time T^*, $P_1 = P_2\beta$. Thus short selling by the rationals will be profitable and will force P_1 into equality with $P_2\beta$.

The two extra conditions are necessary to ensure that an equilibrium exists and that short selling is riskless.[9] If the quasi rationals sell short, and if $P_1 = P_2\beta$, they will believe g_2 is overvalued and will wish to sell it short. Thus

---

[8]This example is discussed in Edwin Elton et al. (1982).
[9]In the finance literature on arbitrage pricing, these two conditions appear as: (1) all investors agree on the state representation; (2) all investors agree on probability zero events.

no equilibrium will exist. The assumption that only rationals sell short is not unreasonable if rationality is associated with professional market participants. It might be called the Marshallian view based on the following from Alfred Marshall:

> The private purchaser of railway shares may know nothing [about its prospects, the ability of its management, and the propriety of its accounts], but he buys with the confidence that all such points have been scrutinized by many keen men with special knowledge, who are able and ready to "bear" the stock if they find it in any weak spot, which . . . had not been allowed for in making up its value. [cited in Mayshar, 1983, pp. 126–127, fn. 25]

The condition that the true mapping be revealed is necessary to create a pure arbitrage opportunity (some chance of gain, no chance of loss). If characteristic stripping is impossible, then knowledge of the true mapping between goods and characteristics is not sufficient to create an arbitrage opportunity. Only if the quasi rationals become informed can the correct price be assured.

Of course, in most nonfinancial markets, characteristic stripping is not costless and short selling is impossible. In these situations (within model 1) quasi rationals do influence prices, and the rational price equilibrium need not obtain.

Production

Up to now we have been assuming that both goods are in fixed supply. To allow for production we will consider three cases: increasing costs, constant costs, and decreasing costs. Formal proofs follow the same lines as above so we just present the results.

Increasing costs. If both goods are produced with technologies involving increasing marginal costs, then the results of the previous section are qualitatively the same. A rational equilibrium can obtain as long as the number of quasi rationals in the economy is small enough.

Constant marginal costs. The constant marginal cost case is a knife-edge situation. Competition assures that price equals marginal cost so both goods can only coexist if the ratio of marginal costs is exactly equal to β. The size of the two groups of consumers is irrelevant.

Decreasing marginal costs. When both goods are produced with economies of scale, then a rational equilibrium can occur with both goods existing. Also, if the quasi rationals are large enough in number and the goods are close enough in efficiency cost, then the quasi rationals can lead to the wrong good being produced. The rationals in this case recognize that it will be cheaper for them to join the quasi rationals than to buy their preferred (ex ante) good.[10]

Comparison with Results in Finance

The models of fixed supply presented so far are very close in structure to a class of models in financial economics first introduced by John Lintner (1969).

In these models, individuals have different beliefs concerning the mean and variance of assets. The reasons for these different beliefs are not investigated so there is no counterpart to our notion of rationality and quasi rationality, but still the market is composed of individuals with different beliefs, and this assumption might be expected to produce similar results.

In an important sense, however, our results are quite different. In the financial models à la Lintner, market prices reflect all beliefs. For that reason Lintner himself found the extension of the model to heterogeneous beliefs basically uninteresting, since everything that was true for homogeneous individuals now became true for the "the market." In the models we discuss, market prices may give zero weight to the beliefs of one class of agents. Why the difference? The reason hinges on special assumptions made in the financial literature which prevent the financial system from breaking up into sub-systems. Because assets are assumed to be joint normally distributed and agents are assumed to have exponential utility functions, all individuals hold all assets. For that reason, asset prices reflect all beliefs. In our model, because there are more goods than characteristics and because the technology is linear, it is possible for rational agents completely to escape the influence of quasi-rational agents by specializing in consumption of the good(s) which the quasi rationals cause to be underpriced. It is precisely this force that can restore rationality to the market. Obviously a necessary condition for this to occur is that there are more goods than characteristics. As the finance examples make clear, this is not sufficient. If, for any reason, all goods are bought by all agents, quasi rationals must influence prices. Thus the examples we discussed earlier are actually biased toward the result that market prices will be fully rational, since they permit rational agents to form their own subeconomies.

AN EXAMPLE

As we emphasized in the introduction, it is generally not possible to prove that any act or set of actions is generated by quasi rational behavior. Differences in tastes and/or information can rarely be ruled out completely. Nevertheless, we

---

[10]A similar problem is analyzed by John Haltiwanger and Michael Waldman (1985). They call increasing costs congestion and decreasing costs synergy.

present here some data from a market where the law of one price (for characteristics) is violated. While a plausible quasi rational explanation can be given, as usual rational-based explanations can also be made. Our purposes, therefore, are just to give an example of how a market might turn out when a quasi rational rule of thumb is widely used, and to use the example to address some other theoretical issues.

Dishwashing Liquid

In 1981 Consumers Union (CU) conducted a study of the price and efficiency of dishwashing liquids. The study was replicated in 1984 with very similar results. We will present the more recent data. Thirty-five brands of dishwashing liquid were tested for their ability to wash dishes. Few differences among brands were discovered on most dimensions, but wide variation was found on the number of dishes a given quantity of the brand could wash. This "dishes washed per squirt" measure was called an efficiency factor. Brands were placed into four groups according to their efficiency factor. Brands in the top group were arbitrarily given an efficiency factor of 1.0. By multiplying the nominal price of the brand by the efficiency factor, a "real cost" was calculated. If the law of one price holds for the characteristic "dishes washed," then the real cost of each brand should be about the same.

Table 1 presents CU's results. As can be seen, the law of one price fails to hold. There is a clear negative relationship between the nominal selling price and the real cost. The most expensive brands are usually the best buys. There may, of course, be other characteristics, such as kindness to hands. However, CU found little difference on these dimensions. Furthermore, the most expensive brands are likely to have more of *all* the (positive) characteristics, so adding more characteristics would probably strengthen the results.

We think the most plausible explanation for this finding is that some consumers confuse the mapping from price per bottle to price per dish washed. It is well known in marketing that many consumers have a general tendency to

TABLE 1 Real Costs of Dishwashing Liquid

Group	Number of Brands in the Group	Average Price	Efficiency Factor	Real Cost
A	8	1.97	1.0	1.97
B	6	1.60	1.4	2.24
C	19	.97	2.7	2.61
D	2	.72	4.7	3.36

SOURCE: *Consumer Reports*, July 1984, p. 413.

buy either the cheapest brand or the most expensive brand. This tendency represents a shopping strategy that greatly reduces decision-making costs at the supermarket. It may well be *rational* to use such a strategy. It would take so long to fully analyze every decision for a single week's family shopping expedition that some simplifying strategies must be used. In cases where quality or taste is easy to judge, a family may learn to make specific alterations to their general strategy ("Don't buy generic cola"). In other cases, such as the dishwashing liquid, a family would have to do some fairly sophisticated testing to determine that its usual "buy cheap" strategy was (in this case) inappropriate.

Since this market has remained stable over the last few years (and probably for much longer), it becomes interesting to ask why the inefficient brands survive. We will consider four forces that could push the (characteristics) market back into equilibrium: arbitrage, entry, education, and tied sales.

Arbitrage and Entry

Arbitrage would be possible if one could profitably buy the expensive brands, dilute them, and sell the diluted product as a cheap brand. However, there is no reason to think this is possible. Entry into the "no frill," generic dishwashing liquid market is relatively free. There are unlikely to be profits to be made by entering this market. The high real cost of these brands probably represents the high fixed cost of packaging and distribution. Literally buying the high-priced brands off the shelf and diluting them for resale is surely an unprofitable venture, and, since the data do not necessarily imply extraordinary profits in any segment, entry alone cannot be expected to solve the problem.

Education

One of the high-price/low-cost brands of dishwashing liquid has, from time to time, run an advertising campaign that stresses the true economy of its brand relative to the low-cost "so-called bargain brands." This is an example of a firm trying to educate the quasi rational segment. Whenever a consumer can be educated at a cost that is less than his potential gain from switching to the efficient product, a profit opportunity exists. However, ironically, this education will not take place if the market is truly competitive. With perfect competition, no one seller can charge a premium above marginal cost and so there is no incentive to pay the costs of education. Only if there is some monopolistic element, such as brand names, will there be a potential return to education. Even then, the educator runs the risk that the education will not be brand specific, so other high-cost brands may be able to free ride at the educator's expense.

Tied Sales

Jerry Hausman (1979) has done a careful study of consumer purchases of air conditioners. He finds, much as in the dishwashing liquid example, that more expensive air conditioners are better buys because they are generally more energy efficient. He reports that the average purchase implies a discount rate of 25 percent after considering utilization rates and energy costs. Furthermore, the implicit discount rates vary systematically with income. Purchases by low-income households imply discount rates of 27 percent, 39 percent, and 89 percent in the three lowest income classes in Hausman's sample. These rates are all much higher than the prevailing borrowing rates (around 18 percent on most credit purchases) at that time.[11]

Hausman discusses several possible solutions to the apparently inefficient purchases being made. One is of particular interest here:

> Another possible type of market solution would be to have utility companies purchase appliances and lease them to their customers. Presumably utilities would be willing to engage in such activity, since they could borrow money to finance the more energy-efficient appliances and then charge a rental rate which would leave the consumer better off. Utilities could develop expertise in choosing the optimal efficiency model in terms of climate and intended utilization and help their customers make a better choice. [p. 51]

While Hausman's idea is along the right lines, it may not go far enough. What the utility would have to do to be sure of getting optimal choices is to rent the air conditioners with the utility costs included in the rental. Only by tying the sale of the air conditioner services with the purchase of the electricity could the possibility of quasi rational choices be ruled out. Of course, other problems such as monitoring utilization might prevent such an arrangement from succeeding. Nevertheless, the theoretical point of interest here is that only by creating a market in the ultimate consumption commodity (the characteristics in the model) can the seller guarantee rational choices.

It is interesting to compare this conclusion with that made by Richard Posner in a similar case:

> The leverage theory (of tie-in sales) held that if a seller had a monopoly of one product, he could and would monopolize its indispensable complements as well, so as to get additional monopoly profits. Thus, if he had a patented mimeograph machine, he would lease the machine at a monopoly price and also require his lessees to buy the ink used in the machine from him and charge them a monopoly price for the ink. This procedure, however, makes no sense as a matter of

---

[11] Air conditioners are rarely purchased by the very poor so most buyers probably have access to at least installment-buying-type credit.

economic theory. The purchaser is buying a service, mimeographing. *The pricing of its components is a mere detail;* it is, rather, the total price of the service that he cares about. If the seller raises the price of one component, the ink, the purchaser will treat this as an increase in the price of the service. If the machine is already being priced at the optimal monopoly level, an increase in the price of the ink above the competitive level will raise the total price of the service to the consumer above the optimal monopoly level and will thereby reduce the monopolist's profits. [1979, p. 929, emphasis added]

Posner, of course, explicitly assumes rational consumers. He says that to do otherwise would be "inconsistent with the premises of price theory." But, if even some consumers are quasi rational, then the way the prices of the various components of a good are framed is no longer a "mere detail." Indeed, framing effects in particular, and quasi rationality generally, open the possibility that repackaging goods via tie-in sales and other similar devices can increase both consumer welfare and monopoly profits. Thus the "Chicago" position on tie-in sales (to permit them) may be right, though for the wrong reasons.

CONCLUSION

When we assume that consumers, acting with mathematical consistency, maximize utility, therefore, it is not proper to complain that men are much more complicated and diverse than that. So they are, but, if this assumption yields a theory of behavior which agrees tolerably well with the facts, it must be used until a better theory comes along. [George Stigler, 1966, p. 6]

There are two possible justifications for the use of maximizing models in applied microeconomics. As Stigler suggests above, one justification is that the models are good predictors. This is the usual "as if" position. The alternative justification is that markets guarantee that only rational behavior can survive. Our reading of the psychology literature referred to earlier suggests that the first justification is frequently violated. Deviations from maximizing behavior are both common and systematic. The implication of the current paper is that the second justification will rarely apply, except (perhaps) in some highly efficient financial markets. Where does that leave us?

First of all, our analysis suggests that research on individual decision making is highly relevant to economics whenever predicting (rather than prescribing) behavior is the goal. The notion that individual irrationalities will disappear in the aggregate must be rejected. However, as Stigler implies, the neoclassical theory will not be abandoned until an acceptable (superior) alternative is available. Such theories will have to be explicitly descriptive rather than normative. The usual approach in economics is to solve for the optimal solution to a problem, and then to *assume* the agents in the model chose accordingly. Thus the model is supposed to be simultaneously normative and descriptive. A model such as Kahneman and Tversky's (1979) prospect theory abandons any claim to normative value. It simply tries to describe human behavior. Thaler and H.M. Shefrin's 1981 self-control theory of saving is in a similar spirit. Both theories seem to fit the data well. It is worth mentioning that both of these models are still basically maximizing. Quasi rationality does not imply random choice.

In the absence of such behaviorally motivated alternative theories, one intermediate step can be taken. A standard practice in applied work is to use the theory to impose restrictions to the empirical estimates. The estimates are then forced to satisfy the restrictions. In the absence of evidence to support the *assumption* that the theory describes behavior, a simple precaution is to do the estimates in an unconstrained fashion whenever that is possible. For example, Grether gave subjects in an experiment a Bayesian revision task in which they *should* equally weight the (given) prior odds and likelihood ration. He then estimated how they *did* combine the data and found that the subjects on average overweighted the likelihood ratio. The model he estimated would outperform an alternative model that assumed proper Bayesian revision. Until better theories are developed, such atheoretical estimation procedures seem appropriate.

Our analysis also has implications for the use of evolutionary arguments in economics. In a review of Richard Nelson and Sidney Winter's 1982 book on this subject, Michael Spence says that "markets discipline agents and modify their behavior." This statement is clearly true for agents within firms, but has limited applicability to individuals acting as consumers or investors. In fact, the more efficient the market, the *less* discipline the market provides. In a fully arbitraged market, all goods (assets) yield the same characteristics per dollar (returns), thus individuals can choose in any manner without penalty. Only in less than fully efficient markets is there any penalty to quasi rationality.

The first version of this chapter was presented at a conference at Cornell University sponsored by the Center for the Study of the American Political Economy. Thaler wishes to acknowledge and thank the Alfred P. Sloan Foundation for financial support. We have received helpful critical comments from Sherwin Rosen, Joachim Sylvestre, Rex Thompson, and Hal Varian. The usual disclaimer applies. The first published version appeared in *The American Economic Review* 75 (1985): 1071–1082. It was revised for this book.

REFERENCES

Arrow, Kenneth. "Risk Perception in Psychology and Economics." *Economic Inquiry* 20 (January 1982): 1–9.

Auld, Douglas. "Imperfect Knowledge and the New Theory of Demand." *Journal of Political Economy* 80 (November/December 1972): 1287–1294.

Becker, Gary S. "A Theory of the Allocation of Time." *Economic Journal* 75 (September 1965): 493–517.

Colantoni, Claude S.; Otto A. Davis; and Malati Swaminuthan. "Imperfect Consumers and Welfare Comparisons of Policies Concerning Information and Regulation." *Bell Journal of Economics* 7 (Autumn 1976): 602–618.

de Finetti, Bruno. *Theory of Probability, Vols. 1, 2.* London: Longmans, 1977.

Einhorn, Hillel J., and Robin M. Hogarth. "Confidence in Judgment: Persistence in the Illusion of Validity." *Psychological Review* 5, 85(1978): 395–416.

Elton, E.; M. Gruber; and J. Rentzler. "Intra Day Tests of the Efficiency of the Treasury Bills Futures Market." Working Paper No. CSFM-38, Columbia Business School, October 1982.

Grether, David. "Bayes Rule as a Descriptive Model: The Representativeness Heuristic." *Quarterly Journal of Economics* 95 (November 1980): 537–557.

Grether, David, and Charles Plott. "Economic Theory of Choice and the Preference Reversal Phenomenon." *American Economic Review* 69 (September 1979): 622–638.

Haltiwanger, John, and Michael Waldman. "Rational Expectations and the Limits of Rationality: An Analysis of Heterogeneity." *American Economic Review* 75 (June 1985): 326–340.

Hausman, Jerry. "Individual Discount Rates and the Purchase and Utilization of Energy-Using Durables." *Bell Journal of Economics* 10 (Spring 1979): 33–54.

Jarrow, Robert. "Beliefs, Information, Martingales and Arbitrage Pricing." Working Paper, Cornell Graduate School of Management, 1983.

Kahneman, Daniel; Paul Slovic; and Amos Tversky. *Judgment Under Uncertainty: Heuristics and Biases.* Cambridge: Cambridge University Press, 1982.

Kahneman, Daniel, and Amos Tversky. "The Framing of Decisions and the Psychology of Choice." *Science* 211 (January 1981): 453–458.

———. "Prospect Theory: An Analysis of Decision Under Risk." *Econometrica* 47 (March 1979): 263–291.

Kunreuther, Howard et al. *Disaster Insurance Protection: Public Policy Lessons.* New York: Wiley, 1978.

Lancaster, Kelvin J. "A New Approach to Consumer Theory." *Journal of Political Economy* 74 (April 1966): 132–157.

Lintner, John. "The Aggregation of Investors' Diverse Judgments and Preferences in Purely Competitive Markets." *Journal of Financial and Quantitative Analysis* 4 (December 1969): 347–400.

Mayshar, Joram. "On Divergence of Opinion and Imperfections in Capital Markets." *American Economic Review* 73 (March 1983): 114–128.

Nelson, Richard, and Sidney Winter. *An Evolutionary Theory of Economic Change.* Cambridge, MA: Harvard University Press, 1982.

Posner, Richard. "The Chicago School of Antitrust Analysis." *University of Pennsylvania Law Review* 127(1979): 925–952.

Samuelson, Paul A. *Foundations of Economic Analysis.* Cambridge, MA: Harvard University Press, 1983.

Stigler, George. *The Theory of Price*. New York: Macmillan, 1966.

Thaler, Richard, and H. M. Shefrin. "An Economic Theory of Self-Control." *Journal of Political Economy* 89 (April 1981): 201–202.

Varian, Hal R. "The Nonparametric Approach to Demand Analysis." *Econometrica* 50 (July 1982): 945–973.

13

DOES THE STOCK MARKET OVERREACT?

Werner F. M. De Bondt and Richard H. Thaler

Research in experimental psychology suggests that, in violation of Bayes' rule, most people tend to "overreact" to unexpected and dramatic news events. This study of market efficiency investigates whether such behavior affects stock prices. The empirical evidence, based on CRSP monthly return data, is consistent with the overreaction hypothesis. Substantial weak form market inefficiencies are discovered. The results also shed new light on the January returns earned by prior "winners" and "losers." Portfolios of losers experience exceptionally large January returns as late as five years after portfolio formation.

As economists interested in both market behavior and the psychology of individual decision making, we have been struck by the similarity of two sets of empirical findings. Both classes of behavior can be characterized as displaying *overreaction*. This study was undertaken to investigate the possibility that these phenomena are related by more than just appearance. We begin by describing briefly the individual and market behavior that piqued our interest.

The term overreaction carries with it an implicit comparison to some degree of reaction that is considered to be appropriate. What is an appropriate reaction? One class of tasks which have a well established norm are probability revision problems for which Bayes' rule prescribes the correct reaction to new information. It has now been well established that Bayes' rule is not an apt characterization of how individuals actually respond to new data (Kahneman et al. [1982]). In revising their beliefs, individuals tend to overweight recent information and underweight prior (or base rate) data. People seem to make predictions according to a simple matching rule: "The predicted value is selected so that the standing of the case in the distribution

Reprinted with permission from *Journal of Finance* 40, 3 (July 1985): 793–808.

of outcomes matches its standing in the distribution of impressions" (Kahneman and Tversky [1982, p. 416]). This rule-of-thumb, an instance of what Kahneman and Tversky call the representativeness heuristic, violates the basic statistical principal that the extremeness of predictions must be moderated by considerations of predictability. Grether [1980] has replicated this finding under incentive compatible conditions. There is also considerable evidence that the actual expectations of professional security analysts and economic forecasters display the same overreaction bias (for a review, see De Bondt [1985]).

One of the earliest observations about overreaction in markets was made by J. M. Keynes: ". . . day-to-day fluctuations in the profits of existing investments, which are obviously of an ephemeral and nonsignificant character, tend to have an altogether excessive, and even an absurd, influence on the market" [1936, pp. 153–154]. About the same time, Williams noted in this *Theory of Investment Value* that "prices have been based too much on current earning power and too little on long-term dividend paying power" [1938, p. 19]. More recently, Arrow has concluded that the work of Kahneman and Tversky "typifies very precisely the exessive reaction to current information which seems to characterize all the securities and futures markets" [1982, p. 5]. Two specific examples of the research to which Arrow was referring are the excess volatility of security prices and the so-called price earnings ratio anomaly.

The excess volatility issue has been investigated most thoroughly by Shiller [1981]. Shiller interprets the Miller-Modigliani view of stock prices as a constraint on the likelihood function of a price-dividend sample. Shiller concludes that, at least over the last century, dividends simply do not vary enough to rationally justify observed aggregate price movements. Combining the results with Kleidon's [1981] findings that stock price movements are strongly correlated with the following year's earnings changes suggests a clear pattern of overreaction. In spite of the observed trendiness of dividends, investors seem to attach disproportionate importance to short-run economic developments.[1]

The price earnings ratio (*P/E*) anomaly refers to the observation that stocks with extremely low *P/E* ratios (i.e., lowest decile) earn larger risk-adjusted returns than high *P/E* stocks (Basu [1977]). Most financial economists seem to regard the anomaly as a statistical artifact. Explanations are usually based on alleged misspecification of the capital asset pricing model (CAPM). Ball [1978] emphasizes the effects of omitted risk factors. The *P/E* ratio is presumed to be a proxy for some omitted factor which, if included in the

---

[1]Of course, the variability of stock prices may also reflect changes in real interest rates. If so, the price movements of other assets—such as land or housing—should match those of stocks. However, this is not actually observed. A third hypothesis, advocated by Marsh and Merton [19], is that Shiller's findings are a result of his misspecification of the dividend process.

"correct" equilibrium valuation model, would eliminate the anomaly. Of course, unless these omitted factors can be identified, the hypothesis is untestable. Reinganum [1981] has claimed that the small firm effect subsumes the P/E effect and that both are related to the same set of missing (and again unknown) factors. However, Basu [1983] found a significant P/E effect after controlling for firm size, and earlier Graham [1973] even found an effect within the thirty Dow Jones Industrials, hardly a group of small firms!

An alternative behavioral explanation for the anomaly based on investor overreaction is what Basu called the "price-ratio" hypothesis (e.g., Dreman [1982]). Companies with very low P/Es are thought to be temporarily "undervalued" because investors become excessively pessimistic after a series of bad earnings reports or other bad news. Once future earnings turn out to be better than the unreasonably gloomy forecasts, the price adjusts. Similarly, the equity of companies with very high P/Es is thought to be "overvalued," before (predictably) falling in price.

While the overreaction hypothesis has considerable a priori appeal, the obvious question to ask is: How does the anomaly survive the process of arbitrage? There is really a more general question here. What are the equilibria conditions for markets in which some agents are not rational in the sense that they fail to revise their expectations according to Bayes' rule? Russell and Thaler [1985] address this issue. They conclude that the existence of some rational agents is not sufficient to guarantee a rational expectations equilibrium in an economy with some of what they call quasi-rational agents. (The related question of market equilibria with agents having heterogeneous expectations is investigated by Jarrow [1983].) While we are highly sensitive to these issues, we do not have the space to address them here. Instead, we will concentrate on an empirical test of the overreaction hypothesis.

If stock prices systematically overshoot, then their reversal should be predictable from past return data alone, with no use of any accounting data such as earnings. Specifically, two hypotheses are suggested: (1) Extreme movements in stock prices will be followed by subsequent price movements in the opposite direction. (2) The more extreme the initial price movement, the greater will be the subsequent adjustment. Both hypotheses imply a violation of weak-form market efficiency.

To repeat, our goal is to test whether the overreaction hypothesis is *predictive*. In other words, whether it does more for us than merely to explain, ex post, the P/E effect or Shiller's results on asset price dispersion. The overreaction effect deserves attention because it represents a behavioral principle that may apply in many other contexts. For example, investor overreaction possibly explains Shiller's earlier [1979] findings that when long-term interest rates are high relative to short rates, they tend to move down later on. Ohlson and Penman [1983] have further suggested that the increased volatility of security returns following stock splits may also be linked to overreaction. The present empirical tests are to our knowledge the first attempt to use a behavioral principle to predict a new market anomaly.

The remainder of the paper is organized as follows. The next section describes the actual empirical tests we have performed. Section 2 describes the results. Consistent with the overreaction hypothesis, evidence of weak-form market inefficiency is found. We discuss the implications for other empirical work on asset pricing anomalies. The paper ends with a brief summary of conclusions.

1. THE OVERREACTION HYPOTHESIS: EMPIRICAL TESTS

The empirical testing procedures are a variant on a design originally proposed by Beaver and Landsman [1981] in a different context. Typically, tests of semistrong form market efficiency start, at time $t = 0$, with the formation of portfolios on the basis of some event that affects all stocks in the portfolio, say, an earnings announcement. One then goes on to investigate whether later on $(t > 0)$ the estimated residual portfolio return $\hat{u}_{pt}$—measured relative to the single-period CAPM—equals zero. Statistically significant departures from zero are interpreted as evidence consistent with semistrong form market inefficiency, even though the results may also be due to misspecification of the CAPM, misestimation of the relevant alphas and/or betas, or simply market inefficiency of the weak form.

In contrast, the tests in this study assess the extent to which systematic nonzero residual return behavior in the period after portfolio formation $(t > 0)$ is associated with systematic residual returns in the preformation months $(t < 0)$. We will focus on stocks that have experienced either extreme capital gains or extreme losses over periods up to five years. In other words, "winner" (W) and "loser" portfolios (L) are formed *conditional upon past excess returns*, rather than some firm-generated informational variable such as earnings.

Following Fama [1976], the previous arguments can be formalized by writing the efficient market's condition,

$$E(\tilde{R}_{jt} - E_m(\tilde{R}_{jt} \mid F^m_{t-1}) \mid F_{t-1}) = E(\tilde{u}_{jt} \mid F_{t-1}) = 0$$

where F_{t-1} represents the complete set of information at time $t - 1$, $\tilde{R}_{jt}$ is the return on security j at t, and $E_m(\tilde{R}_{jt} \mid F^m_{t-1})$ is the expectation of $\tilde{R}_{jt}$, assessed by the market on the basis of the information set F^m_{t-1}. The efficient market hypothesis implies that $E(\tilde{u}_{wt} \mid F_{t-1}) E (\tilde{u}_{L,t}/Ft-1) = 0$. As explained in the introduction, the overreaction hypothesis, on the other hand, suggests that $E(\tilde{u}_{wt} \mid F_t-1) < 0$ and $E(\tilde{u}_{L,t} \mid F_t-1) > 0$.

In order to estimate the relevant residuals, an equilibrium model must be specified. A common procedure is to estimate the parameters of the market model (see, e.g., Beaver and Landsman [5]). What will happen if the equilibrium model is misspecified? As long as the variation in $E_m(\tilde{R}_{jt} \mid F^m_{t-1})$ is small relative to the movements in $\tilde{u}_{jt}$, the exact specification of the equilibrium model makes little difference to tests of the efficient market hypothesis. For, even if we knew the "correct" model $E_m(\tilde{R}_{jt} \mid F^m_{t-1})$, it would explain only small part of the variation in $\tilde{R}_{jt}$.[2]

Since this study investigates the return behavior of specific portfolios over extended periods of time (indeed, as long as a decade), it cannot be merely *assumed* that model misspecification leaves the conclusions about market efficiency unchanged. Therefore, the empirical analysis is based on three types of return residuals: market-adjusted excess returns; market model residuals; and excess returns that are measured relative to the Sharpe-Lintner version of the CAPM. However, since all three methods are single-index models that follow from the CAPM, misspecification problems may still confound the results. De Bondt [1985] formally derives the econometric biases in the estimated market-adjusted and market model residuals if the "true" model is multifactor, e.g., $\tilde{R}_{jt} = A_j + B_j\tilde{R}_{mt} + C_j\tilde{X}_t + \tilde{e}_{jt}$. As a final precaution, he also characterizes the securities in the extreme portfolios in terms of a number of financial variables. If there were a persistent tendency for the portfolios to differ on dimensions that may proxy for "risk," then, again, we cannot be sure whether the empirical results support market efficiency or market overreaction.

It turns out that, whichever of the three types of residuals are used, the results of the empirical analysis are similar, and the choice does not affect our main conclusions. Therefore, we will only report the results based on market-adjusted excess returns. The residuals are estimated as $\tilde{u}_{jt} = R_{jt} - R_{mt}$. There is no risk adjustment except for movements of the market as a whole and the adjustment is identical for all stocks. Since, for any period t, the same (constant) market return R_{mt} is subtracted from all R_{jt}'s, the results are interpretable in terms of raw (dollar) returns. As shown in De Bondt [7], the use of market-adjusted excess returns has the further advantage that it is likely to bias the research design *against* the overreaction hypothesis.[3] Finally, De Bondt shows that winner and loser portfolios, formed on the basis of

---

[2]Presumably, this same reasoning underlies the common practice of measuring abnormal security price performance by way of easily calculable mean-adjusted excess returns [where, by assumption, $E(\tilde{R}_j)$ equals a constant K_j], market-adjusted excess returns (where, by assumption, $\alpha_j = 0$ and $\beta_j = 1$ for all j), rather than more complicated market model residuals, let alone residuals relative to some multifactor model.

[3]We will come back to this bias in Section 2.

market-adjusted excess returns, do not systematically differ with respect to either market value of equity, dividend yield or financial leverage.

We will now describe the basic research design used to form the winner and loser portfolios and the statistical test procedures that determine which of the two competing hypotheses receives more support from the data.

A. Test Procedures: Details

Monthly return data for New York Stock Exchange (NYSE) common stocks, as compiled by the Center for Research in Security Prices (CRSP) of the University of Chicago, are used for the period between January 1926 and December 1982. An equally weighted arithmetic average rate of return on all CRSP listed securities serves as the market index.

1. For every stock j on the tape with at least 85 months of return data (months 1 through 85), without any missing values in between, and starting in January 1930 (month 49), the next 72 monthly residual returns u_{jt} (months 49 through 120) are estimated. If some or all of the raw return data beyond month 85 are missing, the residual returns are calculated up to that point. The procedure is repeated 16 times starting in January 1930, January 1933, . . . , up to January 1975. As time goes on and new securities appear on the tape, more and more stocks quality for this step.

2. For every stock j, starting in December 1932 (month 84; the "portfolio formation date") $(t = 0)$, we compute the cumulative excess returns $CU_j = \Sigma_{t=-35}^{t-0} u_{jt}$ for the prior 36 months (the "portfolio formation" period, months 49 through 84). The step is repeated 16 times for all nonoverlapping three-year periods between January 1930 and December 1977. On each of the 16 relevant portfolio formation dates (December 1932, December 1935, . . . , December 1977), the CU_j's are ranked from low to high and portfolios are formed. Firms in the top 35 stocks (or the top 50 stocks, or the top decile) are assigned to the winner portfolio W; firms in the bottom 35 stocks (or the bottom 50 stocks, or the bottom decile) to the loser portfolio L. Thus, the portfolios are formed conditional upon excess return behavior prior to $t = 0$, the portfolio formation date.

3. For both portfolios in each of 16 nonoverlapping three-year periods $(n = 1, . . . , N; N = 16)$, starting in January 1933 (month 85, the "starting month") and up to December 1980, we now compute the cumulative average residual returns of all securities in the portfolio, for the next 36 months (the "test period," months 85 through 120), i.e., from $t = 1$ through $t = 36$. We find $CAR_{W,n,t}$ and $CAR_{L,n,t}$. If a security's return is missing in a month subsequent to portfolio formation, then, from that moment on, the stock is permanently dropped from the portfolio and the CAR is an

average of the available residual returns. Thus, whenever a stock drops out, the calculations involve an implicit rebalancing.[4]

4. Using the CAR's from all 16 test periods, *average* CAR's are calculated for both portfolios and each month between $t = 1$ and $t = 36$. They are denoted $ACAR_{W,t}$ and $ACAR_{L,t}$. The overreaction hypothesis predicts that, for $t > 0$, $ACAR_{W,t} < 0$ and $ACAR_{L,t} > 0$, so that, by implication, $[ACAR_{L,t} - ACAR_{W,t}] > 0$. In order to assess whether, at any time t, there is indeed a statistically significant difference in investment performance, we need a pooled estimate of the population variance in CAR_t,

$$S_t^2 = [\Sigma_{n=1}^{N}(CAR_{W,n,t} - ACAR_{W,t})^2 + \Sigma_{n=1}^{N}(CAR_{L,n,t} - ACAR_{L,t})^2]/2(N - 1).$$

With two samples of equal size N, the variance of the difference of sample means equals $2S_t^2/N$ and the *t*-statistic is therefore

$$T_t = [ACAR_{L,t} = ACAR_{W,t}]/\sqrt{2S_t^2/N}.$$

Relevant *t*-statistics can be found for each of the 36 postformation months but they do not represent independent evidence.

5. In order to judge whether, for any month t, the average residual return makes a contribution to either $ACAR_{W,t}$ or $ACAR_{L,t}$, we can test whether it is significantly different from zero. The sample standard deviation of the winner portfolio is equal to

$$s_t = \sqrt{\Sigma_{n=1}^{N}(AR_{W,n,t} - AR_{W,t})^2/N - 1}.$$

Since $s_t/\sqrt{N}$ represents the sample estimate of the standard error of $AR_{W,t}$, the *t*-statistic equals

$$T_t = AR_{W,t}/(s_t/\sqrt{N}).$$

Similar procedures apply for the residuals of the loser portfolio.

---

[4]Since this study concentrates on companies that experience extraordinary returns, either positive or negative, there may be some concern that their attrition rate sufficiently deviates from the "normal" rate so as to cause a survivorship bias. However, this concern is unjustified. When a security is delisted, suspended or halted, CRSP determines whether or not it is possible to trade at the last listed price. If no trade is possible, CRSP tries to find a subsequent quote and uses it to compute a return for the last period. If no such quote is available because the stockholders receive nothing for their shares, the return is entered as minus one. If trading continues, the last return ends with the last listed price.

B. Discussion

Several aspects of the research design deserve some further comment. The choice of the data base, the CRSP Monthly Return File, is in part justified by our concern to avoid certain measurement problems that have received much attention in the literature. Most of the problems arise with the use of daily data, both with respect to the risk and return variables. They include, among others, the "bid-ask" effect and the consequences of infrequent trading.

The requirement that 85 subsequent returns are available before any firm is allowed in the sample biases the selection towards large, established firms. But, if the effect under study can be shown to apply to them, the results are, if anything, more interesting. In particular, it counters the predictable critique that the overreaction effect may be mostly a small-firm phenomenon. For the experiment described in Section A, between 347 and 1,089 NYSE stocks participate in the various replications.

The decision to study the CARs for a period of 36 months after the portfolio formation date reflects a compromise between statistical and economic considerations, namely, an adequate number of independent replications versus a time period long enough to study issues relevant to asset pricing theory. In addition, the three-year period is also of interest in light of Benjamin Graham's contention that "the interval required for a substantial underevaluation to correct itself averages approximately 1½ to 2½ years" [1959, p. 37]. However, for selected experiments, the portfolio formation (and testing) periods are one, two, and five years long. Clearly, the number of independent replications varies inversely with the length of the formation period.

Finally, the choice of December as the "portfolio formation month" (and, therefore, of January as the "starting month") is essentially arbitrary. In order to check whether the choice affects the results, some of the empirical tests use May as the portfolio formation month.

2. THE OVERREACTION HYPOTHESIS: EMPIRICAL RESULTS

A. Main Findings

The results of the tests developed in Section 1 are found in Figure 1. They are consistent with the overreaction hypothesis. Over the last half-century, loser portfolios of 35 stocks outperform the market by, on average, 19.6 percent, 36 months after portfolio formation. Winner portfolios, on the other hand, earn about 5.0 percent less than the market, so that the difference in cumulative average residual between the extreme portfolios, $[ACAR_{L,36} - ACAR_{W,36}]$ equals 24.6 percent (t-statistic: 2.20). Figure 1 shows the movement of the ACAR's as we progress through the test period.

The findings have other notable aspects. First, the overreaction effect is asymmetric; it is much larger for losers than for winners. Secondly, consistent with previous work on the turn-of-the-year effect and seasonality, most of the excess returns are realized in January. In months $t = 1$, $t = 13$, and $t = 25$, the loser portfolio earns excess returns of, respectively, 8.1 percent (t-statistic: 3.21), 5.6 percent (3.07), and 4.0 percent (2.76). Finally, in surprising agreement with Benjamin Graham's claim, the overreaction phenomenon mostly occurs during the second and third year of the test period. Twelve months into the test period, the difference in performance between the extreme portfolios is a mere 5.4 percent (t-statistic: 0.77).

While not reported here, the results using market model and Sharpe-Lintner residuals are similar. They are also insensitive to the choice of December as the month of portfolio formation (see De Bondt [1985]).

The overreaction hypothesis predicts that, as we focus on stocks that go through more extreme return experiences (during the formation period), the subsequent price reversals will be more pronounced. An easy way to generate more extreme observations is to lengthen the portfolio formation period; alternatively, for any given formation period (say, two years), we may compare the test period performance of less versus more extreme portfolios,

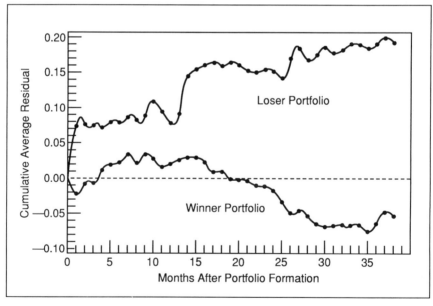

Figure 1. *Cumulative Average Residuals for Winner and Loser Portfolios of 35 Stocks (1–36 months into the test period)*

e.g., decile portfolios (which contain an average 82 stocks) versus portfolios of 35 stocks. Table 1 confirms the prediction of the overreaction hypothesis. As the cumulative average residuals (during the formation period) for various sets of winner and loser portfolios grow larger, so do the subsequent price reversals, measured by $[ACAR_{L,t} - ACR_{W,t}]$ and the accompanying t-statistics. For a formation period as short as one year, no reversal is observed at all.

Table 1 and Figure 2 further indicate that the overreaction phenomenon is qualitatively different from the January effect and, more generally, from seasonality in stock prices. Throughout the test period, the difference in ACAR for the experiment with a three-year formation period (the upper curve) exceeds the same statistic for the experiments based on two- and one-year formation periods (middle and lower curves). But all three experiments are clearly affected by the same underlying seasonal pattern.

In Section 1, it was mentioned that the use of market-adjusted excess returns is likely to bias the research design against the overreaction hypothesis. The bias can be seen by comparing the CAPM-betas of the extreme portfolios. For all the experiments listed in Table 1, the average betas of the securities in the winner portfolios are significantly larger than the betas of the loser portfolios.[5] For example, for the three-year experiment illustrated in Figure 1, the relevant numbers are, respectively, 1.369 and 1.026 (t-statistic on the difference: 3.09). Thus, the loser portfolios not only outperform the winner portfolios; if the CAPM is correct, they are also significantly less risky. From a different viewpoint, therefore, the results in Table 1 are likely to *underestimate* both the true magnitude and statistical significance of the overreaction effect. The problem is particularly severe with respect to the winner portfolio. Rather than 1.369, the residual return calculations assume the CAPM-beta of that portfolio to equal 1.00 only. This systematic bias may be responsible for the earlier observed asymmetry in the return behavior of the extreme portfolios.

To reiterate, the previous findings are broadly consistent with the predictions of the overreaction hypothesis. However, several aspects of the results remain without adequate explanation: most importantly, the extraordinarily large positive excess returns earned by the loser portfolio in January.

One method that allows us to further accentuate the strength of the January effect is to increase the number of replications. Figure 3 shows the ACARs for an experiment with a five-year-long test period. Every December between 1932 and 1977, winner and loser portfolios are formed on the basis of residual return behavior over the previous five years. Clearly, the successive 46 yearly selections are not independent. Therefore, no statistical tests are performed. The results in Figure 3 have some of the properties of a "trading rule." They

---

[5]The CAPM-betas are found by estimating the market model over a period of 60 months prior to portfolio formation.

TABLE 1 Differences in Cumulative Average (Market-Adjusted) Residual Returns Between the Winner and Loser Portfolios at the End of the Formation Period, and 1, 12, 13, 18, 24, 25, 36, and 60 Months into the Test Period

Portfolio Selection Procedures: Length of the Formation Period and No. of Independent Replications	Average No. of Stocks	CAR at the End of the Formation Period		Difference in CAR (t-Statistics)							
		Winner Portfolio	Loser Portfolio	Months After Portfolio Formation							
				1	12	13	18	24	25	36	60
10 five-year periods	50	1.463	−1.194	0.070 (3.13)	0.156 (2.04)	0.248 (3.14)	0.236 (3.17)	0.196 (2.15)	0.228 (2.40)	0.230 (2.07)	0.319 (3.28)
16 three-year periods	35	1.375	−1.064	0.105 (3.29)	0.054 (0.77)	0.103 (1.18)	0.167 (1.51)	0.181 (1.71)	0.234 (2.19)	0.246 (2.20)	NA[c]
24 two-year periods[a]	35	1.130	−0.857	0.062 (2.91)	−0.006 (−0.161)	0.074 (1.53)	0.136 (2.02)	0.101 (1.41)	NA	NA	NA
25 two-year periods[b]	35	1.119	−0.866	0.089 (3.98)	0.011 (0.19)	0.092 (1.48)	0.107 (1.47)	0.115 (1.55)	NA	NA	NA
24 two-year periods[a] (deciles)	82	0.875	−0.711	0.051 (3.13)	0.006 (0.19)	0.066 (1.71)	0.105 (1.99)	0.083 (1.49)	NA	NA	NA
25 two-year periods[b] (deciles)	82	0.868	−0.714	0.068 (3.86)	0.008 (0.19)	0.071 (1.46)	0.078 (1.41)	0.072 (1.29)	NA	NA	NA
49 one-year periods	35	0.774	−0.585	0.042 (2.45)	−0.076 (−2.32)	−0.006 (−0.15)	0.007 (0.14)	−0.005 (−0.09)	NA	NA	NA

[a] The formation month for these portfolios is the month of December in all uneven years between 1933 and 1979.
[b] The formation month for these portfolios is the month of December in all even years between 1932 and 1950.
[c] NA, not applicable.

268

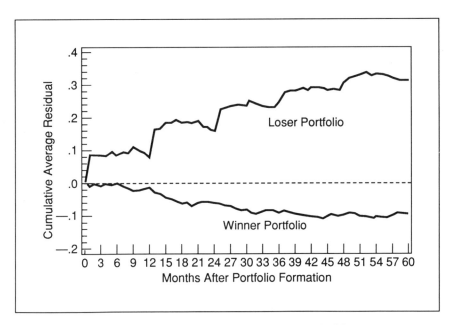

Figure 2. *Differences in Cumulative Average Residual Between Winner and Loser Portfolios of 35 Stocks (formed over the previous one, two, or three years; 1–24 months into the test period)*

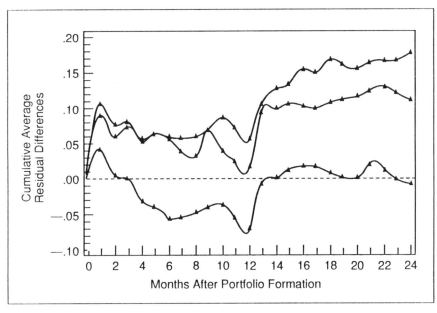

Figure 3. *Cumulative Average Residuals for Winner and Loser Portfolios of 35 Stocks (1–60 months into the test period)*

269

represent the average (cumulative) excess return (before transaction costs) that an investor, aware of the overreaction phenomenon, could expect to earn following any December in which he chose to try the strategy. The effect of multiplying the number of replications is to remove part of the random noise.

The outstanding feature of Figure 3 is, once again, the January returns on the loser portfolio. The effect is observed as late as five Januaries after portfolio formation! Careful examination of Figure 3 also reveals a tendency, on the part of the loser portfolio, to decline in value (relative to the market) between October and December. This observation is in agreement with the naive version of the tax-loss selling hypothesis as explained by, e.g., Schwert [1983]. The winner portfolio, on the other hand, gains value at the end of the year and loses some in January (for more details, see De Bondt [1985]).

B. Implications for Other Empirical Work

The results of this study have interesting implications for previous work on the small firm effect, the January effect and the dividend yield and P/E effects. Blume and Stambaugh [1983], Keim [1982], and Reinganum [1981] have studied the interaction between the small firm and January effects. Their findings largely redefine the small firm effect as a "losing firm" effect around the turn-of-the-year.[6] Our own results lend further credence to this view. Persistently, losers earn exceptionally large January returns while winners do not. However, the companies in the extreme portfolios do not systematically differ with respect to market capitalization.

The January phenomenon is usually explained by tax-loss selling (see, e.g., Roll [1983]). Our own findings raise new questions with respect to this hypothesis. First, if in early January selling pressure disappears and prices "rebound" to equilibrium levels, why does the loser portfolio—even while it outperforms the market—"rebound" once again in the second January of the test period? And again, in the third and fourth Januaries? Secondly, if prices "rebound" in January, why is that effect so much larger in magnitude than the selling pressure that "caused" it during the final months of the previous year? Possible answers to these questions include the argument that investors may wait for years before realizing losses, and the observed seasonality of the market as a whole.

---

[6]Even after purging the data of tax-loss selling effects, Reinganum [1983] finds a (considerably smaller) January seasonal effect related to company size. This result may be due to his particular definition of the tax-loss selling measure. The measure is related to the securities' relative price movements over the last *six months* prior to portfolio formation only. Thus, if many investors choose to wait longer than six months before realizing losses, the portfolio of small firms may still contain many "losers."

With respect to the *P/E* effect, our results support the price-ratio hypothesis discussed in the introduction, i.e., high *P/E* stocks are "overvalued" whereas low *P/E* stocks are "undervalued." However, this argument implies that the *P/E* effect is also, for the most part, a January phenomenon. At present, there is no evidence to support that claim, except for the persistent positive relationship between dividend yield (a variable that is correlated with the *P/E* ratio) and January excess returns (Keim [1982]).

3. CONCLUSIONS

Research in experimental psychology has suggested that, in violation of Bayes' rule, most people "overreact" to unexpected and dramatic news events. The question then arises whether such behavior matters at the market level.

Consistent with the predictions of the overreaction hypothesis, portfolios of prior "losers" are found to outperform prior "winners." Thirty-six months after portfolio formation, the losing stocks have earned about 25 percent more than the winners, even though the latter are significantly more risky.

Several aspects of the results remain without adequate explanation; most importantly, the large positive excess returns earned by the loser portfolio every January. Much to our surprise, the effect is observed as late as five years after portfolio formation.

REFERENCES

The financial support of the C.I.M. Doctoral Fellowship Program (Brussels, Belgium) and the Cornell Graduate School of Management is gratefully acknowledged. We received helpful comments from Seymour Smidt, Dale Morse, Peter Bernstein, Fischer Black, Robert Jarrow, Edwin Elton, and Ross Watts.

Arrow, K.J. "Risk Perception in Psychology and Economics." *Economic Inquiry* 20 (January 1982): 1–9.

Ball, R. "Anomalies in Relationships Between Securities' Yields and Yield Surrogates." *Journal of Financial Economics* 6 (June–September 1978): 103–126.

Basu, S. "Investment Performance of Common Stocks in Relation to Their Price-Earnings Ratios: A Test of the Efficient Market Hypothesis." *Journal of Finance* 3 (June 1977): 663–682.

———. "The Relationship Between Earnings' Yield, Market Value and Return for NYSE Common Stocks: Further Evidence." *Journal of Financial Economies* 12 (June 1983): 129–156.

Beaver, W., and W.R. Landsman. "Note on the Behavior of Residual Security Returns for Winner and Loser Portfolios." *Journal of Accounting and Economics* 3 (December 1981): 233–241.

Blume M., and R. Stambaugh. "Biases in Computed Returns: An Application to the Size Effect." *Journal of Financial Economics* 12 (November 1983): 387–404.

De Bondt, W.F.M. "Does the Stock Market Overreact to New Information?" Unpublished Ph.D. diss., Cornell University, 1985.

Dreman, D.N. *The New Contrarian Investment Strategy.* New York: Random House, 1982.

Fama, E.F., *Foundations of Finance.* New York: Basic Books, 1976.

Graham, B. *The Intelligent Investor, A Book of Practical Counsel,* 3rd ed. New York: Harper & Brothers, 1959.

———. *The Intelligent Investor, A Book of Practical Counsel,* 4th rev. ed. New York: Harper & Brothers, 1973.

Grether, D.M. "Bayes' Rule as a Descriptive Model: The Representativeness Heuristic." *Quarterly Journal of Economics* 95 (November 1980): 537–557.

Jarrow, R. "Beliefs, Information, Martingales, and Arbitrage Pricing." Working Paper, Johnson Graduate School of Management, Cornell University, November 1983.

Kahneman, D., and A. Tversky. "Intuitive Prediction: Biases and Corrective Procedures." In D. Kahneman, P. Slovic, and A. Tversky, eds. *Judgment Under Uncertainty: Heuristics and Biases.* London: Cambridge University Press, 1982.

Keim, D. "Further Evidence on Size Effects and Yield Effects: The Implications of Stock Return Seasonality." Working Paper, Graduate School of Business, University of Chicago, April 1982.

———. "Size-Related Anomalies and Stock Return Seasonality: Further Empirical Evidence." *Journal of Financial Economics* 12 (June 1983): 13–32.

Keynes, J.M. *The General Theory of Employment, Interest and Money.* London: Harcourt Brace Jovanovich, 1964 (reprint of the 1936 edition).

Kleidon, A.W. "Stock Prices as Rational Forecasters of Future Cash Flows." Working Paper, Graduate School of Business, University of Chicago, November 1981.

Marsh, T.A., and R.C. Merton. "Aggregate Dividend Behavior and Its Implications for Tests of Stock Market Rationality." Working Paper No. 1475–83, Sloan School of Management, MIT, September 1983.

Ohlson, J.A., and S.H. Penman. "Variance Increases Subsequent to Stock Splits: An Empirical Aberration." Working Paper, Graduate School of Business, Columbia University, September 1983.

Reinganum, M.R. "Misspecification of Capital Asset Pricing: Empirical Anomalies Based on Earnings' Yields and Market Values." *Journal of Financial Economics* 9 (March 1981): 19–46.

———. "The Anomalous Stock Market Behavior of Small Firms in January." *Journal of Financial Economics* 12 (June 1983): 89–104.

Roll, R. "Vas ist dans?" *Journal of Portfolio Management* 10 (Winter 1983): 18–28.

Russell, T., and R. Thaler. "The Relevance of Quasi Rationality in Competitive Markets." *American Economic Review* 75 (1985): 1071–1082. See Chapter 12 in this book.

Schwert, G.W. "Size and Stock Returns, and Other Empirical Regularities." *Journal of Financial Economics* 12 (June 1983): 3–12.

Shiller, R.J. "The Volatility of Long-Term Interest Rates and Expectations Models of the Term Structure." *Journal of Political Economy* 87 (December 1979): 1190–1219.

———. "Do Stock Prices Move Too Much to be Justified by Subsequent Changes in Dividends?" *American Economic Review* 71 (June 1981): 421–436.

Williams, J.B. *The Theory of Investment Value.* Amsterdam: North-Holland, 1956 (reprint of 1938 edition).

14

FURTHER EVIDENCE ON INVESTOR OVERREACTION AND STOCK MARKET SEASONALITY

Werner F. M. De Bondt and Richard H. Thaler

In a previous paper, we found systematic price reversals for stocks that experience extreme long-term gains or losses: Past losers significantly outperform past winners. We interpreted this finding as consistent with the behavioral hypothesis of investor overreaction. In this follow-up paper, additional evidence is reported that supports the overreaction hypothesis and that is inconsistent with two alternative hypotheses based on firm size and differences in risk, as measured by CAPM-betas. The seasonal pattern of returns is also examined. Excess returns in January are related to both short-term and long-term past performance, as well as to the previous year market return.

In a previous paper (De Bondt and Thaler [1985]), we investigated a simple stock market investment strategy motivated by work in cognitive psychology on intuitive prediction. The strategy is based on the notion that many investors are poor Bayesian decision makers. Experimental and survey evidence indicates that in probability revision problems people show a tendency to "overreact," i.e., they overweight recent information and underweight base rate data. We conjectured that, as a consequence of investor overreaction to earnings, stock prices may also temporarily depart from their underlying fundamental values. With prices initially biased by either excessive optimism or pessimism, prior "losers" would be more attractive investments than prior "winners."

Reprinted with permission from *Journal of Finance* 42, 3 (July 1987): 557–581.

We found considerable evidence consistent with this simple hypothesis.[1] For example, using monthly return data between 1926 and 1982 for stocks listed on the New York Stock Exchange (as compiled by the Center for Research in Security Prices (CRSP) at the University of Chicago), we formed portfolios of the 50 most extreme winners and 50 most extreme losers (as measured by cumulative excess returns over successive five-year formation periods). It was reported that over the following five-year test periods the portfolios of losers outperformed the portfolios of winners by an average of 31.9 percent.

However, many issues regarding the "winner-loser" effect were left unresolved. First, there is a pronounced seasonality in the "price correction." Almost all of it occurs in the successive months of January, especially for the losers. Second, the correction appears to be asymmetric: after the date of portfolio formation, losers win approximately three times the amount that winners lose. Third, the characteristics of the firms in the extreme portfolios were not fully described. This is important since studies by, e.g., Keim [1986] and Reinganum [1983] contain results that suggest that the winner-loser effect may simply be another instance of the well-known size and/or turn-of-the-year effects (for a review, see Schwert [1983]). Finally, the interpretation of our results as evidence of investor overreaction has been questioned. There are at least two alternative explanations, both involving time-varying equilibrium rates of return. Using methodology similar to our own, Vermaelen and Verstringe replicate the winner-loser anomaly for the Belgian stock market. They argue, however, that ". . . this 'overreaction' effect is a rational market response to risk changes" ([1986], p. 13). Their "risk-change hypothesis," also presented by Chan [1986, 1987], states that a decline (increase) in stock prices leads to an increase (decline) in debt-equity ratios and risk as measured by CAPM betas. More recently, Fama and French [1986] again report significant negative serial correlation in stock returns, explaining 25 to 45 percent of three- to five-year return variation. While these authors agree that their findings are consistent with our own (as well as with other models in which prices take long swings away from fundamental values, e.g., Keynes [1936] or Shiller [1984]), they suggest that mean-reverting factor risk premia may be the cause, citing (among other studies) the work of Keim and Stambaugh [1986].

In an effort to reevaluate the overreaction hypothesis, this paper discusses new empirical findings that are relevant to the winner-loser, size, and January effects, as well as to the broader issues of time-varying risk premia and market efficiency. Section 1, based on CRSP data, extends our earlier results and further discusses the seasonality in the return behavior of extreme

---

[1]Other empirical work reporting evidence (on a firm-by-firm basis) consistent with overreaction includes Brown and Harlow [1988] and Howe [1986].

winner and loser portfolios. In addition, we address the issue of whether the winner-loser anomaly can be explained by differences in CAPM-betas. Along with return data, Section 2 uses accounting numbers drawn from COMPUSTAT to characterize the extreme portfolios and to compare and contrast the small firm and winner-loser effects. This section also matches earnings movements to the observed return performance. Stock prices may be thought of as discounted expected earnings, $p = E(c)/\rho$, where c is the earnings stream and ρ is the discount rate. The primary focus of the time-varying expected return explanations is on ρ. Here, we examine the numerator. It is found that, at least for the extreme portfolios, prior stock price performance predicts subsequent reversals in company earnings. The fact that earnings reversals are accompanied by contemporaneous stock price reversals suggests that the market fails to recognize the tendency toward mean reversion in extreme earnings numbers.

While we stress overreaction, we concede that part of the mean reversion in stock prices may also be due to time-varying equilibrium expected returns, and that the tax code may be linked to the unusual January returns. Indeed, these and other valid arguments are not mutually exclusive with overreaction bias. However, our principal motivation remains a concern with the microfoundations of modern finance. Parallel to George Akerlof's approach to economic theory, we aim "to explore the consequences of new behavioral assumptions" ([1984], p. 1).

1. THE WINNER-LOSER EFFECT, STOCK MARKET SEASONALITY, AND RISK

Perhaps the most curious result in our previous paper is the strong seasonality in the test period returns of winners and losers. A large portion of the excess returns occurs in January. Using CRSP monthly return data, we now explore some questions motivated by these earlier findings and other research which links the unusual January returns either to the tax code (e.g., Branch [1977], Chan [1986], Dyl [1977], Reinganum [1983], Roll [1983], and Rozeff [1985]) or to seasonality in the risk-return relationship (e.g., Keim and Stambaugh [1986], and Rogalski and Tinic [1986]). First, are there any seasonal patterns in returns during the formation period? Next, within the extreme portfolios, do systematic price reversals occur throughout the year, or do they occur only in January? Finally, are the January corrections driven by recent share price movements (say, over the last few months), or by more long-term factors? Using the same data set, we also investigate the hypothesis that the winner-loser effect can be explained by changes in CAPM-betas (see Chan [1987] and

Vermaelen and Verstringe [1986]). Before turning to the results, we briefly describe the empirical methods used in this section.

1A. Empirical Methods

1. For every stock j on the CRSP Monthly Return Tape (1926–1982) with at least 61 months of return data (without any missing values in between, and starting in January 1926), we estimate 120 monthly market-adjusted excess returns, $u_{jt} = R_{jt} - R_{mt}$, covering both a five-year portfolio "formation" and a five-year "test" period.[2] An equal-weighted average of the monthly returns on all stocks listed on the NYSE is used for R_{mt}. The procedure is repeated 48 times for each of the ten-year periods starting in January 1926, January 1927, . . . , up to January 1973. Over the years, the various samples grow from 381 to 1245 stocks.

2. For every stock in each sample, we find the cumulative excess return CU_j over the five-year formation period. After that, the CU_j's are ranked and portfolios are formed. The 50 stocks with the highest CU_j's are assigned to a winner portfolio W; the 50 stocks with the lowest CU_j's to a loser portfolio L. In total, there are 48 winner and 48 loser portfolios each containing 50 securities.

3. For some of the descriptive statistics and regression tests below, we combine the 48 winner and 48 loser portfolios into two "master" samples, one of winners and one of losers. These two "master" samples each contain 2,400 observations.

For the correlation tests below, new sets of portfolios are formed as follows. For the five sequences of all nonoverlapping formation periods that start in January 1926, January 1927, . . . , January 1930, the single most extreme winners from each formation period are combined to form group W_1. The stocks that came in second in the formation periods form group W_2, etc. We thus have, for each of five experiments, 50 of what we call "rank portfolios" for winners, $W_1, \ldots, W_{50}$, and 50 "rank portfolios" of losers formed in the same manner. In total, there are 250 winner and 250 loser rank portfolios. Depending on the number of periods, each rank portfolio contains a maximum of either nine or ten stocks.

Average and cumulative average excess returns are found for each rank portfolio. Whenever a return is missing, the average excess return for that portfolio is calculated over the remaining observations. The cumulation

[2]If some or all of the raw return data beyond month #61 are missing, the excess returns are calculated up to that point. No survivorship bias is introduced with this methodology. Firms which drop out before the formation date are not included. For those which drop out during the test period, we use the last entry on the CRSP file to compute the final return, which can be -1 if the shares have no value.

periods include the formation period, the test period, and various subperiods. The tests involve simple, partial, and Spearman rank correlations between relevant pairs of average return performances covering different (sub-)periods.

1B. Excess Returns, Seasonality and Taxes

It is immediately apparent from the plots of test period returns in our previous paper ([1985], Figures 1, 2 and 3) that they contain an important seasonal component. To examine this seasonality in greater detail, and to see whether the formation period returns also show seasonality, Table 1 presents average excess returns earned by both the winner and loser "master" portfolios for various subperiods.[3] During the test period, losers earn virtually all of their excess returns in January (with the last three months of the year offsetting any gains between February and September). Winner excess returns, though smaller (in absolute terms) than for losers, also occur predominantly in January. In the formation period, the January excess returns for winners are about double that of the abnormal performance in other months. For losers, by the last two years of the formation period, the seasonal pattern starts to resemble that of the test period: positive January returns and the larger than usual negative returns toward the end of the year.

One implication of the overreaction hypothesis is a tendency (which Brown and Harlow [1988] call the "magnitude effect") for the most extreme initial

---

[3]The average returns in Table 1 are based on 48 replications with the test periods starting in January of all years between 1931–1978, while our previous paper used the years 1933–1978.

TABLE 1 Average Monthly Excess Returns of Long-Term Winners and Losers for Varying Periods

	Winners				Losers			
Period	All Months	Jan.	Feb.–Sept.	Oct.–Dec.	All Months	Jan.	Feb.–Sept.	Oct.–Dec.
A: FORMATION PERIOD								
$t-4, t$	2.7	4.5	2.6	2.3	−2.1	−.5	−2.1	−2.6
$t-4, t-2$	2.7	5.6	2.6	2.1	−2.0	−1.8	−2.0	−2.2
$t-1, t$	2.6	3.0	2.6	2.7	−2.1	1.6	−2.1	−3.3
B: TEST PERIOD								
$t+1, t+5$	−.2	−.8	−.3	0.0	.6	5.0	.4	−.4
$t+1, t+3$	−.3	−1.3	−.3	.1	.7	6.1	.5	−.5
$t+4, t+5$	−.1	−.1	−.1	−.1	.3	3.3	.1	−.3

NOTE: All entries in the table are average market-adjusted excess returns (in percent) where the return on the market portfolio is measured by an equally-weighted index of all stocks listed on the NYSE, as provided by CRSP. They are based on 2400 observations. See Section 1A for details. Year t represents the last year of the formation period.

winners and losers to exhibit the most extreme subsequent price reversals. Our earlier paper provided supporting evidence by comparing the test period performance of portfolios chosen over formation periods with different durations. The longer the formation period, the greater both the initial price movements and the subsequent reversals. Brown and Harlow's study of the magnitude effect uses a more stringent test. They find that the effect holds even within portfolios of extreme winners and losers. The rank portfolios, described in the empirical methods section above, permit us to investigate this hypothesis as well. In addition, they allow us to focus on the seasonality of the magnitude effect.

We start by calculating Spearman rank correlations between cumulative average excess returns (CAR) for the entire formation period and the first one, two, . . . , five years of the test period. For losers, consistent with overreaction, the average correlations are $-.14$, $-.28$, $-.22$, $-.29$ and $-.30$. A simple bivariate regression (using all 250 loser rank portfolios) of CAR for the formation period on CAR for the test period yields an intercept of $-.205$ (t-statistic: -2.55) and a slope of $-.421$ (-6.67). The R-square (adjusted for degrees of freedom) is $.149$. On the other hand, for winners, there is no evidence of a magnitude effect. None of the equivalent Spearman rank correlations are significantly different from zero, and neither is the slope-coefficient of the bivariate regression.

The previous findings conceal the seasonality of the magnitude effect. Further correlation tests indicate that, except in January, winner and loser excess returns are unrelated to formation period CAR.[4] This raises the question to what extent the exceptional January returns of long-term winners and losers are actually driven by performance over the immediately preceding months, possibly reflecting tax-motivated trading.

Table 2 shows OLS regressions with the excess return in the first January of the test period as the dependent variable. The predictor variables measure relative performance over, respectively, (1) the prior December, (2) the last five months (July through November) prior to December, and (3) the remaining 4½ years of the formation period.[5] Equations A.1 and B.1 indicate that the January excess returns of both winners and losers show significant

---

[4]Using five times 100 rank portfolios, we compute Spearman rank, simple, and partial correlations (controlling for excess returns during the last December of the formation period) between formation period CAR and subperiod CARs for January, February through September, and October through December of each test year. Except for January, no correlations are sizable. For losers, the January correlations are significantly negative. For winners, they are positive for the first January of the test period but generally close to zero for later Januaries. Further regression tests (based on the two "master" samples) indicate that, even though the R-squares are small (varying between .018 and .120), January test period excess returns of both winners and losers are reliably related to return movements in adjacent Januaries.

[5]For the sake of brevity, Table 2 shows only results based on the two "master" samples. The securities in each sample are not independently selected since the formation periods are partially overlapping. However, tests using five subsamples that overcome this problem do not affect our conclusions.

TABLE 2 OLS-Regressions of Winner and Loser Excess Returns for the First January of the Test Period on Selected Variables

Regression #	Intercept	D1 (intercept)	Dec. Excess Return (year t)	D2 (slope)	July–Nov. Cumulative Excess Return (year t)	Cumulative Excess Return (years t − 4 through June of t)	Adj. R-square
A: WINNERS							
A.1	−.011		−.235				.038
	(−3.37)		(−9.76)				
A.2	−.038	.043	−.340	.135			.058
	(−6.95)	(6.21)	(−7.10)	(2.44)			
A.3	−.046		−.214		−.006	.024	.054
	(−6.47)		(−8.88)		(−.58)	(6.01)	
A.4	−.072	.044	−.285	.088	−.009	.023	.073
	(−8.66)	(6.45)	(−5.91)	(1.59)	(−.94)	(5.70)	
B: LOSERS							
B.1	.051		−.704				.130
	(11.45)		(−18.92)				
B.2	.065	−.026	−1.082	.813			.190
	(8.41)	(−2.79)	(−20.27)	(11.09)			
B.3	−.022		−.727		−.144	−.051	.148
	(−1.68)		(−19.68)		(−6.85)	(−4.86)	
B.4	.005	−.023	−1.080	.771	−.108	−.041	.200
	(0.36)	(−2.43)	(−20.37)	(10.52)	(−5.25)	(−4.00)	

NOTE: T-statistics are shown in parentheses. All regressions are based on 2400 observations. See Section IA for details. Dummy variable $D1$ equals one if the equal-weighted return of all NYSE stocks is positive in the last year of the formation period (year t). It is zero otherwise. Predictor variable $D2$ equals the excess return in December of year t multiplied by $D1$.

short-term reversals. For losers, these reversals may reflect tax-loss selling pressure (see, e.g., Branch [1977], Reinganum [1983], and Roll [1983]). For winners, the short-run reversals are consistent with a capital gains tax "lock-in" effect. While we are not aware of any other study documenting turn-of-the-year return reversals for winners, Dyl [1977] and Lakonishok and Smidt [1986] report unusually low trading volume for these stocks in December and unusually high volume in January, facts also consistent with a lock-in effect.

Equations A.3 and B.3 further show a statistically significant link between January excess returns and prior long-term performance. For losers, the long-term effect is negative as predicted by investor overreaction. By its mere presence, the long-term effect contradicts rational tax-loss selling as an explanation of the January seasonal (see also Chan [1986]). For winners, surprisingly, the long-term effect is positive. This observation is in conflict with the overreaction hypothesis.[6]

The economic significance of the long-term effects is substantial. In order to compare it with the economic weight of the short-term effects, we compute the "component contribution" of each predictor variable, i.e., the product of its estimated coefficient and its sample mean. For losers (equation B.3), the average January excess return of 7.9 percent can be decomposed into an unexplained intercept (-2.2 percent), 2.9 percent that is due to a short-term reversal from the previous December, 1.7 percent due to reversals from the previous July through November, and 5.5 percent due to long-term reversals. For winners (equation A.3), the average January excess return equals -1.8 percent and the long-term component is a positive 3.5 percent.

Earlier work (e.g., Rozeff [1985]) suggests that the size of the January excess returns depends on the performance of the market as a whole over the previous year (or previous six months). In order to see whether this applies to our portfolios, intercept and slope dummy variables are added to the OLS-regressions in Table 2. The intercept dummy equals one if R_{mt}, annually compounded, is positive during the last year of the formation period. It is zero otherwise. The slope dummy is defined as the intercept dummy multiplied by the excess return for December. Equations A.2, A.4, B.2, and B.4 show that, on average, following down years, long-term winners perform worse and long-term losers better than they do following years in which the market has risen. For losers, the slope dummy indicates that the December–January

---

[6]OLS-regressions with loser January excess returns for later test years as the dependent variable yield results similar to Table 2. For example, for the 5th January, the coefficient on the excess return for the previous December (i.e., the December of the 4th test year) is $-.462$ (t-statistic: -12.96), while the coefficient on the formation period cumulative residual equals $-.066$ (t-statistic: -6.71)! For winners, the short-term reversals persist (e.g., for the 5th January, the relevant coefficient is $-.169$ (t-statistic: -7.60)) but the (positive) long-term effect disappears beyond the 2nd January of the test period.

reversals are significantly more pronounced following years of market declines. Again, these findings are consistent with tax explanations of the unusual January returns.

1C. Excess Returns and Changing Risk

In our previous paper we investigated whether the excess returns to winner and loser portfolios could be explained by differences in CAPM-betas. The betas were estimated over the formation period. Regardless of the length of the formation period (varying between one to five years), the beta for the loser portfolio was always lower than the beta for the winner portfolio. We therefore concluded that, within the CAPM framework, the reported market-adjusted excess returns were conservative estimates of the "true" risk-adjusted excess returns. However, Chan [1986,1987] and Vermaelen and Verstringe [1986] argue that the usual procedure of estimating betas over a prior period is inappropriate if betas vary with changes in market value. For winners and losers, a negative correlation between risk and market value is plausible because of changes in financial leverage that accompany extreme movements of the value of equity. The implication is that the winner-loser effect may disappear if the risk estimates are obtained during the test period.

To test this hypothesis, we construct "arbitrage" portfolios that finance the purchase of losers by selling winners short, and we regress (using OLS) the annual test period returns $R_{At} = R_{Lt} = R_{Wt}$, on the market risk premium, $R_{mt} - R_{ft}$, i.e., $R_{At} = \alpha_A + \beta_A(R_{mt} - R_{ft}) + \epsilon_{At}$. As before, R_{mt} is the (annually compounded) monthly return on an equal-weighted index of NYSE stocks. R_{ft} is taken from Ibbotson and Sinquefield [18], and it is measured as the (annually compounded) one-month holding period return on U.S. Treasury bills. The constant term α_A is the well-known Jensen performance index; β_A is an estimate of the difference in Sharpe-Lintner CAPM-betas between the loser and winner portfolios. The equation is also estimated separately for the winners and losers with, respectively, $R_{wt} - R_{ft}$ and $R_{Lt} - R_{ft}$ as the dependent variable. Additional regressions include dummy variables that control for the year of the test period. Finally, all the previous regressions are repeated with January and February through December returns as the dependent variables.

The results appear in Table 3. Regression A.1 indicates that, during the test period, the estimated beta for the loser portfolio is indeed .220 greater than the winner-beta. However, this difference in risk is insufficient to explain the return on the arbitrage portfolio since α_A, at 5.9 percent, is significantly positive. Thus, this simple test of the risk-change hypothesis fails to explain the winner-loser effect. Regression B.1 is also of interest because, unlike our previous results, it indicates that, on a CAPM risk-adjusted basis, the winner portfolio has significantly negative excess returns. The coefficients on the dummy variables reveal the familiar pattern of declining excess returns through the test period.

Using alternative methods which allow for time-varying betas, Chan [1987] finds a test period beta of about 0.1 for the arbitrage portfolio, but obtains an alpha insignificantly different from zero. The alpha and beta are average coefficients obtained from separate equations estimated (using monthly data) for each of 18 nonoverlapping three-year experiments. Chan readily admits that the small difference in betas "would appear to have no chance to explain the average monthly return of 0.586 percent" ([9], p. 12). Instead, he explains the combined observations of a small alpha, a small beta, and a large return by positive correlation between the time-varying betas and the market risk premium. The argument is that both the betas and the expected market risk premium may be responding to common state variables.

To further investigate this issue, we recalculate the regressions in Table 3 in a way that permits two betas to be estimated, one for periods when the stock market is rising, and another for when it is falling. Define a dummy variable D which equals one if $R_{mt} > 0$ and zero if $R_{mt} < 0$. The estimated equation for the arbitrage portfolio is now $R_{At} = \alpha_A + \beta_{Au}(R_{mt} - R_{ft})D + \beta_{Ad}(R_{mt} - R_{ft})(1 - D) + \epsilon_{At}$, with similar equations for the winner and loser portfolios.

As shown in Table 4, once betas are allowed to vary with the market, the alphas are no longer significantly positive. These results, which confirm Chan's findings, require careful interpretation. We see in equation A.1 that, while the average CAPM-beta of the arbitrage portfolio was earlier estimated to be .220, the portfolio actually has a positive beta when the market goes up, and a negative beta when it falls. In other words, the arbitrage portfolio does well in both up and down markets. Equations B.1 and C.1 indicate how this happens. For the winner portfolio, the up-beta is .993 while the down-beta is 1.198. For the loser portfolio, the betas are 1.388 and .875. In rising markets, the losers have a tendency to gain more than the winners, while in falling markets, the winners tend to lose more than the losers. Equations A.2, B.2, and C.2 reveal a similar but magnified pattern of returns in January. In contrast, during the rest of the year, the results are muted and the loser alpha is significantly negative.

The risk-change hypothesis claims that during the test period the losers are riskier than the winners, and that this difference in risk is responsible for the apparent excess returns. The above results do not support this view. When risk is measured by CAPM-betas, the risk disparity is insufficient to account for the return gap. Only when the betas are allowed to vary with the level of the market is the alpha of the arbitrage portfolio no longer positive. Furthermore, these time-varying "split" betas are questionable measures of risk. In January, for example, the CAPM-betas are higher for the losers than for the winners (1.469 vs. .931). Yet, it seems odd to say that a portfolio with a beta of

TABLE 3 OLS-Regressions of Annual, January, and February through December Portfolio Risk Premia for the Test Period on Selected Variables

| | | | Independent Variables | | | | |
| | | | Test Year Dummy Variables | | | | |
Regression #	Intercept	$R_m - R_f$	D2	D3	D4	D5	Adj. R-sq.
A: ARBITRAGE PORTFOLIO							
Annual Returns							
A.1	.059 (3.72)	.220 (4.72)					.082
A.2	.121 (3.72)		.021 (.46)	−.020 (−.43)	−.063 (−1.36)	−.081 (−1.77)	.012
A.3	.088 (2.75)	.216 (4.65)	.018 (.40)	−.023 (−.53)	−.060 (−1.36)	−.078 (−1.78)	.092
January Returns							
A.4	.032 (4.40)	.538 (6.94)					.168
February–December Returns							
A.5	.014 (1.08)	.215 (4.78)					.085
B: WINNER PORTFOLIO							
Annual Returns							
B.1	−.033 (−4.47)	1.043 (47.91)					.906
B.2	.130 (2.69)		−.013 (−.19)	.009 (.13)	−.011 (−.15)	.002 (.03)	.000
B.3	−.030 (−1.99)	1.045 (48.06)	−.028 (−1.38)	−.008 (−.39)	.004 (.18)	.016 (.79)	.906

		January Returns						R^2
B.4		.931	−.004					.754
		(26.78)	(−1.37)					
		February–December Returns						
B.5		1.054	−.024					.905
		(47.20)	(−3.76)					

C: LOSER PORTFOLIO

	Annual Returns						R^2
C.1	1.263	.026					.859
	(38.20)	(2.30)					
C.2	.251	.008	−0.11	−.073	−.079		.000
	(4.20)	(.10)	(−.12)	(−.87)	(−.94)		
C.3	1.260	.058	−.011	−.031	−.056	−.062	.860
	(38.24)	(2.55)	(−.34)	(−1.00)	(−1.79)	(−1.98)	

	January Returns						R^2
C.4	1.469	.027					.736
	(25.55)	(5.11)					
	February–December Returns						
C.5	1.269	−.010					.885
	(42.38)	(−1.18)					

NOTE: *T*-statistics are shown in parentheses. In panel A, the dependent variable is, for each of five test years, the return on the winner portfolio. In panel B (panel C), it is the return on the winner (loser) portfolio minus the return on U.S. Treasury Bills. Since our basic experiment is replicated 48 times (covering ten-year periods between 1926–1935, 1927–1936, . . . , through 1973–1982), there are 240 observations. *D2, D3, . . . , D5* are dummy variables that equal one for the 2nd, 3rd, . . . , 5th test year, respectively. They are zero otherwise. The return on the market portfolio is measured using an equally-weighted index of NYSE stocks provided by CRSP. Because we do not have monthly returns for U.S. Treasury Bills beyond December 1981, the regressions with January and February through December returns contain only 235 observations. The last replication of our basic experiment (covering the ten-year period between 1973 and 1982) is dropped.

285

TABLE 4 OLS-Regressions of Annual, January, and February Through December Portfolio Risk Premia on the Market Risk Premium in Up and Down Markets

Regression #	Independent Variables			
	Intercept	$(R_m - R_f)D$	$(R_m - R_f)(1 - D)$	Adj. R-sq.
A: ARBITRAGE PORTFOLIO				
	Annual Returns			
A.1	−.005	.395	−.323	.142
	(−.24)	(6.43)	(−2.36)	
	January Returns			
A.2	.008	.748	−.848	.215
	(.83)	(8.08)	(−2.33)	
	February–December Returns			
A.3	−.032	.376	−.176	.138
	(−1.85)	(6.24)	(−1.60)	
B: WINNER PORTFOLIO				
	Annual Returns			
B.1	−.015	.993	1.198	.908
	(−1.43)	(33.77)	(18.25)	
	January Returns			
B.2	.004	.854	1.439	.763
	(1.04)	(20.39)	(8.73)	
	February–December Returns			
B.3	−.011	1.007	1.168	.906
	(−1.24)	(32.87)	(20.97)	
C: LOSER PORTFOLIO				
	Annual Returns			
C.1	−.020	1.388	.875	.868
	(−1.29)	(31.80)	(8.98)	
	January Returns			
C.2	.012	1.602	.591	.746
	(1.73)	(23.15)	(2.17)	
	February–December Returns			
C.3	−.043	1.384	.992	.892
	(−3.73)	(34.54)	(13.63)	

NOTE: See Table 3. D is a dummy variable which equals one if the return on the market portfolio (as measured by an equally-weighted index of NYSE stocks) is positive. It is zero otherwise.

286

1.602 in up markets and .591 in down markets is riskier than one with up and down betas of .854 and 1.439.[7]

2. THE WINNER-LOSER EFFECT, THE SIZE EFFECT AND OVERREACTION TO EARNINGS

The results so far have utilized only return data. Many questions remain that require additional information. One important issue is whether the winner-loser effect is qualitatively different from the size effect. Are losing firms particularly small? Are small firms for the most part losers? To the extent that the small firm effect (where size is measured by market value of equity) is a losing firm effect, are there any additional excess returns genuinely attributable to company size when size is measured in a way that is independent of short-term price movements? Can we use accounting data to distinguish the overreaction hypothesis from other explanations of the winner-loser effect? To answer these and other questions we turn to the COMPUSTAT tape. Again, we begin by describing our empirical methods.

2A. Empirical Methods

1. Six samples are chosen from the main and delisted (research) files of the Annual Industrial COMPUSTAT tapes for the period between 1965 and 1984. In order to be selected, a company needs complete five-year records prior to (and including) the portfolio formation years 1969, 1971, 1973, 1975, 1977, and 1979 for the following annual data items: #6 (Total Assets; Liabilities and Shareholders' Equity), #12 (Sales), #18 (Income Before Extraordinary Items and Discontinued Operations), #24 (Closing Price for the Calendar Year), #25 (Common Shares Outstanding), #26 (Dividends Per Share by Ex-Date), #27 (Cumulative Adjustment Factor), #58 (Primary Earnings Per Share, Excluding Extraordinary Items and Discounted Operations), and #60 (Common Equity). Also, for each of the five years prior to and including the formation year, the company must have a December fiscal-year end. In addition, it must be listed either on the NYSE or the AMEX. Finally, firms that are part of the S&P 40 Financial Index are excluded. For the six samples listed by formation date, the

---

[7]Rogalski and Tinic use arguments similar to Chan's to explain the January size effect. They show that the CAPM-betas of small firms are higher in January than in other months and that, therefore, "the 'abnormal' returns on these stocks may not, after all, be abnormal" ([1986], p. 63) if proper risk adjustments are made. However, given that so many small firms are losers, we speculate that small firms also have high January betas in up markets and low betas in down markets, a result which would leave the abnormal returns abnormal.

number of companies (and the number of companies listed on the NYSE) are: 1969: 1015 (789); 1971: 1106 (842); 1973: 1262 (931); 1975: 1336 (996); 1977: 1339 (975); and 1979: 1263 (939).

2. For each firm j, annual raw returns R_{jt} and excess returns u_{jt} are computed from COMPUSTAT data (with appropriate adjustments made for stock splits, etc.) for all years between $t - 3$ and $t + 4$, with t representing the final year of the formation period. The excess returns are market-adjusted, $u_{jt} = R_{jt} - Rmt$, where the market return R_{mt} is estimated by compounding (over 12 months) a monthly equal-weighted NYSE index taken from CRSP.

3. Every sample is ordered by each of the following four ranking variables: (a) cumulative excess return (CU_j) over a four-year formation period between the end of year $t - 4$ and the end of year t; (b) market value of equity (MV) at (the end of year) t; (c) market value of equity divided by book value of equity (MV/BV) at t; (d) company assets at t (COMPUSTAT item #6).

4. For each sample and for each ranking variable, with minor adjustments, quintile, decile, and "ventile" (20) portfolios are formed. Average and cumulative average excess returns (CAR) are calculated for the four years between $t - 3$ and t, and for the four years between $t + 1$ and $t + 4$. Subsequently, the (cumulative) average excess returns are averaged once again, either across the six samples, or across two times three samples (formation years 1969, 1973 and 1977, vs. formation years 1971, 1975 and 1979). With CU_j as ranking variable, these two times three samples represent truly independent observations since the formation periods are nonoverlapping.

   For the sake of brevity, the tables below report our findings primarily for the quintile portfolios. However, the statistical tests are done on the basis of ventile or decile portfolios.

5. For each ranking method, portfolio averages and medians are also computed for other variables of interest, most importantly, company income and earnings per share (EPS). The EPS-numbers for different years are adjusted for stock splits, stock dividends, etc.; as a result, they remain strictly comparable through time. In order to improve their cross-sectional comparability, they are scaled by the closing stock price at the end of year $t - 4$.[8]

6. In order to make portfolio comparisons of time-series movements in any given variable X easier, the portfolio averages X_p are indexed by setting them equal to 1.0 in a base year (either t or $t - 4$). Thus, the observations

---

[8]Whenever there are missing data, the portfolio averages and medians are computed over the remaining observations. There are three sources of missing data: (1) fiscal year changes; (2) removal of the company from the COMPUSTAT research files; (3) missing observations in otherwise complete data records. Except in case (3), the stock is removed from all portfolio averages at the same point in time.

may be represented by $X_{pt}^* = (X_{pt}/X_{pb})$ where X_{pb} is the portfolio average in the base year. A simple method to detrend X_{pt}^* (or, in other words, to remove the marketwide component in its movement through time) starts by repeating the above indexation procedure for the whole sample population. Then, if X_{st} stands for the total sample average at t, $X_{st}^* = (X_{st}/X_{sb})$. The next step is to find the detrended X_{pt}^d by dividing X_{pt}^* by X_{st}^* for all t. Tables 7 and 8 below list X_{pt}^d multiplied by 100.

7. Friedman's [15] two-way analysis of variance by ranks is used to test nonparametrically whether, for any ranking method, there is a tendency for the annual excess returns of one portfolio to exceed or to be smaller than the same-year returns of other portfolios. A multiple comparison procedure specifically checks for differences between the extreme decile portfolios. The data are average excess returns during the formation and test periods for twenty portfolios of equal size. The tests are run twice: once for the average excess returns computed with 1969, 1973 and 1977 as the formation years, and again with 1971, 1975 and 1979 as the formation years. We have two times four (years $t - 3 \ldots t$; $t + 1 \ldots t + 4$) independent samples and twenty "treatments" (portfolios). The test statistic is distributed approximately chi-square with nineteen degrees of freedom.

In some cases, Page's [1963] nonparametric test for ordered alternatives provides a more meaningful alternative hypothesis. It checks whether, for any ranking method, the k "treatment" effects are ordered in the following way: $t_1 \leq t_2 \leq \ldots t_k$. If the alternative hypothesis is changed to $t_1 \geq t_2 \geq \ldots \geq t_k$, the test statistic only changes its sign. For large samples, the statistic is distributed approximately as the standard normal. The exact computational formulas for both the Friedman and Page tests can be found in, e.g., Daniel [1978].

2B. Results Comparing the Size and Winner-Loser Effects

Table 5A shows a replication of our original winner-loser experiment using both NYSE and AMEX firms listed on COMPUSTAT for the years 1966–1983. The table shows that even for quintile portfolios (which are less extreme than the deciles or groups of 50 stocks used in our previous study) the losers have positive excess returns and the winners have negative excess returns. Indeed, the Page test does not allow us to reject the hypothesis that the ranking of excess returns in the test period is the inverse of the (forced) ranking during the formation period (see Table 6).

Table 5A also shows the average and median market values for each quintile. It is informative to compare these figures with those in panel B where market value of equity (the usual measure of firm size) is the ranking method, and also with panel D, where the ranking criterion is company assets. The

TABLE 5 Descriptive Statistics for Quintile Portfolios, Ranked by Cumulative Average Residual, Market Value, Market Value Divided by Book Value of Equity, and Assets

Portfolio #	CAR Formation Period	CAR Test Period	Sales	Assets	Market Value	Fin. Lev.	MV/BV	Earnings Yield
A: RANKING CRITERION: CUMULATIVE AVERAGE RESIDUAL (YEARS $t-3$, t)								
				Averages				
1	-.807	.246	n.a.	700	304	n.a.	.962	.023
2	-.323	.122	n.a.	1197	479	n.a.	1.001	.091
3	.003	-.004	n.a.	1335	557	n.a.	1.145	.127
4	.321	-.015	n.a.	1087	561	n.a.	1.455	.180
5	1.264	-.117	n.a.	689	582	n.a.	2.426	.325
				Medians				
1	n.a.	n.a.	200	240	73	.314	.877	.033
2	n.a.	n.a.	204	276	101	.365	.890	.091
3	n.a.	n.a.	215	286	109	.399	.976	.125
4	n.a.	n.a.	216	275	133	.521	1.162	.167
5	n.a.	n.a.	173	174	161	.889	1.848	.245
B: RANKING CRITERION: MARKET VALUE OF EQUITY (YEAR t)								
				Averages				
1	-.111	.299	n.a.	n.a.	9	n.a.	.888	.121
2	.182	.132	n.a.	n.a.	32	n.a.	1.098	.173
3	.180	.116	n.a.	n.a.	96	n.a.	1.325	.166
4	.131	-.090	n.a.	n.a.	288	n.a.	1.592	.156
5	.028	-.209	n.a.	n.a.	2076	n.a.	2.073	.126
				Medians				
1	n.a.	n.a.	35	24	9	.351	.756	.107
2	n.a.	n.a.	93	79	31	.402	.889	.130
3	n.a.	n.a.	177	212	90	.429	1.060	.135
4	n.a.	n.a.	406	558	272	.477	1.194	.117
5	n.a.	n.a.	1470	1769	945	.659	1.437	.102

C: RANKING CRITERION: MARKET VALUE/BOOK VALUE OF EQUITY (YEAR t)

Averages

1	-.258	.407	658	106	n.a.	.361	.100
2	-.030	.226	1219	330	n.a.	.766	.149
3	.163	.095	1260	424	n.a.	1.022	.169
4	.376	.050	1176	594	n.a.	1.427	.180
5	.762	-.013	670	1030	n.a.	3.417	.147

Medians

1	n.a.	136	115	23	.223	.512	.101
2	n.a.	173	234	70	.339	.789	.124
3	n.a.	193	266	103	.439	1.036	.128
4	n.a.	247	295	165	.651	1.437	.128
5	n.a.	187	184	270	1.499	2.766	.103

D: RANKING CRITERION: COMPANY ASSETS (YEAR t)

Averages

1	.217	.237	22	17	n.a.	1.370	.147
2	.228	.143	76	54	n.a.	1.446	.169
3	.146	.091	211	148	n.a.	1.424	.161
4	-.030	-.075	661	431	n.a.	1.463	.136
5	-.110	-.150	4063	1815	n.a.	1.278	.129

Medians

1	n.a.	28	21	10	.526	.958	.121
2	n.a.	95	72	32	.461	1.008	.131
3	n.a.	216	192	93	.462	1.057	.126
4	n.a.	530	592	268	.437	1.136	.109
5	n.a.	1609	2203	755	.350	1.032	.113

NOTE: Year t represents the last year of the formation period. Sales, assets, and market value are measured in $ millions. Financial leverage is measured as market value divided by balance sheet total. Earnings yield is defined as earnings-per-share in year t divided by share price at the end of year $t - 4$ (with appropriate adjustments made for stock splits, etc.). The reported grand averages (grand average medians) are calculated by first (1) averaging (or finding the average median of) the replications with 1969, 1973 and 1977 as the last formation year; then (2) averaging (or finding the average median of) the replications with 1971, 1975, and 1979 as the last formation year; and, finally (3) averaging the averages (or average medians) from steps (1) and (2).

291

firms in both extreme CAR quintiles are smaller than those in the middle portfolios, but they are not unusually small. In fact, the mean for both quintiles is comparable to the 4th quintile of the MV and company assets rankings. (Similar results obtain for the average MV of the extreme deciles and ventiles.) The average market value for the smallest quintile ranked by MV is about 30 times smaller than the average market value for the loser quintile. A comparison of the relevant averages and medians indicates that, while there is some skewness in the distributions, it affects the quintile portfolios more or

TABLE 6 Friedman Two-Way Analysis of Variance by Ranks and Page's Test for Ordered Alternatives

Ranking Variable	Friedman chi-square	Friedman Multiple Comparison Procedure	Page z-statistic
A: FORMATION PERIOD			
CAR $(t - 3, t)$	*	*	*
	*	*	*
MV	8.30	−8.0	−1.08
	29.16	−17.0	−2.39 (−)
MV/BV	67.60 (×)	−32.0 (+)	−8.06 (−)
	65.97 (×)	−30.0 (+)	−8.01 (−)
Assets	8.90	3.0	1.21
	11.91	−1.0	.79
B: TEST PERIOD			
CAR $(t - 3, t)$	41.31 (×)	23.0	5.63 (−)
	15.67	10.0	3.41 (−)
MV	46.76 (×)	33.0 (+)	6.01 (−)
	62.46 (×)	34.0 (+)	7.67 (−)
MV/BV	34.10 (×)	26.0 (+)	5.04 (−)
	37.86 (×)	29.0 (+)	5.48 (−)
Assets	31.66 (×)	22.0	4.79 (−)
	46.50 (×)	29.0 (+)	6.25 (−)

NOTES: (1) The test-statistics in the top (bottom) rows are based on the replications with formation years 1969, 1973, and 1977 (1971, 1975, and 1979). Entries that are significant by construction (the formation period returns for portfolios ranked by cumulative average residuals) are marked with an asterisk. (2) Friedman's test-statistic is distributed chi-square with $k - 1$ degrees of freedom where k, the number of portfolios, equals 20. The null hypothesis can be rejected at the 5 (10) percent level of significance if the test-statistic is greater than or equal to 30.14 (27.20). Entries significant at the 5 percent level are marked with ×. (3) The tests using Friedman's multiple comparison procedure are based on decile portfolios, comparing the returns on portfolios 1 and 10. The critical values for this test are 25.3 ($p = .05$), 23.6 ($p = .10$), 22.7 ($p = .15$) and 21.9 ($p = .20$). Entries significant at the 5 percent level are marked with +. (4) The Page z-statistic is distributed approximately as the standard normal. The computations are based on 20 portfolios. Entries larger than 2.0 are marked with −.

less evenly. Thus, the winner-loser anomaly cannot be accurately described as primarily a small firm phenomenon.[9]

In contrast, it seems more apt to characterize the winner-loser effect as an overvalued-undervalued effect. One traditional measure of under- (or over-) valuation (similar to Tobin's Q) is the ratio of market value to book value of equity (MV/BV). From the MV/BV column in Table 5A, one sees that the ranking by CAR coincides with the ranking of MV/BV. The similarity of the two ranking methods can also be judged by comparing panels A and C where MV/BV is the ranking criterion. Notice that the CARs for the extreme MV/BV portfolios show the familiar winner-loser reversal pattern. The Page test in Table 6 does not allow us to reject such return reversals. Excess returns for portfolios formed on a "book/price" strategy have been reported earlier by Rosenberg, Reid, and Lanstein [1985].

While the losing firm effect cannot be characterized as a small firm effect, one may still ask: To what extent is the small firm effect a losing firm effect?[10] Table 7 provides indexed, detrended measures of MV for portfolios formed on the same criteria used in Table 5. Notice that the companies in the smallest quintile (ranked by MV) have recently shrunk in size relative to other firms in the sample.[11] In fact the V-shaped pattern is similar to that seen for the extreme portfolios ranked by CAR and by MV/BV. It is instructive to compare the MV results with those of Assets. For Assets there is no trend in market value during the formation period. In this sense, Assets is a more permanent measure of firm size than MV.[12]

[9]Fama and French [1986a] also examine the size issue. Using the CRSP monthly return file of NYSE firms, they study winner and loser portfolios containing 35 stocks for 19 nonoverlapping three-year-formation and test periods starting in 1926 and ending in 1982. The market value of the loser portfolio is on average in the 26th percentile, while the market of the winners is in the 58th percentile. Thus, the most extreme NYSE losers tend to be somewhat smaller than average, but not extremely small. There is also considerable variation from one experiment to another and, on occasion, the losers are bigger than the winners. Our COMPUSTAT sample differs in several respects. It includes AMEX firms, covers only the period 1965–84, and the numbers we report in Table 5A are for quintile portfolios (rather than 35 stocks). Even so, the size estimates are roughly comparable. For the subset of periods studied by Fama and French which overlap with out COMPUSTAT sample (1965–1982), the average market value of their losers is $164 million which is larger than the median firm on COMPUSTAT. The number may be usefully compared with the average market value, $234 million, of our most extreme loser ventile (containing, on average, 61 stocks).

[10]Previous research by Reinganum [1983, Table 1] indicates that the smallest MV decile has a disproportionate number of prior short-term losers, and that among the small firms, the losers do particularly well in January. See also Chan [1986, Table 1].

[11]Note that (as explained in Section 2A above) we are detrending relative to the whole sample population, while the CAR's shown in Table 5 were calculated with respect to a NYSE equal-weighted index. That index is likely to underestimate the annual returns to our COM-PUSTAT samples since they include about 26 percent AMEX firms. Thus the moderate fall in returns seen in the second column of Table 5B is not inconsistent with Table 7.

[12]In addition, using Assets to measure firm size avoids any confounding effect introduced by changes in the financial structure of a firm (such as a corporation repurchasing its shares and issuing debt).

TABLE 7 Average Market Value of Equity for Top and Bottom Quintiles, Indexed and Detrended ($MV_{t-4} = 100$)

Ranking Variable	Quintile #	$t-4$	$t-3$	$t-2$	$t-1$	t	$t+1$	$t+2$	$t+3$	$t+4$
						Years				
CAR($t-3$, t)	1	100	85	77	71	59	61	65	74	73
	5	100	118	137	146	170	159	162	154	153
MV	1	100	89	80	72	58	60	69	78	89
	5	100	100	101	101	102	99	96	94	91
MV/BV	1	100	96	90	84	66	67	73	77	85
	5	100	101	107	105	113	110	107	103	99
Assets	1	100	97	95	98	101	104	118	133	134
	5	100	100	99	99	98	96	93	91	89

NOTE: Year t represents the last year of the formation period. All entries are indexed and detrended averages for six replications with 1969, 1971, 1973, 1975, 1977, and 1979 as the last formation year. See Section 2A for details.

294

Since the size effect, as measured by MV, is partly a losing firm effect, it is interesting to see whether there are still excess returns to small firms if another measure of size such as Assets (or Sales) is used. In Tables 5 (panel D) and 6, we show that, in fact, excess returns are still significantly related to size. (Similar results, not reported here, are obtained if Sales (COMPUSTAT item #12) is used as the ranking criterion).

2C. Excess Returns and Overreaction to Earnings

In contrast to the risk-change and time-varying discount rate explanations of the winner-loser effect, one interpretation of the overreaction hypothesis stresses misperceptions of future cash flows for extreme winners and losers.[13] The hypothesis entails that investors, on average, have an excessively short-term orientation: They focus on the recent past and do not look beyond the immediate future. An implication of the hypothesis is that there should be a close correspondence between stock returns and short-term changes in the earnings outlook. Of course, if earnings were to follow a random walk (even in the tails of the cross section of firms), then myopic forecasts could coincide with rational expectations (in the absence of other information). However, if earnings are mean-reverting in the tails, as suggested by, e.g., Brooks and Buckmaster [1976], then stock prices influenced by myopic forecasts will show mean reversion as earnings realizations systematically diverge from earlier expectations. Therefore, paradoxically, extreme stock price increases and decreases should be predictive of subsequent earnings reversals. If this pattern is not observed, then at least this simple form of the overreaction hypothesis can be rejected.

Table 8 shows average and median earnings per share, normalized by share price at the end of year $t - 4$, detrended, and indexed to be equal to 100 at the beginning of the test period. The results for the portfolios formed by CAR are consistent with the overreaction hypothesis. Both winners and losers show the predicted reversal pattern.[14,15] The same pattern is observed for the MV/BV

---

[13]Overreaction behavior could be manifest in other ways as well. Investors might be overly sensitive to perceived risks, producing normatively excessive risk premia. Alternatively, some investors' decisions might be influenced by temporary fads, as proposed by Shiller [1984].

[14]A comparison of the average and median EPS makes it clear that the averages are somewhat affected by outliers. Preliminary work suggests that there is similar cross-sectional skewness in the test period returns of securities that make up the extreme portfolios. Simple binomial tests further indicate that, for a majority of test periods starting each year between 1970 and 1980, the percentage of firms in the loser decile portfolio that experience above-average earnings growth is significantly larger than the equivalent percentage in the winner decile.

[15]Since the samples are selected from both the main and delisted (research) files of COMPUSTAT, they do not suffer from "ex post selection" (survivorship) bias as it is normally understood in the literature (see, e.g., Banz and Breen [1986]). However, for our purposes, the earnings pattern of companies *after* they leave the research file is still relevant. If there were unusual attrition in the extreme quintile portfolios, the earnings trends documented in Table 7

ranking criterion, which is another proxy for market price deviations from fundamental value. One intriguing aspect of these results is that the reversal of earnings is much larger for the losers than for the winners. This offers one possible explanation of the similar asymmetry in excess returns. If the anomalous price behavior is driven by earnings surprises, then the returns pattern should be similar to the earnings pattern.[16]

In contrast, both size measures, MV and Assets, show distinctly different patterns. Small firms, by either measure, show faster earnings growth than large firms throughout both the formation and test periods. This suggests that one possible explanation for the size effect is a failure by the market to recognize the small firms' higher growth potential. This and other related hypotheses are investigated by Givoly and Lakonishok [1984], but are not pursued any further here.

3. SUMMARY AND CONCLUSIONS

The principal findings of this study are:

1. Excess returns for losers in the test period (and particularly in January) are negatively related to both long-term and short-term formation period performance. For winners, January excess returns are negatively related to the excess returns for the prior December, possibly reflecting a capital gains tax "lock-in" effect.
2. The winner-loser effect cannot be attributed to changes in risk as measured by CAPM-betas. While the (zero-investment) arbitrage portfolio has a positive beta of .220, this is insufficient to explain its average annual (test period) return of 9.2 percent. Further analysis shows that the arbitrage portfolio has a positive beta in up markets and a negative beta in down

---

would be biased in a direction that unduly favors the overreaction hypothesis. We doubt that this is actually happening in an important way. Summed over the six samples, each quintile portfolio contains 1452 companies in the formation year. With CAR as the ranking criterion, the loser portfolio still contains 1349 (92.9 percent) companies at the end of year $t + 3$. For the other quintiles, the relevant percentages are 93.9, 94.9, 95.2, and 93.3 (with the extreme winner portfolio last). While the reasons for delisting may differ, it is also important to note at this point that the number of firms removed from COMPUSTAT because of financial difficulty is "substantially smaller than the number delisted because of merger or limited distribution" (McElreath and Wiggins [1984, p. 74]).

[16]For a sample of COMPUSTAT firms, Beaver, Lambert, and Morse also study the relationship between price changes and earnings changes. They conclude that prices behave "as if earnings are perceived to be dramatically different from a simple random walk process" ([1980, p. 3]). In particular, the market expects events that cause positive or negative earnings surprises to induce additional earnings changes later on. These findings are consistent with overreaction.

TABLE 8 Average and Median Earnings Per Share, Indexed and Detrended

Ranking Variable	Years								
	$t-4$	$t-3$	$t-2$	$t-1$	t	$t+1$	$t+2$	$t+3$	$t+4$
DECILE PORTFOLIOS: [EPS$(t-4)$/P$(t-4)$] = 100									
				Average Earnings-Per-Share					
CAR$(t-3,t)$									
1	100.0	55.1	15.3	−2.6	0.1	17.6	35.4	41.9	52.4
2	100.0	80.8	73.6	34.8	43.6	57.1	63.3	71.0	79.0
3	100.0	81.6	73.5	68.1	57.4	56.6	61.8	66.4	66.1
8	100.0	99.3	98.6	100.9	101.6	97.9	93.4	88.7	90.6
9	100.0	149.2	164.8	186.6	185.3	185.0	176.8	177.3	175.1
10	100.0	164.2	216.4	262.3	277.5	266.8	250.4	239.5	239.0
QUINTILE PORTFOLIOS: [EPS$(t-4)$/P$(t-4)$] = 100									
				Median Earnings-Per-Share					
CAR$(t-3,t)$									
1	n.a.	197.0	151.9	114.1	100.0	106.3	118.0	137.2	126.6
5	n.a.	83.3	91.5	99.2	100.0	97.3	94.0	92.7	94.6
				Average Earnings-Per-Share					
CAR$(t-3,t)$									
1	n.a.	361.1	257.8	66.3	100.0	185.9	248.7	284.7	334.5
5	n.a.	66.8	82.1	96.5	100.0	96.7	89.7	87.9	87.7
MV									
1	n.a.	83.3	94.9	88.0	100.0	101.5	120.9	115.3	125.6
5	n.a.	114.5	106.7	100.2	100.0	100.0	98.2	100.7	95.0
MV/BV									
1	n.a.	142.1	128.0	104.3	100.0	104.4	119.2	112.8	124.4
5	n.a.	69.8	83.5	89.3	100.0	110.1	111.4	111.4	108.2
Assets									
1	n.a.	72.5	89.6	89.1	100.0	102.9	110.4	114.7	118.2
5	n.a.	125.9	117.0	109.7	100.0	102.2	96.2	100.1	97.7

NOTE: See Table 7. The earnings-per-share data are adjusted for stock splits and stock dividends. Before portfolio averaging, they are scaled by the closing stock price on the last trading day of year $t-4$.

297

markets, a combination that would not generally be considered particularly risky.

3. The winner-loser effect is not primarily a size effect.
4. The small firm effect is partly a losing firm effect, but even if the losing firm effect is removed (by using a more permanent measure of size, such as assets) there are still excess returns to small firms.
5. The earnings of winning and losing firms show reversal patterns that are consistent with overreaction.

What conclusions seem warranted at this time? Many puzzles remain, especially regarding the seasonality in excess returns. We have no satisfactory explanation for the January effects, rational or otherwise.

On the more positive side, the reversal pattern documented by our earlier paper has now been replicated by many other researchers (Brown and Harlow [1988], Chan [1987], Fama and French [1986a and b], Howe [1986]), and there is plenty of evidence that stock returns vary over time in a manner that can be predicted by variables that reflect levels of asset prices (Keim and Stambaugh [1986]).

According to Fama and French [1986, p. 24], "Whether predictability reflects market inefficiency or time-varying expected returns generated by rational investor behavior is, and will remain, an open issue." In fact, they conclude that the issue is not resolvable. How then can progress be made? In our view, students of financial markets have little choice but to broadly examine the evidence on return predictability and make a judgment regarding which type of model offers the most parsimonious explanation of the facts.

This paper has made contributions to this task in two different directions. First, two plausible explanations of the winner-loser effect, namely those based on the size or risk characteristics of the winning and losing firms, have been examined. The data do not support either of these explanations. Second, the paper provides new evidence consistent with the simple behavioral view that investors overreact to short-term (i.e., a few years) earnings movements. Certainly, within the framework of the efficient market hypothesis, it is distinctly puzzling that a dramatic fall (rise) in stock prices is predictive of a subsequent rise (fall) in company-specific earnings.

As to time-varying discount rates, we certainly agree that they may play a role in explaining the observed price reversals. However, even if time-varying discount rates can be shown to offer a coherent explanation of the winner-loser effect and other anomalies, for the "market rationality hypothesis" (Merton [24]) to be accepted, it will also be necessary to demonstrate that these fluctuations in discount rates can be characterized as rational responses to economic conditions rather than emotional shifts in the mood of market participants.

REFERENCES

We thank K. C. Chan, Alan Kraus, Josef Lakonishok, Theo Vermaelen, and members of the Cornell and Wisconsin finance workshops for helpful comments. Graham Lemke and Charles Lee provided expert computational assistance. All remaining errors are our own. We would like to acknowledge financial support from the Pete Johnson Fund for Research in Finance at the University of Wisconsin-Madison (De Bondt) and from the Behavioral Economics Program of the Alfred P. Sloan Foundation (Thaler).

Akerlof, George A. *An Economic Theorist's Book of Tales*. London: Cambridge University Press, 1984.

Banz, Rolf W., and William J. Breen. "Sample-Dependent Results Using Accounting and Market Data: Some Evidence." *Journal of Finance* (September 1986): 779–793.

Beaver, William, Richard Lambert, and Dale Morse. "The Information Content of Security Prices." *Journal of Accounting and Economics* 2 (1980): 3–28.

Branch, Ben. "A Tax Loss Trading Rule." *Journal of Business* (April 1977): 198–207.

Brooks, LeRoy D., and Dale A. Buckmaster. "Further Evidence of the Time Series Properties of Accounting Income." *Journal of Finance* (December 1976): 1359–1373.

Brown, Keith C., and W. V. Harlow. "Assessing the Magnitude and Intensity of Stock Market Overreaction." *Journal of Portfolio Management* (1988): 6–13.

Chan, K. C. "Can Tax-Loss Selling Explain the January Seasonal in Stock Returns?" *Journal of Finance* (December 1986): 1115–1128.

———. "The Use of Information in Market Values for Estimating Time-Varying Stock Betas." Working Paper, Faculty of Finance, Ohio State University, June 1986.

———. "On the Return of the Contrarian Investment Strategy." Working Paper, Faculty of Finance, Ohio State University, January 1987.

Daniel, Wayne W. *Applied Nonparametric Statistics*. Boston: Houghton Mifflin, 1978.

De Bondt, Werner F. M., and Richard H. Thaler. "Does the Stock Market Overreact?" *Journal of Finance* (July 1985): 793–805.

Dyl, Edward A. "Capital Gains Taxation and Year-End Stock Market Behavior." *Journal of Finance* (March 1977): 165–175.

Fama, Eugene F., and Kenneth R. French. "Permanent and Temporary Components of Stock Prices." Working Paper No. 178, Graduate School of Business, University of Chicago, July 1986.

———. "Common Factors in the Serial Correlation of Stock Returns." Working Paper, Graduate School of Business, University of Chicago, October 1986.

Friedman, Milton. "The Use of Ranks to Avoid the Assumption of Normality Implicit in the Analysis of Variance." *Journal of the American Statistical Association* 32 (1937): 675–701.

Givoly, Dan, and Josef Lakonishok. "Earnings Growth and the Firm-Size Anomaly."

Working Paper No. 832/84, The Leon Recanati Graduate School of Business Administration, Tel Aviv University, November 1984.

Howe, John S. "Evidence on Stock Market Overreaction." *Financial Analysts Journal* (July/August 1986): 74–77.

Ibbotson, R. G., and R. A. Sinquefield. *Stocks, Bills, and Inflation: The Past and the Future*. Charlottesville, VA: The Financial Analysts Research Foundation. University of Virginia, 1982.

Keim, Donald B. "Size Related Anomalies and Stock Return Seasonality." *Journal of Financial Economics* (June 1983): 13–32.

Keim, Donald B., and Robert F. Staubaugh. "Predicting Returns in the Stock and Bond Markets." *Journal of Financial Economics* (1986): 357–390.

Keynes, John Maynard. *The General Theory of Employment, Interest and Money*. London: Harcourt Brace Jovanovich, 1964 (reprint of 1936 edition).

Lakonishok, Josef, and Seymour Smidt. "Volume for Winners and Losers: Taxation and Other Motives for Stock Trading." *Journal of Finance* (September 1986): 951–974.

McElreath Robert B., Jr., and C. Donald Wiggins. "Using the COMPUSTAT Tapes in Financial Research: Problems and Solutions." *Financial Analysts Journal* (January/February 1984): 71–76.

Merton, Robert C. "On the Current State of the Market Rationality Hypothesis." Working Paper No. 1717-85, Massachusetts Institute of Technology, October 1985.

Page, E. B. "Ordered Hypothesis for Multiple Treatments: A Significance Test for Linear Ranks." *Journal of the American Statistical Association* 58 (1963): 316–330.

Reinganum, Marc R. "The Anomalous Stock Market Behavior of Small Firms in January: Empirical Tests for Tax-Loss Selling Effects." *Journal of Financial Economics* (June 1983): 89–104.

Rogalski, Richard J., and Seha M. Tinic. "The January Size Effect: Anomaly or Risk Measurement?" *Financial Analysts Journal* (November/December 1986): 63–70.

Roll, Richard. "Vas ist Das? The Turn-of-the-Year Effect and the Return Premia of Small Firms." *Journal of Portfolio Management* (Winter 1983): 18–28.

Rosenberg, Barr, Kenneth Reid, and Ronald Lanstein. "Persuasive Evidence of Market Inefficiency." *Journal of Portfolio Management* (Spring 1985): 9–16.

Rozeff, Michael S. "The December Effect in Stock Returns and the Tax-Loss Selling Hypothesis." Working Paper No. 85-18, College of Business Administration, University of Iowa, May 1985.

Schwert, William. "Size of Stock Returns, and Other Empirical Regularities." *Journal of Financial Economics* (June 1983): 3–12.

Shiller, Robert J. "Stock Prices and Social Dynamics." *Brookings Papers on Economic Activity* (1984): 457–510.

Vermaelen, Theo, and Marc Verstringe. "Do Belgians Overreact?" Working Paper, Catholic University of Louvain, Belgium, November 1986.

15

DO SECURITY ANALYSTS OVERREACT?

Werner F. M. De Bondt and Richard H. Thaler

It has long been part of the conventional wisdom on Wall Street that financial markets "overreact." Both casual observation and academic research support this view. The October crashes of 1987 and 1989 reinforce the research by Shiller and others which suggests that stock prices are too volatile. Also, Shiller's (1987) survey evidence reveals that investors were reacting to each other during these crashes, rather than to hard economic news. A similar conclusion is reached by French and Roll (1986) who find that prices are more volatile when markets are open than when they are closed.

Our own prior research (De Bondt and Thaler, 1985, 1987) argued that mean reversion in stock prices is evidence of overreaction. In our 1985 paper we showed that stocks that were extreme "losers" over an initial three to five-year period earned excess returns over the subsequent three to five years. In the 1987 paper we showed that these excess returns cannot easily be attributed to changes in risk, tax effects, or the "small firm anomaly." Rather, we argued that the excess returns to losers might be explained by biased expectations of the future. We found that the earnings for losing firms had fallen precipitously during the formation period (while they were losing value), but then rebounded strongly over the next few years. Perhaps, we speculated, "the market" did not correctly anticipate this reversal in earnings. This hypothesis, of excessive pessimism about the future prospects of companies that had done poorly, was suggested by the work of Kahneman and Tversky on the psychology of prediction. They found that people's intuitive forecasts have a tendency to overweight salient information such as recent news and under-weight less salient data such as long-term averages.

Of course, there are many reasons to be skeptical that actual investors—many, stock market professionals—are subject to the same biases as student subjects in laboratory experiments. Definitely, the market professionals are experts in their field, they have much at stake, and those who make systematic errors may be driven out of business. Therefore, we present here a study of the expectations of one important group of financial market professionals: security

Reprinted with permission from *American Economic Review* 80, 2 (May 1990): 52–57.

analysts who make periodic forecasts of individual company earnings. This is an interesting group to study on three counts. First, other investigators have repeatedly found that earnings forecasts (and forecast revisions) have an important influence on stock prices. Second, past work suggests that analysts are rather good at what they do. For example, analyst forecasts often outperform time-series models (see, e.g., Conroy and Harris, 1987). Finally, the precision of analyst expectations represents a natural upper bound to the quality of the earnings forecasts of less sophisticated agents. After all, most investors do not have the time or the skill to produce their own predictions and, accordingly, they buy (rather than sell) earnings forecasts. Thus, for all of the above reasons, it is particularly interesting to see whether market professionals display any of the biases discovered in studies of nonexpert judgment.

We specifically test for a type of generalized overreaction, the tendency to make forecasts that are too extreme, given the predictive value of the information available to the forecaster. This tendency is well illustrated by an experiment conducted by Kahneman and Tversky (1973). Subjects were asked to predict the future grade point average (GPA) for each of ten students on the basis of a percentile score of some predictor. Three predictor variables were used: percentile scores for past GPA, for a test of mental concentration, and for a test of sense of humor. Obviously, a measure of past GPA is a much better predictor of future GPA than is a measure of mental concentration which, in turn, is much more reliable than information on sense of humor. Therefore, subjects should give much more regressive forecasts in the latter two conditions; that is, the forecasts should be less variable. The results indicated that people were not nearly sensitive enough to this consideration. Subjects that were given a nearly useless predictor (the "sense of humor" condition) made predictions that were almost as extreme in variation as those given a nearly perfect predictor (the "past GPA" condition). This pattern leads to a systematic bias: forecasts that diverge the most from the mean will tend to be too extreme, implying that forecast errors are predictable.

This study asks whether security analysts display similar biases. Our focus is on forecasted changes in earnings per share (EPS) for one- and two-year time horizons. We study two questions. The first question is whether forecast errors in EPS are systematically linked to forecasted changes. In particular, are the forecasts too extreme? Are most forecast revisions "up" ("down") if the analysts initially projected large declines (rises) in EPS? Clearly, under rationality, neither forecast errors nor forecast revisions should ever be predictable from forecasted changes. The second question is whether the bias in the forecasts gets stronger as uncertainty grows and less is (or objectively can be) known about the future.

Several of the regressions reported below are of the form $AC = \alpha + \beta FC$ where AC is the actual change and FC is the forecasted change. The null hypothesis of rational expectations is that $(\alpha, \beta) = (0, 1)$. The two alternative behavioral hypotheses sketched above are:

H1. Forecasted changes are too extreme, so actual changes are less (in absolute value) than predicted: $\beta < 1$.
H2. The estimated β for the two-year forecasts is less than the β for the one-year forecasts.

The next two sections describe the data and the empirical results. We find considerable support for the behavioral view. We then briefly discuss the sources of the systematic forecast error.

1. DATA

The analysts' earnings forecasts are taken from the Institutional-Brokers-Estimate-System tapes (IBES) produced by Lynch, Jones & Ryan, member of the New York Stock Exchange. We study forecasts between 1976 and 1984. Lynch, Jones & Ryan contacts individual analysts on a regular basis and computes summary data such as means, medians, or standard deviations. The summary data which we analyze are sold to institutional investors. Updates are available each month but here we only work with the April and December predictions of EPS for the current as well as the subsequent year. The April forecasts are approximately one- and two-year forecasts since we only consider companies with a fiscal year ending in December. For these firms, actually realized earnings are typically announced sometime during the first few months of the following calendar year.

We match the earnings forecasts for each company with stock returns and accounting numbers. The returns are provided by the Center for Research on Security Prices (CRSP) at the University of Chicago. The accounting data are listed on the annual industrial (main or delisted) COMPUSTAT files, sold by Standard & Poor's. Since all data sources contain full historical records, no survivorship biases affect the sample selection. Care is taken to adjust for stock splits and stock dividends so that all current and past returns, earnings figures, and forecasts are expressed on a comparable basis. When necessary, forecasts of fully diluted EPS are converted to forecasts of primary EPS (excluding extraordinary items).

While some IBES data are available for approximately 2300 to 2800 companies each year, our annual samples contain many fewer observations. For example, for the one-year forecasts, the number varies between 461 and 785. This follows from the data selection criteria that we use. Companies only qualify if they have (1) records on IBES, CRSP and COMPUSTAT; (2)

returns on CRSP for three years prior to the forecast month; (3) EPS numbers on COMPUSTAT for ten years prior to the forecast month; (4) a December fiscal year; and (5) the data needed to compute the variables in the regressions described below. Despite the stringent data requirements, our sample (in firm-years) is the largest we know of that has been used to study the rationality of earnings forecasts (e.g., Brown, Foster, and Noreen, 1985).

2. METHODS AND RESULTS

Much of the regression analysis is based on three sets of variables: forecasted changes in EPS (FC1, FC2, and FC12); actual changes in EPS (AC1, AC2, and AC12); and forecast revisions (FR1, FR2, and FR12). The "consensus" one- and two-year forecasts of earnings per share (FEPS(t) and FEPS($t + 1$)) that we study are defined as the cross-sectional means or medians of analyst forecasts reported in April of year t ($t = 1976...1984$). Forecasted changes are then computed as FC1(t) = FEPS(t) − EPS($t − 1$), FC2(t) = FEPS($t + 1$) − EPS ($t − 1$), and FC12(t) = FEPS($t + 1$) − FEPS(t) where EPS(t) represents actually realized earnings per share. We find actual earnings changes in a way that is similar to the forecasted changes. For example, AC1(t) = EPS(t) − EPS ($t − 1$). Eight-month forecast revisions (FR1) subtract the April forecast of EPS(t) from the equivalent forecast in December. Twenty-month forecast revisions (FR2) subtract the April forecast of EPS($t + 1$) from the December forecast in year $t + 1$. Finally, FR12 subtracts the April FC12(t) from the equivalent FC12(t) in December of year t.

The regressions in Table 1 use mean consensus forecasts. All variables are normalized by the standard deviation of earnings per share between years $t = 10$ and $t − 2$.[1] Even though we also ran the regressions year by year, the results in Table 1 are based on the pooled samples. There are three main findings. Forecasts are too optimistic, too extreme, and even more extreme for two-year forecasts than for single-year predictions.

Equation 1 refers to the one-year forecasts. We regress the actual change in earnings on the April forecasted change. The intercept is significantly negative, indicating that the forecasts are too optimistic. This excessive optimism also appears in Equation 3 for the two-year forecasts. The negative intercepts in Equations 2 and 4 reveal that there is a general tendency for forecasts to be revised downwards between April and December.

The finding of unrealistic optimism seems consistent with the experimental research of Weinstein (1980) and others who find such biases in the expecta-

---

[1] We also tried other normalization procedures, such as dividing by company assets per share at the end of year $t − 1$, the stock price on the last trading day of year $t − 5$, and the standard deviation of EPS between $t − 5$ and $t − 2$. Results are qualitatively the same for all methods.

tions of individuals in everyday life. However, we do not want to push this argument too far for two reasons. First, if we consider the nine individual year-by-year regressions, the intercepts are positive four times. Second, optimism bias also has a plausible agency interpretation. Many analysts work for brokerage houses which make money by encouraging trading. Since every customer is potentially interested in a buy recommendation, while only current stockholders (and a few willing to go short) are interested in sell recommendations, optimistic forecasts may be preferable. Indeed, it is well known that buy recommendations issued by brokerage houses greatly exceed sell recommendations.

All six regressions in Table 1 present evidence supporting the hypothesis that forecasts are too extreme. Ignoring the constant term in Equation 1, actual EPS changes average only 65 percent of the forecasted one-year changes. For the two-year forecasts (Equation 3), this statistic falls to 46 percent.[2] In the year-by-year regressions equivalent to Equations 1 and 3, the slope coefficients are less than one every single time.

Note that Equations 1 and 3 could be rewritten with the forecast errors (AC1 − FC1 and AC2 − FC2) on the left-hand side and with the forecasted

TABLE 1 Tests for the Rationality of Earnings Per Share Forecasts

Equation	Variables	Constant Term	Slope	Adj. R^2 #Observations
1	AC1, FC1	−.094	.648	.217
		(−3.7)	(−21.7)	5736
2	FR1, FC1	−.120	−.181	.041
		(−6.7)	(−15.6)	5736
3	AC2, FC2	−.137	.459	.071
		(−2.3)	(−19.5)	3539
4	FR2, FC2	−.192	−.381	.074
		(−3.9)	(−16.8)	3538
5	AC12, FC12	.153	−.042	.000
		(2.4)	(−16.9)	3520
6	FR12, FC12	.348	−.439	.153
		(19.4)	(−25.3)	3562

NOTE: All variables are as defined in the text. The dependent variable is listed first. T-values appear in parentheses beneath the regression coefficients and test whether they differ from zero. However, for the slopes of Equations 1, 3, and 5, the t-statistics test whether the coefficients differ from one.

---

[2]The two-year regressions are open to criticism because the sampling interval (one year) is shorter than the forecast interval (two years) creating a non-independence across data points. To remove this problem, we break the sample in two, and replicate Equation 3 using forecasts just from every other year, so that the time periods are non-overlapping. Results are comparable.

changes as the regressors. The new slope coefficients then equal the betas in Table 1 *minus* one, while the *t*-statistics remain the same. The new slopes have a straightforward interpretation: The larger the forecasted changes, the larger is the forecast error in the opposite direction. The R^2s of these regressions are .076 and .097.

The previous findings all suggest that forecast revisions should also be predictable from forecasted changes, and indeed they are, as shown in Equations 2 and 4. In these regressions, rationality implies that β should be equal to zero. In actuality, the slopes are significantly negative. By December, the average reversal of the one-year forecasts made in April equals 18 percent of the original predicted changes. For the two-year forecasts, the reversal amounts to 38 percent.

As expected, the results are stronger for the two-year and second-year forecasts. The two-year results are clearly driven by the predicted changes for the second year (see Equations 5 and 6). With the R^2 for Equation 5 equal to zero, actual changes are simply unrelated to forecasted changes in EPS from year t to $t + 1$. On average, any non-zero prediction, either positive or negative, is pure error. By December, the analysts have reversed their April forecasted changes for the second year by 44 percent.

In sum, the above results are consistent with generalized overreaction. However, a different interpretation is based on the problem of errors in variables. If our measure of forecasted changes in earnings contains error, then the slope coefficients are biased downward. In evaluating this argument, one should consider the most likely sources of error. One possibility is IBES data entry errors. Following O'Brien (1988), we removed any data points for which the predicted change in EPS or the forecast revision was greater than $10. The results in Table 1 reflect this error screen. In addition, we also recomputed regressions 1 and 3 using a smaller sample of firms for which the consensus forecast is based on the individual predictions of three analysts or more. For this subset, we then used the median forecasted earnings change as the regressor. The β's increased but were still significantly less than one.

A second potential source of error stems from the fact that the forecasts on the IBES tape may be stale. In fact, O'Brien (1988) finds that the average forecast in the IBES sample is 44 days old. Stale forecasts are troublesome if the forecasters do not know the earnings for year $t - 1$ when they make their predictions for year t. For example, a forecaster who thinks that year t earnings will remain unchanged from year $t - 1$ will appear to be predicting a change in earnings if his estimate of $t - 1$ earnings is wrong. We cannot completely rule out this interpretation of the results but we selected April as the month to study with an eye toward minimizing the problem. We chose the longest possible forecast horizon where we could still be reasonably confident that the forecasters would know the previous year's earnings. The April forecasts are issued in the third week in April so that, by O'Brien's estimate, the average forecast was made in early March. At this point, the analysts should either know the past year's earnings exactly or have a very good estimate. Thus it seems unlikely that such a large bias could be produced by errors of this type.

Another reason for confidence in the results reported here is that others have obtained similar results in previous studies of professional forecasters, both security analysts and economists. Using just the 1976–8 years of the IBES data, Elton, Gruber, and Gultekin (1984) estimated regressions similar to ours, and obtained slope coefficients less than one in each year. In a study of exchange rate expectations, Froot and Frankel (1989) also found evidence consistent with overreaction or, what they call, "excessive speculation." Forecast errors are regressed on forecasted changes in exchange rates. The slope coefficients which, under rationality, should equal zero, are always significantly different from zero. When an instrumental variables technique is used to correct for errors-in-variables, the results do not change. Finally, Ahlers and Lakonishok (1983) studied economists' forecasts of ten macroeconomic variables, using the Livingston data set. In regressions similar to our Equation 1 they find slope coefficients significantly less than one for each of ten variables being forecast. In other words, predicted changes were more volatile than actual changes, consistent with overreaction.

We have documented generalized overreaction. However, an interesting question remains: What causes excessive optimism or pessimism in earnings forecasts? We considered several variables that might explain EPS forecast errors. Two variables that are of interest in light of our previous work include a measure of market valuation, MV/BV, the ratio of the market value of a company's equity to its book value (at the end of year $t - 1$), and earnings trend (the growth rate of earnings over the years $t - 6$ to $t - 2$). Both variables were significantly related to forecast error in the expected direction, that is, excessive optimism for high MV/BV and high earnings growth firms, and excessive pessimism for firms low of these measures. Unfortunately, neither factor explained much of the variation in the forecast errors.

3. CONCLUSION

Formal economic models of financial markets typically assume that all agents in the economy are rational. While most economists recognize that, in fact, not everyone is fully rational, the existence of an irrational segment of the economy is often dismissed as irrelevant with the claim that there will be enough rational arbitragers to assure that rational equilibria will still obtain. Whatever the theoretical merits of this position (for a critique see De Long et al., forthcoming; Russell and Thaler, 1985), an interesting empirical question is whether the presumed smart money segment actually can be identified. This paper investigates one possible source of rationality in financial markets, namely security analysts.[3]

The conclusion we reach from our examination of analysts' forecasts is that they are decidedly human. The same pattern of overreaction found in the predictions of naive undergraduates is replicated in the predictions of stock market professionals. Forecasted changes are simply too extreme to be considered rational. The fact that the same pattern is observed in economists' forecasts of changes in exchange rates and macroeconomic variables adds force to the conclusion that generalized overreaction can pervade even the most professional of predictions.

The proper inference from this, we think, is to take seriously the behavioral explanations of anomalous financial market outcomes. When practitioners describe the recent October crashes as panics, produced by investor overreaction, perhaps they are right. After all, aren't these practitioners the very same "smart money" that is supposed to keep markets rational?

REFERENCES

We thank Dale Berman from Lynch, Jones & Ryan and Bart Wear from First Wisconsin Asset Management for providing the data used in this study. We also gratefully acknowledge financial support from the Research Foundation at the Institute of Chartered Analysts (De Bondt) and the Russell Sage Foundation (Thaler). Helpful comments and advice have been provided by Josef Lakonishok, though, of course, errors are our own responsibility.

Ahlers, David, and Josef Lakonishok. "A Study of Economists' Consensus Forecasts." *Management Science* 29 (October 1983): 1113–1125.

Brown, Philip, George Foster, and Eric Noreen. *Security Analyst Multi-Year Earnings Forecasts and the Capital Market*. Sarasota, FL: American Accounting Association, 1985.

Conroy, Robert, and Robert Harris. "Consensus Forecasts of Corporate Earnings: Analysts' Forecasts and Time Series Methods." *Management Science* 33 (June 1987): 725–738.

De Bondt, Werner F.M., and Richard H. Thaler. "Does the Stock Market Overreact?" *Journal of Finance* 40 (July 1985): 793–805.

———. "Further Evidence on Investor Overreaction and Stock Market Seasonality." *Journal of Finance* 42 (July 1987): 557–581.

De Long, Bradford, Lawrence H. Summers, Andrei Shleifer, and Robert Waldmann. "Noise Trader Risk in Financial Markets." *Journal of Political Economy* 98 (1990): 703–738.

---

[3]Northcraft and Neale (1987) find that professionals in a different financial market—real estate agents with, on average, seven years of experience—are just as subject to a judgmental bias in the appraisal of house values as are naive student subjects.

Elton, Edwin J., Martin J. Gruber, and Mustafa N. Gultekin. "Professional Expectations: Accuracy and Diagnosis of Errors." *Journal of Financial and Quantitative Analysis* 19 (December 1984): 351–365.

French, Kenneth R., and Richard Roll. "Stock Return Variances: The Arrival of Information and the Reaction of Traders." *Journal of Financial Economics* 17 (September 1986): 5–26.

Froot, Kenneth A., and Jeffrey A. Frankel. "Forward Discount Bias: Is It an Exchange Risk Premium?" *Quarterly Journal of Economics* 104 (February 1989): 139–161.

Kahneman, Daniel, and Amos Tversky. "On the Psychology of Prediction." *Psychological Review* 80 (1973): 237–251.

Northcraft, Gregory B., and Margaret A. Neale. "Expert, Amateurs, and Real Estate: An Anchoring-and-Adjustment Perspective on Property Pricing Decisions." *Organizational Behavior and Human Decision Processes* 39 (February 1987): 84–97.

O'Brien, Patricia C. "Analysts' Forecasts as Earnings Expectations." *Journal of Accounting and Economics* 10 (January 1988): 53–83.

Russell, Thomas, and Richard H. Thaler. "The Relevance of Quasi Rationality in Competitive Markets." *American Economic Review* 75 (December 1985): 1071–1082.

Shiller, Robert J. "Investor Behavior in the October 1987 Stock Market Crash: Survey Evidence." Working Paper, Cowles Foundation, Yale University, November 1987.

Weinstein, Neil. "Unrealistic Optimism about Future Life Events." *Journal of Personality and Social Psychology* (1980): 806–820.

16

INVESTOR SENTIMENT AND THE CLOSED-END FUND PUZZLE

CHARLES M.C. LEE, ANDREI SHLEIFER, and RICHARD H. THALER

This paper examines the proposition that fluctuations in discounts of closed-end funds are driven by changes in individual investor sentiment. The theory implies that discounts on various funds move together, that new funds get started when seasoned funds sell at a premium or a small discount, and that discounts are correlated with prices of other securities affected by the same investor sentiment. The evidence supports these predictions. In particular, we find that both closed-end funds and small stocks tend to be held by individual investors, and that the discounts on closed-end funds narrow when small stocks do well.

Modern theories of finance are based on the fundamental premise that capital markets are efficient. The efficient market hypothesis (EMH) states that the price of a security is equal to its "fundamental value"; that is, the present value of its expected future cash flows, conditional on all currently available information. In this form, the hypothesis has proven difficult to test because assumptions about future cash flows and discount rates needed to compute fundamental value are not clear cut; witness Kleidon's (1986) and Marsh and Merton's (1986) critiques of Shiller's (1981) procedures for computing value in his volatility tests. The difficulties of identifying appropriate assumptions about future cash flows and the discount rates are unfortunate, since in the absence of acceptable measures of value, the EMH becomes an unsupported claim.

Reprinted with permission from *The Journal of Finance* 46, 1 (March 1991).

There is one type of security for which value is relatively easy to observe—a closed-end mutual fund. Unlike the more popular open-end fund, a closed-end fund issues a fixed number of shares and then invests the proceeds in other securities. Because the number of shares is fixed an investor must sell shares to someone else to liquidate a holding. The investor cannot, as in the case of an open-end fund, simply redeem his shares, in which case his proportional asset holdings are liquidated and he is given the proceeds. Rather, the amount that a shareholder of a closed-end fund receives if he sells his holdings is equal to the price at which these shares trade in the market.

Since the earnings assets of a closed-end fund are typically other traded securities, the value of the fund is presumably the market value of its portfolio of securities. This amount, net of any liabilities, is known as the fund's net asset value (NAV). The EMH can then be easily tested by comparing the market price of a closed-end fund to its net asset value. The surprising result—which remains a challenge to the EMH—is that closed-end funds typically sell at discounts: prices below net asset values. Discounts of 20 percent are common, and even higher discounts are sometimes observed. So, in the one case where value is actually observed, the EMH appears to be rejected.

Several past studies have attempted to solve the puzzle by pointing out that the methods used to value the securities in the portfolio might overstate the true value of the assets. Three factors are often cited as potential explanations: agency costs, tax liabilities, and illiquidity of assets. The agency costs theory states that management expenses incurred in running the fund are too high and/or the potential for subpar managerial performance reduces asset value. The tax explanation argues that capital gains tax liabilities on unrealized appreciations (at the fund level) are not captured by the standard calculation of NAV. Finally, because some funds hold restricted or letter securities which have trading restrictions, the argument has been made that such assets are overvalued in the calculation of NAV. While each of these explanations is logical and may explain some portion of the observed discounts, we show below that even collectively these factors fail to account for much of the existing evidence.

Our primary purpose is to evaluate empirically an alternative explanation for the closed-end fund puzzle presented by Zweig (1973) and Delong, Shleifer, Summers, and Waldmann (1990) (DSSW). Zweig (1973) suggests that discounts on closed-end funds reflect expectations of individual investors. DSSW develop a model in which rational investors interact in financial markets with noise traders who are less than fully rational. An important feature of their model is the existence of unpredictable fluctuations in "noise trader sentiment," defined as the component of expectations about asset returns not warranted by fundamentals. Investor sentiment can represent trading on noise rather than news (Black (1986)) or trading on popular models (Shiller (1984)). In the case of closed-end funds, fluctuations in investor sentiment can lead to fluctuations in demand for closed-end fund shares which are reflected in changes in discounts. In addition to Zweig's early idea that fund discounts reflect investor sentiment, the DSSW model explains why funds can sell at discounts even if investors are not, on average, pessimistic. Our paper reviews and extends the implications of this model, and then presents empirical evidence largely consistent with these implications.

Before the various explanations of closed-end fund pricing can be evaluated, it is important to provide a more complete description of the facts. There are four important pieces to the puzzle which together characterize the life cycle of a closed-end fund:

1. Closed-end funds start out at a premium of almost 10 percent, when organizers raise money from new investors and use it to purchase securities (Weiss (1989) and Peavy (1990)). Most of this premium is a natural derivative of the underwriting and start-up costs which are removed from

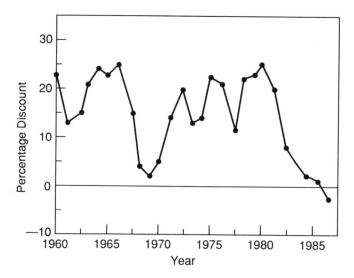

Figure 1. *Percentage discount or premium of Tricontinental Corporation at the end of each year during 1960–1986. The percentage discount is computed as 100 × (NAV − SP); where NAV is the per share net asset value and SP is the share price of the fund. The mean (median) of the percentage discount or premium is 14.43 (15.0). The maximum (minimum) value is 25.0 (−2.5) and the standard deviation is 8.56.*

the proceeds, thus reducing the NAV relative to the stock price. The reason that investors pay a premium for new funds when existing funds trade at a discount is the first part of the puzzle to be explained.

2. Although they start at a premium, closed-end funds move to an average discount of over 10 percent within 120 days from the beginning of trading (Weiss (1989)).[1] Thereafter, discounts are the norm. For illustrative purposes, Figure 1 shows the year-end discounts on the Tricontinental Corporation (TRICON) fund during 1960–1986. Tricontinental is the largest closed-end stock fund trading on U.S. exchanges, with net assets of over $1.3 billion as of December 1986. Although there are some periods where the fund sells at a premium relative to the NAV, most of the time it sells at a discount, which frequently hovers around 20 percent.[2]

3. As Figure 1 illustrates for TRICON, discounts on closed-end funds are subject to wide fluctuations over time. During 1960–1986, year-end discounts for TRICON ranged from 25 percent to a premium of 2.5 percent. It is by no means the case that the discount is a constant fraction of net asset value (or a constant dollar amount). The fluctuations in the discounts appear to be mean reverting (Sharpe and Sosin, 1975). Thompson (1978), Richards, Fraser, and Groth (1980), Herzfeld (1980), Anderson (1986), and Brauer (1988) all document significant positive abnormal returns from assuming long positions on funds with large discounts.

4. When closed-end funds are terminated through either a liquidation or an open-ending, share prices rise and discounts shrink (Brauer, 1984, Brickley and Schalheim, 1985). Most of the positive returns to shareholders accrue when discounts narrow around the announcement of termination. A small discount persists, however, until final termination or open-ending.

Our purpose is to understand this four-piece puzzle. In Section 1 we argue that standard explanations of the puzzle cannot, separately or together, explain all four pieces of the puzzle. We review the DSSW explanation of the puzzle in Section 2 and discuss some implications of this explanation. Section 3 covers data and variables description. Section 4 presents our tests of the new implications, and Section 5 deals with some objections. Section 6 presents supplementary evidence bearing on this explanation of closed-end fund discounts, and Section 7 concludes.

---

[1] The sample in the Weiss study is closed-end funds started during 1985–87. The average discount figure cited relates to stock funds investing in U.S. companies.

[2] Throughout this paper, discounts are expressed in terms of percentage of NAV. Positive discounts reflect stock prices which are below NAV.

1. STANDARD EXPLANATIONS OF THE CLOSED-END FUND PUZZLE

Agency costs, illiquidity of assets, and tax liabilities have all been proposed as potential explanations of closed-end fund discounts. However, these arguments, even when considered together, do not explain all four pieces of the closed-end fund puzzle. This section reviews these arguments.

A. Agency Costs

Agency costs could create discounts for closed-end funds if management fees are too high or if future portfolio management is expected to be subpar (Boudreaux, 1973). There are several problems with agency costs as a theory of closed-end fund pricing. First, neither current nor future agency costs can account for the wide fluctuations in the discounts. Management fees are typically a fixed percentage of NAV and certainly do not fluctuate as much as do discounts. The present value of future management fees can in principle fluctuate with interest rates. However, as we show later (Table 9), changes in discounts are not significantly correlated with interest rate changes. Second, agency costs cannot explain why rational investors buy into closed-end funds *initially* at a premium, since they should expect the funds to sell at a discount eventually. For that matter, agency and trading costs cannot explain why new and seasoned funds ever sell at premia. Third, agency costs do not seem to explain much of the cross-sectional variation in discounts. Malkiel (1977) did not find a significant relationship between management fees and/or fund performance and discount levels. By grouping funds into two groups, based on their discounts, Roenfeld and Tuttle (1973) did find, in a very small sample, marginal support for a contemporaneous relationship between fund performance and discounts. However, assuming rational expectations, a more appropriate test is to check for a relation between discounts and *future* NAV performance of funds, not past or current performance. Lee, Shleifer, and Thaler (1991) show that there is, if anything, a positive correlation between discount levels and future NAV performance; funds with large discounts tend to have higher subsequent NAV performance than those with low discounts. This result is the opposite of what might be expected from rational discounting of agency costs.

B. Illiquidity of Assets

Two other theories posit that the NAV published by the funds exaggerates the true asset value. The first theory, the *restricted stock hypothesis*, says that funds hold substantial amounts of letter stock, the market value of which is lower than its unrestricted counterpart, and that such holdings are overvalued in the calculation of NAV.[3] This idea can be ruled out immediately as a general explanation of discounts since many of the largest funds that trade at discounts hold only liquid publicly traded securities. For example, TRICON does not have any significant restricted holdings. An examination of the annual financial statements of TRICON reveals that for the years during the period studied, the assets which either required Board of Directors' valuation or were marked as "unidentified" common stocks are always less than 0.5 percent of the total NAV of the fund.

The effect of holding restricted stocks is also mitigated by regulation, which requires the funds to discount such securities in computing NAV to an amount which their Boards of Directors have determined (and publicly attested) is a fair market value equivalent. Nevertheless, there is a small but significant relationship in the cross section between the level of restricted holdings and the level of discounts (see, for example, Malkiel (1977) and Lee, Shleifer, and Thaler (1991)). Apparently, the market does not believe the funds have adequately discounted these securities. Restricted stock holdings can thus explain a portion of the discount on certain specialized funds, but it offers no explanation for the substantial discounts of large, diversified funds.

Another version of the illiquidity argument, the *block discount hypothesis*, is based on the observation that reported NAV's are computed using the trading price of a marginal share. Since closed-end funds sometimes hold substantial blocks of individual securities, the realizable proceeds from a liquidation would be much lower than the reported NAV. Like the restricted stock hypothesis, this argument runs counter to the evidence that large abnormal positive returns are realized when closed-end funds are open-ended (Brauer (1984), Brickley and Schallheim (1985)). Also, neither theory makes any contribution to explaining the other parts of the puzzle.

C. Capital Gains Tax Liabilities

The NAV of a closed-end fund does not reflect the capital gains tax that must be paid by the fund if the assets in the fund are sold.[4] The tax liability associated with assets which have appreciated in value would reduce the liquidation value of the fund's assets. This theory runs into a serious problem

---

[3]Letter, or restricted, stock refers to securities of a corporation which may not be publicly traded without registration under the Securities Act of 1933, because they have not been previously registered. A fund acquires these securities through private placement and agrees to a "letter" contract restricting their resale to the public within a specified time period. These securities can be resold privately with the letter attached.

[4]The fund has a choice of retaining or distributing its net realized capital gains. If the fund distributes these gains, owners of the fund's shares must pay tax on the distributions according to their own personal tax status. If the fund retains a portion of its net realized capital gains, it is required to pay taxes in accordance with the highest marginal personal tax rate. A tax receipt is then issued to the shareholders which is deductible from personal income taxes.

with the evidence in Brauer (1984) and Brickley and Schallheim (1985). These papers show that on open-ending, closed-end fund prices move up to net asset values rather than the net asset values falling down to the fund share prices, as would be the case if the measured net asset values were too high.[5] Moreover, Malkiel (1977) demonstrates that under fairly generous assumptions, the tax liabilities can account for a discount of no more than 6 percent.[6] Also, the tax theory suggests that discounts should widen when the market rises (since unrealized appreciation tends to increase in a bull market), contrary to the evidence we present below.

To summarize, standard explanations have been marginally successful (for some funds) in explaining Part 2 of our 4-part puzzle, i.e., the existence of discounts. However, the existing theories do not provide satisfactory explanations for the other parts of the puzzle: why funds get started, why the discounts fluctuate over time, and why large positive abnormal returns are realized when the fund is open-ended. Perhaps most important, each of these explanations deals with the puzzle of closed-end funds selling at discounts and fails to explain why sometimes funds sell at premia, particularly when they are started. Even taken collectively, these explanations cannot account for all the evidence. In the next section, we present an alternative explanation that not only accommodates these apparent anomalies, but also yields further testable hypotheses.

2. INVESTOR SENTIMENT

A. Noise Trader Risk

DSSW (1990) present a model of asset pricing based on the idea that the unpredictability of the opinions of not-fully-rational investors (or noise traders) impounds resale price risk on the assets they trade. In this model, there are two types of investors: rational investors and noise traders. Rational investors form rational expectations about asset returns. In contrast, noise traders' expectations about asset returns are subject to the influence of sentiment: they overestimate the expected returns (relative to the rational

---

[5] As pointed out to us by Jeffrey Pontiff, the evidence from open-ended funds is subject to selection bias. Another possibility, which is difficult to test, is that the NAV is properly measured only for the funds that open-end.

[6] The key assumptions in this calculation are the percentage of unrealized appreciation in the assets, the period of time before the asset is sold by the fund, and the holding period of the investor after the sale. Malkiel assumed the unrealized appreciation was 25 percent of the fund's assets and, in the worst case, the asset was sold immediately by the fund and the shares were sold immediately thereafter by the investor (which would maximize his tax liability) to arrive at the 6 percent amount. A more probable estimate, given the 25 percent unrealized appreciation, would be around 2 percent.

expectation) in some periods and underestimate them in others. Each period, rational investors and noise traders trade the assets based on their respective beliefs. Because assets are risky and all investors are risk averse, the equilibrium price reflects the opinions of both the rational investors and the noise traders.

DSSW then make two crucial assumptions. First, they assume that rational investors' horizons are short, so that they care about the interim resale prices of the assets they hold, not just the present values of dividends. This assumption is realistic. Portfolio managers are subject to frequent, periodic evaluations which shorten their horizons while individuals often have liquidity needs for selling. Also, the longer a rational investor keeps his trade open the higher are the cumulative transactions costs if either cash or assets have to be borrowed for that trade. Short sales, in particular, are difficult and costly over any long horizon. These costs of arbitrage tend to shorten investors' horizons and make them concerned with interim resale prices (Shleifer and Vishny, 1990).

Second, DSSW assume that noise traders' sentiment is stochastic and cannot be perfectly forecasted by rational investors. In particular, a rational investor cannot perfectly forecast how optimistic or pessimistic noise traders will be at the time he wants to sell the asset. Because rational investors care about the resale prices of assets, the unpredictability of noise trader sentiment impounds an additional risk on the assets they trade. The extra risk is that at the time a rational investor wants to sell an asset, noise traders might be bearish about it, causing its price to be low. As long as a rational investor might want to sell the asset in finite time, the risk of an adverse sentiment shift is every bit as real as fundamental risk of low dividends. This noise trader risk is borne by both rational investors and noise traders.

If different noise traders traded randomly across assets, the risk their sentiment would create would be diversifiable, just as idiosyncratic fundamental risk is diversifiable in conventional pricing models. However, if fluctuations in the same noise trader sentiment affect many assets and are correlated across noise traders, then the risk that these fluctuations create cannot be diversified. Like fundamental risk, noise trader risk arising from the stochastic investor sentiment will be priced in equilibrium. As a result, assets subject to noise trader risk will earn a higher expected return than assets not subject to such risk. Relative to their fundamental values, these assets will be underpriced.

DSSW discuss closed-end funds as an interesting application of their model. Suppose that noise traders' expectation about future returns is subject to unpredictable changes. Some of the time noise traders are optimistic about returns on these securities and drive up their prices relative to fundamental values. For securities where fundamental values are hard to observe, the effects of this optimism will be hard to identify. But in the case of closed-end funds, investor optimism will return in their selling at premia or at smaller discounts. Other times, noise traders are pessimistic about returns on these securities, drive down their prices, and so closed-end funds sell at larger discounts. In this way, stochastic changes in demand for closed-end funds by investors with unpredictably changing expectations of returns cause stochastic fluctuations in the discounts.

In this model, the risk from holding a closed-end fund (and any other security subject to the same stochastic sentiment) consists of two parts: the risk of holding the fund's portfolio and the risk that noise trader sentiment about the funds changes. In particular, any investor holding a closed-end fund bears the risk that the discount widens in the future if noise traders become relatively more pessimistic about closed-end funds. As long as this risk from the unpredictability of future investor sentiment is systematic, i.e., if investor sentiment affects many assets at the same time, this risk will be priced in equilibrium. When investor sentiment risk is systematic, it will affect a wide range of securities which includes, but is not limited to, closed-end funds. Investor settlement in the DSSW model, therefore, reflects expectations which are market-wide rather than closed-end fund specific.

B. Individual Investor Sentiment

One additional element is needed in applying the DSSW model to closed-end funds—differential clienteles. Specifically, it is necessary to assume that noise traders are more likely to hold and trade closed-end funds than the underlying assets in the funds' portfolios. If the same investors are investing in both the underlying securities and in the fund shares, then any change in investor sentiment will affect both the NAV and the share price, resulting in no change in the discount. Changes in the discount reflect not the aggregate effect of investor sentiment changes but the differential effect of the sentiment of the closed-end fund investing clientele relative to the investing clientele of the underlying assets. In this chapter, we speculate that the discount movements reflect the differential sentiment of individual investors since these investors hold and trade a preponderance of closed-end fund shares but are not as important an ownership group in the assets of the funds' investment portfolio.

There is ample evidence that closed-end funds are owned and traded primarily by individual investors. For example, Weiss (1989) found that three calendar quarters after the initial offering of new closed-end funds, institutions held less than 5 percent of the shares, in comparison to 23 percent of the shares of a control sample of IPO's for operating companies. Similarly, we found the average institutional ownership in the closed-end funds in our sample (Appendix 1) at the beginning of 1988 to be just 6.6 percent (median 6.2 percent). For the sake of comparison, average institutional ownership for a random sample of the smallest 10 percent of NYSE stocks is 26.5 percent (median 23.9 percent), and 52.1 percent (median 54.0 percent) for the largest

10 percent of NYSE stocks. Using intraday trading data, we have also found that in 1987, 64 percent of the trades in closed-end funds were smaller than $10,000. This number is 79 percent for the smallest 10 percent of NYSE stocks and only 28 percent for the largest 10 percent of NYSE stocks.[7] Collectively, the evidence strongly indicates that closed-end funds are both held and traded primarily by individual investors.

This evidence leads us to conjecture that the sentiment that affects closed-end fund discounts should also affect other securities that are held and traded predominantly by individual investors. As the evidence cited above shows, one set of such securities is small firms. If smaller capitalization stocks are subject to the same individual investor sentiment as closed-end funds, then fluctuations in the discounts on closed-end funds should be correlated with the returns on smaller stocks. When enough stocks in addition to closed-end funds are affected by the same investor sentiment, risk from this sentiment cannot be diversified and is therefore priced.

C. Arbitrage

The notion that holding a closed-end fund is riskier than holding its portfolio runs into an obvious objection. Why can't a rational arbitrageur buy the fund selling at a discount and sell short its portfolio? Since the fund costs less than its underlying assets, there is wealth left over after this perfectly hedged transaction, and the dividends that the fund distributes will cover the dividends on the investor's short position. In practice, however, there are several problems with this strategy.

First, if the fund changes its portfolio, the arbitrageur must similarly change the portfolio that is sold short. This may be difficult to accomplish in a timely manner. Second, investors do not get the full proceeds of a short sale: the hedge is not costless.[8] Third, even if these practical problems could be solved, the hedge would not be a pure arbitrage opportunity unless the arbitrageurs have an infinite time horizon and are never forced to liquidate their positions.[9] If, in contrast, an arbitrageur might need to liquidate at some finite time, then he faces the risk that the discount has widened since the time

---

[7]Decile membership is based on total market capitalization at the beginning of each year. Firms are sorted by CUSIP, and every third firm is selected to form the random sample. Inclusion in the final sample is subject to availability of data. There were 44–48 firms in each decile portfolio of the final sample. Percentage institutional ownership is based on the first issue of the *Standard and Poor's Stock Report* in each year after adjusting for known closely-held shares and block holdings. That is, the values reported are percentages of institutional holdings, divided by (100 − percent of closely-held or block shares). The intraday trading data is from the Institute for the Study of Security Markets (ISSM) based at Memphis State University.

[8]See Herzfeld (1980) for a similar strategy that can be implemented using call options.

[9]For an analysis of the conditions necessary for arbitrage to eliminate irrationality, see Russell and Thaler (1985).

the arbitrage trade was put on. If the discount widens, the arbitrage trade obviously results in a loss. Arbitrageurs would never need to liquidate their positions if they received the full proceeds from the initial short sales, since the initial investment would have been negative, and all future cash flows would be zero. But, since arbitrageurs do not get full proceeds, they might need to liquidate to obtain funds. In such cases, bearing noise trader risk is unavoidable. As long as arbitrageurs do not have infinite horizons, arbitrage against noise traders is not riskless because the discount can widen. Because of this risk, arbitrageurs take only limited positions, and mispricing can persist.

A possible alternative to the "buy and hold" arbitrage is a takeover of a closed-end fund, followed by a sell-off of its assets to realize the net asset value. The theoretical impediment to such takeovers has been identified by Grossman and Hart (1980) who show that free-riding fund shareholders would not tender their shares to the bidder unless they receive full net asset value. Because making a bid is costly, the bidder who pays full NAV cannot himself profit from the bid, and so no bids will take place. In practice, managerial resistance and regulatory restrictions represent formidable hurdles for the would-be bidder. For example, by 1980 the Tricontinental and Lehman funds had each defeated four attempts at reorganization (Herzfield, 1980). More recently, in 1989 the Securities and Exchange Commission helped block the takeover of the Cypress fund. If acquires' profits from closed-end fund takeovers are meager after transaction costs, then it is not surprising that such takeovers have not been more common.

D. Investor Settlement and the Four Part Puzzle

Changing investor sentiment has a number of empirical implications for the pricing of closed-end funds. Most importantly, because holding the fund is riskier than holding its portfolio directly, and because this risk is systematic, the required rate of return on assets held as fund shares must, on average, be higher than the required return on the same assets purchased directly. This means that the fund must, on average, sell at a discount to its NAV to induce investors to hold the fund's shares. Note that to get this result we do not need to assume that noise traders are, on average, pessimistic about funds: the average underpricing of closed-end funds comes solely from the fact that holding the fund is riskier than holding its portfolio. This theory is therefore consistent with the main puzzle about closed-end funds: they sell at a discount.

The theory is also consistent with the other three pieces of the puzzle. First, it implies that when noise traders are particularly optimistic about closed-end funds (and other assets subject to the same movements in investor sentiment), entrepreneurs can profit by putting assets together into closed-end funds and selling them to the noise traders. In this model, rational investors do not buy closed-end funds at the beginning. On the contrary, if they could borrow the shares they would sell the funds short.[10] It seems necessary to introduce some type of irrational investor to be able to explain why anyone buys the fund shares at the start when the expected return over the next few months is negative. Noise traders, who are sometimes far too optimistic about the true expected return on the fund shares, serve that purpose in the model. In this theory, then, there is no "efficiency" reason for the existence of closed-end funds. Like casinos and snake oil, closed-end funds are a device by which smart entrepreneurs take advantage of a less sophisticated public.

Second, the theory implies that discounts on closed-end funds fluctuate with changes in investor sentiment about future returns (on closed-end funds and other securities). In fact, this theory *requires* that discounts vary stochastically since it is precisely the fluctuations in the discounts that make holding the fund risky and therefore account for average underpricing. If the discounts were constant, then the arbitrage trade of buying the fund and selling short its portfolio would be riskless even for a short horizon investor, and discounts would disappear.

Third, the theory explains why funds' share prices rise on the announcement of open-ending and why discounts are reduced and then eliminated at the time open-ending or liquidation actually occurs. When it is known that a fund will be open-ended or liquidated (or, as Brauer (1988) points out, even when the probability of open-ending increases appreciably), noise trader risk is eliminated (or reduced), and so is the discount. Notice that this risk is largely eliminated when open-ending or liquidation is announced, since at that time any investor can buy the fund and sell short its portfolio knowing that upon open-ending his arbitrage position can be profitably closed for sure. The risk of having to sell when the discount is even wider no longer exists. The small discount that remains after the announcement of open-ending or liquidation can only be explained by the actual transactions costs of arbitrage (the inability to receive short-sale proceeds or the unobservability of the fund's portfolio) or the effect of some of the standard explanations mentioned earlier. The investor sentiment theory thus predicts that the discounts which remain after the announcement of open-ending or liquidation should become small or disappear eventually.

E. Additional Implications

The investor sentiment explanation of discounts on closed-end funds appears to perform better than alternative theories in explaining the key stylized facts. More interestingly, it has a number of additional implications which have not been derived or tested in the context of other theories of discounts. As with the

[10]Peavy (1990) shows that underwriters of closed-end funds buy shares in the aftermarket to support the price. Discussions we had with a professional trader of closed-end funds indicate that short selling of closed-end fund IPO's is extremely difficult.

implications discussed above, the new implications are derived from the idea that discounts on closed-end funds reflect widespread changes in investor sentiment rather than idiosyncratic changes in such fund's management or operations.

The first implication is that levels of and changes in discounts should be highly correlated across funds. Since the same sentiment drives discounts on all funds as well as on other securities, changes in this sentiment should determine changes in discounts.

Second, the observation that funds can get started when noise traders are optimistic about their returns can be taken further. Specifically, to the extent closed-end funds are substitutes, the model predicts that new funds should get started when investors favor seasoned funds as well, i.e., when old funds sell at a premium or at a small discount. This effect might be obscured by short-selling constraints on new funds, and the fact that new funds are not perceived as perfect substitutes for seasoned funds. Nevertheless, we test this implication by examining the behavior of the discounts on seasoned funds when new funds are started.

The third implication of the theory is perhaps the most interesting and surprising. The theory requires that for investor sentiment to affect closed-end fund prices, despite the workings of arbitrage, the risk created by changes in investor sentiment must be systematic. The same investor sentiment that affects discounts on closed-end fund must affet other assets as well which have nothing to do with closed-end funds. For example, returns on some portfolios of stocks might be correlated with changes in the average discount on closed-end funds, controlling for market returns. Portfolios affected by the same sentiment as closed-end funds should do well when discounts narrow and poorly when discounts widen. The theory itself does not specify which securities will be influenced by the same sentiment as closed-end funds. However, as we argued above, smaller capitalization stocks are good candidates since individual investors specialize in holding both smaller stocks and closed-end funds.

Other models of closed-end fund discounts are either silent about these predictions, or else they yield opposite results. The evidence we present below, then, is either orthogonal to alternative theories, or else enables us to differentiate between them and the investor sentiment explanation of discounts.

3. DATA AND VARIABLE DESCRIPTION FOR THE BASIC ANALYSIS

Our closed-end fund data were collected from two main sources. Information on annual discounts and net asset values, as well as background information on each fund, was obtained from the 1960 to 1987 editions of Wiesenberger's

Investment Companies Services annual survey of mutual funds. We were also able to obtain the year that each fund started from these sources.[11] A total of 87 funds were initially identified through this source, of which 68 were selected for monthly analysis because they were known to have CUSIP identifiers.[12] For these funds, we collected the weekly net asset value per share, stock price, and discount per share as reported by the *Wall Street Journal* (WSJ) between July, 1956 and December, 1985 (inclusive). Each week, generally on Monday, the WSJ reports Friday closing prices, NAV, and discounts. To convert the data into a monthly series, the Friday which was closest to each month end was taken, so each observation is within 3 days of the last day of the month.[13] The NAV per share information from the WSJ was then combined with the number of shares outstanding at the end of each month (obtained from the monthly master tape of the Center for Research of Security Prices (CRSP)) to arrive at the total net asset value for each fund.

For several of the tests which follow we constructed a value-weighted index of discounts (VWD) both at the annual and monthly levels as follows:

$$VWD_t = \sum_{i=1}^{n_t} W_i\, DISC_{it},$$

where

$$W_i = \frac{NAV_{it}}{\sum_{i=1}^{n_t} NAV_{it}}, \quad NAV_{it} = \text{net asset value of fund } i \text{ at end of period t}$$

$$DISC_{it} = \frac{NAV_{it} - SP_{it}}{NAV_{it}} \times 100,$$

SP_{it} = stock price of fund i at end of period t

n_t = the number of funds with available $Disc_{it}$ and NAV_{it} data at the end of period t

---

[11]More detailed information, such as the composition of the TRICON portfolio, were obtained by examining the financial statements of the fund. Also, to ensure that funds which were open-ended during our period of study were included in the count of fund starts, we checked funds reported in Wiesenberger against the list of funds in Brickley and Schallheim (1985) as well as Brauer (1984).

[12]We are indebted to Greg Brauer for providing us with this list of funds.

[13]The use of a monthly interval allows for comparison with other macroeconomic variables. Various validity checks were employed both during the data collection and later analysis to ensure the integrity of this data. The inputting of a NAV and stock price, for example, generated an automatic discount calculation on the input screen which was checked against the figure reported in the WSJ. After input, univariate statistics were computed on all large funds to check for outliers, and unusual observations were traced back to the WSJ. Occasional inaccuracies in the WSJ figures were corrected through appeal to numbers reported in adjacent weeks. There were two weeks for which the WSJ did not appear to have reported this data. In constructing the monthly series the next closest Friday's close was used.

We also computed changes in the value-weighted index of discounts (ΔVWD). For this measure, we computed VWD in a similar fashion, except we required that each fund included in the index must have the DISC and NAV data available for months t and t − 1, so that monthly changes in the index are computed over the same asset base. In other words, we require common membership in adjacent months. We then defined ΔVWD to be:

$$\Delta VWD_t = VWD_t - VWD_{t-1}$$

The change in the value-weighted index of discounts (ΔVWD) was computed both annually and with monthly data. For the monthly series, we computed this variable several ways. In the first case we excluded funds which specialize in foreign securities, specifically the ASA Fund and the Japan Fund. In the second case we excluded bond funds (funds which invest primarily in debt securities). The results were similar irrespective of the ΔVWD measure used. The reported findings were based on ΔVWD computed using both foreign and domestic stock funds (i.e., excluding bond funds but including both the ASA Fund and the Japan Fund). This time-series spanned 246 months (7/65 to 12/85).

Of the original sample of 68 funds, 18 were either missing data from the WSJ or did not have shares information available on CRSP and 30 others were bond funds. This left a total of 20 stock funds which participated in the monthly ΔVWD series (see Appendix I for listing). Of these remaining funds, some had relatively short life spans, others may occasionally have missing data points, so the actual number of funds included in computing VWD and ΔVWD varied from month to month. The stock fund ΔVWD series had monthly memberships ranging from 7 funds to 18 funds. In the vast majority of months, at least 10 funds were in the index. We show later that the key findings in this paper are relatively insensitive to the choice of funds which are included in the value-weighted index.

4. EVIDENCE

A. Co-movements in Discounts of Different Funds

The investor sentiment model predicts that the discounts on closed-end funds will be correlated. Figure 2 shows the levels of discounts for all closed-end stock funds at the end of each year during 1960–1986. The clear impression is that discounts on individual funds are highly correlated. In fact, the average pairwise correlation of *year-end discounts* for domestic funds is 0.497 (0.607 for diversified domestic funds). Individual pairwise correlations range from insignificant with specialized funds to above 0.8 for some diversified domestic funds. The average pairwise correlation of *annual changes* in discounts among domestic stock funds is 0.389.

The same conclusion emerges from an examination of monthly pairwise correlations. Tables 1 and 2 present the monthly correlations of both levels and changes in discounts for several major funds. The ten funds in these tables have the highest number of available observations over the study period. With the notable exception of American South African (ASA) Fund and the Japan Funds (two foreign funds), and perhaps Petroleum Resources (a fund specializing in oil and gas stocks), the levels of discounts on different funds show a high level of correlation.[14] The average pairwise correlation of month-end discounts for domestic funds is 0.530 (0.643 for diversified domestic funds). The average pairwise correlation of monthly changes in discounts among domestic stock funds is 0.248 (0.267 for diversified domestic funds). That this comovement is captured by the VWD variable is seen in the strong correlation of this variable to the discounts of each individual fund. This is true even for the two foreign funds.

---

[14]The reasons for the low correlations of discounts of foreign and domestic funds may have to do with special influences on foreign funds, such as exchange and trading controls, and possibly with different investor sentiments about foreign funds. ASA also has unique risks in that it specializes in South African gold stocks.

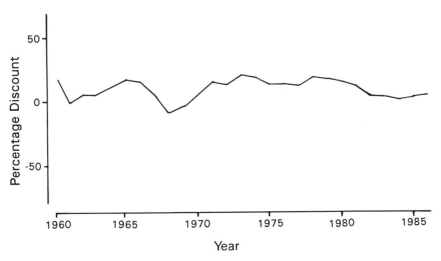

Figure 2. *Percentage discount or premium at the end of the year for all closed-end stock funds during 1960–1986. The percentage discount is computed as 100 × (NAV − SP); where NAV is the per share net asset value and SP is the share price of the fund. The sample includes all 46 stock funds reported in the* Wiesenberger Investment Companies Services *Annual survey during this period. The discount on a value-weighted portfolio of these funds is represented by the solid line.*

TABLE 1 Correlation of Monthly Discounts of Individual Funds

Correlation between levels of discounts at month end for nine individual funds, the discount on a value-weighted portfolio of all closed-end stock funds (VWD), and the total value of all New York Stock Exchange firms, NYVAL (7/65 to 12/85). The pairwise Pearson product-moment correlation and p-value for two-tailed test of the null hypothesis of zero correlation are shown, as is the number of observations.

	AdExp	ASA	CentSec	GenAm	Japan	Lehman	Niag	Petr	TriCon	VWD
AdExp	—									
ASA	0.266 0.0001 225	—								
CentSec	0.654 0.0001 159	−0.286 0.0003 155	—							
GenAm	0.737 0.0001 242	0.065 0.3279 227	0.596 0.0001 159	—						
Japan	0.430 0.0001 239	0.235 0.0004 225	0.512 0.0001 158	0.395 0.0001 241	—					

Lehman	0.830 0.0001 240	0.303 0.0001 225	0.693 0.0001 159	0.785 0.0001 242	0.643 0.0001 239	—			
Niag	0.596 0.0001 242	0.106 0.1104 227	0.266 0.0007 158	0.633 0.0001 244	0.533 0.0001 241	0.753 0.0001 242	—		
Petr	0.378 0.0001 243	0.165 0.0129 226	0.159 0.0447 159	0.254 0.0001 243	−0.084 0.1947 240	0.230 0.0002 241	0.198 0.0019 243	—		
TriCon	0.651 0.0001 241	0.075 0.2630 226	0.651 0.0001 157	0.459 0.0001 243	0.533 0.0001 240	0.666 0.0001 241	0.671 0.0001 243	0.279 0.0001 242	—	
VWD	0.810 0.0001 243	0.427 0.0001 228	0.539 0.0001 159	0.711 0.0001 245	0.651 0.0001 242	0.893 0.0001 243	0.767 0.0001 245	0.281 0.0001 244	0.805 0.0001 244	—
NYVAL	−0.019 0.7721 243	0.477 0.0001 228	−0.860 0.0001 159	−0.254 0.0001 245	−0.053 0.4130 242	−0.046 0.4714 243	−0.084 0.1891 245	−0.016 0.7976 244	−0.316 0.0001 244	−0.056 0.2787 246

TABLE 2 Correlation of Changes in the Monthly Discounts of Individual Funds

Correlation of changes in the monthly discounts between nine individual funds, a value-weighted portfolio of all closed-end stock funds (ΔVWD) and the monthly return on a value-weighted portfolio of all New York Stock Exchange firms—VWNY (7/65 to 12/85). The pairwise Pearson product-moment correlation and *p*-value for two-tailed test of the null hypothesis of zero correlation are shown, as is the number of observations.

	AdExp	ASA	CentSec	GenAm	Japan	Lehman	Niag	Petr	TriCon	ΔVWD
AdExp	—									
ASA	−0.054 0.3687 207	—								
CentSec	0.424 0.0001 155	0.037 0.6530 149	—							
GenAm	0.301 0.0068 237	−0.622 0.3687 211	0.063 0.4374 155	—						
Japan	−0.028 0.6732 232	0.0189 0.7870 208	−0.0311 0.7030 153	0.0181 0.7831 235	—					

					Lehman	Niag	Petr	TriCon	ΔVWD
Lehman	0.304 0.0001 235	0.061 0.3808 210	0.339 0.0001 155	0.406 0.0001 238	0.037 0.6700 233	—			
Niag	0.173 0.0075 237	0.082 0.236 211	0.178 0.028 153	0.188 0.0034 241	0.118 0.0719 235	0.263 0.0001 238	—		
Petr	0.269 0.0001 239	0.051 0.4650 209	0.056 0.4884 155	0.247 0.0001 239	0.173 0.0081 234	0.173 0.0077 236	0.249 0.0001 239	—		
TriCon	0.358 0.0001 235	-0.171 0.0133 209	0.238 0.0033 151	0.242 0.0002 239	0.053 0.4187 233	0.309 0.0011 236	0.247 0.0001 239	0.201 0.0018 237	—	
ΔVWD	0.419 0.0001 239	0.384 0.0001 213	0.300 0.0001 155	0.435 0.0001 243	0.165 0.0109 237	0.629 0.0001 240	0.413 0.0001 243	0.381 0.0001 241	0.561 0.0001 241	—
VWNY	0.159 0.0138 239	-0.143 0.037 213	0.199 0.0131 155	0.059 0.3638 243	-0.241 0.0002 237	0.1061 0.3229 240	0.225 0.0004 243	-0.027 0.6760 241	0.120 0.0629 241	0.013 0.8446 245

It seems clear from Tables 1 and 2 that discounts of different domestic funds tend to move together. In fact, these high correlations between discounts justify the construction of the value-weighted discount. The positive correlations are consistent with the hypothesis that discounts on different funds are driven by the same investor sentiment. Tables 1 and 2 also illustrate the point that neither the levels nor the changes in discounts on closed-end funds are related very strongly to levels of stock prices or stock returns. The correlation between the returns on the value-weighed market index (VWNY) and the changes in the value-weighted discount index (ΔVWD) is not significantly different from zero. A similar result was obtained by Sharpe and Sosin (1975). Thus, if discounts are driven by movements in investor sentiment, this sentiment is not strongly correlated with the aggregate stock market returns. As we argued above, these movements reflect the differential sentiment of individual investors.

B. When Do Funds Get Started?

The investor sentiment approach to the pricing of closed-end funds predicts that new funds get started when old funds sell at premiums or at small discounts. Testing this hypothesis presents several problems. First, over most of the period we examine, very few funds get started. Although this fact makes sense given that funds almost always trade at a discount during this period, it makes testing more difficult. Second, it takes time to organize and register a fund, which means that funds can start trading much later than the time they are conceived. These delays also raise the possibility that fund offerings are withdrawn when market conditions change, creating a bias in the time series of fund starts. Third, new funds tend to be brought to market with features which distinguish them from existing funds. In the early 1970s the funds which got started were primarily bond funds and funds specializing in restricted securities, types that had not previously existed. In the bull market of 1985–87, numerous foreign funds and so called "celebrity funds" (funds managed by well-known money managers) came to market. The former offered easy access to markets in specific foreign countries, and the latter offered an opportunity to cash in on the expertise of famous managers. To the extent seasoned funds and existing funds are not seen as perfect substitutes, new funds could get started even when seasoned funds sell at discounts.

In this chapter, we do not delve deeply into fund organization and marketing issues but rather present some simple statistics. Figure 3 plots the number of stock funds started each year against the VWD at the beginning of the year. Note that fund starts tend to be clustered through time. Periods when many funds start roughly coincide with periods when discounts are relatively low. Table 3 compares the value-weighted discounts on seasoned funds in years when one or more new stock funds begin trading and in years where no stock funds begin trading. Between 1961 and 1986, there are 12 years in which one or more stock funds get started and 14 years in which no stock funds start. The average beginning-of-year discount in the former years is 6.40 percent, and the average beginning-of-year discount in the latter years is 13.64 percent. The difference between the average discounts in the two subsamples of years is significant at the 1 percent level. This result lends some support to the argument that new funds get started when discounts on old funds are lower, though the discounts are nontrivial even in the years with new start-ups. Given the caveats discussed above, the evidence on start ups of new funds appears at least consistent with the investor sentiment hypothesis.

C. Discount Movements and Returns on Portfolios of Stocks

In this subsection, we present evidence on perhaps the least obvious prediction of the theory, namely that changes in the discounts on closed-end funds should be correlated with returns on baskets of stocks that may have nothing to do with the funds themselves. In particular, we look at portfolios of firms with different capitalizations, under the theory that the individual investors are significant holders and traders of smaller stocks, and so changes in their

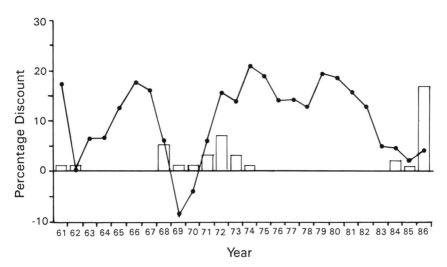

Figure 3. *The number of closed-end stock funds started and the discount on stock funds at the beginning of the year. This graph shows the number of closed-end stock funds started during the year and the percentage discount on a value-weighted portfolio of closed-end stock funds at the beginning of each year during 1961 to 1986. The line graph represents the percentage discount at the beginning of the year. The bar graph represents the number of stock funds started during the year.*

sentiment should affect both closed-end funds and smaller stocks. Since we have established that discounts on different funds move together, we use the change in the value weighted discount (ΔVWD) as a proxy for discount changes. Our measure of market returns are returns on the value-weighted index of NYSE stocks. Finally, the portfolios of stocks we consider are ten size-ranked portfolios. The first portfolio (Decile 1) are the 10 percent of all stocks that have the smallest equity value on NYSE, and the tenth portfolio (Decile 10) are the 10 percent with the largest equity value. The portfolio rebalancing algorithm used to compute decile portfolio returns follows Chen, Roll, and Ross (1986). Membership of each decile was determined at the beginning of each year and kept constant for the rest of the year. The returns of each firm in the decile were weighted by its beginning-of-month market capitalization. In case of missing returns, a firm was excluded from the portfolio for the current and following month.[15]

TABLE 3 Statistical Comparison of the Value-Weighted Discount at the Beginning of the Year for Years with Fund Starts and Years Without Fund Starts

Statistical comparison of the value-weighted discount at the beginning of the year for years in which one or more closed-end stock funds were started versus the years in which no stock funds started.*

	Years in Which One or More Stock Funds Started	Years in Which No Stock Funds Started
Mean Value-weighted Discount at the Beginning of the Year	6.40	13.64
Number of Years	12	14
t-statistic for a Test of a Difference in Means Between Two Random Samples Assuming Unequal Variance	−2.51*	
t-statistic for a Test of a Difference in Means Between Two Random Samples Assuming Equal Variance	−2.63*	
z-statistic for the Wilcoxon Rank Sum Test of a Difference in Means Between Two Random Samples	−2.24*	

*Significant at the 1 percent level in one-tailed tests (5 percent in two-tailed tests).

[15] Since discounts are reported as of each Friday's close, the use of full monthly returns introduces a potential timing problem. We correct for this by computing the monthly market returns and the returns of the decile portfolios using the exact dates on which the discounts are computed. Slightly weaker results than those of Table 4 would obtain if full monthly returns are used, although the coefficient on ΔVWD would still be significant in all deciles at the 1 percent level (two-tailed), except for Decile 9, which is significant at the 2 percent level. Special thanks to Raymond Kan for suggesting this improvement.

Table 4 presents the results of time series regressions of returns of decile portfolios on market returns and on changes in VWD. As in previous studies, we find that all portfolios have market betas in the neighborhood of 1, with the smallest firms having a beta of 1.3 and largest firms having a beta of 0.93. Beta estimates are almost identical when these regressions are run without the VWD variable. For all portfolios, we also find evidence of a correlation between returns and changes in the VWD holding market returns constant. For Decile 10, the largest firms, we find that stock prices do poorly when discounts narrow. For the other nine portfolios, stocks do well when discounts shrink.[16] The signs of the effects are as expected. When individual investors become optimistic about closed-end funds and smaller stocks, these stocks do well and discounts narrow. When individual investors become pessimistic about closed-end funds and smaller stocks, smaller stocks do badly and discounts widen.[17]

For Decile 1, a drop of one percent in the monthly value weighted discount index is accompanied by an extra return of 0.67 percent per month. Since the median absolute change in the monthly discount index over our study period is 1.40, this means in a typical month the discount factor is associated with a monthly fluctuation of 0.94 percent in the Decile 1 returns. The median monthly absolute return for Decile 1 firms over this period is 3.912 percent. Thus, in a typical month, approximately 24 percent of the monthly small firm returns is accountable by discount changes, even after controlling for general market movements. For Deciles 2 through 9, the effect is in the same direction but weaker. The effect on the returns of Decile 10 firms, while statistically significant, is of a different sign and much smaller; in a typical month, about five percent of the total return is accountable by discount changes.[18]

The coefficients on the change in VWD are monotonic in portfolio size. For the smallest stocks, which typically have the highest individual ownership, the comovement with closed-end funds is the greatest. For larger capitalization stocks, which have lower individual ownership, this comovement is weaker. Finally, the largest stocks, which by the end of this period had over 50 percent institutional ownership, seem to move in the opposite direction from the discounts. We have replicated these findings using equal-weighted rather than

---

[16]In Table 4, the American South-Africa (ASA) Fund is included in the calculation of the VWD. The results do not materially change if this fund is excluded.

[17]The evidence presented thus far is inconsistent with the unmeasured capital gains tax liability hypothesis of discounts. This theory predicts that when stocks do well, closed-end funds should accrue unrealized capital gains, and discounts should in general widen, holding the turnover rates on fund assets constant. However, Table 2 shows that the correlation between returns on the market and changes in discounts is about zero (the statistically insignificant correlation is negative which goes against the tax theory). Table 4 also indicates that discounts narrow when small stocks do well which is also inconsistent with the tax explanation.

[18]Based on $(1.40 \times 0.10)/2.534$, where 2.534 is the median absolute return on the Decile 10 portfolio.

TABLE 4 The Time-Series Relationship Between Returns on Size-Decile Portfolios, the Market Return, and Changes in Closed-End Fund Discounts

The time-series relationship (7/65 to 12/85) between monthly returns on decile portfolios (dependent variables), changes in the monthly discount on a value-weighted portfolio of closed-end stock funds (ΔVWD), and the monthly return on a value-weighted portfolio of New York Stock Exchange firms (VWNY). Decile 10 contains the largest firms, Decile 1 the smallest. Membership in each decile is determined at the beginning of year and kept constant for the rest of the year. Returns of each firm are weighted by the beginning-of-month market capitalization. In case of missing returns, a firm is excluded from the portfolio for the current and following month. The dependent variable in the last row is the excess return of small firms over large firms, computed by subtracting Decile 10 returns from Decile 1 returns. The number of observations is 245. t-statistics are shown in parentheses.

Return on the Decile Portfolio	Intercept	ΔVWD	VWNY	Adjusted R^2
1 (smallest)	0.0062	−0.0067 (−4.94)	1.238 (18.06)	58.7
2	0.0042	−0.0049 (−4.83)	1.217 (23.66)	70.3
3	0.0036	−0.0039 (−4.20)	1.202 (26.09)	74.0
4	0.0033	−0.0038 (−5.07)	1.163 (30.64)	79.7
5	0.0027	−0.0029 (−4.12)	1.148 (32.90)	81.8
6	0.0024	−0.0028 (−4.65)	1.124 (37.08)	85.1
7	0.0013	−0.0015 (−3.03)	1.134 (45.30)	89.4
8	0.0015	−0.0015 (−3.45)	1.088 (51.32)	91.5
9	0.0003	−0.0010 (−3.14)	1.057 (66.93)	94.8
10 (largest)	−0.0005	0.0010 (3.84)	0.919 (71.34)	95.4
1–10	0.0067	−0.0077 (−4.93)	0.319 (4.05)	13.5

334

value-weighted market returns and found the same monotonicity of coefficients. When an equal-weighted market index is used, however, the five portfolios of largest firms all show negative comovement with the value-weighted discount, while the five smaller portfolios all have positive coefficients. These results are consistent with the view that what is relevant about size in our regressions is individual ownership. Firms which are smaller (larger) than "average" comove positively (negatively) with discounts on closed-end funds because they have a higher (lower) concentration of individual investors than the "average" firm in the market index.

A final piece of evidence germane to this analysis comes from the seasonal pattern of discounts. Brauer and Chang (1990) present the striking result that prices of closed-end funds exhibit a January effect even though prices of the funds' portfolios do not. We confirmed this result in our data: the mean January ΔVWD is significantly negative, meaning discounts shrink in January. Interestingly, Ritter (1988) documents that 40 percent of the year-to-year variation in the turn-of-the-year effect is explained by the buy-sell activities of individual investors. These findings, of course, accord well with the notion that closed-end fund prices are affected by individual investor trading, some of which occurs at the end of the year, and not just by fundamentals. However, to ensure that Table 4 results are not restricted to the turn-of-the-year, we performed the same regressions with January and December observations removed. The coefficients on ΔVWD remained significant for all ten deciles at the 1 percent level and the monotonicity is preserved.

To summarize, the evidence suggests that discounts on closed-end funds narrow when smaller stocks do well. This correlation is stronger, the smaller the stocks. These results are consistent with the hypothesis that individual investor sentiment is particularly important for the prices of smaller stocks and of closed-end funds. In the next section, we test the robustness of this finding.

5. FURTHER EVIDENCE ON SIZE PORTFOLIOS

A. Do Closed-end Funds Hold Small Stocks?

Our finding that smaller stocks do well when discounts on closed-end funds narrow runs into an objection. Suppose that closed-end funds holdings are concentrated in smaller stocks which are thinly traded. Then prices used in the calculation of net asset value are often stale, whereas closed-end fund prices are relatively fresh. This means that when smaller stocks do well, closed-end funds that hold these stocks appreciate, but the net asset value does not rise by as much as it should because some of the smaller stock prices used to compute the NAV are stale. Reported NAV's could also be stale if closed-end funds report changes in NAV sluggishly. The effect would be the same as if assets were infrequently traded. In their case, the discount narrows (i.e., the stock price of the fund moves up relative to its NAV) precisely when smaller stocks do well. The key finding of the previous section could then result from the mismeasurement of the net asset value.

This objection relies on the critical assumption that closed-end funds invest in smaller stocks (so their stock prices move together with the prices of smaller firms). This assumption is suspect in light of Brauer and Chang's (1990) finding that the portfolio holdings of closed-end funds do not exhibit a January effect. To evaluate this assumption more directly, we examine the portfolio of TRICON. Table 5 describes TRICON's holdings, distributed by decile, every 5 years starting in 1965. It is clear from this table that TRICON's holdings are concentrated in stocks in the largest two deciles, which, together with short-term holdings and cash equivalents, represent about 80 percent of the fund's holdings. Short-term holdings and stocks in the top 5 deciles typically represent over 90 percent of the fund's earning assets. In contrast, the fund typically holds less than 4 percent of its assets in stocks from the bottom five deciles. Since the stocks in the top two deciles are virtually never mispriced because of nontrading, and since the stocks in the top five deciles are rarely mispriced, it is hard to believe that TRICON's portfolio is subject to large mistakes in the calculation of net asset value because of nontrading or sluggish reporting.

In Table 6 we again regress decile returns on VWNY and changes in discounts as in Table 4, but this time changes in TRICON's discount are used instead of the changes in the value-weighted discount (ΔVWD). The results are very similar to those in Table 4 although parameter estimates are closer to zero, presumably because of a larger idiosyncratic component to TRICON's discounts. Nonetheless, it remains the case that smaller stocks do well when TRICON's discount narrows even though TRICON is holding virtually no small stocks. This finding is inconsistent with the hypothesis that our results can be explained by nontrading or delayed reporting.[19] Incidentally, TRICON itself is a Decile 8 stock, and its comovement with small stocks cannot be explained by the size of its own market capitalization.

---

[19]We also regressed the difference between the small and large firm returns (Decile 1 returns minus Decile 10 returns) against market movements and the change in discounts for each of ten major funds. For all ten funds, the coefficient on the discount variable was negative, significantly so for eight of the funds. Thus the relationship between small firm excess returns and discount changes is relatively insensitive to the choice of the fund. However, the t-statistics on ΔDISC$_i$ for individual funds are lower than the t-statistics on ΔVWD in Table 4, suggesting the portfolio approach was successful in removing idiosyncratic variations in the individual fund discounts.

TABLE 5 Composition of the Tricontinental Corporation Investment Portfolio

Composition of the investment portfolio of Tricontinental Corporation (TRICON) at the end of the year, distributed by the total market capitalization of the individual investments. To construct this table, each holding in the TRICON portfolio for each of the years listed was identified from the financial statements of the fund. For the majority of holdings, market capitalization was obtained through the CRSP tapes; market capitalization for the remainder were traced to Moody's Security Manuals and manually checked against decile cutoffs for each year. Values are shown in thousands of dollars. Decile cutoffs for each year are the same as those used on earlier regressions and are obtained from CRSP. Cash and short-term holdings include government T-bills and corporate debt instruments, net of short-term liabilities of the fund. Other holdings represent equity securities for which the market capitalization was not readily obtainable.

	1985		1980		1975		1970		1965	
Decile 1	0.0	0.0	0.0	0.0	2902.4	0.5	3644.7	0.6	8486.8	1.5
Decile 2	0.0	0.0	3316.5	0.4	548.5	0.1	7514.0	1.2	5856.0	1.0
Decile 3	2793.8	0.2	0.0	0.0	3507.9	0.6	125.8	0.0	0.0	0.0
Decile 4	0.0	0.0	7000.0	0.8	2051.2	0.4	1575.0	0.3	0.0	0.0
Decile 5	2477.9	0.2	19125.0	2.2	9840.5	1.7	9715.5	1.6	8016.2	1.4
Decile 6	4575.0	0.4	38519.2	4.4	5903.5	1.0	14304.3	2.4	0.0	0.0
Decile 7	63575.5	5.3	58238.9	6.6	28283.5	5.0	21934.8	3.7	23832.0	4.3
Decile 8	118981.2	10.0	88204.4	10.1	53320.2	9.4	51241.0	8.5	76452.2	13.7
Decile 9	306874.7	25.7	181298.3	20.7	69407.0	12.2	49787.5	8.3	82263.8	14.7
Decile 10	558993.8	46.8	391753.9	44.7	344500.4	60.7	371398.4	61.7	336612.2	60.2
Short-term Holdings and Cash Equivalents	128745.1	10.8	67978.2	7.8	41905.7	7.4	60690.5	10.1	17940.0	3.2
Other Holdings	8143.2	0.7	20890.9	2.3	5474.4	1.0	9702.1	1.6	0.0	0.0
Total Value of Portfolio	1195160.3	100.0%	876325.3	100.0%	567645.2	100.0%	601633.6	100.0%	559459.2	100.0%

337

**TABLE 6 The Time-Series Relationship
Between Returns on Size-Decile Portfolios, the Market Return,
and Changes in the Discount of Tri-Continental Corporation**

The time-series relationship (7/65 to 12/85) between monthly returns on decile portfolios (dependent variables), changes in the monthly discount of Tri-Continental (TRICON) and the monthly return on a value-weighted portfolio of New York Stock Exchange firms (VWNY). Decile 10 contains the largest firms, Decile 1 the smallest. Membership in each decile is determined at the beginning of year and kept constant for the rest of the year. Returns of each firm is weighted by the beginning-of-month market capitalization. In case of missing returns, a firm is excluded from the portfolio for the current and following month. The dependent variable in the last row is the excess return of small firms over large firms, computed by subtracting Decile 10 returns from Decile 1 returns. The number of observations is 241. t-statistics are shown in parentheses.

Return on the Decile Portfolio	Intercept	TRICON	VWNY	Adjusted R^2
1	0.0062	−0.0026	1.263	56.0
(smallest)		(−2.74)	(17.52)	
2	0.0044	−0.0021	1.236	68.9
		(−2.98)	(23.11)	
3	0.0039	−0.0017	1.214	72.9
		(−2.70)	(25.46)	
4	0.0036	−0.0013	1.174	78.3
		(−2.41)	(29.39)	
5	0.0030	−0.0011	1.156	81.0
		(−2.40)	(31.96)	
6	0.0025	−0.0014	1.135	84.6
		(−3.41)	(36.28)	
7	0.0014	−0.0009	1.142	89.4
		(−2.76)	(44.99)	
8	0.0016	−0.0010	1.097	91.7
		(−3.54)	(51.41)	
9	0.0004	−0.0007	1.062	94.8
		(−3.21)	(66.21)	
10	−0.0006	0.0005	0.916	95.4
(largest)		(2.94)	(69.80)	
1–10	0.0069	−0.0031	0.347	8.1
		(−2.85)	(4.20)	

338

B. The Stability of Results over Time

A further concern about our analysis is whether the results are stable over time. In Table 7 we reproduce the results from Table 4 except we split the sample in the middle (September 1975). For the earlier subsample, the results are stronger than in Table 4, with both the significance and the monotonicity of coefficients reemerging. For the second half, the results are significantly weaker. Although the coefficients on the change in the value-weighted discounts are negative for the first nine decile portfolios and positive for the tenth, their magnitude and statistical significance are much smaller than in the first half of the sample.

What can cause this instability of coefficients over time? One possibility is that the variation in the VWD was smaller in the later subperiod, yielding less explanatory power. Indeed, the standard deviation of ΔVWD falls from 2.40 to 1.95 from the first subperiod to the second. However, there is a more basic economic reason why the second period results might be different—the steady increase in institutional ownership of small firms. As we mentioned earlier, 26.5 percent of the shares of the smallest decile firms were held by institutions by 1988. An examination of a random sample of the smallest decile firms in 1980 revealed that institutions held only 8.5 percent of the shares. In just 8 years, institutions had more than tripled their holdings in first decile firms. At the same time, institutions continued to avoid closed-end funds, presumably because money managers are reluctant to delegate money management. One possible interpretation of the evidence, then, is that in the second half of our sample, individual investors became relatively less important in determining stock prices, particularly for the stocks of smaller firms. As a result, individual investor sentiment, which continues to be reflected in the discounts on closed-end funds, was no longer as strongly reflected in the pricing of smaller stocks.

To test this conjecture, we formed a portfolio consisting of all NYSE firms, other than closed-end funds, which had less than 10 percent institutional ownership in 1985.[20] We looked at these firms in 1985 because over time institutional holdings have increased, and so firms that have less than 10 percent institutional ownership in 1985 are likely to have even lower institutional ownership before 1985. In other words, the ownership structure of these firms is similar to that of closed-end funds. In 1985, there were only 56 such firms on NYSE, of which we found CUSIP numbers for 52. Interestingly, 37 (71 percent) of these stocks are public utilities which are not fundamentally related to closed-end funds in any obvious way. It is also of interest that only

---

[20]More precisely, we required that the total of institutional and closely-held shares, as reported by the January issue of the *Standard and Poor's Stock Report*, be less than 10 percent of a firm's outstanding common shares.

TABLE 7 Stability of the Time-Series Relationship Between Returns on Size-Decile Portfolios, the Market Return, and Changes in Closed-End Fund Discounts

Analysis of the stability of the time-series relationship between monthly returns on decile portfolios (dependent variables), changes in the monthly discount on a value-weighted portfolio of closed-end stock funds (ΔVWD) and the monthly return on a value-weighted portfolio of New York Stock Exchange firms (VWNY). Decile 10 contains the largest firms, Decile 1, the smallest. Membership in each decile is determined at the beginning of year and kept constant for the rest of the year. Returns of each firm is weighted by the beginning-of-month market capitalization. In case of missing returns, a firm is excluded from the portfolio for the current and following month. The dependent variable in the last row is the excess return of small firms over large firms, computed by subtracting Decile 10 returns from Decile 1 returns. The number of observations for the first period is 122, the second period is 123. t-statistics are shown in parentheses.

Return on the Decile Portfolio	First 123 months (7/65 to 9/75)				Second 123 months (10/75 to 12/85)			
	Intercept	ΔVWD	VWNY	Adj. R^2	Intercept	ΔVWD	VWNY	Adj. R^2
1 (smallest)	0.0054	-0.0101 (-5.50)	1.355 (13.83)	63.2	0.0079	-0.0022 (-1.08)	1.140 (12.08)	54.9
2	0.0015	-0.0070 (-4.89)	1.303 (16.97)	71.1	0.0078	-0.0022 (-1.52)	1.129 (16.79)	70.3
3	0.0016	-0.0057 (-4.60)	1.269 (19.18)	75.6	0.0064	-0.0014 (-1.00)	1.137 (17.80)	72.5
4	0.0022	-0.0050 (-4.88)	1.206 (21.99)	80.2	0.0048	-0.0022 (-1.98)	1.123 (21.16)	79.1
5	0.0010	-0.0042 (-4.59)	1.193 (24.27)	83.1	0.0050	-0.0010 (-0.95)	1.104 (22.29)	80.5
6	0.0014	-0.0038 (-4.58)	1.184 (26.79)	85.6	0.0041	-0.0016 (-1.81)	1.060 (25.71)	84.7
7	0.0006	-0.0021 (-2.90)	1.184 (31.04)	88.8	0.0025	-0.0009 (-1.31)	1.080 (33.44)	90.3
8	0.0016	-0.0018 (-2.98)	1.123 (35.67)	91.3	0.0017	-0.0012 (-1.89)	1.053 (36.56)	91.8
9	0.0000	-0.0013 (-2.82)	1.084 (44.58)	94.3	0.0009	-0.0007 (-1.52)	1.027 (50.93)	95.6
10 (largest)	-0.0002	0.0014 (4.16)	0.902 (50.18)	95.5	-0.0010	0.0004 (1.11)	0.937 (50.12)	95.4
1–10	0.0056	-0.0115 (-5.47)	0.4530 (4.04)	25.2	0.0089	-0.0027 (-1.12)	0.2038 (1.87)	2.5

8 (15 percent) of these firms are in the smallest size decile and 26 firms (50 percent) are in Deciles 5 and higher, so this is not a portfolio of small firms. Given our conjecture that individual ownership, rather than size per se, causes comovement with closed-end fund discounts, we expect a positive correlation between the returns of these stocks held largely by individuals and the changes in discounts on closed-end funds.

Table 8 presents the regression of the portfolio returns of individual-owned firms on market returns and the change in the value-weighted discount. For the whole period, and for both of the two subperiods, the coefficients on ΔVWD are significant, even after controlling for market movements. Firms held primarily by individuals do well, controlling for the market, when discounts on closed-end funds narrow. This finding corroborates our explanation of the weaker correlation between changes in discounts and returns on smaller stocks in the second subperiod. Specifically, individual investors, whose sentiment closed-end fund discounts capture, became less important in holding and trading small firms. Thus, the weaker results in Table 7 for the second subsample, as well as Table 8 results for individual-owned firms, both support the individual investor sentiment interpretation of the evidence.

**TABLE 8 The Time-Series Relationship
Between Returns of Firms with Low Institutional Ownership,
the Market Return, and Changes in Closed-End Fund Discounts**

The time-series relationship between the monthly returns on a portfolio of firms with low institutional ownership (the dependent variable), changes in the monthly discount on a value-weighted portfolio of closed-end stock funds (ΔVWD), and the monthly return on a value-weighted portfolio of New York Stock Exchange firms (VWNY). The dependent variable is the equally-weighted mean monthly return on a portfolio of firms whose total institutional ownership of common stocks outstanding is 10 percent or less. Membership in the portfolio is based on the total shares held by institutions and insiders as reported in the January, 1985 edition of the S&P Stock Report. A total of 52 firms is in the portfolio. Number of observations is 245, 122, and 123, respectively, for the three time periods. t-statistics are shown in parentheses.

Time Period	Intercept	ΔVWD	VWNY	Adjusted R^2
All Months (7/65–12/85)	0.0012	−0.0035 (−4.30)	0.744 (18.67)	59.8
First 123 Months (7/65–9/75)	−0.0020	−0.0042 (−3.74)	0.790 (13.50)	60.9
Second 123 Months (10/75–12/85)	0.0051	−0.0025 (−2.17)	0.677 (12.60)	57.5

6. ARE DISCOUNTS A SENTIMENT INDEX?

We have interpreted the discount on closed-end funds as an individual investor sentiment index. This section presents further evidence to substantiate this interpretation. First, we examine the relationship between this index and the risk factors identified by Chen, Roll, and Ross (1986). If the discounts are highly correlated with measures of fundamental risk, then our interpretation may be suspect. Second, we check whether the discounts are related to the net withdrawals from open-end funds and to the volume of initial public offerings of stocks other than closed-end funds. The latter tests are comparisons of discounts with other indices of investor sentiment.

A. Relationship of Discount Changes to Other Macroeconomic Factors

One question raised by our empirical evidence is whether the sentiment factor that we identify with the VWD is a new factor or whether it just proxies for macroeconomic factors previously identified in the literature. Chen, Roll, and Ross (1986) present a number of macroeconomic variables that affect stock returns in time-series regressions and expected returns in cross-section regressions. They interpret the variables to be risk factors. The variables include "innovations" in: industrial production, risk premia on bonds, the term structure of interest rates, and expected inflation. Table 9 presents the monthly correlations of changes in these factors with changes in the value-weighted discount (ΔVWD).

The main pattern that emerges from this table is that changes in discounts are not highly correlated with changes in "fundamental" factors. The correlations with "hard" macroeconomic variables such as production are very small. There is some correlation (0.157) between the changes in the discount and changes in the expected inflation rate (DEI). When expected inflation rises, so does the discount. We know of no fundamental explanation for this finding. Notice that changes in discounts are not correlated with the unanticipated change in the term structure (UTS). This result is counter to the agency cost argument which predicts that when long rates fall the present value of future management fees rise, so discounts should increase.

Another way to see whether the discount is an independent factor is to add this variable to an equation explaining returns using the other risk factors. Table 10 presents results of regressions of the monthly difference in returns between smallest and largest deciles of firms on changes in various factors. The results show that, even when changes in Chen, Roll, and Ross's "fundamental" factors are controlled for, changes in the VWD still have a pronounced and significant effect on the difference in returns between small and large firms. In

TABLE 9 Correlation Between Changes in the Value-Weighted Discount and Innovations in Various Macroeconomic Variables

Correlation between the monthly change in the discount on a value-weighted portfolio of closed-end stock funds, innovations in various macroeconomic variables, and the excess return earned by small (Decile 1) firms over large (Decile 10) firms for the period 7/65 to 12/85. The pairwise Pearson product-moment correlation and p-value for two-tailed test of the null hypothesis of zero correlation are shown. The number of observations is either 245 or 246. The macroeconomic variables are obtained from Chen, Roll, and Ross (1986) and are briefly described here. ΔVWD is the monthly change in the discount on a value-weighted portfolio of closed-end stock funds. DECSIZ is the monthly return on the smallest decile firms (Decile 1) minus the monthly return on the largest decile firms (Decile 10). EWNY and VWNY are the returns on equal-weighted and value-weighted portfolios of NYSE firms, respectively. MP($t+1$) is the monthly change in industrial production, as measured by $\log(\text{IP}(t+1)) - \log(\text{IP}(t))$, where IP($t$) is the seasonally unadjusted production at month t. YP($t+12$) is the yearly change in industrial production as measured by $\log(\text{IP}(t+12)) - \log(\text{IP}(t))$. UPR($t$) is the unanticipated change in risk premia at month t, measured by UBAA $-$ LGB where UBAA is the return of under Baa bonds at month t, and LGB is the return on long term government bonds at month t. UTS(t) is the unanticipated change in term structure at month t, as measured by LGB $-$ TB where LGB is the return on long term government bonds at month t and TB is the Treasury-Bill return of month t as observed at the end of month $t-1$. DEI(t) is the change in expected inflation measured by EI($t+1$) $-$ EI(t) where EI is the expected inflation for month t as at month $t-1$. UI(t) is computed by subtracting expected real interest of month t (Fama-Gibbons (1984)) from the T-Bill return of month t. UI(t) is unanticipated inflation measured by I(t) $-$ EI(t) where I(t) is the realized inflation for month t (CRSP SBBI), and EI(t) is the expected inflation for month t as at month $t-1$.

	DECSIZ	EWNY	VWNY	MP	YP	UPR	UTS	DEI	UI
ΔVWD	-0.268	-0.093	-0.0126	-0.003	-0.006	-0.053	-0.052	0.157	0.057
	0.0001	0.1489	0.8446	0.9571	0.9303	0.4099	0.4207	0.0137	0.3721

343

TABLE 10 The Relationship between Small Firm Excess Returns, Macroeconomic Innovations, and Changes in the Value-Weighted Discount

The time-series relationship (7/65 to 12/85) between the excess return earned by small (Decile 1) firms over large (Decile 10) firms, innovations in various macroeconomic variables and the monthly change in discount on a value-weighted portfolio of closed-end stock funds shown as ΔVWD. The number of observations is 245 and t-statistics are shown in parentheses. The macroeconomic variables are obtained from Chen, Roll, and Ross (1986) and are briefly described here. The dependent variable is the monthly return on the smallest decile firms (Decile 1) minus the monthly return on the largest decile firms (Decile 10). EWNY and VWNY are the returns on equal-weighted and value-weighted portfolios of NYSE firms, respectively. $MP(t+1)$ is the monthly change in industrial production, as measured by $\log(IP(t+1)) - \log(IP(t))$, where $IP(t)$ is the seasonally unadjusted production at month t. $YP(t+12)$ is the yearly change in industrial production as measured by $\log(IP(t+12)) - \log(IP(t))$. $UPR(t)$ is the unanticipated change in risk premia at month t measured by UBAA minus LGB where UBAA is the return of under Baa bonds at month t, and LGB is the return on long term government bonds at month t. UTS(t) is the unanticipated change in term structure at month t as measured by LGB − TB where LGB is the return on long term government bonds at month t and TB is the Treasury-Bill return of month t as observed at the end of month t − 1. DEI(t) is the change in expected inflation measured by $EI(t+1) - EI(t)$ where EI is the expected inflation for month t as at month t − 1 computed by subtracting expected real interest of month t (Fama-Gibbons (1984)) from the T-Bill return of month t. UI(t) is unanticipated inflation, measured by $I(t) - EI(t)$ where I(t) is the realized inflation for month t (CRSP SBBI), and EI(t) is the expected inflation for month t as at month t − 1.

Model	Intercept	VWNY	EWNY	YP	MP	DEI	UI	UPR	UTS	ΔVWD	Adj. R^2
1	0.0086	—	—	0.0150	0.4212	0.768	-3.793	0.789	0.480	—	12.1
				(0.23)	(3.07)	(0.16)	(−1.98)	(4.26)	(2.84)		
2	0.0090	—	—	—	0.4256	0.851	-3.774	0.799	0.489	—	12.5
					(3.14)	(0.18)	(−1.98)	(4.44)	(2.99)		
3	-0.0002	—	0.7400	—	0.3572	-6.210	-0.391	-0.129	-0.464	—	43.8
			(11.61)		(3.28)	(−1.64)	(−0.25)	(−0.78)	(−3.00)		
4	0.0064	0.2973	—	—	0.4439	-2.004	-2.989	0.518	0.166	—	15.2
		(2.92)			(3.32)	(−0.43)	(−1.57)	(2.57)	(0.85)		
5	0.0084	—	—	—	0.4332	3.347	-3.643	0.731	0.463	-0.0068	17.9
					(3.28)	(0.73)	(−1.97)	(4.16)	(2.91)	(−4.08)	
6	-0.0005	—	0.7264	—	0.3670	-3.907	-0.344	-0.173	-0.471	-0.0060	48.1
			(11.82)		(3.49)	(−1.06)	(−0.23)	(−1.09)	(−3.16)	(−4.53)	
7	0.0055	0.3294	—	—	0.4546	0.317	-2.77	0.415	0.103	-0.0072	21.2
		(3.34)			(3.51)	(0.07)	(−1.51)	(2.12)	(0.54)	(−4.40)	

fact, in Model 7, which includes the value-weighted NYSE index, the Chen, Roll, and Ross factors, and the change in the value-weighted discount, the discount variable has the highest t-statistic. The value-weighted discount seems to be a factor with an independent influence on returns. Even if changes in investor sentiment are (weakly) correlated with changes in "fundamental" factors, they still have a large influence of their own.

B. Evidence from Open-End Funds Redemptions

Malkiel (1977) found that discounts on closed-end funds narrow when purchases of open-end funds outstrip redemptions. His interpretation of this finding is similar to our own—similar market forces drive the demand for both open- and closed-end funds.

To examine this issue more closely, we have extended Malkiel's sample through the entire 246 months of our study period (7/65 to 12/85), and performed a similar analysis. After February 1982, there is an enormous increase in net purchases of open-end funds. Since this appears to be a regime change relative to the previous experience, we have estimated our regressions separately for two periods: 1965–1981 and 1965–1985. The results are presented in Table 11.

The results in Table 11 confirm Malkiel's finding that discounts increase with net redemptions from open-end funds. The ratio of redemptions to sales is significant in both time periods, and the difference in redemptions and sales is significant if the last 3 years of the sample are excluded. Although the overall explanatory power of these regressions is low, these results lend further credence to the view that changes in closed-end fund discounts reflect changes in individual investor sentiment. In this case, the evidence suggests that the investors whose sentiment changes are also investors in open-end funds. These tend to be individual rather than institutional investors.

C. Evidence from Initial Public Offerings

Another domain in which individual investors are important is the initial public offerings of corporations other than closed-end funds (IPO's). The investor sentiment hypothesis suggests that these IPO's should be more prevalent in times when individual investors are optimistic, so the stocks will fetch high prices relative to their fundamental values. While institutional investors are more important buyers of IPO's than they are of closed-end funds (Weiss (1989) estimates that, on average, 23 percent of IPO stocks are held by institutions three quarters after the offering). Individuals still account for over 75 percent of buying of IPO's, and we expect their sentiment to affect the timing of these offerings.

To measure the intensity of IPO activity we use the annual number of IPO's from Ibbotson, Sindelar, and Ritter (1988). We regress this measure of IPO volume on the beginning of the year value-weighted discount. Of course, IPO activity might be responsive to fundamentals as well. For example, firms might go public to raise capital when the future looks particularly bright. To control for this factor, we also include the dividend price ratio of the S&P 500, a measure of the expected growth rate of dividends. The regressions are run on an annual rather than a monthly basis to alleviate the strong serial correlation in monthly IPO's, although monthly results are similar. The results are displayed in Table 12 and Figure 4.

The first regression shows that in fact IPO volume is highly correlated with the VWD. The coefficient is significant at the 1 percent level, and the adjusted R-square of the regression is 41 percent. The significance of this relationship is also apparent from Figure 4. When the value-weighted discount shrinks from 15 percent to zero, the number of IPO's in the subsequent year rises by

TABLE 11 The Relationship between Net Redemption on Open-End Funds, the Market Return, and Changes in the Value-Weighted Discount

The time-series relationship between net redemption on open-end funds (dependent variable), the monthly return on a value-weighted portfolio of New York Stock Exchange firms (VWNY), and changes in the monthly discount on a value-weighted portfolio of closed-end stock funds (ΔVWD). The net redemption on open-end funds is measured two ways: by the monthly ratio of net redemptions to sales on open-end funds (R/S) and by the monthly net redemption on open-end funds expressed as a percentage of total fund assets at the beginning of the month (NRED). R/S is computed as redemptions/sales. NRED is computed as (redemptions-sales)/total fund assets. Monthly redemptions, sales, and fund assets data are obtained from the Investment Companies Institute and represent all open-end funds with long-term investment objectives (i.e., exclude money market and short-term municipal bond funds.) t-statistics are shown in parentheses.

Model	Dep. Var.	Intercept	VWNY	ΔVWD	Adj. R^2	No. of Obs.
		Panel A—7/65 to 12/85				
1	R/S	0.855	−1.864	0.029	4.9	245
			(−3.03)	(2.35)		
2	NRED	−0.005	−0.044	0.0001	3.0	245
			(−3.05)	(0.38)		
		Panel B—7/65 to 2/82				
1	R/S	0.949	−1.417	0.034	4.5	199
			(−2.18)	(2.53)		
2	NRED	−0.001	−0.009	0.0003	3.6	199
			(−1.73)	(2.50)		

**TABLE 12 The Relationship Between Number of IPO's,
the Dividend-to-Price Ratio on S&P500, and the Value-Weighted Discount
at the Beginning of the Year**

The time-series relationship between the annual number of Initial Public
Offerings (dependent variable), the dividend to price ratio of S&P500
stocks at the beginning of the year expressed as a percentage (Div/Price),
and the level of the value-weighted discount on a portfolio of closed-end
funds at the beginning of the year (VWD_{t-1}). The computation of the
dividend to price ratio on the S&P500 index follows Fama and French
(1988). The number of observations is 20. t-statistics are shown in
parentheses.

Intercept	VWD_{t-1}	Div/Price	Adjusted R^2
456.9	−19.3	—	40.9
	(−3.76)		
230.1	−21.8	61.8	41.5
	(−3.90)	(1.09)	

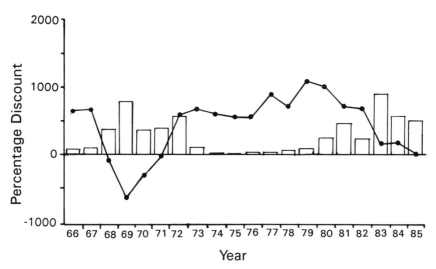

Figure 4. *The number of IPO's and the discount at the beginning of the year. This graph
shows the number of Initial Public Offerings (IPO's) during the year and the percentage
discount on a value-weighted portfolio of closed-end funds at the beginning of the year during
1966 to 1985. The line graph represents the value-weighted discount at the beginning of the
year × 50. The bar graph represents the number of IPO's during the year (source for IPO
data: Ibbotson, Sindelar, and Ritter (1988)).*

347

approximately 300 which is roughly one standard deviation. The second regression shows, to our surprise, that the dividend price ratio on the S&P 500 index does not affect the pace of the IPO activity. The regressions seem to suggest that individual investor sentiment is important in determining when companies go public, but the expected growth rate is not. The IPO evidence is consistent with our interpretation of discounts on closed end funds as a measure of individual investor sentiment.

7. SUMMARY
AND BROADER IMPLICATIONS

Closed-end mutual funds are not a very important financial institution in and of themselves. Together they represent a tiny fraction of the assets traded in organized security market. However, closed-end funds present a unique opportunity to investigate the validity of the efficient market hypothesis since their fundamental values are known and do not appear to be equal to their prices.

We have tested the theory that the changing sentiment of individual investors toward closed-end funds and other securities explains the fluctuations of prices and discounts on closed-end funds. In this theory, discounts are high when investors are pessimistic about future returns, and low when investors are optimistic. Average discounts exist because the unpredictability of investor sentiment impounds a risk on any investor in a closed-end fund in addition to the risk inherent in the fund's portfolio. The theory appears to be consistent with the published evidence on closed-end fund prices, and several new predictions of the theory have been confirmed. The evidence suggests that discounts on closed-end funds are indeed driven by changes in small investor sentiment, and that the same sentiment affects returns on small capitalization stocks.

The basic conclusion of this chapter is that closed-end fund discounts are a measure of the sentiment of small investors. That sentiment is sufficiently widespread to affect the prices of small stocks in the same way that it influences the prices of closed-end funds. Changing investor sentiment makes funds riskier than the portfolios they hold, and so causes average underpricing of funds relative to fundamentals. The same investor sentiment affects small stocks as well, so small stocks must be subject to the same risk as closed-end funds. *Therefore, small stocks must also be underpriced relative to their fundamentals.*

The fact that small investor sentiment has a disproportionately large impact on small firms implies that small firms are riskier than our current pricing models would imply. Therefore, controlling for the fundamental risk of the small stocks, their average returns will appear too high. Of course, this result is the well-established small-firm effect. Thus, an additional, less obvious implication of our theory is that the small firm effect may, in part, be clientele-related.

While our findings do not imply risk-free arbitrage opportunities, they do point to the existence of nonfundamental risks within the market. The fact that such risks are priced yields two important implications:

1. Securities subject to such risks will trade, on average, at discounts from their fundamentals.
2. Movements in security prices (i.e., stock returns) may be attributable to movements in investor sentiment.

The noise trader model of DSSW does not limit underpricing to small firms, since all firms subject to sentiment fluctuations should trade at discounts relative to their fundamentals. However, the clientele of closed-end funds is such that our empirical results pertain only to small firms. There may, of course, be other sentiment measures (institutional investor sentiment?) that affect security prices. Changes in such sentiments would influence returns on particular segments of security markets, those segments favored or disfavored by the investors in question, and would lead to systematic mispricing.

Since it is harder to observe fundamental value in other market segments, establishing the existence of mispricing will be difficult. But because it is so easy to observe the fundamental value of a closed-end fund, the pervasive evidence of mispricing in this domain is especially surprising. For what other security does the *Wall Street Journal* publish deviations from fundamental value every Monday morning? If securities as simple as these are mispriced, what should our prior be that the EMH holds for more complicated assets, such as the stocks of large, diversified firms. Indeed, the prediction of security underpricing offers a possible explanation for another Wall Street puzzle: the premium paid when one firm buys another. Just as the market value of a closed-end fund might be worth less than the value of its underlying assets, the market value of a firm could be less than the fundamental value of all of its component parts.

APPENDIX I List of the Twenty Closed-end Stock Funds Used in Constructing the Monthly Changes in the Value-Weighted Index of Discounts (earlier name in parentheses)

ASA Ltd. (American South African)
Abacus Fund, Inc.
Adams Express Co.
Advance Investors Corp.
American International Corp.

Carriers and General Corp.
Dominick Fund, Inc.
Eurofund International, Inc. (Eurofund, Inc.)
General American Investors, Inc.
MA Hanna Co.
International Holdings Corp.
Japan Fund, Inc.
Lehman Corp.
Madison Resources, Inc. (Madison Fund, Inc.)
Niagara Shares Corp.
Petroleum and Resources Corp. (Petroleum Corp. of America)
Surveyor Fund, Inc. (General Public Service Corp.)
Tricontinental Corp.
United Corp.
United States and Foreign Securities Corp.

REFERENCES

Lee is Assistant Professor of Accounting at the School of Business, University of Michigan, Shleifer is Professor of Economics at Harvard University. Thaler is the Henrietta Johnson Louis Professor of Economics at the Johnson Graduate School of Management, Cornell University. We would like to acknowledge helpful comments from Greg Brauer, Eugene Fama, Ken French, Raymond Kan, Merton H. Miller, Sam Peltzman, Mark Ready, Sy Smidt, René Stulz, Lawrence Summers, Robert Vishny, Robert Waldmann, and an anonymous referee, and financial support from Russell Sage Foundation and Social Sciences and Humanities Research Council of Canada. Thanks also to Greg Brauer, Nai-Fu Chen, Thomas Herzfeld, and Jay Ritter for providing data, and Sheldon Gao and Erik Herzfeld for research assistance.

Anderson, Seth C. "Closed-end Funds Versus Market Efficiency." *Journal of Portfolio Management* (Fall 1986):63–67.

Black, Fischer. "Presidential address: Noise." *Journal of Finance* 41 (1986):529–543.

Boudreaux, K. J. "Discounts and Premiums on Closed-end Mutual Funds: A Study in Valuation." *Journal of Finance* 28 (1973):515–522.

Brauer, Gregory A. "Open-ending Closed-end Funds." *Journal of Financial Economics* 13 (1984):491–507.

———. "Closed-End Fund Shares' Abnormal Returns and the Information Content of Discounts and Premiums." *Journal of Finance* 43, (1988):113–128.

———, and Eric Chang. "Return Seasonality in Stocks and their Underlying Assets: Tax Loss Selling Versus Information Explanations." *Review of Financial Studies* 3 (1990):257–280.

Brickley, James A., and James S. Schallheim. "Lifting the Lid on Closed-End

Investment Companies: A Case of Abnormal Returns." *Journal of Financial and Quantitative Analysis* 20 (1985):107–118.

Chen, Nai-Fu, Richard Roll, and Stephen Ross. "Economic Forces and the Stock Market." *Journal of Business* 59 (1986):383–403.

De Long, J. B., A. Shleifer, L. H. Summers, and R. J. Waldmann. "Noise Trader Risk in Financial Markets." *Journal of Political Economy* 98 (1990):703–738.

Fama, Eugene F., and Michael Gibbons. "A Comparison of Inflation Forecasts." *Journal of Monetary Economics* 13 (1984):327–348.

———, and Kenneth R. French. "Dividend Yields and Expected Stock Returns." *Journal of Financial Economics* 22 (1988):3–26.

Grossman, Sanford J., and Oliver D. Hart. "Takeover Bids, the Free-rider Problem, and the Theory of the Corporation." *Bell Journal of Economics and Management Science* (Spring 1980):42–64.

Herzfeld, Thomas J. *The Investor's Guide to Closed-end Funds* (New York: McGraw-Hill, 1980).

Ibbotson, Roger G., Jody L. Sindelar, and Jay R. Ritter. "Initial Public Offerings." *Journal of Applied Corporate Finance* 1 (1988):37–45.

Lee, Charles M. C., Andrei Shleifer, and Richard H. Thaler. "Explaining Closed-end Fund Discounts." Unpublished Manuscript. University of Michigan, Harvard University, and Cornell University.

Malkiel, Burton G. "The Valuation of Closed-End Investment Company Shares." *Journal of Finance* 32 (1977):847–859.

———. *A Random Walk Down Wall Street*, 4th ed. (New York: Norton, 1985).

Peavy, John W. "Returns on Initial Public Offerings of Closed-End Funds." *Review of Financial Studies* 3 (1985):695–708.

Richards, R. M., D. R. Fraser, and J. C. Groth. "Winning Strategies for Closed-end Funds." *Journal of Portfolio Management* (Fall 1980):50–55.

Ritter, Jay R. "The Buying and Selling Behavior of Individual Investors at the Turn of the Year." *Journal of Finance* 43 (1988):701–717.

Roenfeldt, Rodney L. and Donald L. Tuttle. "An Examination of the Discounts and Premiums of Closed-end Investment Companies." *Journal of Business Research* (Fall 1973):129–140.

Russell, Thomas and Richard H. Thaler. "The Relevance of Quasi Rationality in Competitive Markets." *American Economic Review* 75 (1985):1071–1082.

Sharpe, William F., and Howard B. Sosin. "Closed-end Investment Companies in the United States: Risk and Return." In B. Jacquillat, ed. *European Finance Association 1974 Proceedings* (Amsterdam: North Holland, 1975):37–63.

Shiller, Robert J. "Stock Prices and Social Dynamics." *Brookings Papers on Economic Activity* 2 (1984):457–498.

Shleifer, Andrei, and Robert W. Vishny. "Equilibrium Short Horizons of Investors and Firms." *American Economic Review Papers and Proceedings* 80 (1990):148–153.

Thompson, Rex. "The Information Content of Discounts and Premiums on Closed-end Fund Shares." *Journal of Financial Economics* 6 (1978):151–186.

Weiss, Kathleen. "The Post-offering Price Performance of Closed-end Funds." *Financial Management* (Autumn 1989):57–67.

Wiesenberger, A. *Investment Companies Services*, annual surveys 1960–1986. (New York: Warren, Gorham, and Lamont).

Zweig, Martin E. "An Investor Expectations Stock Price Predictive Model Using Closed-end Fund Premiums." *Journal of Finance* 28 (1973):67–87.

INDEX

Page numbers in **boldface** refer to tables and figures.

353